Where are National Capitalisms Now?

Also by Jonathan Perraton

GLOBAL TRANSFORMATIONS: Politics, Economics and Culture (*1999, with David Held, Anthony McGrew and David Goldblatt*)

Also by Ben Clift

FRENCH SOCIALISM IN A GLOBAL ERA: The Political Economy of the New Social Democracy in France (*2003*)

Where are National Capitalisms Now?

Edited by

Jonathan Perraton
*Lecturer in Economics and Deputy Director, Political Economy
Research Centre, University of Sheffield, UK*

and

Ben Clift
Lecturer in International Political Economy, Warwick University, UK

First published 2004 by
PALGRAVE MACMILLAN
Houndmills, Basingstoke, Hampshire RG21 6XS and
175 Fifth Avenue, New York, N.Y. 10010
Companies and representatives throughout the world

PALGRAVE MACMILLAN is the global academic imprint of the Palgrave
Macmillan division of St. Martin's Press, LLC and of Palgrave Macmillan Ltd.
Macmillan® is a registered trademark in the United States, United Kingdom
and other countries. Palgrave is a registered trademark in the European
Union and other countries.

ISBN 0–333–92894–6

This book is printed on paper suitable for recycling and made from fully
managed and sustained forest sources.

A catalogue record for this book is available from the British Library.

Library of Congress Cataloging-in-Publication Data
    Where are national capitalisms now? / edited by Jonathan Perraton and
Ben Clift.
        p. cm.
    Includes bibliographical references and index.
    ISBN 0–333–92894–6
        1. Economic policy – Case studies. 2. Comparative economics. 3. Capitalism.
    4. Deregulation. 5. Free trade. 6. Financial institutions. 7. Financial crises.
    8. Business cycles. 9. International economics integration. 10. Globalization –
    Economic aspects. 11. Globalization – Political aspects. 12. Nationalism.
    I. Perraton, Jonathan, 1964– II. Clift, Ben.

HD87.W47 2003
330.9'049—dc21   2003053646

10 9 8 7 6 5 4 3 2 1
12 11 10 09 08 07 06 05 04 03

Printed and bound in Great Britain by
Antony Rowe Ltd, Chippenham and Eastbourne

Contents

List of Tables and Figures

Tables

Figures

Acknowledgements

This book arises from a conference of the Political Economy Research Centre at the University of Sheffield. Financial support for the conference was provided by the Barings Foundation, Carfax Publishers and Polity Press and we thank them all. All the conference participants provided most useful comments and insights; we are particularly grateful to Aidan Foster-Carter, Dominic Kelly, Michael Moran, Renee Prendergast, Jim Tomlinson and Alex Wadden for their contributions as discussants. Andrew Gamble and Anthony Payne both played a key role in facilitating the conference. Sylvia McColm, the PERC administrator, organized the conference with her customary efficiency and good-humour: we remain in her debt. Chapter 8 originally appeared in the *Journal of Economic Issues* and we thank the Association for Evolutionary Economics for permission to reprint it here.

JONATHAN PERRATON
BEN CLIFT

List of Contributors

Claire Annesley is Lecturer in European Politics at the University of Manchester. She has written on social exclusion in Europe, New Labour welfare policies and the political economy of contemporary Germany.

Ben Clift is Lecturer in International Political Economy of Warwick University. He is the author of several articles on French politics, European social democracy and corporate governance. He is the author of *French Socialism in a Global Era: The Political Economy of the New Social Democracy in France* (2003).

Andrew Gamble is Professor of Politics and Director of the Political Economy Research Centre, University of Sheffield. His works include *Britain in Decline* (4th edition, Palgrave, 1994), *The Free Economy and the Strong State* (2nd edition, Palgrave, 1994), *Hayek: The Iron Cage of Liberty* (1996) *Politics and Fate* (2000) and *Between Europe and America: The Future of British Politics* (Palgrave, 2003).

Barry Gills is Reader in International Politics, University of Newcastle. He researches international political economy theory, historical analysis of social systems and social change and globalization with particular reference to the politics of resistance, reform in South Korea and the political economy of development.

Dong-Sook Gills is Senior Lecturer in Politics and International Studies at the University of Sunderland. She researches the sociology of development, particularly gender issues in East Asia. Her publications include *Rural Women and Triple Exploitation in Korean Development* (1999).

Kazuyoshi Matsuura is a University Lecturer in Economics at Matsuyama University, Japan.

Rory O'Donnell is Director of the National Economic and Social Council in Dublin and was formerly Professor of Business Administration at University College Dublin. His publications include (with Brigid Laffan and Michael Smith) *Europe's Experimental Union: Rethinking Integration* (2000).

Jonathan Perraton is Lecturer in Economics and Deputy Director of the Political Economy Research Centre, University of Sheffield. He has written extensively on globalization and is co-author, with David Held *et al.*, of *Global Transformations: Politics, Economics and Culture* (1999).

Michael Pollitt is a University Senior Lecturer at the University of Cambridge, UK.

Geoff Pugh is Principal Lecturer in European Economics at Staffordshire University Business School. He has written several papers on European economics and is co-author, with Thomas Lange, of *The Economics of German Unification* (1998).

Hugo Radice is Senior Lecturer in International Political Economy at the University of Leeds. He is author of numerous articles on globalization, international and comparative political economy, transnational corporations and economic developments in East-Central Europe.

Ryoji Takada is a Professor of Commerce at the University of Marketing and Distribution Sciences, Japan.

Satoru Tanaka is a University Lecturer in Economics at the Kobe City University of Foreign Studies, Japan.

Grahame Thompson is Professor of Political Economy at the Open University. Amongst other works, he is author of *Between Hierarchies and Markets: The Logic and Limits of Network Forms of Organization* (2003) and, with Paul Hirst, of *Globalization in Question* (1999) and editor of *Economic Dynamism in the Asia-Pacific* (1998).

David Tyrrall is Lecturer in Accounting and Finance at Cass Business School, London. His main research interests are in international accounting and finance.

Juhana Vartiainen is Researcher at the Labour Institute for Economic Research. He has written extensively on the Scandinavian economies, labour economics, wage bargaining and the political economy of economic policy.

Linda Weiss is Professor in the Department of Government and International Relations, University of Sydney. She has written extensively on the comparative and international politics of economic development, particularly globalization and governance, comparative capitalism and developmental states in East Asia. Her books include *States in the Global Economy* (2003), *The Myth of the Powerless State* (1998) and, with John Hobson, *States and Economic Development* (1995).

1
Introduction

Jonathan Perraton and Ben Clift

If, as is often claimed, capitalism is the only game in town, does it matter *which* capitalism we live under? The claim that capitalism is the only feasible economic system left is often conflated with the claim that only its neo-liberal Anglo-Saxon variant is viable. We, and the contributors to this volume, dispute this latter claim for reasons set out below.[1] Debates on national capitalisms have often become polarized between those who see convergence onto an Anglo-Saxon norm as inevitable and those who stress continuities in different national models. Nevertheless, although differences between national economies clearly remain, many of the features of national economies that would have been identified around, say, 1980 have since undergone a major change. In the light of this, the Political Economy Research Centre at the University of Sheffield convened a conference to consider the following questions:

- How far do existing models of national capitalism (chiefly, Anglo-Saxon, Rhineland and East Asian) remain accurate characterizations of national economies?
- How can we analyze the impact of international integration on national models of capitalism beyond simply asking whether convergence is inevitable?
- How have different countries responded to the ways in which international integration has changed the relative costs of different policy options?

The chapters below are revised versions of papers for that conference and each represents their authors' attempts to move the national capitalisms debate forward.

There has been a lively popular and academic debate at least since the 1980s on the merits of different varieties of capitalism, with antecedents in Shonfield (1965) and originating in Polanyi (1944). For proponents of Continental European (especially Rhineland) capitalism it combines an innovative national economy with high levels of social inclusion (Albert, 1993;

Hutton, 1995, 2002). Some proponents of Japanese capitalism proclaimed its superiority in terms of productivity alone, but others have claimed further that this form of capitalism promotes social cohesion, particularly within the firm, and low unemployment (Dore, 2000). The East Asian model of capitalism, exemplified particularly by Korea and Taiwan, is not a simple replica of the Japanese model but it was notable before the 1997 exchange rate crises for combining high growth rates with relatively egalitarian income distribution (World Bank, 1993). Anglo-Saxon capitalism retained many proponents on standard economic grounds that flexible markets, especially for labour, promote growth and employment. Further, many features of the Anglo-Saxon model – notably privatization and a decline in active industrial policy, financial deregulation, more flexible labour and product markets and limits to welfare provision – have been adopted elsewhere, often by social democratic governments.

For some commentators the 1990s decisively settled the debate over national capitalisms in favour of the Anglo-Saxon model. The United States experienced its longest postwar boom and unemployment fell to levels not seen in a generation. The budget deficit was brought under control and a falling dollar reduced the trade deficit to the surprise of many observers outside the economics profession. By contrast, the European economies experienced slow growth, high unemployment and widespread debate about the viability of their welfare systems. Japan spent much of the decade in stagnation or outright recession, whilst the 1997 currency crisis exposed apparent problems with other variants of the East Asian model. Indeed some commentators argue that the very features of the Japanese model often identified as being central to its postwar success – notably, industrial policy, long-term relations between firms, lifelong employment relations and management practices – are now major fetters to its performance (Porter et al., 2000).

We do not believe that the 1990s experience settled the national capitalisms debate in this fashion. Such conclusions exemplify a common problem with this debate, that of generalizing from short-term trends – the evidence of earlier decades can readily be used to tell quite different stories. The end of the US 1990s boom and its continued structural imbalances, particularly the trade deficits, vindicates Grahame Thompson's careful analysis of US 1990s performance in his chapter. Some of these imbalances can be seen in other Anglo-Saxon economies, so that the United Kingdom continues to run trade deficits despite fiscal balance and at the end of 2002 Australian household debt stood at 127 per cent of disposable income, even higher than in the United States.[2] Emphasizing negative aspects of the European models overlooks the role of restrictive macroeconomic policy in Europe's poor performance in the 1990s, particularly German unification and the efforts to meet the Maastricht criteria for EMU. With Japan and other East Asian countries one can hardly deny their growth performances until recent years. It is also hard to see how any model could have dealt easily with

Japan's problems in the 1990s of massive bad bank debt, a collapse in consumer confidence and deflation. The jury remains out on how far the 1997 East Asian currency crisis was caused by structural failings of these economies and how far it was driven by investor panic (Chang *et al.*, 1998; Radelet and Sachs, 1998; Wade, 1998). Subsequently the leading East Asian economies have shown clear signs of bouncing back. Furthermore, if Anglo-Saxon capitalism is the optimal model we would also expect its examples besides the United States – Britain, Canada, Australia and New Zealand – to display a clearly superior performance, which they have not.

There are deeper grounds for questioning much of the national capitalisms debate. In a major recent contribution, Coates (2000) assesses the economic contributions which query whether the institutional features of developed economies have a major impact on their economic performance. There is a range of evidence that globally institutions have a significant impact on performance, but this is less clear between developed economies. At least as a first approximation, Freeman (2000) argues that institutions make little difference to growth and unemployment in developed economies but they do have a major impact on the distribution of income and employment. Trying to use enduring differences in national institutions to explain differences in growth or unemployment rates for a particular decade is therefore likely to be fruitless.

Which institutions matter?

So many different contributors to the national capitalisms literature have emphasized so many different institutional features of national economies and produced so many different classifications of different countries the researcher can easily fail to see the wood from the trees. Some clarity is attempted here.

Until recently many economists tended to either ignore the role of institutions or largely see them as impediments to the free operation of markets. The emergence of the 'new institutional economics' of Douglass North (e.g. North, 1990) and others highlight the importance of embedded institutional arrangements in underwriting the functions of business and the market economy within a broadly orthodox economic framework. This work overlaps with an older institutionalist tradition that develops its analysis from alternative conceptions of economic agency (e.g. Hodgson, 1988, 1999). There are key differences and similarities between the two approaches (Rutherford, 1994), but for our purposes the similarities are more important. From either a 'new' or 'old' institutionalist perspective these arrangements are enduring and exhibit path dependence. Both approaches would share the broad assumption that market activities rest upon non-market arrangements between actors. Empirical applications of institutionalist theory to explaining differences in economic performance tend to invoke similar variables whatever the initial perspective (e.g. Hodgson, 1996). These non-market arrangements structure incentives for activity and profoundly affect the distribution of the output. In Douglass North's classic statement:

> Institutions are the rules of the game in a society or, more formally, are the humanly devised constraints that shape human interaction. In consequence they structure incentives in human exchange, whether political, social or economic. Institutional change shapes the way societies evolve through time and hence is the key to understanding historical change. ... Institutions reduce uncertainty by providing a structure to everyday life. They are a guide to human interaction, so that when we wish to greet friends on the street, drive an automobile, buy oranges, borrow money, form a business, bury our dead or whatever, we know (or can learn easily) how to perform these tasks. We would readily observe that institutions differ if were trying to make the same transactions in a different country. (North, 1990: 3–4)

Institutional arrangements reflect the history, politics and culture of a country. We would therefore expect to see – and do, indeed, see – a diversity of institutional arrangements across national economies and would not necessarily predict convergence either in response to common exogenous developments or in response to apparent differences in performance (Hodgson, 1999: ch. 6).

The national capitalisms literature itself is difficult to summarize on the question of which institutions matter most. This is for two reasons. First, as noted above, there is a wide range of institutional arrangements considered in the literatures by different authors. Second, many accounts see the institutional arrangements as part of a system operating in a mutually reinforcing way (Hollingsworth, 1997a). This approach – criticized for its functionalism in Hugo Radice's chapter – thus rejects the notion that one can analyze institutions in isolation; the ensemble of a nation's institutions is crucial. Nevertheless, whilst remaining initially agnostic as to whether a systemic approach is needed we can class institutional arrangements in the following broad categories: those that govern relations between the state and the private actors, chiefly business and labour; those that govern relations between business and labour; those that govern relations between firms and those that govern relations between finance and industry. This is similar to, for example, Ruigrok and Tulder (1995) distinguishing between firm's bargaining relations within and outside the value chain.

States, markets and business

In an important sense state intervention is ubiquitous: states set the laws that govern economic activity. Under the Westphalian system, nation states were assumed to be sovereign in their law making, but contemporary international integration has tempered this so that the states are increasingly subject to international legal principles (Held, 1995; Held *et al.*, 1999: ch. 1). Laws governing economic activity provide clear examples of this: regional trading arrangements, such as the European Union (EU) and the North American Free Trade Agreement, provide international legal frameworks for economic activity whilst the World Trade Organization is attempting to stipulate certain global principles for the conduct of international trade.

State intervention in the economy is more usually conceived in terms of direct government expenditure and specific interventions to shape economic outcomes, industrial policy loosely speaking. Total government activity, contrary to some more extreme or 'hyper-globalization' views,[3] has generally either continued to grow as a proportion of national income or at least stabilize. Furthermore, there remain significant and persistent differences between countries in the shares of government expenditure in economic activity. This book pays only limited attention to the welfare state, although it does consider the resources available for funding the welfare state. Books are written on trends in the welfare state and we cannot fully do justice to it. Little consideration is given to short-term macroeconomic policy and whether international economic integration has reduced the possibilities for government activism (but see Webb, 1995 for evidence that it has).

The decline in state activism as industrial policy is probably most obvious. Governments have privatized state-owned enterprises and deregulated markets. The ability to set trade barriers or subsidize favoured firms has been severely curtailed. Industrial policy – conceived as 'policy aimed at *particular industries* (and firms as their components) to achieve outcomes that are *perceived by the state* to be *efficient for the economy as a whole*' (Chang, 1996: 60, emphases in original) – has been in general decline. Nevertheless, one must be cautious here for three reasons. First, as several of the chapters (especially on France and the East Asian developmental states) emphasize, the decline in industrial policy can easily be overstated as states find innovative means to influence the economy. Second, no major economy – the United States definitely included – conforms to a neo-liberal model; all retain significant degrees of state intervention. Third, the deregulation process has not been a simple case of removing legal restrictions on economic activity: in each country it entailed new legislation designed by governments to influence the outcome. How far governments were successful in this remains a key question.

Business and labour

Relations between business and labour can be conceived at the firm level, particularly styles of management, and at the macroeconomic level, particularly different systems of wage bargaining. Most of the chapters pay limited attention to different management styles, but other studies suggest that the differences are significant for economic performance and distribution

(Gordon, 1996; Marsden, 1999; Whitley, 1999) and Chapter 5 by Annesley, Pugh and Tyrrall considers the implications of this for Germany.

There is a well-known literature proposing that the nature of national wage bargaining between business and labour has a significant impact on outcomes of unemployment and inflation. In particular, according to Calmfors and Driffill (1988) the best outcomes have been expected in those countries with the most decentralized *and* the most centralized systems of wage bargaining. The former group essentially comprises the Anglo-Saxon countries, at least after the reduction in trade union power over the 1980s, and the latter group comprises those economies usually classified as corporatist – particularly those in Scandinavia. The chapters on the United States, Britain and the Scandinavian countries in particular examine the role of bargaining wage systems.

Relations between firms

General contributions to the national capitalisms literature often stress differences between business-to-business relations across countries. Continental European countries are expected to have closer and more cooperative relations between firms – a point often stressed in the burgeoning literature on industrial districts – in contrast to the arms-length transactions underwritten by extensive legal contracts that are said to characterize the Anglo-Saxon system. Greater collective organization by employers in the Rhineland countries particularly is said to make it easier for employers to create institutions for collective goods, notably the provision of training. Close relations between firms and their suppliers are also often claimed to be at the heart of East Asian capitalism: the just-in-time management techniques of Japanese manufacturing require close coordination and cooperation between large firms and their suppliers. Nevertheless, although we do not dismiss the importance of these relations our contributors do not examine them in detail and the lack of readily available information prevents us from examining this in any detail in our concluding chapter.

Finance and industry

Relations between finance and industry have been central to many of the key contributions to the national capitalisms debate, notably Dore (1987, 2000), Albert (1993) and Hutton (1995, 2002). These emphasize not only the dominant forms of industrial finance and the terms on which this finance is provided, but also patterns of corporate ownership and governance. The 'exit' nature of Anglo-Saxon systems, with their emphasis on liquidity and corporate governance through the threat of takeover, is contrasted with the 'loyalty' nature of Continental European and Japanese financial systems where stock market capitalization is much lower and hostile takeovers are rare. In the latter systems, effective corporate governance is often largely attributed to long-term relations between banks and firms. The provision of 'patient' finance is said to enable firms to construct long-term relations with other stakeholders, particularly other firms and labour. Several of the chapters analyze these relations in detail and this is explored further in the concluding chapter.

The chapters

In addition to the questions above that frame this study, we suggested to the country chapter authors that they consider how they would have described the key institutional features of the country around 1980 in order to examine what has changed since and which features remain fundamental.

Grahame Thompson examines the unprecedented growth of the US economy in the 1990s. Many commentators attributed this to a combination of the impact of new technologies through the 'new economy' and higher global economic integration. The careful examination of the evidence in this chapter raises scepticism that these changes can account for much of the growth and locates it closer to home. Under the Reagan administration the reversal of the New Deal historic compromise laid the basis for the 1990s boom in profits as real wages for many workers barely grew. This, combined with the judicious macroeconomic management of the 1990s, was central to business expansion. Importantly this shows that some of the neo-liberal characteristics of the US economy are not long run embedded features, but the result of politically engineered changes over the past 20 years. Proponents of the neo-liberal ideal often effectively conflate it with the US economy, but there remain important differences between this ideal and American reality.

In his chapter on Britain, Andrew Gamble examines how the UK model has changed since 1980 in terms of relations between capital and labour, industry and finance and the state and capital. There was widespread agreement on the dimensions of the problems facing the UK economy at the start of the 1980s, but little consensus over the solutions. Unquestionably the Conservative administrations of the 1980s transformed relations between capital and labour and between the state and capital. Although less often noted, it also transformed aspects of the financial system through the 1986 'Big Bang' deregulation programme. It is arguable that a British government was uniquely placed to effect such fundamental institutional changes since it could exercise strong central power through a parliamentary majority despite only attracting a minority of the popular vote. Nevertheless, there are important continuities with the pre-Thatcher past, particularly in finance–industry relations. Further, whilst the new Labour administrations since 1997 have not reversed much of the Conservative legacy, its policies are significantly different from those administrations. Globalization might be expected to have a particularly strong impact on the UK economy as Britain has particularly high levels of international economic integration fom a major economy. Such an impact can clearly be seen in some sectors, particularly with the transformation of some British industries through inward direct investment. However, Andrew Gamble emphasizes the most contentious issue in British politics for a generation – the impact of integration with the EU. The EU legal regime provides a framework for economic activity that, at least arguably or potentially, reflects continental European practice and has already had a profound impact on the British political economy. Indeed sections of the British right now openly advocate British withdrawal from the EU and alignment with the North American Free Trade Agreement instead to preserve the Anglo-Saxon character of the British economy. Continued membership of the EU, with its projected widening and deepening, is likely to entail further changes to British economic institutions (see, further, Hutton, 2002).

Echoes of the British debate on European integration can be seen in the Irish debates over economic reform in the 1980s and exceptional growth in the 1990s. Too often in the comparative national capitalisms literature Ireland is either ignored completely or lazily tagged as just another Anglo-Saxon economy. In his chapter, Rory O'Donnell emphasizes the importance of collective agreements amongst social groups in the 1980s once it was generally acknowledged that Ireland's postwar economic underperformance should not be allowed to persist. Ireland's 'Celtic Tiger' record as the fastest growing EU economy of the 1990s is well known. Two points stand out here. First, the social compact was constructed over a few years in the 1980s. Most comparative national capitalisms literature views successful compacts as being hard to construct, usually emerging out of major crises (economic depression or the aftermath of war) and taking years to establish and maintain the levels of trust required. Second, this social compact comprises a wide range of groups, including some outside formal economic activity, instead of just employers and organized labour of the traditional models. Rory O'Donnell sees a strange symmetry between the Irish 'Euro-sceptics' critique of the Irish economy's reliance on EU integration and the dependency theory critique that sees the Irish economy as occupying a subordinate ('screw-driver assembly') position in the world economy. Neither critique has much empirical force and the Irish economy's successful social compact offers useful wider lessons.

The next three chapters examine continental European economies, although the differences are as important as the similarities. Claire Annesley, Geoff Pugh and David Tyrrall outline the key institutional features of West Germany's postwar economic success. They then construct a model to illustrate how Germany's consensus culture aided the generation of innovation and appropriation of its gains. In the 1990s, the German economy faced the challenge of unification, as well as the more general challenges of globalization and the new economy. On several macroeconomic counts, particularly unemployment levels, the German economy performed poorly in the 1990s.

However, the macroeconomic failures mask the continued innovative capacity of German firms. The authors argue that proposals to reform German model risk undermining the consensual culture that has sustained innovation. This is not to deny the need for some reform. In particular the insider–outsider structures in the labour market limit employment generation. Nevertheless, they argue, reform needs to be sensitive to existing German institutions.

France never fitted comfortably into a classic account of postwar Continental European capitalism. Lacking the levels of social organization for collective goods characteristic of Germany, France's postwar regime saw high levels of state intervention administered by a political elite with close ties to the business elite. Many accounts see France as having undergone a major transformation towards the Anglo-Saxon model after the abandonment of the Mitterand's radical policies of the early 1980s. Ben Clift's chapter, drawing on a wide range of sources, offers a more nuanced account. The 1980s and 1990s did indeed see far-reaching policies of privatization and financial deregulation with the consequent abandonment of much of the earlier industrial policy. However, these changes were designed in detail by state authorities. The governance and behaviour of French corporations show clear continuities with the past whilst the French government expenditure remains relatively high and the French state continues to intervene in key areas. The 35-hour working week policy is a good example of this and is examined in some detail in Ben Clift's chapter.

Juhana Vartiainen's chapter examines the four Scandinavian economies of Denmark, Finland, Norway and Sweden. As small open economies with highly developed welfare states funded by high tax levels and centralized wage bargaining, they might be thought to be most vulnerable to globalization. Juhana Vartiainen argues instead that their welfare states are a rational response to international integration and remain politically viable. Although the wage bargaining systems are under some pressure and these economies have lost their exceptionally good employment records of the 1980s, this does not imply the need for wholesale deregulating of their economies or abandonment of the bargaining systems.

The chapter on Japan by Kazuyoshi Matsuura, Michael Pollitt, Ryoji Takada and Satoru Tanaka directly considers change since the 1980s. They date the start of transformation of Japan's economy from the 1985 Plaza agreement for managing the Yen–Dollar exchange rate that was followed by the rise and fall of the 'bubble' economy and the ensuing recession. This financial instability was accompanied by external pressure on Japan for liberalization, growing multinationalization of production and an ageing population, which have combined to place strains upon key aspects of postwar institutional arrangements in the Japanese economy. Drawing on a wide range of sources, they show how the 'main' bank system, lifetime employment and seniority wages, inter-corporate relations and industrial policy operated in the postwar period to aid Japanese economic development and how structural change since the mid-1980s has acted to undermine these relations.

The issue of state intervention in open economies is central to Linda Weiss's chapter. She examines the relative performance of Korea and Taiwan in the 1990s. In the aftermath of the 1997 East Asian crisis many commentators prophesied the end of the East Asian model of capitalism, particularly its levels of state intervention. Linda Weiss takes issue with this interpretation. She argues that financial liberalization was largely driven by internal pressures, whilst Taiwan's relatively cautious approach left it less exposed to sudden shifts in market sentiments and thus better able to ride out the 1997 crisis. As the dust from the 1997 crisis has settled many key aspects of the developmental state remain in place in both of these countries. This is part of her wider argument that state activism remains viable in the world economy (Weiss, 1998).

Barry and Dong-Sook Gills's chapter on Korea might at first sight seem to contradict aspects of Linda Weiss's chapter, but their perspectives are largely complementary. This chapter puts more emphasis on globalization processes as leading to shifts in economic policy and is more sceptical about the viability of the developmental state. However, both chapters share the view that the economic reform programme in Korea since the 1997 crisis faces basic contradictions. Barry and Dong-Sook Gills's chapter focuses more on the role of labour and business. Whilst some of the economic reform processes – for example, reducing the power of the large business conglomerates the *chaebol*; increased product market competition – are not obviously detrimental to labour, other reforms threaten its interests. The ongoing process of democratization creates pressures to incorporate labour into decision-making and expand welfare provision, the neo-liberal nature of economic reforms may undermine this and the *chaebol* retain considerable powers to frustrate efforts to reform them. This makes for an unstable process and the character of the emerging Korean model remains open.

The penultimate chapter by Hugo Radice provides a bridge between the country case study chapters and our concluding chapter. He provides a brief but critical survey of the main themes in the comparative national capitalisms literature. He makes three key criticisms of this literature. The first is that the methodology of this literature by focusing on country studies is bound to emphasize national diversity and downplay common trends. His second point is that as businesses become more international, they develop relations – with overseas suppliers, customers, workforces and governments – that are essentially those that the national capitalisms literature theorizes at the national level. The stretching of business relations internationally means that some institutions can no longer be seen as neatly bounded by national borders (if, indeed, they ever were). Hugo Radice's final point is that accounts of national capitalism are often functionalist in the sense that each feature is mutually reinforcing the overall national system. As a social scientific explanation for the emergence and evolution of such institutions, this functionalism is inadequate.

In the concluding chapter, we pick up the themes outlined here and analyze the changes in these features across the developed countries. The chapter starts with a theoretical analysis of institutional features of national capitalism before considering in detail government expenditure and state intervention; financial systems and corporate governance; industrial relations; systems of wage bargaining. As well as drawing on the contributors' chapters, a wide range of data is produced across the developed countries to examine how far they have converged and how far national differences persist. This enables us to analyze the forces driving these trends.

Notes

1. The viability of other economic systems besides capitalism is not considered here, but see Hodgson (1999).
2. 'The Lucky Country: Is Australia's Economic Miracle Sustainable?', *The Economist*, 8 March 2003, p. 85.
3. On 'hyper-globalization' and other perspectives see Held *et al.* (1999) and Hirst and Thompson (1999).

2
The US Economy in the 1990s: The 'New Economy' Assessed

Grahame Thompson

Introduction

This chapter traces the course of the US economy over the 1990s, which saw a sustained upward swing in its fortunes. Over 1991–99 the average real growth rate was over 3.5 per cent, and this was accompanied by minimal inflation and historically low unemployment levels. These features led many commentators to predict that the traditional four-stage business cycle of prosperity, transition, recession and finally recovery – one that had typified the course of much of the post-Second World War US economy – was now over (Weber, 1997). It had entered a completely new era – the era of the 'New Economy' – in which there was no business cycle, only sustained growth. What is more, the argument went, this new era would see the global resurgence of the United States with the emergence of another American economic miracle to parallel that at the beginning of the twentieth century, and one to rival that of the now exhausted German and Japanese economic miracles of the 1960s and 1980s, respectively (Zuckerman, 1998). Growth rates of over 4 per cent in the late 1990s fuelled the sentiment amongst business leaders and commentators that there really was a new paradigm governing economic activity in the United States. The good times were back again, and here to stay!

This chapter takes the issue of the 'new era' as the central point of reference and examines the arguments both for and against it. This provides an opportunity to assess the late 1990s state of the economy and what might have changed during the 1990s.[1]

Changing contours of the US macroeconomic position

We begin this assessment with the broad macroeconomic characteristics of the economy. The growth rate of US Gross Domestic Product (GDP) has been strong over the entire 1990s, but it was particularly impressive after 1995. Compared to its main competitors the US position was even more

12

Table 2.1 Comparative US economic indicators, 1990–99

	1990–95	1996–99
Real GDP growth (yearly % changes)		
USA	1.9	4.1
EU15	1.5	2.5
Japan	1.9	1.1
Gross capital formation (as % of GDP)		
USA	16.3	19.7
EU15	19.7	20.1
Japan	30.0	27.6
Investment in machinery and equipment (as % of GDP)		
USA	7.5	—
EU15	8.4	—
Japan	11.0	—
Net savings (as % of GDP)		
USA	4.1	—
EU15	7.4	—
Japan	17.4	—
Unemployment (as a % of labour force)		
USA	6.4	4.8
EU15	9.4	9.6
Japan	2.5	3.9
Inflation (% change per year)		
USA	3.5[1]	2.2
EU15	4.2[1]	2.0
Japan	1.6[1]	0.6
Government sector balance (as % of GDP)		
USA	−4.4[2]	−0.5
EU15	−5.4	−2.3[3]
Japan	−0.1	−5.4
Trade balance (as % of GDP)		
USA	−1.2	−2.4[4]
EU15	0.7	1.6[4]
Japan	1.7	2.4[4]

Notes
[1] 1989–95.
[2] 1990–94.
[3] Excludes Luxembourg.
[4] 1996–97.

Sources: Compiled from *OECD Historical Statistics*, 1960–95 (Paris: OECD, 1995) *Economic Outlook*, No. 73 (2003) *European Economy*, No. 65, Convergence Report 1998, EU Luxembourg 1998; *OECD Main Economic Indicators*, February 1999.

impressive, as shown in Table 2.1. In addition, the United States had improved its position a little in terms of gross capital formation, although it still lags behind the European Union (EU) and Japan. Moreover, this remains true in the case of machinery and equipment investment as well. Japan

(16.3 per cent investment to GDP ratio in 1999) still demonstrated a superior position to that of the United States (12.3 per cent) even as its, and the EU's (16 per cent), relative advantage faded. This is confirmed in the case of net savings. The US savings rate plummeted, particularly between 1991 and 1994. Estimates put personal savings rates at almost zero in 1998 (still under 2 per cent of GDP in 1999), so that it was corporate and particularly public savings that contributed the bulk of the 6 per cent overall ratio in 1998. For the time being at least the great personal savers in the international system remain the Japanese.

Turning to consider unemployment and inflation, these also cast the United States in a favourable light. Unemployment was back to its levels of the 1960s, while inflation seemed to have been almost completely driven out of the system. Not since the 1960s had there been a period of such strong economic growth combined with such low levels of unemployment and inflation. In the case of the other main economies, on the unemployment front both the EU and Japan turned in a deteriorating performance over the entire 1990s, with the EU's unemployment rate double that of the United States between 1996–99. A major element in the 'triumph of the US economy' story in the 1990s is made up of this difference to the European experience. The Europeans were accused of not having either created the jobs that the United States had done, nor to have solved their unemployment problem. It was also claimed that the Japanese might soon be heading for double digit unemployment if their recession matured into a full-blown depression.

Turning now to two final indicators; the famous 'twin deficits' of the federal government balance and the balance on the external accounts that confronted the United States throughout the 1980s. Here, the United States seemed to have almost solved its budget deficit problem by 1999, as the account swept into the black, while budget deficits in the EU also diminished considerably towards the end of the 1990s. That of Japan rose, however, as a consequence of the essentially 'Keynesian' policies adopted by successive Japanese governments in response to the emerging recession in their own economy (though without much success).

On the other hand, the United States has not solved the trade deficit problem. Indeed, this has burgeoned. The merchandise trade deficit was around US$450 billion in 2000 and the current account deficit was over US$400 billion or about 4.2 per cent of GDP. Japan's trade surplus continued to expand: the formidable Japanese production machine rolls on. The EU as a bloc was essentially in balance on its external account in the latter part of the period.

What these data signal is the reasons for the optimistic mood in the United States about the economy. US citizens had seen their economy growing, their personal net wealth increasing (as the stock market boomed), and they had embarked upon a consumption boom as a result (hence the low personal savings rate). This in turn had stimulated an improved aggregate investment record, but a further serious deterioration in the balance of payments as imports were sucked in to feed the consumption boom. The rise in the value of the dollar after 1995 also added to the stimulus for consumption as the price of imported goods fell. Now we need to examine this story in greater detail.

A booming economy?

What were the reasons put forward for the booming economy in the United States? Here two basic determinants have been identified: technological developments and globalization. As we shall see, the story is considerably more complicated, involving much more than just these two elements, but for the moment we examine these in turn.

Technological developments

The argument about technological developments can be illustrated by Table 2.2. This indicates the importance of investment in the 1990s boom, relative to that of previous post-war expansions, and the negligible contribution of government's expenditure. In particular, it is producers' durable equipment that stands out as the significant major change from previous expansions. Whilst the overall record in fixed equipment was not particularly encouraging for the United States relative to other countries, its investment in 'information processing equipment' soared as their prices fell. In 1995–96 alone it grew by 21 per cent in real terms. Adding in the growth of software capital reinforces the overall importance of IT in the boom, particularly after 1995 (Jorgenson and Stiroh, 2000: 139–40, figures 3 and 4).

Thus the United States is in the middle of a profound 'technological revolution' it is argued, involving computers, semiconductors and other high-technology production, which is itself based upon advances in communication and information technology. The United States leads in many areas of information processing, which is driven by the re-equipment of its

Table 2.2   Contributions to per cent growth in GDP in US postwar expansions

Year	Percentages			
	Private consumption	Private fixed non-residential investment	Government	Net exports
1961–69	61.8	16.1	18.4	−2.6
1982–90	65.1	11.6	18.7	−5.2
1992–99	68.4	28.9	5.7	−12.6

Source: *Economic Report to the President*, 2001 table B-5.

domestic economy. This is having profound implications for all economic activity, it is suggested. US firms now account for over 40 per cent of the world's investment in computing, spending twice as much on 'infotech' as do European firms, and eight times the global average.

The United States thus dominates the knowledge industries of the future, it is claimed, and its exporting successes reflect this advantage. Exports are growing in advanced semiconductors, computer network servers, personal computers, software and services, entertainment, finance and telecommunications; as well as in a small number of the more traditional high-tech sectors like completed civilian aircraft. Basically, what the information technology revolution is producing, according to the optimistic advocates of a new economy, is a dramatic increase in productivity. This part of their story we return to below.

'Globalization'

The 'technological revolution' explanation for the unusually strong and sustained growth record is bolstered by an argument about the advent of 'globalization' and the way the American economy has both contributed to – and reacted to – this trend. There is a good deal of dispute about exactly what globalization means, and whether it genuinely represents a new structural stage in international capitalism (Hirst and Thompson, 1999; Held *et al.*, 1999). I avoid this discussion here and simply define 'globalization' as the increasing internationalization of economic relationships, involving a growth in interdependence and integration across national borders for all aspects of economic activity.

During most of the post-Second World War period, it is argued, the US economy remained relatively isolated from economic interdependencies and international integration. The United States was a very large 'continental' economy, trading and investing mainly within its own national boundaries. In 1970, for instance, the United States traded only 8 per cent of its GDP (sum of imports plus exports as per cent of GDP), and despite the growth of its overseas multinational corporations, these still centred the vast bulk of their investment activity on the domestic territory. In addition, although the dollar operated as the main international currency, the internationalization of financial markets was also limited as countries maintained capital controls and heavily regulated their national economies and exchange rates.

All this changed during the 1970s and 1980s, and it was in the 1990s that 'globalization' really took off. Liberalization, privatization and deregulation proceeded apace during the 1980s in particular, and became a worldwide phenomenon under an American sponsored global neo-liberal policy agenda. By 1999, the US economy was trading nearly 24 per cent of its GDP, a threefold increase on the 1970 position. In addition, there was a surge in US investment abroad as well as foreign investment into the United States (clearly, there has been a deficit since the 1980s). So the United States too had now entered the global economy, but with a vengeance. From the perspective of the 'new economics' this full-blown entry of the United States into the global economy is another reason why the economy had rapidly expanded. It capitalized on the opening up of other economies, inserting US business practices and financial acumen into the markets and organizations of what were previously sheltered and relatively isolated national economies. Here the globalization and technological revolution arguments fuse as US businesses were shocked out of their own complacency by a newly invigorated international competition. Restructuring, re-engineering, downsizing and vigorous cost-cutting were the response, it is suggested, so that now American companies have become vastly more efficient. The twin pressures of international competition and rapid technological change combined to announce a new era, to which American corporations were almost uniquely able to respond positively. Moreover, since the introduction of information technology and the process of globalization are only just beginning, there is a no obvious limit on the expansion of American capitalism either domestically or abroad.

Here it was a new version of the 'heroic entrepreneur' that served to fulfil the American dream once again. A culture of rugged individualism, entrepreneurialism, pragmatism and novelty – this time embodied in the small start up company which rapidly rose to stock market flotation, personified by the likes of Bill Gates at Microsoft – is invoked as the underlying microeconomic foundation of the positive macroeconomic results just described.

Questioning the 'new economics'

There are a number of ways to tackle a review and critical assessment of the 'new paradigm'. Broadly speaking these fall into two broad categories; those that look to the international position of the economy and which particularly emphasize financial and monetary measures in this respect, and those that focus upon the domestic economy and which tend to concentrate upon 'real economy' measures (e.g. Katz and Krueger, 1999; Zarnowitz, 1999). In the main, I stick to these two approaches in what is discussed below.

A productivity miracle?

A central plank in the new economics approach relies upon the positive consequences of introducing information technology for productivity growth. Here we return to a long running issue in the modern history of the American economy namely the 'riddle of productivity' (see Thompson, 1999a,b).

The recent record on US productivity is given in the first part of Table 2.3. This shows a single measure (output per hour worked), but the results are similar if other productivity measures are used. It is clear that for the

Table 2.3   US business sector productivity, 1980–2000

	Annual percentage change						
	1980–90	1990–95	1995	1996	1997	1998	1999	2000
Output per hour worked	1.7	1.5	0.7	2.8	2.3	2.8	2.8	4.2
Non-farm business	1.5	1.5	0.9	2.5	2.0	2.7	2.6	4.3
Manufacturing	2.9	3.2	3.8	3.5	4.3	5.4	4.5	6.9

Source: US Government, *Statistical Abstract of the United States,* 2001: 399, table 613.

economy as a whole the growth in output per hour worked was modest over 1990–98, with rates of under 1 per cent per year being recorded between 1990 and 1995. The differences between the overall non-farm business sector and that for manufacturing as a part of this sector are also revealing. Clearly, productivity in manufacturing has been increasing at a much faster rate than that for the business sector as a whole, with impressive rates of growth in manufacturing in the second half of the 1990s.

On the surface, however, this might seem odd, given the emphasis on the growth in investment in computing technology and informatics, and the decline of manufacturing as the key part of the US economy, as stressed by the 'new paradigm' story outlined above. With the growth of a post-industrial 'service economy', we might have expected productivity in the overall non-farm business sector to have led that in manufacturing. Clearly, however, what is still classified as manufacturing now involves a great deal of service type activities as well (see also Williams *et al.*, 1999).

This issue of productivity has come under even more intense scrutiny as the US long boom matured in the late 1990s (e.g. Gordon, 1999, 2000; Jorgenson and Stiroh, 2000; Oliner and Sichel, 2000). In particular, the differences between the record for the whole economy and that for the manufacturing sector have again exercised commentators. A detailed disaggregated breakdown for this sector shows that the bulk of the growth for the sector as a whole can be accounted for by a single small industry, computer manufacturing (Gordon, 1999). Between 1995:Q4 and 1999:Q1 output per hour productivity increased by a staggering 41.7 per cent per annum for this industry alone. The comparisons with other non-farm businesses and with other historical periods are shown in Table 2.4. Thus, while computer manufacturing comprised just 1.2 per cent of total US output, its prodigious productivity record accounts for the bulk of the growth shown in Table 2.2. The record for the rest of the sector, and indeed for the economy as a whole, remained modest. However, this should not deflect us from acknowledging the fact that things might change rapidly in the future.

Table 2.4   Output per hour, by sector, alternative intervals
1950–99 (percentage growth rate per annum)

	1950:2–1972:2	1972:2–1995:4	1995:4–1999:1
Non-farm private business	2.63	1.13	2.15
Manufacturing	2.56	2.58	4.58
durables	2.32	3.05	6.78
computers		17.83	41.70
non-computers	2.23	1.88	1.82
non-durables	2.96	2.03	2.05
Non-farm, non-durables	2.68	0.80	1.50

Source: Adapted from Gordon (1999: 28, table 1).

Table 2.5   International comparisons of GDP
and productivity: 1989/90 and 1997

Real per capita GDP (USA 5 100)	1989	1997
Japan	75.5	83.8
France	73.6	72.6
Germany	78.3	81.4*

Output per hour worked in manufacturing	% change 1990–97
USA	3.2
Japan	3.0
Germany	3.0
Italy	3.4
Sweden	5.0
Netherlands	4.1
UK	2.6

Note: * West Germany only. All Germany, 72.6.

Source: Adapted from Krugman (1998: 43) and
Statistical Abstract of the United States, 1999.

Investment in ICT could produce its major benefits down the line, as it
becomes a critical mass in the economy overall.

In addition, given the emphasis on the United States's advantage in the
new technology investment stakes, we might have expected its productivity
growth to have outstripped that of its main economic rivals. Here the evidence is mixed. Comparative productivity data are presented in Table 2.5.

Table 2.6   Investment in ICT, G7 countries

	Canada	France	Germany	Italy	Japan	UK	USA
Per cent share in non-residential gross fixed capital formation: IT equipment							
1985	6.9	6.1	3.4	3.4	3.4	5.2	6.3
1990	7.3	5.0	3.5	4.1	3.8	7.5	8.7
1996	10.1	6.0	6.1	4.2	4.6	11.7	13.4
Communication equipment							
1985	4.2	4.0	3.7	2.4	0.8	5.2	5.8
1990	5.3	3.8	3.7	3.6	1.5	5.8	7.0
1996	6.1	4.9	4.8	5.4	3.5	6.6	6.5
Average annual rate of growth of constant price expenditure on: IT equipment							
1985–90	17.2	16.2	18.8	20.8	23.6	25.5	19.6
1990–96	17.6	11.0	18.6	12.9	14.5	17.6	23.8
Communication equipment							
1985–90	20.6	19.0	18.4	25.6	34.7	20.3	16.7
1990–96	4.3	2.1	3.4	9.2	15.0	2.2	5.1

Source: OECD (2000a: 184, Table V.3).

In terms of real GDP per person, Japan and Germany improved their position as against the United States between 1989 and 1997, if only modestly, while France slipped a little. In terms of annual growth rates of productivity, between 1990 and 1997 many of the European countries did better than the United States in the manufacturing sector while Japan and Germany performed a little less well. Even for ICT investment, a number of other OECD countries have had a similar performance to the United States, as Table 2.6 shows. The experience in the United States over the 1990s is not unique (though see Gust and Marquez, 2000 for a slightly different conclusion).

What these data indicate is that the United States's record in terms of productivity is not as outstanding as is implied by the 'new economy' thesis. Indeed, in many ways they demonstrate a productivity record over the 1990s no better than for much of the post-Second World War period before the 1990s (see Gordon, 1999: 29–30, tables 2 and 3; Thompson, 1999a: tables 5.6 and 5.7). Improvements in the United States have been modest – with the exception of the manufacturing sector and computer manufacturing in later years – and the United States has not greatly improved in respect of its comparative international position. Moreover, the fact that, in part at least, the

United States has held its own against its economic competitors is more the result of the lacklustre performance of those rivals over the same period. So why has this promised breakthrough so far failed to emerge? Here many of the arguments that characterized the debate about the productivity slowdown in the 1970s and 1980s have resurfaced. The 'new economics' authors suggest that there are measurement errors which fail to record all the real productivity gains that have accrued in the service sector in particular. Indeed, the mismeasurement issue has become the main focus for the optimists with respect to the future prospects for the economy. However, this is difficult to sustain since the new paradigm optimists make no quarrel with the GDP figures – which are celebrated – and productivity is simply these GDP figures divided by various measures of employment. Moreover, any mismeasurement of output has been a perennial problem not something just confined to the 1990s.

In fact, there were a lot of methodological and cyclical changes that can account for much of the modest productivity growth over the early 1990s. Underlying gains in 'total factor productivity' (that productivity growth not accounted for solely by either increased capital input or the quantity of labour used but due to the way these two factors are better organized) were as low as 0.3 per cent a year between 1990 and 1996 (US Government Printing Office, 1999a: 75). In addition, some of the modest improvement in productivity recorded was itself the result of measurement changes which boosted productivity growth by anything up to 0.4 percentage points a year.[2] Table 2.7 gives a typical estimate of labour productivity changes and total factor productivity changes over the various cyclical periods.

One explanation for the limited impact of computer investment is that despite the torrid pace of such investment, and the US superior record internationally, it still represented a very small share of the overall capital employed in the economy; less than 5 per cent of the total net stock of equipment and less than 2 per cent of net non-residential fixed capital in 1998 (ibid., 75).

Probably the best explanation relates to the still early nature of ICT investment. It may be that there is a long learning curve before the benefits of this become apparent, and only after a critical mass of such investment has been

Table 2.7   Consensus estimates of labour productivity and total factor productivity

Per cent change per year	1959–74	1973–95	1995–99
Average labour productivity	2.95	1.42	2.58
Total factor productivity	1.01	0.34	0.99

Source: Jorgenson and Stiroh (2000: 217).

built up in the economy over time. Thus rising productivity follows major technical innovations with a considerable lag and so the promised benefits will only appear sometime in the future. Of course, this may help sustain the booming economy, something we return to below. But again there are dissenting voices. Gordon (2000) argues, for instance, that much of the productivity benefits shown in Table 2.7 are *cyclical* and thus *not* sustainable over the long term.

Increased globalization?

The other main reason for economic growth given by the new paradigm is that the United States is now a fully globalized economy, competing not only with the OECD countries of Western Europe and the Far East but also increasingly with developing countries. There are a complex set of issues that arise here, not all of which can be dealt with in this chapter so I concentrate upon a few main and illustrative ones only.

There can be little doubt that the United States has indeed increased its level of interdependence with the international economy over the 1990s period. But all economies have done this, and many to a much greater extent than the United States has done (Hirst and Thompson, 1999, 2000; Held *et al.*, 1999). Table 2.8 gathers together a range of measures of trade, direct investment and financial activity, which summarize the extent of the international integration of the US economy in the mid-1990s.

The question is whether the levels of integration and internationalization indicated by these figures amount to a new era of global openness for the US economy. To some extent, this is a matter of judgement. Clearly, the trade to GDP ratio having passed 20 per cent in the 1990s is the highest percentage shown, but this is still low by developed country standards [Line 1]. In addition, less than 10 per cent of US GDP represented trade with the developing countries (excluding oil exporters) [Line 2]. Most commentators have argued that this is too small a percentage to be effective in putting much downward competitive pressures on either domestic US labour costs or on the prices of its manufacturing output (e.g. Krugman and Lawrence, 1994; Borjas *et al.*, 1997).

If we now turn to the activities of MNCs, the absolute growth of the FDI flows can be misleading because when expressed as a percentage of GNP these amounted to only 1.2 per cent for inflows and 1.6 per cent for outflows in 1997 [Line 3]. The percentages for stocks of FDI (the accumulation of past inflows and outflows) were higher, but again only around 10–12 per cent in 1997 [Line 4]. And the share of FDI inflows in overall capital formation was just 8 per cent, so 92 per cent of domestic investment was generated from domestic sources in 1997 [Line 5]. Furthermore, the overall capital flows into the United States over the 1990s resulting from its current account deficit was no more than about 1.2 per cent of GDP per year on average [Line 6].

Table 2.8   Measures of US economic openness and
internationalization, 1990–2000

	%
Trade (imports + exports) as a % of GDP (1996)	19
Trade (imports + exports) with LDCs as a % of GDP (1996)	7
FDI flows as a % of GNP (1997)	
In flows	1.2
Out flows	1.6
FDI stocks as a % of GNP (1997)	
Inward	9.3
Outward	11.8
Share of inward FDI as a % of gross fixed capital formation (1996)	7.0
Net capital flows (absolute value of current account as % of GDP – average 1990–96)	1.2
Foreign assets and liabilities of commercial banks as a % of their total assets (1996)	
Assets	2.6
Liabilities	8.2
Institutional investors' overseas assets holdings as a % of total security holdings (1993)	4.7
Percentage of financial assets finally held by households in overseas securities (end 1995)	11.0
Overseas holdings of US equities (end 1996)	5.0

Sources: All derived from statistics collected in Hirst and
Thompson (1999: chapters 2–4).

The rest of the data in Table 2.8 refer to measures of the internationalization of US financial markets and institutions. Looking at the commercial
banks first, their foreign assets and liabilities were still a small fraction of
their overall assets in 1996 [Line 7], and this was likewise the case for institutional investors (pension and mutual funds) [Line 8]. This relatively low
foreign asset holding by financial institutions was reflected in the amount
of financial assets households held in the form of overseas securities. Finally,
the reverse of this, the foreign holdings of US securities, was just 7 per cent
at the end of 2000 [Line 10].

Overall then, we might conclude from the brief review of the 'globalization' of the US economy that it had not proceeded that far by the mid-1990s.

Although more integrated than in the 1970s, the level of increased integration is unlikely to have been sufficient to account for much of the GDP growth experienced in the 1990s. This is not to argue that the impact was nil, only that it does not represent a sufficiently large structural change to have the impact attributed to it. Of course the US economy may integrate much further and faster in the near future, but then, as in the case of technological benefits discussed above, the growth would also accrue sometime in the future.

Thus such that it might be in order to invoke 'international interdependencies' as a key factor in explaining the 1990s US growth record it is more appropriate that they appear as 'cyclical' indicators than as 'structural' ones. Here we could point to a number of important features. These would include the appreciating currency after 1995, which made imports cheaper and helped stimulate domestic consumption (the corollary of this, low domestic interest rates, added to this effect and stimulated investment); until very recently declining world prices of commodities and a favourable turn in the US terms of trade; strong overseas demand for US securities and the United States as an attractive location for FDI (in 1998, FDI inflows were US$193bn – of which US$155bn was M&As investment – while FDI outflows were US$133bn, making the United States a net importer of FDI–UNCTAD 1999). This strong attraction of the United States as a location for inward direct investment is often argued to be an important reason for the continuation of the boom, but the corollary of this is the trade deficit. However, as long as these favourable macroeconomic conditions hold, the boom might continue. Therefore, the question is whether these represent a sufficient explanation for the boom, or whether there are a set of more fundamental reasons that account for it. We return to this below.

Other explanations for the growth record

If we cannot explain the growth record of the US economy during the 1990s simply in terms of investment in new technologies and globalization what alternatives are available? Here we can revisit some of the issues raised when considering the macroeconomic performance of the economy as in the section, 'Changing contours of the US macroeconomic position'. Whilst many of these have also been mentioned in the context of the 'new paradigm' discussion, they do not figure as centrally there as will be stressed here.

Government spending

A key change in the trajectory of the US economy during the 1990s was the turnaround in the government finances, as the federal government moved from a deficit to a surplus (between 1969 and 1997, there had been a continual deficit). There was a close correlation between the degree of federal government savings and net domestic investment; if the 'crowding out' thesis is to be believed it was this change in government savings that in effect financed the expansionary investment cycle (as well as by borrowing overseas). Net private, and State and Local government savings, whilst positive over this period, declined slightly as a share of GDP, mainly as a result of the collapse in household savings commented upon above.

The reasons for this change around are basically twofold. After 1990, there was a 'peace dividend' associated with the ending of the Cold War. This enabled the rate of federal military expenditures to be cut back. For instance, calculated in real dollar terms, the 1999 defence budget called for a spending limit of $270 billion – down $50 billion from the Cold War average (and down $100 from the 1980s' average of the Reagan Presidency). International Affairs spending was also cut (involving items like official development assistance, military aid, spending on US diplomatic efforts and UN activity).

The other main area of expenditure savings has been in the social security budget. This did not strongly emerge until after 1994, as the welfare participation rate dropped sharply. The decline in the welfare rate seems closely correlated with the drop in the unemployment rate, but the former was probably aided as much by the passing of President Clinton's controversial Personal Responsibility and Work Opportunity Reconciliation Act (PRWORA) into law in 1996. This dramatically changed the welfare rules in the United States, making assistance work-focused and time-limited. It also shifted greater responsibility for welfare management to States and localities. The consequence has been a nationwide reduction in welfare caseloads. Of course, this was aided by the generally buoyant nature of the economy and the job market. The PRWORA has been judged as a success, however; it has meant less people on welfare, more in jobs and no seeming increase in deprivation – a virtuous trade-off. However, the real crunch will come if (or when) the economy experiences a contraction, particularly in respect to welfare benefit deprivation.

Financial developments and the company sector

A second set of favourable developments during the 1990s involved financial conditions, broadly considered. Obviously, the main manifestation of this was the booming stock market outlined above. This itself was fed by the rapid securitization of American private savings which was itself partly the result of the liberalization of the domestic (and international) financial system. In addition, there had been another merger boom, with record numbers in 1996 and 1997, which also fuelled the stock market.

Added to this was a robust growth in corporate profits between 1993 and 1997 (Zarnowitz, 1999), a declining trend in interest rates and the plentiful availability of external financial capital (because of the decline in the federal government deficit and the appreciating dollar). All these features helped stimulate the favourable corporate investment climate. These developments – the decline in interest rates, combined with low inflation and moderate monetary growth – enabled the Fed to claim a good deal of the credit for carefully steering the economy along the path to growth. Such that there were exogenous shocks to the system, these were expertly handled by the Chairman of the Fed, Alan Greenspan, who gained a reputation as an astute manager of the system, complementing President Clinton's own cautious and basically conservative approach to economic matters.

International crises and reactions

This concentration on domestic matters should not divert attention from important developments at the international level. Here, it is the US economy's sheer size and importance in the world on the one hand, and yet its still relatively and internationally isolated nature on the other, that enable it to ride out many potentially threatening events originating from overseas. The international financial crises of the 1990s had a relatively small impact on the United States. The series of crises starting with East Asia over 1997–98, followed by Russia in August 1998 and Brazil in January 1999 affected the United States the most, and it led important 'rescue packages' in response to the latter two. The United States mobilized international support, put its weight behind the IMF initiated short-term 'stabilization policies' by granting extra funds to the IMF (US$18bn in 1998); pressed for long-term 'policy reforms' in the emerging market economies to promote market-led recovery; adjusted its domestic interest rates to restore confidence and liquidity; and, finally, arranged support mechanisms for domestic financial institutions that got into difficulties as a consequence of the crises (e.g. in the case of the hedge fund, Long Term Capital Management, where the FED helped arrange a US$3.6bn support loan in September 1998). All these measures undoubtedly helped stem the possibilities of wider disruption in the domestic economy and potential contagion effects throughout the international economy.

The size and importance of the economy and its underlying growth momentum also allowed the United States to take a policy of benign neglect with respect to its exchange rate. The dollar fell against other main currencies up until 1995, but between mid-1995 and September 1998 it appreciated against both European and East Asian currencies in both nominal and real terms (a modest depreciation set in again in late 1998). As we have seen, the strong appreciation of the dollar since 1995 helped keep import prices down, especially for oil and other commodities, contributing to the drop in inflation and the improvement in the US terms of trade (a measure of the prices of exports relative to imports, so an increase in the terms of trade translates into an increased purchasing power of US goods in world markets and higher real US income). The strong dollar also supported the low interest rate policy pursued by the FED. But the strong dollar meant that exports were more difficult to sell abroad, so, combined with the increase in imports, the balance of payments continued to deteriorate. And the failure of domestic savings to meet the needs of investment meant the United States continued its borrowing abroad, so its net international investment position deteriorated further during the 1990s. The United States remains the world's largest debtor country.

Overall, however, what is striking about these international developments is that up until 1999 at least, they failed to seriously dent the shine of the US growth trajectory. The potentially quite adverse international crises were coped with and their affects shrugged off after only temporary interruptions to domestic economic activity.

Developments in the labour market

Between January 1993 and the end of 1998 the US economy created a remarkable 17.7 million new jobs (US Government Printing Office, 1999a: 1). This is where the characteristics of the US's legendary 'labour market flexibility' become important, and nowhere is this more clearly demonstrated than in the case of wages.

The basic trends can be seen in Table 2.9. Between 1990 and 1995, real hourly wages in the United States fell almost every year. Only in 1997 did real wages begin to expand again, and then slowly. Thus, the bulk of the US growth record over the first six years of the 1990s was built on the backs of a declining average real wage for those employed by businesses. This experience is almost unprecedented in modern advanced economies. In conventional economic theory, reductions in real wages are thought to lead to an increased demand for labour, hence the growth in employment. Clearly, there has been an enormous downward pressure put on real wages, so that the hourly incomes of those in the wage-earning sector have declined. This has led to the emergence of longer working hours, second (even third) jobs, and larger numbers of multi-earner households in an attempt to maintain overall family incomes. In part this can also account for the drop in the personal saving rate as these households used any surpluses they could generate in the face of declining incomes to maintain their consumption levels

Table 2.9   US hourly real compensation rates of change, 1998–2000

	Annual percentage change						
	1990	1995	1996	1997	1998	1999	2000
Real hourly compensation	0.6	−0.4	0.4	0.9	3.9	2.4	1.6
Non-farm business	0.4	−0.4	0.3	0.8	3.8	2.3	1.6
Manufacturing	−0.2	−0.4	−1.4	−0.2	3.8	1.9	1.8

Source: US Government, *Statistical Abstract of the United States*, 2001: 399, table 613.

and patterns (though in part, the decline in the savings ratio could also be taken as a sign of consumer confidence and positive expectations).

A further result of this process is the growth of income and especially wealth inequality over the 1990s. The OECD concluded that between 1975 and 1995 there was a general growth in income inequality within most OECD countries, but this was particularly marked in the case of the United States, which also displayed one of the highest inequality *levels* by the mid-1990s (OECD, 1997a).

The OECD finding is confirmed for the 1990s by the data in Table 2.10, which shows the distribution of aggregate incomes for each fifth of US families, and that received by the top 5 per cent. Note how the lowest 80 per cent all lost shares in the 1990s, whilst only the top fifth increased their share, and how there was a marked increase in the income share of the top 5 per cent of income earners. A remarkable 47.3 per cent of incomes went to just the top fifth of earners in 1998.

Table 2.11 presents data on the development of incomes amongst the different ethnic groups in the United States. Clearly, there are significant and entrenched inequalities in median family income for different ethnic groups. In terms of all families, the point made above about the reduction in average real incomes is shown in the first column. Only in 1997 did

Table 2.10   Percentage distribution of aggregate income, 1960–97

	Lowest 5th	Second 5th	Third 5th	Fourth 5th	Highest 5th	Top 5%
1960	4.8	12.2	17.8	24.0	41.3	15.9
1965	5.2	12.2	17.8	23.9	40.9	15.5
1970	5.4	12.2	17.6	23.8	40.9	15.6
1975	5.6	11.9	17.7	24.2	40.7	14.9
1980	5.3	11.6	17.6	24.4	41.1	14.6
1985	4.8	11.0	16.9	24.3	43.1	16.1
1988	4.6	10.7	16.7	24.0	44.0	17.2
1989	4.6	10.6	16.5	23.7	44.6	17.9
1990	4.6	10.8	16.6	23.8	44.3	17.4
1991	4.5	10.7	16.6	24.1	44.2	17.1
1992	4.3	10.5	16.5	24.0	44.7	17.6
1993	4.1	9.9	15.7	23.3	47.0	20.3
1994	4.2	10.0	15.7	23.3	46.9	20.1
1995	4.4	10.1	15.8	23.2	46.5	20.0
1996	4.2	10.0	15.8	23.1	46.8	20.3
1997	4.2	9.9	15.7	23.0	47.3	20.7
1998	4.2	9.9	15.7	23.0	47.3	20.7
1999	4.3	9.9	15.6	23.0	47.2	20.3

Source: US Government, *Statistical Abstract of the United States*, 1975, 1981, 1998, 1999 and 2001 editions.

Table 2.11   Median household in constant dollars, 1980–99

	All	White	Black	Asian/ Pacific Islands	Hispanics
1980	35 851	37 822	21 790	—	27 634
1985	36 568	38 565	22 945	—	27 041
1989	38 836	40 852	24 295	48 505	29 452
1995	37 251	39 099	24 480	44 397	24 990
1996	37 686	39 459	24 934	45 952	26 445
1997	38 411	40 453	26 002	46 969	27 640
1998	39 744	41 816	25 911	47 667	28 956
1999	40 816	42 505	27 910	51 205	30 735

Source: US Government, Statistical Abstract of the United States, 2001: 433, table 661.

median real family income exceed its 1989 level. In 1997, Whites and Blacks had returned to, or bettered, their pre-1989 position, but it was still lower for Asian/Pacific Islanders and Hispanics. The result for Blacks is itself interesting and important because it looks at last as though this particularly disadvantaged ethnic group may be beginning to show a relative gain in its economic position. However, the downside is that Hispanics may now be replacing Blacks as the most heavily disadvantaged group in America.

Here we also need to focus on the actual business strategies of US corporations in their dealings with labour. The period after the 1980s saw an unprecedented attack on labour from business interest. Analyzing this raises a set of more structural issues, including the role of bargaining power and collective action, not all of which can be accounted for simply by short-term changes in labour market conditions. A longer-term perspective is necessary.

The period from the New Deal to the mid-1970s in the United States was one of a strategic compromise between business and labour, marked by an acceptance of the legitimate interests of each in the conduct of business activity and in terms of a broad social accommodation in economic policy-making more generally (Roe, 1994: part III; Gates, 1998). However, this compromise was deliberately broken in the mid-1970s just at the time when the increases in inequality referred to above also began to emerge.

The break in the historical compromise saw a renewed attack on the working conditions of American labour, and a release of the constraints on managerial prerogatives and managerial salaries. The late David Gordon has documented the consequences of this in detail (Gordon, 1996). His argument is that despite a rhetoric of 'downsizing' by American management, the actual facts go against this. There has been an increase in the numbers and levels of supervisory and management personnel. In addition, the wage bill for this managerial group has expanded at the expense of those very workers they are supervising and managing. In this context, a corporate strategy of deliberately undermining the wages of production workers and shop floor employment cutbacks has emerged. This is borne out by data on the distribution of reasons for losing a job amongst those who actually lost a job between 1981 and 1995 (Farber, 1997).

What is striking about these data is that the job loss rate actually accelerated dramatically in the 1993–95 period despite the sustained economic expansion and decline in the unemployment rate. This result is consistent with the claims of a secular decline in job security and an increase in job 'churning'. Workers are experiencing a faster turnover in jobs, as they lose their job and (perhaps) find another one. What is more, this increased turnover was procyclical – it increased as the economic cycle took an upturn (rather than diminished, as in previous cycles). The growth of the category 'other reasons' for job loss from 20 per cent or less in the 1980s to more than a quarter in the first half of the 1990s is intriguing, and not readily explainable. But Farber (1997) suggests that combined with the 'position abolished' category together accounting for around a half of job losses over 1991–95, it implies an increased trend for internal corporate restructuring in which labour bears the brunt of the uncertainty and restructuring costs. In addition, Farber's analysis demonstrates that it is those who lost their job who suffer the severest decline in wages as and when they found other work. The decline in real weekly earnings for displaced works if they found another job was about 13 per cent for all re-employed displaced workers over the period 1989–95. Thus not only did job security decline in America during the 1990s, it was this job loss mechanism that undermined real wages to the greatest extent. As a footnote to this last point, however, it should be noted that the job displacement rate analyzed fell between 1995 and 1997 (from 15 per cent to 12 per cent) – though it was still a third higher than it had been in 1987–89, when the unemployment rate was at a similar level. In addition, the reduction in weekly earnings among those re-employed was only 5.7 per cent, much lower than for the previous periods in the 1990s (US Government Printing Office, 1999a: 122, chart 3–12).

However, at the same time this released the restraint on corporate management from rapidly increasing its own remuneration. The coincidental securitization of American savings and the stock market boom has additionally fed the incomes of stockholders and the well off. The outcome is the growth in inequality in the United States.

Here we have the seeds of an alternative explanation for much of the turn against the unskilled worker and the reduction of real wages in the United States. What is more is this is an explanation that is 'domestic' in origin. It provides an account for the surge in US growth rates, as wages were depressed and profits increased, that centres its account firmly in the domestic economic arena rather than in the more fashionable global one. Of course, the consequences of this 'turn against labour' in the United States can be partly seen in the labour productivity and TFP statistics. Although

ITC investment undoubtedly added to the acceleration in productivity growth over the very late 1990s, the statistics also reveal the key contribution of labour to this (Jorgenson and Stiroh, 2000: 143, table 2; Oliner and Sichel, 2000: 10, table 1). Longer working hours accounted for the bulk of the average labour productivity increases, and the 'hidden' effects of all the job security issues must have contributed to the ability of employers to ratchet up TFP.

However, the explanation offered by these 'labour sweating' advocates is not without its own problems. They probably underestimate the extent of downsizing that has actually occurred in the United States. They also ignore the increase in high-skilled jobs being driven by the growth in technical grade workers in more sophisticated manufacturing processes, who tend to be classified in the supervisory and managerial grades. This might also account for the emphasis on the importance of so-called 'symbolic analysts' (those engaged in conceptual rather than manual tasks) to the American future as stressed by the likes of Robert Reich (who was Labour Secretary for much of the first Clinton administration – see Reich, 1992).

In addition, analysis by Katz and Kruger (1999) casts some doubt on the 'loss of worker security' explanation for the downward pressure on wages, though their main objective is to use this to explore the reasons for the decline in unemployment. However, in this respect, they also note that some 2 per cent of the US labour force is incarcerated, and this prison population is one of the more vulnerable groups in terms of unemployment possibilities.

Conclusions

The new economic paradigm with which we began this chapter painted a very rosy picture for the future of the US economy. However, its twin candidates for the determinants of the booming 1990s' economy – a technological revolution in informatics leading to major productivity gains, and the rapid 'globalization' of the US economy – turned out to be only partly convincing. Indeed the whole picture of a prosperous and booming economy for all looked increasingly shaky as the growing inequalities in income and wealth were uncovered. The consumption boom that led the economic growth trajectory must have been at best largely confined to the better off sections of the population. The high import propensity of this section of the population also added to the balance of payments problems. Only in the very latter years of the decade was there any indication that prosperity might be becoming more widely spread.

However, this widening of the benefits of the US growth decade was surely also threatened by the prospects of an economic downturn in the economy. The only real debate was whether the deceleration would be gradual and orderly or abrupt and disruptive. The structural problem confronting the US economy at the turn of the century was clearly indicated by the data above. Switching attention from the supply side of the economy (investment and productivity growth) to the demand side, indicates that the maintenance of aggregate demand can only be accomplished by re-distributing incomes away from the rich and back to the poor and median income households. There is a limit to how much further income inequality could advance if overall demand is to be sustained, since the wealthy have a lower long-term propensity to consume than the less well off, and their consumption demands are highly import elastic.

However, perhaps it would be churlish to end this chapter on such a negative note. In many ways the sustained economic growth rate found in the economy as a whole was a significant achievement, one for which much of the rest of the world could be grateful. It helped the rest overcome their own crises and downturns, minimizing the damage to their own living standards.

Notes

1. For an analysis of the course of the US economy over the post-Second World War period before 1990, see Thompson (1989, 1999a).
2. *Financial Times*, 29 October 1999; 'A Spanner in the Productivity Miracle', *The Economist*, 11 August 2001, pp. 63–4.

3
British National Capitalism since the War: Declinism, Thatcherism and New Labour

Andrew Gamble

In 1980 British capitalism was widely thought to be in a serious condition. Speculation about decline and its causes was in full flood, and the short-comings of British national capitalism were widely canvassed. All national capitalisms suffered from the mid-1970s economic downturn and the acceleration of inflation, but Britain appeared to be worse affected and to respond more slowly than other countries to the same external pressures. Unemployment doubled to over a million; inflation accelerated, reaching a peak of 26 per cent in 1975; growth and productivity were stagnant, and there were record deficits on the balance of payments. All the main targets of postwar economic management were being missed simultaneously. This was accompanied by a resurgence of industrial militancy, an unstable currency and widening fiscal deficits. There were widely expressed fears that the country was becoming ungovernable and that government itself was becoming overloaded.

Observers had claimed Britain's relative economic decline for much of the century. A much-debated question at the time was whether Britain's experiences were a local instance of a general crisis of capitalism, or whether they reflected a particular crisis of British capitalism. This notion that there was a crisis of British capitalism separate from the crisis of capitalism as a global system of accumulation goes to the heart of the models of capitalism debate (Coates, 2000) and to much of the declinist literature (English and Kenny, 2000). The idea of British decline assumes a British economy which can be distinguished as a separate entity from the global economy and meaningfully compared with other units within it. It also implies that there is a distinctive British national capitalism, which can be compared with other national capitalisms, and which therefore can be said to compete with them. This view has been contested from different theoretical perspectives (Overbeek, 1990; Krugman, 1996), but it receives support from historical institutionalist approaches which argue that between national jurisdictions there are important variations in institutions, political cultures and organizations which lead to differences in performance and outcomes (Hall,

1986; Kelly, 1998; Weiss, 1998). For historical institutionalists global capitalism has been inseparable from national jurisdictions and the competition between them has been one of the most important factors in the development of the global capitalist economy (Arrighi, 1994).

What were the specific features of British national capitalism in 1980? Its shortcomings were acknowledged on all sides. However, there were very different economic and political constructions of what the problem was that needed to be remedied. Conservatives argued that it was the British variant of Keynesian social democracy which had existed since the 1940s which was in crisis and should be stripped away to allow the true character of British capitalism to re-emerge (Joseph, 1976). Restoring vigour to British capitalism required the removal of obstacles to enterprise by reducing the state sector and confronting union power. Many on the left also thought that the post-war Keynesian regime was tottering, but they argued that what was needed was stronger government intervention and direction to remedy the chronic underinvestment by British industry in new technology, new plant and the skills of the workforce (Holland, 1975). These disputes were embedded in complex understandings of the legacies from the historical development of British national capitalism, which emphasized the institutions and capacities which allowed Britain to emerge from its minor kingdom status on the edge of Europe in medieval times to a position of world hegemony, the centre of the financial and commercial circuits of the nineteenth-century global economy and the largest world empire (Hobsbawm, 1968; Gamble, 1994a). From a historical institutionalist perspective it is this history which, by accounting for the many distinctive features and peculiarities of British national capitalism, helps explain the reasons both for British dominance and for British decline (Kennedy, 1988). The peculiarities, which once were strengths, became weaknesses in the very different circumstances of the American dominated world order after 1945.

These debates now overlap with debates on globalization and regionalization, and their implications for national capitalisms (Gamble and Payne, 1996; Held *et al.*, 1999). For some analysts globalization represents a stage of development of the global capitalist economy which increases pressures for convergence on a single model of capitalism. David Coates, for example, has argued that as capital becomes increasingly mobile, local peculiarities and institutions become costly to sustain and therefore vulnerable and subject to political attack (Coates, 2000). Others disagree that convergence pressures will be any greater than in the past, and argue that so long as separate national jurisdictions exist, national capitalisms will persist (Hirst and Thompson, 1999). Rising international competition still leaves states with considerable autonomy in deciding the best strategy to make their economies globally competitive.

Alongside this debate has been the question of Europe. It has sometimes been confused with the debate on globalization, but it is important to disentangle them. The convergence which the European Union (EU) threatens is of a different kind. The EU is best understood as a new jurisdiction which in some areas overrides the British national jurisdiction. If Britain participates fully in the process of European integration some of the distinctive features of British national capitalism may gradually disappear. There is some evidence that this is beginning to happen, particularly as the Single European Market and European social legislation take hold and change the behaviour, constraints and opportunities for British companies. However, this is primarily a political and legal process internal to the EU, and is quite different from the argument that all national capitalisms are converging as a result of global economic competition. As a political issue, moreover, it is still unresolved and Britain could still choose to re-establish an independent national jurisdiction within the global market.

The first section of this chapter will review the main institutional features of British capitalism as they appeared in 1980 at the height of the decline debate in terms of three central relationships between capital and labour, industry and finance and the state and capital. The second section will then examine to what extent these have changed in the last 20 years in the context of the new debates on globalization and on Europe. The conclusion will sum up where British national capitalism is today.

Peculiarities of British capitalism

Capital and labour

A distinctive feature of British national capitalism in 1980 was the industrial strength and political influence of its trade unions. One of the key legacies of Britain's imperial and economic dominance was the size of the urban working class (Gamble, 1994a). The strength of the organized working class in Britain compelled legal and political recognition of its interests. This was done by granting the unions special immunities from prosecution under the provisions of common law. British labour was also distinctive for its culture and strong communities. The world of labour in Britain was a world apart from that of capital and the traditional institutions of the British state to an extent which was unusual, and this in part reflected the sheer size and weight of the British working class within the occupational structure (Hobsbawm, 1968). The other side of this unity, however, was sectionalism. In 1980 the workforce of each industry was still often fragmented between several different unions, whose origins lay in different crafts and skills (Kilpatrick and Lawson, 1980). As a result of this it often proved difficult to deal with inter-union disputes or to forge an overall policy for the union movement as a whole.

The main historical tradition of the trade unions, still alive and well in 1980, was to negotiate wages and other conditions with their employers through free collective bargaining. Trade unions were instinctively hostile both to employers and to the state, and tried to remain independent of both. This tradition rested on an adversarial conception of the company and of the social order, in which labour was pitted against capital (Clift *et al.*, 2000); however much the interests of the two might be accommodated through negotiation, the fundamental opposition could never be overcome. Trade unionists were therefore suspicious of entering into collaboration with employers or with government, even when the government in question was formed by their own Labour Party.

There was a conflict at the heart of the British labour movement between its industrial and political wings, which became more pronounced as time went on, and had reached a particularly acute phase by 1980, and was responsible for so much of the despairing comment on the future of social democracy and of British capitalism. The problem was reconciling the very considerable capacity of the trade unions to defend the immediate interests of their members with a social democratic programme for ensuring economic growth and universal welfare spending. The pursuit of the latter regularly impelled Labour administrations to seek ways of incorporating trade unions within national policy-making in order to ensure that trade union strength was not used destructively, but in support of social democratic objectives (Gamble and Kelly, 2000c). What the 1970s revealed starkly was the difficulty of making a British form of corporatism work. Those trade union leaders willing to participate in corporatist arrangements often found it hard to control their members, and always risked being outflanked by those calling for a return to free collective bargaining and independence. Supporting incomes policies and social contracts proposed by the government was always capable of being represented as support for a policy that favoured the employers. In an adversarial conception of the relationship between capital and labour, the state by definition had to come down on one side or the other. The argument of the left in the trade unions was that Labour governments were in this respect little different from Conservative governments and always in the end supported capital rather than labour. Conversely, employers feared that corporatism would institutionalize greater power for unions and undermine the right to manage, whilst they remained suspicious of government intervention. Further, UK employers' organizations lacked the cohesion of the counterparts in other European countries like Germany.

The tradition of trade union independence had always been nourished by an attitude to the company which was quite content to maintain a rigid divide between employers and employees. An adversarial conception of industrial relations also meant an adversarial conception of the company. Trade unionists were in general content to accept the dominant legal form of the company as a private association. They had no wish to make the company a constitutional body as had occurred in Germany, which gave workers formal rights of representation in the company. British trade unions preferred a strict separation between labour and capital, while pressing politically through the Labour Party for the transfer of companies from private to public ownership (Clift *et al.*, 2000).

Even following nationalization, however, unions continued to see the public sector managements in the same way that they had viewed private management, and still insisted on keeping their independence and their right to free collective bargaining. This was a highly unstable situation, since in conditions of full employment as existed through the 1950s and 1960s the bargaining position of unions was considerably enhanced against employers, but they failed to develop a political strategy of the kind developed for instance by the Swedish labour movement. The attempts that were made ended in failure. The strong movement for industrial democracy, for example, which led to the setting up of the Bullock Committee in 1976 foundered partly because the unions were very divided upon its proposals for giving, employees direct representation on company boards (Clift *et al.*, 2000). Similarly, the 1974 social contract between the unions and the Labour government eventually broke down and was followed by the industrial unrest of the winter of 1978/79. Those events became a symbol through the way they were constructed by the Conservative media of the failure of the postwar social democratic regime. It certainly marked the end of the attempts to establish a system of corporatist decision-making for the economy which had been developing over the previous 50 years (Middlemas, 1979), and appeared to confirm that British national capitalism had failed to find a way to function with strong unions. By 1980 solving the union problem had become a main plank of the Conservative programme for reversing British decline.

Industry and finance

A second distinctive feature of British national capitalism in 1980 was the relationship between industry and finance, and in particular the relative weakness of the former and strength of the latter. From being the pioneer of industrialism, the workshop of the world, Britain had become an economy dominated by financiers and rentiers. Capital it was said was increasingly diverted from productive uses to maximize returns for the growing class of rentiers. What is now generally agreed is that British capitalism was always predominantly commercial and financial, and that this did not change even at the height of British industrial dominance in the nineteenth century (Ingham, 1984; Anderson, 1987; Cain and Hopkins, 1993; Arrighi, 1994). The ascendancy of finance over industry is therefore not a new phenomenon, but a deep-seated aspect of the character of British capitalism (Shonfield, 1965; Landes, 1969), but one which does not in itself place British capitalism at a disadvantage (Rubinstein, 1993; Arrighi, 1994).

In 1980, however, the weakness of British manufacturing was regarded as one of the main explanations for relative economic decline. A strong capitalist economy was held to require a strong manufacturing base. Because of its short-term financial orientation British capitalism was seen as increasingly marginal to the way in which the leading capitalist economies were organized, and apparently incapable of adapting sufficiently to the new Fordist patterns of production that radiated out from the United States to all parts of the global economy (Jessop *et al.*, 1988; Chandler, 1990; Overbeek, 1990). Many modern industries had been established in Britain in the twentieth century. In the 1970s, however, there was a general malaise in British industry which affected not only the old staple industries of the nineteenth century like shipbuilding and steel but also several of the twentieth-century mass production industries like cars (Elbaum and Lazonick, 1986; Owen, 1999). The British seemed unable to succeed at manufacturing, as industry after industry was forced to cut costs and restructure in the face of foreign competition (Williams *et al.*, 1983; Coates, 1994).

The global economic downturn in the 1970s revealed that Britain no longer had the financial and political strength it once possessed to compensate for its industrial weakness. But the prosperity of the City of London and the financial services sector were little affected. The City had shown itself adept at moving into new markets like Eurodollars, and increasingly detaching itself from the failing British economy. Although the City was no longer the dominant financial centre in the world, it had remained one of the leading centres, and was assisted in doing so by successive British Governments (Strange, 1971; Ingham, 1984; Helleiner, 1994).

The British economy therefore presented a contradictory picture in 1980. On the one hand there was a large manufacturing sector, much of which was failing to compete and was wracked with problems. Britain had patently failed to create the kind of successful mass manufacturing base using American models of mass production which many other countries had succeeded in doing. In this sector, based mainly in the north and midlands of England, and in Wales and Scotland, unemployment was rising, the rate of job creation and new business creation was low. At the same time there was another British economy, based on the City of London, but radiating out through the Home Counties and the South East of England which was prosperous and expanding, creating jobs and new businesses. This sector was also allied to profitable parts of manufacturing, including pharmaceuticals, aeronautics and defence. All these sectors were dominated by transnational companies. Britain had long been the base for more leading transnational companies than any other national capitalism apart from the United States, as well as attracting strong inward investment by foreign transnational companies (Fine and Harris, 1985: ch. 3).

The state and capital

The third distinctive feature of British national capitalism in 1980 was the role played by the state. Much writing on decline identifies the British state as a key part of the problem. This is obviously true of those approaches like the Conservative view cited above that the chief reason for poor British economic performance was the degree of intervention by the state in the economy. But it is also true of those accounts which argue that the problem is not too much state intervention but too little. What Britain lacked according to an influential diagnosis is a developmental state (Marquand, 1988; Hutton, 1995). States elsewhere have succeeded in establishing a clear framework for planning and steering the development of the national economy. Governments are proactive in seeking to create the conditions for successful economic performance (Coates, 2000: ch. 7). Failure of such initiatives in Britain was often attributed to the character of the British state itself, the nature of its institutions and the attitudes they fostered (Nairn, 1977; Hall, 1986).

Some critics of the British state claimed it had a bias against modernization and significant reform, despite the constant political rhetoric to the contrary. It was a closed elitist structure which had been constructed for the very different task of managing a world Empire and maintaining Britain's dominant financial and commercial position in the global economy. It was never designed, except in so far as military capability was concerned, to promote domestic industry, in the way that so many states learned to do after 1880, and again after 1945. Although the critics acknowledged that the British state had expanded enormously in the course of the twentieth century and developed a huge administrative apparatus, they argued that much of the effort was dissipated because of the antiquated constitutional structure within which ministers and civil servants were obliged to work.

In 1980 the organization of the state still bore many of the hallmarks of its nineteenth century past. The Treasury, despite challenges, remained the key department of the state, its orientation reflecting the priorities of financial rather than industrial capital. Traditionally, it had seen the preservation of Britain's world role as its main duty, and therefore gave priority to maintaining the value of the pound and the institutions of a liberal world order, rather than sustaining domestic jobs and businesses. The Department of Industry still retained the traditional orientation of the Board of Trade, which it had absorbed. Labour Governments on two occasions had tried to create a department which would be specifically concerned with the national economy and with the manufacturing base, rather than with the transnational economy in which a lot of British firms were engaged. Both attempts were short lived (Brittan, 1971). The extension of universal programmes of health, education and social security created departmental empires with very extensive remits, but these were primarily spending and administrative departments. Strategic issues and budgetary issues were reserved for the Treasury. There was little attempt to coordinate the work of these departments or to set clear targets for outputs and the main concern of the Treasury was to keep tight financial control over expenditure.

In its macroeconomic policies the stance of British Governments since 1945 had been formally Keynesian, but in practice had not been put to the test, because demand was so full, and employment so high. When inflation began to accelerate in the 1960s British Governments tried to contain cost and demand pressures while preserving public spending programmes. The failure to do this when external pressures mounted in the 1970s brought the wreckage of this policy and the adoption with full Treasury approval of a monetarist approach, which gave higher priority to the control of inflation and public spending than to reducing unemployment.

In its industrial policy the Government up to 1980 had remained interventionist, although its interventions were marked by many confusing changes of policy and the absence of any long-term coherent strategy (Hall, 1986). The nationalized sector which had been greatly extended under the postwar Attlee Government was extended again by Conservative and Labour Governments in the 1970s. However, there was much disagreement as to how the sector should be used, whether it should be further expanded, and how it might be integrated in a developmental strategy. Yet the original rationale for such a large public sector was to enable the state to plan the national economy, and ensure that levels of investment were increased. By 1980 the failure to develop a clear national strategy undermined the point of having so many nationalized industries (Fine and Harris, 1985: part II). Critics of the British state also pointed in particular to its relative failure to do more to foster education and training, building up the skills base of its citizens and developing their human capital. British national capitalism in 1980 was notable for the poor quality not just of physical capital but also of human capital, and many of these shortcomings were ascribed to the failure of state policies.

However, the picture is uneven. The developmental state thesis has been criticized for ignoring the instances of a much more proactive role by the British state, particularly in relation to defence and agriculture. Defence had always been central to the British state and to its success, going back to the naval shipyards of the seventeenth century. The pursuit of an expansionary commercial and imperial policy from the seventeenth century onwards required heavy expenditure on military capacity, and this has continued to the present, with state protection and support of the defence sector. So in relation to defence, and to a lesser extent to agriculture since 1940, the British state has been a developmental state, and a successful developmental state (Edgerton, 1991).

From Thatcher to Blair: the revival of British capitalism

In the last 20 years there have been significant changes in British national capitalism and in the nature of the political economy debate about it, arising from a combination of external pressures and an internal realignment of forces. The most important external pressures have arisen on the one hand from the deepening process of European integration, and second from the restructuring of capital across global markets. European integration which produced the single market in the 1980s and the single currency in the 1990s has proved an important threat to the survival of a separate British national capitalism because by creating a new jurisdiction it has established a set of political and legal processes which mean that full participation in Europe means accepting increasing harmonization of its institutions and policies with those in the rest of Europe. Britain, the most reluctant member of the EU, continues to drag its feet on further integration, but the convergence that has already taken place through the implementation of the Single European Market programme and the provisions of the Treaties of Maastricht and Amsterdam, is considerable, and more is on the way. By degrees some aspects of British national capitalism are being transformed in ways which will make it more like national capitalisms elsewhere in Europe. This is a political choice, so far not repudiated by any British government, as to the arrangements which will best secure British prosperity in the future.

The other important external factor has been global restructuring and the emergence of new technologies and (potentially) new leading sectors. This has not only underlain the huge shifts in employment and the growth and decline of different sectors in the last 20 years, it has also transformed the competitive position between national capitalisms.

In 1980, as already noted, Britain had a relatively high level of international integration. This continued over the next two decades with external economic liberalization, notably the abolition of exchange controls as one of the first acts of the incoming Thatcher government. On most measures Britain has higher levels of trade, international investment and financial flows relative to national income than the other leading economies (Held et al., 1999; Hirst and Thompson, 1999, 2000). As well as the continued external orientation of many large British firms, inward investment has been central to the transformation of British industry and finance over the past 20 years.

In the 1980s, the economies of Britain and the United States performed less well than the economies of either Germany or Japan, and the balance of economic advantage and even of world leadership appeared to be tilting away from the United States (Kennedy, 1988). In the 1990s, however, the rise of new knowledge industries centred on information technology and genetics have helped the United States regain its position as the leading economy (see further, Grahame Thompson: ch. 2), while Germany and Japan have both suffered severe recessions and much slower growth. These developments have helped to restore faith in American capitalism and, by extension, British capitalism as well, at least in respect of certain features which both now share, including flexible labour markets, shareholder value and short-term financial markets. This has enabled both the Conservative and Labour Governments in the 1990s to posture as defenders of the virtues of British capitalism against European capitalism, and explains some of the reluctance in Britain to embark on deeper integration with Europe.

Internally changes in British capitalism have been assisted through a major redrawing of the political terrain, brought about first by Thatcherism, then by New Labour. The Conservative Government between 1979 and 1997 and the Labour Government after 1997 were different in certain respects in their policies and attitudes from earlier postwar administrations. It is easy to exaggerate both the novelty of the Thatcher government, since many of its policies were foreshadowed by previous British Governments of the 1970s, and the continuity and coherence of its programme which contained many inconsistencies and changes in direction (Marsh and Rhodes, 1992). Moreover, the argument that there has been a continuous neo-liberal administration in Britain for the last 20 years, undisturbed by Labour's election victory in 1997, ignores the many ways in which the direction of policy has shifted under Labour (Gamble and Kelly, 2000c). These qualifications aside, the Thatcher Government did pursue a radical programme of economic modernization which explicitly challenged many of the institutional features of the postwar economic regime, and sought to purge British national capitalism of certain aspects, notably its strike-prone workers, inefficient nationalized industries, anti-enterprise culture, the size of its welfare state, the pretensions of its special interests and professions and the scope of government intervention (Gamble, 1994b). The shock which Thatcherism administered to the British economy and the British state had lasting effects and helped create a new political terrain. When Labour eventually returned to government in 1997 it did not seek to reverse these changes by renationalizing industries, reviving corporatist institutions or repealing the Conservative trade union laws. It accepted many of the Conservative reforms, but developed them in new directions by beginning the slow process of rebuilding the legitimacy of both unions and public services and thus embedding markets once more in a social context.

Capital and labour

Some of the most dramatic changes since 1980 have taken place in the position of labour. The policies of the Thatcher Government played their part in this, but at least as important were the long-term changes in the structure of economic activity (Marsh, 1992). The Thatcher Government, however, partly inadvertently, hastened the process. The combination of the second oil price hike which pushed sterling to very high levels (Britain was now an independent oil producer through the North Sea fields), and the government's tough monetary stance which raised interest rates, created a sharp squeeze on profits and a severe recession, with the result that investment and output plummeted and unemployment soared, eventually peaking at over 3 million. This economic collapse weakened the bargaining position of the unions, and the Government took full advantage of this by driving through successive trade union laws which placed heavy new restrictions on trade union activity, and supported employers in fighting industrial disputes, winning some major victories, including those over the miners in 1984/85 and the newspaper printers in 1986. Along with mining there was a huge shakeout of traditional industrial and manufacturing jobs during the Thatcher years; shipbuilding, cars, steel and engineering were all major losers. The power of public sector trade unions, often identified by Conservative thinkers as key to the 'British union problem', was undermined by privatization, public expenditure controls and changes to union law.

The Thatcher Government resurrected the traditional disciplines of bankruptcy and unemployment to restructure the economy and liquidate the positions of many established groups of workers and industries. The result was a substantial redrawing of the map of British capitalism. Manufacturing employment shrank (by a third to 21 per cent of the workforce by 1992) with the loss of more than 3 million full-time jobs, and with it one of the most important bases of British trade unionism. Trade unions membership plunged from 12 million in 1980 to less than 8 million in 1992. Many of the new jobs which were subsequently created were part-time and low paid, and in sectors with low union membership, or from which unions were excluded (Marsh, 1992; Coates, 2000).

What also declined, particularly in the 1990s, were strikes. From having one of the highest records of strikes in the 1960s and 1970s, in the 1990s Britain experienced one of the lowest. The reassertion of managerial dominance and the undermining of union power both in terms of national collective bargaining and the influence of the shop floor were lasting changes and marked a substantial transformation of British national capitalism. These changes were not a direct result of the union legislation, but by removing the legal privileges which trade unions had enjoyed since 1906, and subjecting them once again to the threat of legal action if they sanctioned strike action, it helped consolidate the swing in the balance of power to the employers that was happening anyway.

Another major change was that the Thatcher Government sought to reverse the tide towards corporatism which had been proceeding since the 1920s. It was particularly successful in dismantling corporatist institutions at the national level. Trade unions were effectively excluded from any participation in national decision-making. All machinery for incomes policy and industrial planning, even eventually the National Economic Development Council itself (in 1992), were scrapped. The unions ceased to be one of the state's governing institutions, and this change was ratified by Labour. After 1987 Labour began to distance itself from the trade unions, and gradually accepted the Thatcherite union reforms. It promised however to redress the balance against employers by giving workers new individual rights. These plans were eventually embodied in a white paper, *Fairness at Work*

(DTI, 1998) and subsequent legislation. It marked an important strengthening of the position of employees against employers, but did so by creating a legal framework for the rights of individual workers rather than through the reintroduction of legal privileges and immunities for trade unions as corporate bodies. This shift was consolidated through the ratification of the Social Chapter of the Maastricht Treaty, from which the Conservatives had previously secured an opt out.

The logic of Labour's position suggested further moves down the road to providing employment protection through similar institutional and legal means to those in other European capitalisms (Taylor, 1998). Its introduction of a minimum wage was a sign of this new thinking. However, Labour remained committed to the concept of flexible labour markets, and was opposed to some of the regulatory burdens and costs which were imposed on European employers. Its employment-centred welfare policy, the New Deal, aimed at encouraging the unemployed back into long-term employment, was an active labour market policy but one which remained significantly different from active labour market policies elsewhere in Europe notably through its emphasis on flexible labour markets. The structure of employment in Britain with the proliferation of low-paid, part-time jobs was significantly different than in many other European countries, but Labour's election meant that convergence towards a European pattern of strong individual employment rights became more likely.

Progress on reforming the company was even slower, but here too the combination of initiatives from business itself in proposing new forms of self-regulation, the European directives on the company and the pressure for common standards of external regulation in areas like the environment, had begun to create a new climate. The Labour Government established a Company Law Review in 1998, and although a radical overhaul of company law was not in prospect, recognition of the need to clearly articulate a legal framework for the company which could recognize its public responsibilities had become powerful (Parkinson, 2000; Gamble and Kelly, 2000b).

Industry and finance

The relationship between industry and finance also underwent some major changes after 1980. The huge shakeout in manufacturing had the effect of strengthening those sectors of the economy based around the financial and service core of the South East and the major MNCs in oil, electrical engineering, pharmaceuticals and defence. The course the restructuring took entailed enormous dislocation in many regions away from the South East, and loaded huge costs on to them (Martin and Tyler, 1992; Rowthorn, 2000). It made possible a big expansion of the financial and service sectors, and was aided by a big inflow of foreign investment which helped to reorganize some industries by introducing new work practices and management styles (Hood and Young, 1997). The contraction in manufacturing employment occurred in every national capitalism, but the speed of the contraction as a result of the policies of the Thatcher Government was exceptionally rapid, and left Britain with a much smaller manufacturing sector measured by employment share than either Germany or Japan.

The extreme fears that de-industrialization practised on this scale would permanently unbalance the British national capitalism and lead to an uncontrollable decline, as the manufacturing base would be too small to generate the exports needed to sustain a high level of employment were not realized (Rowthorn and Wells, 1987). This led the proponents of the neo-liberal strategy to proclaim an economic miracle, a major increase in productivity and lower inflation creating the basis for the soar away boom of the late 1980s (Walters, 1986). The boasts were premature when the economy overheated, in part because the Government had fuelled it through tax cuts, and plunged into a deep recession which pushed unemployment above 3 million again and took several years to overcome. Many economists also questioned whether the productivity gains could be sustained (Healey, 1992; Glyn, 1992b).

The resumption of growth, however, after the ERM exit in 1992, proved more durable, and the British economy entered into one of its longest periods of sustained expansion, accompanied by falling unemployment and low inflation (Crafts, 1997; Kelly, 1997). The increase in productivity was modest, far short of a miracle, but it was significant, and laid the basis for rising living standards and the opportunity to increase public spending, which the Labour Government was able to capitalize on in the spending plans it announced in July 2000.

There still remained major shortcomings in British capitalism, not least the low levels of investment in plant and technology, and the weaknesses in infrastructure, particularly education, training and health (Kitson and Michie, 1996). The outcome of the neo-liberal strategy under the Conservative Governments was the creation of a large sector of low-wage, low-skill jobs. This was reinforced by the priority which was generally given to cutting taxes whenever possible and restraining public spending (Wilks, 1993). Labour began to reverse this priority after 1997 and to give new importance to the formation of human capital, but the accumulated deficiencies of supply-side policy meant that it would be a long time before Britain equipped its workers with the same skills and training as those of other European capitalisms. Underinvestment in both human and physical capital remains a marked characteristic and weakness of British capitalism (Hay, 1999; Coates, 2000). Education spending under Labour, for example, although it rose in real terms, was still below what it had been as a percentage of GDP under the Major Government.

The shake-up initiated by the Thatcher Government was not confined to industry. The privileges of several professions, including lawyers and doctors, were curtailed. Although the financial services sector was one of the main beneficiaries of Thatcherite economic policy it too was subjected to reorganization, and the exposure of restrictive practices, most notably through the major deregulation ('Big Bang') of financial markets in the 1980s (Moran, 1991; Augar, 2000). As a result the City was subjected to much fiercer competition and forced to change quite radically. Its position as a leading financial centre was preserved, at the cost of opening the City to a major influx of foreign capital and foreign banks. By the end of the 1980s the City had one of the highest levels of foreign ownership of any sector of the British economy.

Another area where the neo-liberal industrial strategy had a major impact was the programme of privatization which from small beginnings grew until it became a flagship policy of Thatcherism. By the time the Conservatives left office there were very few industries left in the public sector. Telecommunications, gas, electricity, steel, cars, aerospace, coal, water, shipbuilding and rail had all been privatized. From one of the largest public sectors among leading national capitalisms Britain ended the century with one of the smallest (Rowthorn, 1992; Juhana Vartiainen: ch. 7). The change was however less dramatic than sometimes portrayed. First, although the Conservative Governments succeeded in reducing the budget deficit – even moving into surplus during the late 1980s – whilst cutting income and corporate tax rates, total government expenditure continued to rise in real terms and as a proportion of GDP. Second, since commercialization of the nationalized sector was already far advanced and new regulatory regimes had to be introduced for many of these industries. The real substance of the change was therefore a shift towards the creation of a regulatory state (Vogel, 1996; Loughlin and Scott, 1997), another development that brought British capitalism more into line with European capitalism (Majone, 1994, 1996). It created new thinking about the role and limits of government, and the way in which the public interest should be defined and enforced.

State and capital

The role of the state has changed in the last 20 years through this major redrawing of the boundaries between the public and the private sectors, but also through the need to determine a strategy for survival in a fast changing global environment. One of the first steps of the Thatcher Government was to end all exchange controls, an early signal of its determination to pursue a neo-liberal strategy. The government believed that only by opening the British economy fully to global markets would British industry become competitive once again. One result was a sharp increase both in British investment abroad, and in foreign direct investment in Britain. The neo-liberal diagnosis of Britain's problem was that ever since the suspension of the gold standard in 1931 the British economy had become uncompetitive, sheltered behind protectionist walls, and that the only way to overcome this was to get rid of all forms of domestic protection and subsidy. This logic was not applied to defence and to agriculture, whilst the pharmaceuticals industry continued to benefit from the major home market provided by the National Health Service.

Another key question was Britain's relationship to the EU, and the deepening process of European integration. The period after 1983 saw a switch in the positions of the two main parties on the value of Britain's membership. The Conservative Party, which had been the architects of entry, became increasingly divided over the merits of further integration, and by the end of the 1990s the Eurosceptic wing had gained effective control of the party. The Labour Party which had campaigned in 1983 on a manifesto pledging to withdraw from the EU moved after 1987 first to cautious acceptance, and then to strong enthusiasm not only for membership but also for further integration (Gamble and Kelly, 2000a).

The Conservative switch is explained by the particular free-market strategy to which the party became committed under Margaret Thatcher. This strategy not only re-established some aspects of the former free trade and sound money programme traditionally associated with British national capitalism. It was also strongly nationalistic, in believing that retention of national sovereignty was vital to preserve the distinctive features of British national capitalism, and so safeguard Britain's future prosperity. The Thatcherite vision was for Britain to regain its status as a trading nation, relying on enterprise, low taxation and maximum economic freedom, and sloughing off collectivism and socialism. Such a programme ran however counter to full participation in the EU, unless the EU was prepared to endorse Thatcherite economic policies. There was never much chance of that, which meant that frictions were bound to grow between the Thatcher Government and the EU. The inescapable logic of the Thatcherite position was and is a withdrawal from the EU, since economic sovereignty as the Thatcherites understand it rules out any transfer of sovereignty beyond the creation of a free trade area, and the EU has never been just about that, but the creation of a new jurisdiction which in certain areas supersedes the old national jurisdictions.

The Labour position has become the obverse of this. The reason why so much Labour opinion was initially opposed to the Common Market was because it was seen as a capitalist club dominated by right of centre governments whose rules would prevent the realization of a state-led industrial recovery plan for Britain. What changed this position was the growing awareness that the space for that kind of national protectionism had largely disappeared, and that the EU offered many positive advantages, not least employment protection, labour rights and quality of public services far in advance of anything enjoyed by workers in Thatcher's Britain. Many in the Labour Party became enthusiastic about the EU because European capitalism with its commitment to long-term investment in both people and infrastructure seemed more like the kind of capitalism they wanted to achieve for Britain (Gamble and Kelly, 2000a).

Another big change in the 1990s was the return to low levels of inflation and declining, although still quite high levels of unemployment. The new international monetary regime first established in the 1970s laid down rules which were eventually adopted by all national capitalisms in response to the demands of economic management in the new global environment. Keynesianism was far from dead, however, nor could it be when state expenditure continued to be so high a proportion of GDP. Active state policies to manage the economy could not be dispensed with, but the focus did switch on to the supply side of the economy, on how to assist in the formation of human and physical capital, but also more broadly on how to facilitate the emergence of institutional frameworks which could encourage growth. This was accompanied by new concerns as to how markets and particular sectors should be regulated, and how public interest agendas on environmental protection and on equal opportunities and human rights could be embedded in market and fiscal rules and in organizational cultures. This terrain was not obviously a neo-liberal one and offered major new opportunities for initiatives from the Centre-Left (Krieger, 1999).

Conclusion

It is easy to exaggerate the changes through which British capitalism has passed since 1980, but some of them do appear to be real. Some of the distinctiveness of British capitalism has disappeared, and that process will accelerate if Britain continues to participate in European integration and joins the euro. The opponents of the euro, however, form a powerful coalition which seeks not just to prevent the disappearance of the pound, that ultimate symbol of British greatness and independence (Stephens, 1996; Thompson, 1996), but also to preserve the distinctiveness of British national capitalism from other capitalisms in Europe. The distinctiveness which came from Britain's hegemonic role in the nineteenth century was steadily eroded during the twentieth century. Britain is however still different enough from its European partners, not least in the degree of its economic integration in the Union, to make the idea of a British capitalism standing outside an increasingly integrated European economy not entirely fanciful (Holmes, 1996).

If Britain were to become detached from the EU, the scope would then exist for making British capitalism much more distinctive once again, using the powers of a national jurisdiction to reject many of the changes which have been agreed as a result of European integration over the last 30 years. It is the gradual enlargement of a European jurisdiction which has circumscribed the distinctiveness of capitalisms throughout Europe, assisted by the increasing interpenetration and cooperation of European business and finance, as shown by such developments as the merger in 2000 of the London and Frankfurt stock exchanges. The pressure does not of course come only from Europe, but from many global regulatory bodies as well, which are keen to agree common standards for accounting, trade, property rights and much more. This pressure is unlikely to abate, whether or not Britain is part of the EU inner core. However, if it were outside, there would undoubtedly be greater scope for pursuing its own course.

The argument on the right for such an outcome is that only if Britain retains economic sovereignty can it maintain a capitalism which is enterprising and free, with low taxation, weak unions and minimal state intervention (Holmes, 1996). It would also be a capitalism with widening income inequalities, low wages and low skills. The argument on the left is that such a British national capitalism is worth preserving to ensure an independent social and economic policy, which is not constrained by the deflationary policies of an unaccountable European Central Bank (Gamble and Kelly, 2000a).

If the argument eventually goes against the sceptics Britain will still be distinctive in many ways from other European capitalisms, but the differences will become less marked. Much will depend on how sub-national jurisdictions develop within the EU, and how many powers are devolved, permitting the emergence of new forms of institutional diversity. However, the changes to British national capitalism which have already occurred in the last 20 years mean that many of its traditional peculiarities have gone forever.

4
Ireland: Social Partnership and the 'Celtic Tiger' Economy

Rory O'Donnell[1]

Introduction

Ireland presents an intriguing challenge for any attempt to identify and assess the national model of capitalism. For over a century and a half, the country could not achieve sufficient economic development to retain its population. Yet, in the 1990s Ireland has been one of the fastest growing developed economies. Rapid growth of exports, output and employment have led market analysts to describe Ireland as the 'Celtic Tiger'.[2]

This chapter focuses on two institutional aspects of Ireland's approach, industrial policy and social partnership. Since 1987, Ireland has conducted economic and social policy by means of social partnership between the state and economic and social interests. This provided the framework within which industrial development policy achieved a significant measure of success.[2]

The next section outlines the outward-looking strategy adopted in the late 1950s and identifies the strengths and weaknesses of Irish industrial policy from 1960 to the late 1980s. It briefly describes the deep economic, social and political crisis of the 1980s and reports a variety of recent interpretations of Ireland's economic failures. The section, 'Social Partnership' outlines the social partnership approach developed in the late 1980s and pursued through the 1990s. The next section summarizes economic performance under social partnership, revised industrial policy and deeper European integration. The remainder of the chapter is concerned with interpretation of the Irish case. In the section 'Developmental or dependent state?', I ask whether Ireland is better understood as a developmental state or a case of dependency. The next section discusses the interpretation of Irish social partnership. I outline its analytical underpinnings and the arguments against it advanced by the country's more orthodox economists. I discuss Ireland's structural unsuitability for neo-corporatism and, drawing on the self-understanding of Irish partnership, suggest that it is not adequately captured by the concept of neo-corporatism. Some conclusions are outlined in the last section.

Development strategy and industrial policy

Achievements and limits

The background to the remarkable developments of the past decade is Ireland's difficult economic and political history. The nineteenth century saw de-industrialization, agrarian crisis, famine and emigration, which more than halved Ireland's population. Political independence was used, from the early 1930s to the early 1960s, to pursue a strategy of protection. Although protection increased employment in industry, it failed to solve the underlying developmental problem. The switch to an outward-orientated strategy was prompted by the severe balance of payment difficulties, recession and emigration of the 1950s. The switch coincided with, and was encouraged by, the emergence of economic growth, which continued strongly until 1973. Ireland's decision, in the late 1950s and early 1960s, to switch from protectionism to outward orientation, was a highly conscious one. It was intended to achieve an exporting economy by modernizing and reorienting the indigenous economy and attracting inward investment. Industrial policy combined strong fiscal and financial incentives to both inward investment and indigenous enterprises – an approach that has continued to this day.

The new economic strategy had four significant successes from 1960 to 1987 (NESC, 1996). After a century and a half of virtual stagnation, Ireland achieved relatively strong economic and demographic growth. There was a dramatic structural adjustment of the economy. In 1960, agriculture, forestry and fishing accounted for almost 37 per cent of employment. By 1987, this had fallen to 14 per cent, reflecting Ireland's success in attracting inward investment from the United States and continental Europe. These achievements were accompanied by a distinct modernization. The period after 1960 saw a strong increase in living standards and expectations. Incomes, wages and welfare provisions converged on those in the United Kingdom.

However, these successes were qualified in important ways. The development of viable, employment-generating, businesses outside of agriculture was in doubt. The adjustment of indigenous enterprises to international competition failed more often than it succeeded. By default, Ireland's economic strategy came to rely heavily on inward investment. While Ireland proved an attractive location, it was not clear that this was an adequate basis for development. An ongoing concern was the fact that MNCs located only certain stages of production in Ireland, retaining high value-added functions at headquarters or in other advanced countries. Indeed, during the 1970s, the weakness of *linkages* from foreign-owned enterprises to the indigenous economy became a major subject of research and policy concern (O'Malley, 1981, 1986). It was feared that the only significant impact of the MNCs on Ireland was the hiring of labour and the relaxation of the balance of payments constraint. This impression was reinforced by evidence that employment in each foreign-owned plant tended to decline after a number of years. The extent and persistence of differences between foreign-owned and indigenous enterprises – in technology, export orientation, product quality, scale – prompted many to describe Ireland as a 'dual economy'. This raised questions about the adequacy of the industrial policy and prompted arguments for a greater focus on building strong indigenous enterprises and sectors (NESC, 1982).

Demographic and economic growth and international comparison created increased aspirations, distributional conflict, new social needs and intensified political competition. Ireland's strong recovery from the recession of 1974–75 was largely driven by increased public spending and borrowing. Buoyant domestic growth in the 1960s and 1970s postponed the day of reckoning for much indigenous manufacturing industry and cloaked the problems of Ireland's political economy. The underlying weaknesses were cruelly exposed in the profound economic, social and political crisis of the 1980s. The period 1980–87 was one of recession, falling living standards and a dramatic increase in unemployment. Total employment declined by almost 6 per cent and employment in manufacturing by 25 per cent. While the proximate causes of the crisis were international recession, domestic fiscal correction and deflation, the major shakeout in indigenous enterprises and employment can be interpreted as a delayed adjustment to international competition, particularly European integration.

Foreign-owned, grant-aided, export-orientated industries – in chemical, pharmaceutical and electronic machinery – experienced continuous expansion, and rapid export growth, throughout the period of EEC/European Union (EU) membership. Irish firms which relied on the domestic market faired well in the 1970s, when domestic demand was buoyant, but suffered severe contraction in the 1980s. Domestic firms in internationally traded sectors suffered secular decline after the removal of tariff protection. Many of Ireland's relatively large manufacturing firms were in these sectors. The drastic removal of these industries – and their replacement by foreign-owned firms in high-technology segments of chemicals, pharmaceuticals and electrical machinery – constituted a much more significant inter-industry adjustment than was found elsewhere in the EEC (Pelkmans, 1982; NESC, 1989). It created an enormous increase in unemployment, and induced a sharp reduction in average manufacturing firm size, thereby reversing a slow process of industry concentration that had operated since the 1930s. This seemed to further reduce the possibility of building a large-scale indigenous industrial sector (NESC, 1989; Krugman, 1991).

The debate on Ireland's economic failure

The severity of this experience in the 1980s altered perceptions of the Irish economy. Expectations of medium and long-term prosperity became extremely weak, which encouraged rent-seeking and profit-taking behaviour.

This was evident in the extent of capital flight and the tendency for various government incentives to produce rent-seeking financial manipulation rather than increased business initiative. The emergence of the so-called 'black hole' in the balance of payments and national accounts, and the coincidence of rapidly growing exports with falling living standards and employment, produced fears that the modern Irish economy was fundamentally fictitious.[3] The failure, once again, of indigenous development gave rise to a number of major studies of Ireland's 'economic failure'.

Crotty (1986) argued that Ireland should be compared with third world countries, in which the social and political structures established under colonialism are used by the state in ways which favour entrenched elites. O'Hearn (1989) traced Ireland's long-run failure to its outward-looking free market strategy, which made Ireland a 'classic case of "dependent" relations: slow growth and inequality caused by foreign penetration'. Although supportive of inward investment, O'Malley (1989) argued that Ireland, as a late-developing country, faced, and still faces, significant barriers-to-entry created by the scale, market power or technological lead of established firms in larger, more developed economies.

Others attributed poor economic performance to failings in national culture, political institutions and administration (Garvin, 1981; Inglis, 1987; Kennedy *et al.*, 1988; Girvin, 1989; Lee, 1989; Breen *et al.*, 1990). Mjoset's work for National Economic and Social Council (NESC) synthesized these studies, suggesting a dynamic interaction of economic and social structures, global political factors, and cultural and attitudinal patterns. In his view, Ireland's 'basic vicious circle starts from two facts: the weak national system of innovation and population decline via emigration. The mechanism whereby these two features reinforce each other must be sought in social structure. These mechanisms are highlighted by studying contrasts which emerge from the comparison with the other... countries' (Mjoset, 1992).

Changes in industrial policy

The crisis of the 1980s reinforced the criticisms of industrial policy, noted above, and during that decade, the focus and delivery of industrial policy was quietly changed. There was increased emphasis on developing indigenous enterprises, and separate agencies for FDI and indigenous development were created. Industrial policy became more selective and demanding. The development agencies worked closely with firms in devising and implementing company development strategies. The National Linkage Programme was created to increase the number and capability of Irish sub-suppliers to MNCs. Science and technology policy was reorganized and new sector-specific agencies were created. The approach to inward investment became more selective, targeting leading firms in the high-growth, high-technology sectors: computers, pharmaceuticals, medical equipment and software. The argument for a greater focus on building strong indigenous firms and sectors – including Porter-style clusters – received a measure of official support (Industrial Policy Review Group, 1992). EU structural funding provided resources for innovative approaches and the Irish agencies became part of emerging networks at the EU level. The conception of industrial policy was widened and the business implications of public policy in telecommunications, education and regulation was recognized.

Social partnership

In a context of deep despair in Irish society in the mid-1980s, the social partners – acting in the tripartite NESC – hammered out an agreed strategy to escape from the vicious circle of real stagnation, rising taxes and exploding debt. NESC's *Strategy for Development* (1986) formed the basis upon which a new government and the social partners quickly negotiated the Programme for National Recovery to run from 1987 to 1990 (NESC, 1986). This was to be the first of five agreements which have recently brought Ireland to more than a decade of negotiated economic and social governance. Each social partnership programme is preceded by an NESC *Strategy* report, setting out the shared perspective of the social partners (NESC, 1990, 1993, 1996, 1999).

The content and process of Irish social partnership has evolved significantly since 1987. All five programmes included agreement between employers, unions and government on the rate of wage increase in both the private and public sectors for a three-year period. The first partnership programme enlisted trade union support for a radical correction of the public finances. In return, the government accepted that the value of social welfare payments would be maintained, and income tax would be reformed to reduce the burden on workers. Given the high average tax rate on earned income, which resulted from earlier attempts to reduce the fiscal deficit by tax increases, the exchange of moderate wage increases for tax reductions has remained an important feature of Irish social partnership. Beyond pay and tax, the partnership programmes have contained agreement on an ever-increasing range of economic and social policies. A consistent theme has been the macroeconomic parameters of fiscal correction, ERM membership, the Maastricht criteria and EMU. While partnership began by addressing a critical central issue, looming insolvency and economic collapse, it has since focused more and more on a range of complex supply-side matters. This is reflected in a dense web of working groups, committees and task forces, which involve the social partners in the design, implementation and monitoring of public policy.

Another consistent theme has been employment creation and the problem of long-term unemployment. The 1990 agreement led to the creation of local partnership companies – involving the social partners, the community and voluntary sector and state agencies – to design and implement more coordinated, multidimensional, approaches to social exclusion. An OECD evaluation considered that the partnership approach to local development constituted an experiment in economic regeneration and participative democracy which is of international significance (Sabel, 1996).

An important feature of Irish social partnership has been a concern to widen the partnership process beyond the traditional social partners. A new forum was established and membership of existing deliberative bodies was gradually widened to include representatives of the community and voluntary sector. Reflecting this, the 1996 and 2000 programmes were negotiated in a new way, involving representatives of the unemployed, women's groups and others addressing social exclusion. These agreements also included measures to promote partnership at enterprise level and agreement on action to modernize the public service. New institutional arrangements were created to monitor the implementation of the partnership programmes.

Economic performance under social partnership, revised industrial policy and deeper European integration

The period of social partnership has been one of unprecedented economic success in Ireland. The country not only escaped from the deep economic, social and political crisis of the 1980s, but also may have significantly addressed its long-term developmental problems of emigration, unemployment, trade deficits and weak indigenous business development.

The success of the economy since the start of the partnership experiment in 1987 is illustrated in Table 4.1. It shows the principal macroeconomic variables since 1987 and allows comparison with the five years from 1982 to 1986. Under partnership, growth resumed, inflation continued to decline, the budget deficit fell sharply, employment began to recover, but unemployment initially stayed stubbornly high. The UK and European recessions of the early 1990s, and the ERM crisis of 1992–93, interrupted Ireland's recovery somewhat. Strong growth after 1993 produced a dramatic increase in employment, huge budget surpluses and, eventually, a big reduction in unemployment. The combination of economic growth, tax reductions, reduced interest rates and wage increases yielded a substantial increase in real take-home pay. Between 1987 and 1999, the cumulative increase in real take-home pay for a person on average manufacturing earnings was over 35 per cent.

The performance of the Irish economy since 1996 has been exceptionally strong. In the period 1997 to 1999, Irish GDP growth of 9.4 per cent per year compares with 2.4 per cent in the Euro-zone and 2.9 per cent in the OECD. Ireland's astonishing rate of employment growth, 6.5 per cent per year, compares with 1.3 per cent in both the Euro-zone and OECD. Indeed, between 1994 and 1999, Ireland achieved a 28 per cent increase in employment, while the EU as a whole produced a 3 per cent increase.

Table 4.1   Selected macroeconomic variables for Ireland, 1987–99

	GDP growth %	Inflation (GDP deflator) %	Employment growth %	Unemployment (% of labour force)	General government balance, % of GDP
1982–86	1.8	8.7	−1.3	15.0	−11.2
1987	4.7	2.2	1.3	16.6	−8.2
1988	5.2	3.2	0.1	16.1	−4.3
1989	5.8	5.5	0.0	14.7	−1.7
1990	8.5	−0.7	4.4	13.4	−2.8
1991	1.9	1.8	−0.3	14.8	−2.9
1992	3.3	2.8	0.6	15.4	−3.0
1993	2.6	5.2	1.4	15.6	−2.7
1994	5.8	1.7	3.0	14.3	−2.0
1995	9.5	2.7	4.8	12.3	−2.5
1996	7.7	2.3	3.4	11.6	−0.2
1997	10.7	3.5	4.8	9.9	0.6
1998	8.9	5.7	10.2	7.8	2.2
1999	8.6	3.5	4.5	5.7	3.4

Source: OECD *Economic Outlook*, June and December 1999a; *Economic Review and Outlook*.

In interpreting and assessing the Irish model it is clearly of interest to estimate the role of social partnership and a revised industrial policy in the apparent economic transformation since 1987. It is also important to ask whether – using partnership, a modified industrial policy and membership of the EU – Ireland has overcome the deep developmental constraints which have bedevilled it for many decades. These questions are addressed below.

Developmental or dependent state?

The striking economic growth since 1987 poses interesting challenges to any attempt to characterize the Irish variant of capitalism. O'Hearn (1998) argues that the rapid growth since 1987 actually reinforces Ireland's position as a dependent location within the globalized system of transnational production and trade. He argues that Irish growth is dominated, to an even greater extent, by the output and exports of US companies. 'In the main, the Irish tiger economy boils down to a few US corporations in IT and pharmaceuticals' (O'Hearn, 2000: 75). Indeed, he suggests that much of Ireland's growth is an illusion, reflecting the inflated output of key firms in a few sectors, such as computers, pharmaceuticals and software. Little real breakthrough has been achieved by indigenous enterprises. The social partnership agreements represent an effort by government and trade unions to create macroeconomic stability, through suppression of wages and other neoliberal policies, in order to enhance the profitability of both foreign and domestic capital. Increased inequality is an integral part of this pattern of dependent development. Job growth since 1987 largely reflects a process of deregulation and casualization. Thus, he disputes whether Ireland can validly be compared to the Asian Tigers, and sees Irish growth as neither sustainable nor generalizable. The Irish economy remains vulnerable to a crisis in the IT or pharmaceutical sectors or to a change of strategy by leading US multinationals. Ireland can only achieve real development by exerting greater control over capital and much greater direct state intervention in industry. Given that the EU is a neo-liberal arrangement that 'limits the developmental options of small states', such a strategy cannot be achieved without 'a break from the EU' and a 'reversal of global liberalisation'.

In order to assess the adequacy of the dependency interpretation, we need to take a view on a range of factual, policy and developmental issues. Is it correct to describe Irish growth as largely fictitious and mainly a product of MNC production? Does this interpretation provide a plausible account of the options that Irish actors faced and the approaches they adopted? Does dependency theory provide an adequate conceptualization of the nature of globalization, emerging patterns of economic activity and the development models available to semi-peripheral and small counties? I address each of these questions in turn.

Is there no indigenous element in the Celtic Tiger?

It is undoubtedly true that MNCs account for a very large proportion of Ireland's increased output, employment and exports. However, not all these MNCs can be seen as export platforms with little developmental impact on the Irish economy. Some, such as Ericsson and Digital, undertake high-grade functions and are relatively deeply embedded within the Irish economy. More importantly, the predominance of MNC output and exports should not be allowed to occlude the very significant improvement in the capabilities and performance of indigenous firms in both manufacturing and services. Employment in Irish-owned manufacturing enterprises increased by more than 10 per cent between 1987 and 1997 (O'Malley, 1998). This employment growth is not only greater than has been achieved in Ireland in the past, but significantly outpaces manufacturing employment growth in other developed economies. This employment growth is not dependent on sub-supply to MNCs; exports of Irish firms increased faster than employment through the 1990s, despite slower growth in overseas markets than in the Irish economy. Indeed, the greatest growth in employment in Irish manufacturing firms occurred in the more highly traded and internationally competitive sectors. Having been virtually stagnant between 1980 and 1987, the output of Irish-owned manufacturing increased by an average of 4.0 per cent per year from 1987 to 1995 – more than twice the OECD average. O'Riain points out that industrial R&D spending in the whole economy increased in real terms by 15 per cent among foreign firms and 16 per cent among Irish-owned firms (O'Riain, 2000). O'Malley's judgement on the performance of indigenous manufacturing is that 'the scale and durability of this improvement is without precedent in twentieth century Ireland' (1998: 35).

Nor is it accurate to portray the growth in Irish employment as predominantly an expansion of 'bad' jobs. While the Irish economy has certainly been creating part-time jobs at a rapid pace, there has been a very significant increase in full-time employment and the largest number of new jobs are managers and professionals (Tansey, 1998). As O'Riain says, the employment growth has been characterized by an overall upgrading of the occupational structure combined with a significant polarization of occupations and wages (O'Riain, 2000).

What about the patterns of organization and industrial relations in the MNCs and Irish-owned enterprises? As noted above, differences between the technological and managerial profile of foreign-owned and indigenous companies were a cause of much research and concern in the 1960s and 1970s. However, in those decades there was considerable uniformity in industrial relations. An adversarial model, based on collective bargaining and arms-length dealings between unions and management, diffused throughout much of industry and services. This reflected the willingness of incoming MNCs to recognize trade unions and adapt to local traditions of industrial relations (Kelly and Brannick, 1985). However, research by Roche shows that in the 1980s and 1990s there has been profound fragmentation and divergence in industrial relations practices. Four distinct industrial relations models have emerged: a non-union human resource (HR) model, a 'new industrial relations' or 'partnership' model, an approach of managerial unilateralism and deregulation and, in some sectors of the economy, continued adversarialism with only piecemeal innovation (Roche, 1998). This fragmentation arises, in large part, because the MNCs arriving in the late 1980s and 1990s have adopted the non-union HR approach (Roche and Geary, 1996).

This fragmentation of previously prevalent adversarial model is confirmed by research which shows distinctly different rates of adoption of a range of human resource management and work organization practices in foreign-owned and Irish-owned enterprises (Geary and Roche, 2001). The emergence of a significant *difference* between the industrial relations practices of foreign and indigenous firms should not be allowed to conceal the degree of *change* within Irish firms. The proportion of Irish workplaces experimenting with new work practices 'is impressive and compares favourably with other countries' (Geary, 1999: 879) – although there is a lively debate on the depth, scope and economic significance of workplace innovation in Ireland.[4] The ongoing dynamic is described by Roche and Geary as follows:

Notwithstanding the significant differences in the level of adoption of human resource practice between foreign- and Irish-owned workplaces, there is evidence ... of a 'spill-over-effect' where the latter are increasingly introducing new HR practices most often associated with MNCs ... In that sense, the HR practices of MNCs may well have acted as an important catalyst and exemplar for change amongst Irish-owned companies. (Geary and Roche, 2001: 125)

The emergence of new HR and industrial relations approaches in Irish enterprises is consistent with the other trends noted above: their improved output and export performance, their enhanced profitability, the increasing educational profile of the working-age population, the involvement of many companies in either sub-supply to MNC or international networks of production and innovation and the creation of the National Centre for Partnership (located in the Prime Minister's Department) under the 1996 agreement.

In combination, these trends cast doubt on O'Hearn's view that the 'the Celtic Tiger boils down to a few US corporations in IT and pharmaceuticals'.

The policy options and strategies of Irish actors

Does the dependency view provide a convincing account of the options which Irish actors faced and the approaches they adopted? Although the dependency perspective on Irish development clearly has some historical validity, a number of reservations remain. These particularly concern the policy alternative which is implicit within the dependency account.

First, for all the limitations of inward investment as the engine of Ireland's development strategy, O'Hearn fails to demonstrate how it has actually *impeded* indigenous development. His answer would be that foreign investment, *in combination with free trade*, impeded development. However, this only brings us to a second general difficulty, concerning protectionism. O'Hearn is no doubt correct to say that Irish protectionism, in place from 1932 to 1965, was insufficiently strategic. But he skips lightly over the limits of a protectionist strategy in Irish circumstances, particularly the small size of the domestic market (O'Hearn, 1998: 162). Irish people have experienced protection and closure and have no appetite for either. It is simply incorrect to cast this as a view confined to a narrow policy elite or social group beholden to international capital. Indeed, the third general reservation is that, even in the desperate 1980s, dependency studies, which identified the EU and the international system as the source of Ireland's problem, were never seen as offering a basis for action. At the end of the 1980s the new ideas and action were in exactly the opposite direction: supporting *deeper* economic integration in the EU and transition to EMU (O'Donnell, 1993).

If the policy options facing Irish actors are not adequately appreciated, then the policy choices they made are simply misdescribed. In part, this is because O'Hearn paints with such a broad brush: Ireland has followed a neo-liberal path in the 1980s and 1990s, the EU is a neo-liberal arrangement that 'limits the developmental options of small states', the jobs created in Ireland in the past decade are 'low paying with poor conditions of employment'. These broad strokes leave no room for analysis of the *different* strategies followed by Ireland and, for example, the United Kingdom, over the past decade. It is hard to accept that the differences between British Thatcherism and Irish social partnership, British macroeconomic and exchange rate policy and Irish participation in ERM and EMU, and many other differences, are irrelevant details within a single neo-liberal strategy.

On Europe and many other issues there is an uncanny similarity between O'Hearn's approach and that of the small group of Irish neo-liberal economists: a disbelief that anything deep has, or can, change in the indigenous Irish economy, an unwillingness to discuss the role of social partnership in the performance of the past 14 years, opposition to EMU, instinctive dislike of European integration and reluctance to explore its details or nature, and a particular notion of the link between economics and politics. The statist and neo-liberal extremes not only resemble each other, but they need each other, in order to keep the irrelevant 'state versus market' debate going. Meanwhile, Irish actors live in between: seeking a basis for macro discipline which does not sacrifice social solidarity, seeking to make industrial policy relevant to firms in new kinds of market, seeking to reorganize Irish unions and companies, seeking to repair the personal and social damage of high unemployment, seeking to revitalize local initiative and community involvement. The complex mixture of success and failure in these endeavours cannot be uncovered with blunt global analytical instruments provide by dependency theory.

The adoption of a global and strongly structural political economy prevents an adequate account of Irish social partnership. O'Hearn (1998: 169) says that 'the more successful the IDA has become in attracting MNCs, the weaker popular organizations and trade unions have become at the heights of the economy where they are always unwelcome, and the less input they have had on public policy'. This might surprise the Irish trade unions, community organizations and voluntary groups that negotiated the 1997 and 2000 partnership agreements participate in numerous state and EU-funded projects.

If we were to adopt a systemic/structural theory, it is hard to see that it would support emulation of the Asian Tigers in the Irish case. Ireland emerged in the ambit of British imperialism, American democracy and Europe. So, what were its options? What might a developmental state look like in this very different context? O'Hearn never asks these questions – assuming, it seems, that it would look just like Korea or Taiwan (O'Hearn, 1998: 162). However, Irish actors and the Irish people had no choice but to ask and answer these questions. Their unambiguous and unswerving answer has been that, precisely because of Ireland's structural position and the play of power in the international system, Ireland benefits from membership of a law-based international order such as the EU, which constrains the naked use of political and economic power and significantly protects small states in international negotiation.

Conceptualizing the Irish developmental state

There can be no doubt that Irish development poses challenges to existing conceptual frameworks. Ireland's economic breakthrough has not been driven by a developmental state which protects the local economy in order to incubate strong localized enterprises capable of competing in the international economy. Yet, the state has been a key player in economic development. Irish social partnership is not founded on social democratic hegemony (or even class-based parties), is not confined to labour and capital, and does not exchange wage moderation for active demand management at national level and co-determination at enterprise level. Yet, partnership seems a key element in the remarkable economic success since 1987.

The first of these conceptual challenges is addressed in O'Riain's recent work on the Irish software industry and Irish economic development (O'Riain, 2000). He builds on Evans' view that developmental states are characterized by 'embedded autonomy' (Evans, 1995). Such states are embedded in local capital by close ties between state bureaucrats and domestic business. Although an educated labour force is critical, labour is typically excluded from the key institutions of the state. These developmental states retain their autonomy because they have a classical Weberian bureaucracy. While embeddedness allows the state to gather information and mobilize resources, autonomy guarantees that national development goals remain central to state action. O'Riain labels the developmental states of East Asia as *bureaucratic developmental states*.

While the theory of the developmental state has shed a great deal of light on Asian development, it is relatively weak in explaining the role of the state in newly emerging economies such as Ireland and Israel. O'Riain suggests that it be extended along its three underlying dimensions – state intervention in the globalization process, conditions of embedded autonomy and threats to state intervention that emerge dynamically during the development process – to create a conception of a remade *flexible developmental state* (FDS) (O'Riain, 2000):

The FDS is defined precisely by its ability to create and animate post-Fordist networks of production and innovation and international networks of capital, and to link them together in ways that promote local and national development. The FDS can attempt to do this in two primary ways. It can connect to existing flows of capital by attracting FDI and then building local networks of production (typically sub-supply) and innovation (much more rarely) around this 'imported' industrial organisation. It can also attempt to foster indigenous networks of innovation and then encourage them to internationalise, but from a position of relative strength. In either case, the state development strategy is to connect the local and the global economy in such a way that local industrial transformation, accumulation, and development can take place. The FDS plays a key role in fostering 'better' connections to the global. (O'Riain, 2000: 165)

He shows how the Irish state – through a complex and flexible set of agencies and policies – both attracted the leading MNCs in software and acted as 'midwife' in the creation of a group of innovative Irish software firms.

The software sector is perhaps the clearest example of what O'Riain describes as the 'two globalizations' that characterize the Irish economy of the past decade. The first of these derives from the attraction of FDI and, to a limited degree, embedding in the local economy: 'The global goes local'. The second – and, as O'Riain notes, most surprising in the context of Irish economic history – is the emergence of a local network of indigenous firms that have become integrated into international business and technology flows and have become successful in international markets: 'The local goes global'. These are complemented by what O'Riain sees as a third mode of integration into the global economy: the social partnership arrangements by which 'the national level mediates local adjustment to the global' (O'Riain, 2000: 184). To see how this has operated it is necessary to look at Irish social partnership in more detail.

Social partnership: neo-corporatism or post-corporatist concertation?

How should we interpret the emergence, success and persistence of social partnership in Ireland since 1987? While it is clearly tempting to see it as a version of 'neo-corporatism', there are several difficulties with this view. This section begins with an outline of the economic analysis which underpinned social partnership after 1987. It then considers Ireland's structural unsuitability for neo-corporatism and reports the interesting debate within Ireland on the correct way to characterize and interpret the partnership since 1987.[5]

Analytical underpinnings and the neo-liberal critique

In 1990, NESC set out the analytical framework of partnership. It argued that there are three requirements for a consistent policy framework in a small, open, European democracy:

(i) The economy must have a macroeconomic policy approach that guarantees low inflation and steady growth of aggregate demand.
(ii) There must be an evolution of incomes that ensures continued improvement in competitiveness, and which handles distributional conflict in a way which does not disrupt the functioning of the economy.

(iii) There must be a set of complementary policies which facilitate and promote structural change, in order to maintain and improve competitiveness in an ever-changing external environment.

It was argued that, in the Irish case, the first of these requirements is best met by adherence to the ERM, a non-accommodating exchange rate and, as soon as possible, transition to membership of EMU. The second requirement is best met by a negotiated determination of incomes and, to be really effective, such a negotiated approach must encompass not only the evolution of pay, but also taxation, the public finances, exchange rate and monetary policy, the main areas of public provision and social welfare. In pursuit of the third requirement, the Council advocated a major programme of structural reform in taxation, social welfare, housing, industrial policy, manpower policy and the management of public enterprises. It argued that such reforms can only succeed with the active consent and participation of those who work in the agencies and institutions concerned (NESC, 1990).

The international orientation of Irish social partnership was further underlined in the NESC's 1996 *Strategy*. While globalization has undoubtedly undermined many elements of national economic policy, even in large countries, there remain several areas where national policy remains crucial, and may even have become more significant. Indeed, study of current economic conditions clarifies the policy approaches which can be effective in a small, open, European democracy like Ireland:

(i) Most of the policies which affect national prosperity are *supply-side* policies;
(ii) Given rapid economic change, national policies must produce *flexibility*;
(iii) Successful national supply-side policies, directed towards innovation and competitiveness, depend on 'the high level social cohesion and co-operation that the state can both call upon and develop' (Hirst and Thompson, 1992).

This implies that the main focus of policy analysis and development should be the supply-side measures that influence competitive advantage, and the institutional arrangements which encourage discovery and implementation of such measures (NESC, 1996).

While the evolution of Irish economic policy in the past 14 years has been marked by a high level of consensus – between the social partners and across the political spectrum – the more liberal and orthodox economists have stood outside the consensus. Some have objected to the politicization of industrial relations because it 'adds to the bargaining power of trade unionism on an ongoing basis' (Durkan, 1992). Others have argued that the social partners are 'insiders', whose pay and conditions have been protected at the expense of 'outsiders who would work for less', and that social partnership has had the effect of 'raising the level of unemployment and emigration'

(Walsh and Leddin, 1992). An aspect of the strategy that has particularly provoked orthodox and neo-liberal economists is EMU. A preference for the British model of economic and social policy (of the 1980s) is combined with a preference for sterling rather than the euro (O'Leary and Leddin, 1996; Neary and Thom, 1997). Having failed to shake the consensus on EMU, they argued that EMU requires abandonment of centralized wage bargaining.[6]

Adopting the partnership approach, Ireland made major advances in economic management and economic performance. In particular, consensus on this long-run strategy took the exchange rate, and therefore inflation, outside day-to-day party political competition and industrial relations conflict. This can be contrasted with an approach in which short-termism rules in economic policy, business decisions and wage setting. It has led, in the United Kingdom, to short bursts of fast economic growth, followed by deep recessions imposed in order to reduce inflation. Ireland's experiment since 1987 has, for the first time in its history, partly inoculated it from the, strikingly unsuccessful, combination of macro policy and income determination pursued in Britain for many years. Ireland finally escaped the most negative effects of Britain's political business cycle and, in the process, also rejected the neo-liberal approach to social policy and regulation adopted in Britain between 1979 and 1997. As a result, it has preserved a higher level of social solidarity, which seems a pre-requisite to sustaining redistributive policies and addressing issues of structural change and reform in a non-conflictual way.

Ireland's structural unsuitability for neo-corporatism

The Irish case is also challenging to existing theories of neo-corporatism. Important conditions which facilitated neo-corporatist 'political exchange' in Austria, Sweden and Norway – such as a dominant social democratic party, cohesive employers organizations and a trade union movement with a high degree of authoritative centralization – were not met in Ireland (Hardiman, 1988). This led some to doubt the possibility of partnership in Ireland. Others disputed that the Irish experiment could be viewed as *social* corporatism, arguing that the trade union elite agreed a programme of severe measures to adjust the Irish economy, first to fiscal crisis, and then to European integration (Teague, 1995). In addition, it was pointed out that social partnership at the national level was weakly reflected in workplace industrial relations (Taylor, 1996).

There can be no doubt that structures and procedures which sustain national tripartite arrangements were weak in Ireland *when compared with the classical neo-corporatist models*. However, Irish partnership has prompted important institutional developments – particularly the establishment of a central monitoring system – that has improved the effectiveness of tripartite concertation and that go some way to overcoming the indecisiveness and clientelism which can arise within the Irish party system. Unlike the 1970s, the agreements of the 1980s and 1990s have been based on a shared understanding of the problems facing the Irish economy and society and the main lines of policy required to address them. While the Irish case involves an unusual balance between national-level and enterprise-level partnership, the 1997 agreement, Partnership 2000, gave rise to a significant initiative on enterprise-level partnership (O'Donnell and Teague, 2000).

In any case, comparison with the classical, Northern European, neo-corporatist cases may have lost some of its relevance. International developments suggest some revision of traditional ideas on both the *conditions for* and the *nature of* neo-corporatism (O'Donnell, 1993). It seems more relevant to compare the Irish experiment with approaches to social concertation in other European countries in recent years, rather than the heyday of postwar neo-corporatism (Crouch, 1994; O'Donnell and O'Reardon, 1997, 2000). The Irish approach bears definite similarities to the social pacts emerging in a number of EU countries in the late 1990s (Pochet and Fajertag, 2000; Compston and Greenwood, 2001).

In assessing the merits and potential of the social partnership experiment, note should be made of the political context. It might once have been believed that the social partnership model was dependent on the dominant position of the centre-left, catchall, political party, Fianna Fail. However, since 1987, the party composition of Irish government has gone through rapid changes, such that all political parties of any significance have been in government in various coalitions. The social partnership approach has not only survived this, but also gained the support of the Labour Party and the second largest party, Fine Gael. Indeed, the evolution of social partnership has seen a co-evolution in Irish party politics – towards a system of permanent, but frequently renegotiated, coalition. This brings Ireland nearer to a European system of governance, which does not have the 'winner takes all' and 'oppositional' characteristics of the British system.

The self-understanding of Irish social partnership

The development of social partnership in Ireland since 1987 has involved a wide range of economic and political actors in a complex process of negotiation and interaction. A detailed and shared analysis of economic and social problems and policies has been a key aspect of this process. On occasions, that analysis has focused on the partnership system itself (NESC, 1996; NESF 1997). That examination revealed some severe difficulties in making an inclusive system of partnership work, but also a new view of social partnership. Our focus here is on four central arguments that emerged in the Irish discussion and that may have a bearing on the way in which the re-emergence of concertation or social partnership in other EU member states should be interpreted.

A distinction was made between two conceptions, or dimensions, of partnership:

• Functional interdependence, bargaining and deal making.
• Solidarity, inclusiveness and participation.

Effective partnership involves both of these, but cannot be based entirely on either. There is a third dimension of partnership, which transcends these two. Partnership involves the players in a process of deliberation that has the potential to shape and reshape their understanding, identity and preferences. The partners describe the process as 'dependent on a shared understanding', and 'characterised by a problem-solving approach designed to produce consensus'. This third dimension has to be added to the hard-headed notion of bargaining (and to the idea of solidarity), to adequately capture the process.[7] Indeed, despite the difficulties of an inclusive partnership system, there are limited preconditions for effective social partnership of that sort. The key to this would seem to be the adoption of 'a problem-solving approach'. As one senior trade unionist put it, 'The society expects us to be problem-solving.' This problem-solving approach is a central aspect of the partnership process, and is critical to its effectiveness.

This emphasis on problem-solving is combined with observation of three trends which demand a further revision of conventional ideas of neo-corporatism (NESF, 1997). First, the nature and role of social partners is changing. Traditional characteristics of partners in neo-corporatist systems – monopoly representation, a functional role in the economy, centralized structures for representing and disciplining members (Cawson, 1986) – are giving way to new ones: *information* as the key resource, new forms of public advocacy: *analysis, dialogue* and *shared understanding*. Second, we are also witnessing an historical shift in the role of the centre and national government. The traditional roles – allocating resources, directing the operation of departments and administering complex systems of delivery and scrutiny – are giving way to new ones: policy entrepreneurship, monitoring, facilitating communication and joint action between social interests, and supporting interest group formation. Third, the relationship between policy-making, implementation and monitoring is changing, in ways which place monitoring, of a new sort, at the centre of policy development (Dorf and Sabel, 1998).

The evolution of Irish social partnership reflects these changes. Over time, the emphasis has shifted from macroeconomic matters to structural and supply-side policies, and the range of supply-side issues has widened to address key constraints on Irish growth, such as childcare and lifelong learning. This change in the substantive emphasis of partnership has involved a parallel change in method. While macroeconomic strategy can be agreed in high-level negotiation, complex cross-cutting policies on social exclusion, training, business development or childcare can only be devised and implemented with the active participation of all the relevant actors. There have been considerable institutional innovations in policies addressing long-term unemployment, rural and urban re-generation and business development (Sabel, 1996).

Conclusions

In seeking more effective policies for indigenous development over the past 20 years, Irish studies drew on various models: the Japanese firm, the industrialization of Korea and other late-developing economies, flexible specialization, the industrial districts of Italy and Germany, the neo-corporatist concertation of Northern Europe, the National System of Innovation of successful and small European countries, Porter's clusters and the networks of resurgent Danish and other regions. Now that some competitive success is emerging, it turns out not to conform to any of these models (O'Donnell, 1998). Apart from the need to be sceptical of model social and economic systems, what does this tell us?

Given Ireland's small size and extreme openness, it would be inappropriate to identify an 'Irish model'. Nevertheless, there are two reasons why the Irish case should be taken seriously in attempts to formulate policy approaches and conceptualize patterns of economic and social development in the early twenty-first century. The first is the scale of transformation achieved since 1987: a country with a history of de-industrialization under British colonial rule, continued failure of indigenous development after independence, virtual economic collapse in the 1980s and repeated crises of unemployment and emigration, has increased its employment by 37 pcr cent in the 1990s and by 46 per cent since 1987, becoming a significant centre of high technology manufacturing and advanced services. Second, the study of an economy and society which is unusually open to international flows of capital, labour and technology might reveal some important features of the emerging global system, and disclose new possibilities for economic and social life.

As regards business and economic development, the Irish case raises questions about some influential theories of indigenous agglomeration and clustering, on the one hand, and FDI and globalization, on the other. Successful sectors show limited clustering, of the sort advocated by Porter, and Irish-owned firms do not seem to have a 'home base' in Porter's sense (Clancy *et al.*, 1998; O'Donnell, 1998). Instead, the firms that succeed are often those that integrate themselves, with the help of Irish government agencies, into international networks. O'Riain's analysis suggest that two broad modes of integration into the global economy can co-exist, each 'combining local and global networks in different ways' (O'Riain, 2000: 160). It highlights the multiple roles which a flexible developmental state can play in fostering more advantageous connections to the global.

As regards concertation and partnership, the Irish case raises questions about traditional theories of neo-corporatism. It suggests that concertation is possible without social democratic hegemony and without the political, interest-group and enterprise-level *structures* found in the classical Northern European postwar cases of neo-corporatism. It confirms that national level partnership can be highly effective in small countries, as has been noted in earlier studies (Katzenstein, 1985; Crouch, 1994). However, it also highlights the limited ability of centralized national-level partnership, involving only the traditional social partners, to address the wide range of complex cross-cutting social and economic problems which confront society now. These problems require more decentralized systems of interest representation, mediation, implementation and monitoring (Dorf and Sabel, 1998); they also benefit from supranational policy development and coordination, such as that emerging at the EU level. The Irish case, and current developments in other EU countries, suggests that there is a partnership or 'corporatist' road to these new policy systems. Decentralization, delegation and contracting should not be the preserve of neo-liberal approaches to public sector reform. But, since the emerging partnership approach differs so much from the old social democratic model, it should probably be seen a 'post-corporatist', rather than neo-corporatist.

An unresolved problem, both practically and analytically, is how the two globalizations of business, as described by O'Riain, can be linked to the partnership approach in a way which not only supports business success (which has been done), but also addresses social exclusion (more effectively) and reduces inequality (which has not been achieved).

Several important aspects of Irish development have not been discussed in this chapter, but should be noted. The first is the role of the EU in Ireland's economic transformation. There is no doubt that the European Monetary System, EMU, the internal market and the Structural Funds had a significant impact (O'Donnell, 2000). Ireland's belated success suggests that a small, peripheral, less-advanced, post-colonial country can catch-up with the leading European post-imperial nations. It also shows that regional integration, of the sort developed in Europe, can facilitate such a catch up. This is all the more significant, now that the protectionist, authoritarian and non-democratic Asian models of catch-up and industrialization are faltering, and new countries look to the EU. The second aspect which has not been discussed is the astonishing set of social and cultural changes which occurred in Ireland since the 1960s, but particularly since the mid-1980s. The most dramatic has been in the role of women in society, the economy and public life. However, others include increased inequality, the collapse of the influence of the Catholic Church, the discovery of the Irish diaspora, a revival of Irish culture and the emergence of entrepreneurialism.

Notes

1. The views expressed in this chapter are those of the author and should not necessarily be attributed to the National Economic and Social Council.
2. Two important dimensions not explored in this chapter are the place of European integration in Ireland's development and the role of social and cultural change. See O'Donnell (2000).
3. This is captured well in the title of Fintan O'Toole's book *Black Hole, Green Card: The Disappearance of Ireland* (Dublin: New Island Books, 1994).
4. See Sabel (1996); McCartney and Teague (1997); European Foundation (1997); Geary (1999); Roche and Geary (2000); O'Donnell and Teague (2000).
5. In addition to those cited in the text, see: O'Donnell (1995), O'Donnell and Thomas (1998) and O'Donnell and O'Reardon (2000).
6. For the partners' response to these arguments see NESC (1996).
7. A recent study has characterized Dutch social partnership in remarkably similar terms. See Visser and Hamerijck (1997).

5
The German Economic Model: Consensus, Stability, Productivity and the Implications for Reform

Claire Annesley, Geoff Pugh and David Tyrrall[1]

Introduction: the German economic model

During the second half of the twentieth century, a distinct form of capitalism developed in West Germany. This model of capitalism – commonly referred to as the German Model – managed to secure and sustain high levels of stability, productivity and economic growth throughout most of this period. The literature that has emerged to account for the success of this model of capitalism highlights different distinctive features of this model; some focus on the relationships between finance and industry while others are more concerned with the relationship between labour and industry. A common aspect in all these accounts is that the German Model is a negotiated form of capitalism, which is facilitated by a culture of consensus and consensus-building institutions.

The task of this chapter is to highlight the aspects of culture and institutions of consensus that underpin the German Model and to argue that the culture and institutions that promote consensus have been fundamental determinants of stability and productivity in the economy. In this endeavour we develop a formal model to deepen understanding of the connections between the cultural and institutional features that distinguish Germany's social market economy and its characteristic stability and productivity performance. We argue further that the institutional interconnectivity is fundamental to the success of the German economy, and that deviation from this growth path will undo the aspects that underwrote its postwar success.

We then go on to consider the fate of the German Model in the current capitalist phase. During the 1990s, economic growth stalled and unemployment rose and at this time the culture of consensus was both named as a likely cause of the decline in economic performance and held responsible for the apparent inability of the German economy to solve its problems. The chapter therefore considers the state and fate of the consensual German Model in the new economic conditions. While recognizing that consensus was the guarantor of stability, productivity and growth in the second half of the twentieth century, commentators have questioned whether this will be the case under conditions of increasing global integration, in new areas of economic activity and for unified Germany. We argue here that in spite of increased emphasis in the 1990s on profitability and shareholder value in Germany's large listed companies, the culture of consensus continues to permeate German business practice and consensus-building institutions are integrated into business organizations (Vitols *et al.*, 1998). We argue here that the culture of consensus need not be abandoned nor should the institutions that promote consensus be dismantled. Rather, we argue that the problems of the 1990s highlight the imperative to reform.

We take up the issue of reform in the concluding section. We argue that reform should be undertaken in accordance with, rather than against, the institutions of consensus in the social market. A reform process consistent with the cultural and institutional environment will be the most effective in moving Germany towards full employment while maintaining its ultimate source of productivity growth. Reforms introduced in conflict with social market institutions – hence, in opposition to at least one of the participating social partners – will undermine the cultural and institutional source of Germany's productivity advantage.

The German Model and consensus

Germany's social market economy is based on a culture of consensus and consensus-building institutions (Grosser, 1970: 304; Müller-Armack, 1990: 17; Lange and Pugh, 1998: 4–5). In this section we consider the rationale for making consensus a priority in the postwar reconstruction of the German economy and briefly describe the institutions that were set up to promote such a culture. Then, we set out a formal model of the connection between consensus and productivity performance.

Consensus features highly in the German national culture and this also permeates into corporate culture. Postwar German political culture developed through a conscious effort to apply lessons from German history to institutional and policy design. Pre-war social conflict and political polarization had led to fascism, war and the division of Germany. Therefore, the promotion of consensus permeated institutional design in postwar Germany. Private ownership and competition were combined with institutions designed to minimize conflict and secure consensus. The aim was and is to combine market dynamism with cooperation and stability and, in the long term, this was to perpetuate the legitimacy and, hence, dynamism of the market economy.

The best-known institutions of Germany's social market economy are codetermination (industrial democracy), the Bundesbank (monetary policy), and highly clustered, export-oriented manufacturing industry (embracing both global giants and small- and medium-size firms, the *Mittelstand*), which draws competitive advantage from a highly skilled workforce provided by the 'Dual' system of vocational training. The concept of the social market embraces social partnership and the concept of stakeholders, and has an affinity with quasi-corporatist institutions in the labour market.[2] Cooperation between capital and labour was to be promoted through institutions of social partnership, including industrial democracy. This is seen in the existence of works councils, labour representation on supervisory boards and national wage determination by social partners.

The consensus-promoting institutions developed in Germany have a positive impact on competitive advantage for two reasons. First, consensus increases the pace and stability of innovation and productivity growth, which in turn contributes to macroeconomic stability by minimizing supply-side shocks. This is demonstrated below by applying X-efficiency (XE) theory and strategic management theory to model the means by which German national culture helps firms to generate innovation, productivity growth and sustainable competitive advantage. Second, consensus culture erects barriers to imitation from firms from outside the culture, because non-consensus cultures will find it difficult to imitate innovations that are either culture dependent or path dependent.

Consensus, stability and productivity

German firms generate a relatively high and stable pace of innovation and productivity growth. This is consistent with the aggregate, national data presented in Figure 5.1.[3]

The German preference for stability found its best-known economic expression in the Bundesbank, which made Europe's youngest national currency into the world's most stable (Pugh and Carr, 1993). According to the intellectual pioneers of Germany's social market concept, monetary stability meant not only macroeconomic stability but also an efficiently operating price mechanism to provide investors with undistorted price signals and so facilitate the most efficient allocation of resources (Owen-Smith, 1994: 17). Correspondingly, in the real economy, Germany experienced a relatively stable productivity growth. Figure 5.2 documents Germany's relatively strong productivity growth performance over the period 1950–96 in comparison with the four other major OECD economies.[4] Relative to the United States, Germany (here, the former West Germany) underwent steady convergence until the mid-1990s when, on this measure, it replaced the United States as the productivity leader. Relative to the United Kingdom, whose productivity is indexed to 100, Germany's substantial lead was eroded in the early and mid-1980s but has again increased since the late 1980s.

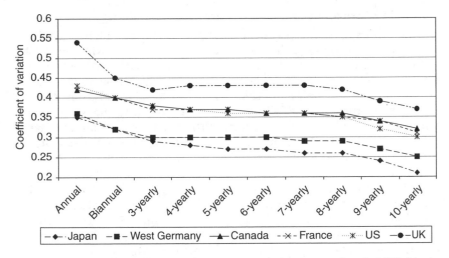

Figure 5.1   Volatility of labour productivity growth (output per hour), 1974–94: six main OECD economies (coefficient of variation of annual to 10-yearly growth rates)

Source: DTI calculations from ONS, OECD and Eurostat data (own calculations).

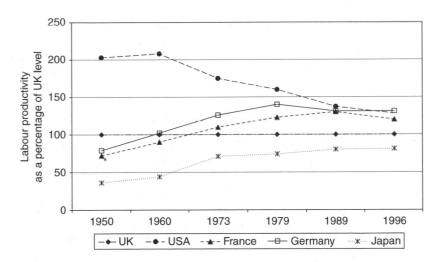

Figure 5.2   Growth of labour productivity in the five major OECD economies relative to the UK (UK = 100) (1950–96)

Source: O'Mahony, 1999, p. 5.

Cultural influences on productivity growth and stability

What role does consensus play in ensuring the stability and high productivity of the German economy? This issue can be tackled by drawing on the XE theory. This is concerned with internal inefficiencies of the firm, where inefficiency is defined as 'deviation between intended attainable results and the actual outcome' (Leibenstein, 1987: 5). Below, we draw also on strategic management theory to develop a dynamic extension to the XE theory in which culture and institutions influence the rate of innovation and hence productivity growth. Dynamic X-*in*efficiency means that the actual rates of innovation and productivity growth are below their maxima.

In Leibenstein's static model of the firm (1987: 18 and 232), employee effort is a function of internal or hierarchical pressure, and is modelled using the inverted-U curve. Relationships of the inverted-U type relate stimulus to response and are well known in psychology (Frantz, 1997: 59). The horizontal (x) axis may be pressure, motivation, stress or anxiety, while the vertical (y) axis may be effort, performance, effectiveness or quality of decisions. Effectiveness increases with pressure up to a peak, and then decreases as pressure continues to increase, that is, there are diminishing returns to pressure. In our dynamic extension of the model, we hypothesize that effective innovation is also a function of pressure.

Porter suggests an explicit relationship between innovation and pressure (1990b: 75–7): '[I]nnovation usually requires pressure, necessity and even adversity.' The 'essential ingredients' for achieving international competitive success are 'the pressures on companies to invest and innovate'. However, Porter does not provide a testable model of this relationship (Grant, 1991). We explicitly model a relationship between internal pressure and the pace of effective innovation, which synthesizes insights from strategic management literature with the XE theory. This inverted-U relationship is illustrated in Quadrant 1 of the model outlined in Figure 5.3, which is then developed counterclockwise.

Quadrant 1: internal pressure and the pace of innovation

Internal pressure is the independent (x-axis) variable. We assume that this is effective internal pressure, in the sense that an increase in pressure by management does elicit increased value-adding activity up to a point. However, as explained above, excessive pressure is counterproductive, so that the relationship has a maximum at P_m. We also assume, following Leibenstein, that the level of effective internal pressure within the firm is strongly related to the degree of *external* pressure upon the firm, whether from microeconomic sources (competition) or from macroeconomic sources (the business cycle, exchange rate changes and so forth). The pace of innovation is the dependent (y-axis) variable. We assume that this is effective innovation in that it is beneficial for the firm. By pace of innovation we mean a flow of innovation

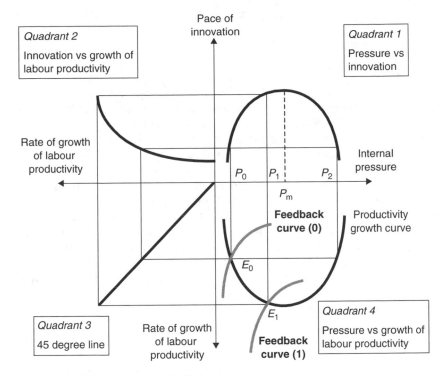

Figure 5.3 Model of dynamic X-efficiency

per period. The pace of innovation determines, *ceteris paribus*, a corresponding rate of productivity growth.

Quadrant 2: innovation and the rate of growth of labour productivity

This Quadrant shows the effects of varying the pace of innovation upon the rate of labour productivity growth. Labour productivity (LP) is defined as the value of output per unit of labour input:[5] i.e.,

$$LP = \frac{Q \times P}{L}$$

where Q is units of output, P is sales price per unit, and L is labour input. In rates of change, this becomes

$$\%\Delta LP = \%\Delta Q + \%\Delta P - \%\Delta L$$

where % Δ is percentage change. This simplifies to

$$\%\Delta LP = \%\Delta TR - \%\Delta L \qquad (5.1)$$

where TR is total (sales) revenue.

The RHS terms of Equation (5.1) may be related to product innovation and process innovation. Product innovation (via, e.g., improvements in quality) permits the firm to increase price per unit (premium pricing) and hence achieve total sales revenue growth (%ΔTR). Process innovation enables the firm to produce the same output more efficiently, so that labour input per unit of output falls ($-\%\Delta L$). We assume that both of these relationships are subject to diminishing returns. Hence, the resulting labour productivity growth curve (%ΔLP) displays diminishing returns.

Because the pressure versus innovation curve in Quadrant 1 is an inverted U, every pace of innovation other than the maximum has two associated levels of pressure (a high and a low level). However, the innovation versus growth of labour productivity curve in Quadrant 2 rises with innovation. Accordingly, as internal pressure rises firms first move up the innovation versus growth of labour productivity curve, but then slide back down it if pressure becomes excessive.

Quadrant 3

The 45° line in panel 3 is a diagrammatic device to project rates of productivity growth into Quadrant 4.

Quadrant 4: internal pressure, the rate of growth of labour productivity, and the feedback curve

Quadrants 1–3 show how productivity growth is generated as another inverted-U function of internal pressure in Quadrant 4. Different pressure levels (P_0, P_1 and P_2) are associated with unique rates of innovation (Quadrant 1) and productivity growth (Quadrant 2) and, hence, with unique points defining the productivity growth curve in Quadrant 4. Thus far, the model shows how varying pressure within firms generates varying rates of productivity growth. Following Leibenstein in his static model, we complete our dynamic model by introducing a feedback curve into Quadrant 4.

The feedback curve reverses the direction of causation of the productivity growth curve so that labour productivity growth becomes the independent (*x*-axis) and internal pressure the dependent (*y*-axis) variable. The *slope of the feedback curve* shows that pressure is inversely related to productivity growth because, *ceteris paribus*, higher productivity growth lowers the constraint concern (i.e. attention and response to the external environment) within the firm. In turn, this decreases intra-firm pressure and employee effort to innovate and hence increase productivity. The reverse effect also obtains.

Thus the feedback curve shows pressure as inversely related to productivity growth.

Together, the productivity growth curve and the feedback curve move the model towards equilibrium.[6] The firm's dynamic equilibrium depends upon the location of its feedback curve. The two feedback curves 0 and 1 illustrate differing equilibria at E_0 and E_1. These are stable combinations of internal pressure and productivity growth, because in each case the level of internal pressure generates a rate of productivity growth that enables the firm to cope with external pressure, which means that the rate of productivity growth is consistent with the level of internal pressure. (Outside equilibrium, the initial level of pressure causes a rate of productivity growth that is either too low, which induces a higher level of internal pressure so as to raise the rate of productivity growth, or too high, which induces a lower level of internal pressure and so lowers the rate of productivity growth.) Note that equilibrium – that is, the pair of mutually consistent values of pressure and productivity growth – for any firm may not necessarily be the maximum possible pace of innovation and productivity growth. The maximum possible rate of productivity growth that the firm can attain will depend on the location of its feedback curve.

The role of consensus on the firm and the location of the feedback curve

The model yields predictions about the impact of consensus on firms' productivity growth, because different corporate cultures support different locations of the firm's feedback curve. Accordingly, we now turn to cultural factors that govern *the location of the feedback curve*.

The principles are illustrated using a representative firm with a two-level hierarchy of managers and employees. Formal, incomplete employment contracts are filled out by relational (or implicit) contracts that allow exchange where the details are too complicated to be specified in written or formal contracts (Leibenstein, 1987: 35; Milgrom and Roberts, 1992: ch. 5). In particular, they allow conventions (i.e. social norms or standards) to constrain discretion. Employees have discretion over their motivation and effort including those aspects of effort and motivation directed towards effective innovation and change. Managers have discretion over both rewards (including both pay and job security) and pressure (Leibenstein, 1978: 13; Milgrom and Roberts, 1992: 179; Frantz, 1997: 56).[7] When each group maximizes its own self-interest conditional upon the other groups' behaviour, the dominant strategy for both groups is adversarial (i.e. to cheat). If managers offer the highest rewards, then employees gain by reducing effort, including that directed towards innovation. Conversely, if workers maximize effort, then managers gain by reducing rewards.

In a non-consensual culture, management is less likely to assume trust and more likely to attempt to achieve productivity growth by reducing individual discretion through increased managerial and organizational control. Even if bureaucratization succeeds in reducing static X-inefficiency, productivity growth is likely to be made suboptimal by the absence of motivational factors, 'such as enthusiasm', since 'a mixture of routine *and* discretion (i.e., trust) is likely to produce more efficient behaviour than routine alone' (Leibenstein, 1987: 162), especially with respect to innovation. Where employer/employee contracts are governed by managerial controls that reduce employee discretion, there will be limited opportunities for innovative behaviours. Indeed, a strategy of direct control over employees indicates that management have little confidence in employee abilities and decision-making, and so contributes to disunity and conflict rather than commitment and innovation. Thus, mutual distrust is a sufficient condition for the prisoners' dilemma outcome of minimum effort, minimum innovation, minimum productivity growth and hence minimum reward growth (Leibenstein, 1982, 1987: 43–59; Frantz, 1997: 45–55).

In contrast, a consensual culture favours trust (Kay, 1993: 60 and 326). In particular, shared values, especially those that receive institutional expression, are conducive to confidence in other people's behaviour. Thus in Germany, an institutional context based on the principle of consensus constrains even those firms inclined not to collaborate with trade unions and/or employee representatives – including affiliates of UK and US multinationals – to establish either high-trust relationships with works councils or some 'functional equivalent' with employees (Muller, 1998: 738–9). If management is trusted to adhere to established norms on pay, workloads and job security, employees reciprocate with commitment and motivation – hence maintaining intra-firm pressure and employee efforts to search out and utilize knowledge, and to accept or even initiate changes – as a necessary response to external pressure (Leibenstein, 1987: 241). Accordingly, the nature of the conventions under which a firm operates may allow it to escape the prisoners' dilemma, by permitting Nash equilibrium at some higher level of innovation, productivity growth and reward growth.[8] This favourable outcome is particularly likely in German firms, because firm-specific training and employee investment in firm-specific skills are not only an outcome of trust but also promote long-term employment relationships (Adnett, 1996: Table 5.1) within which learning and reputation effects enable the building of trust. In contrast, shorter-term Anglo-American employment relationships favour a 'one-shot game' in which the prisoners' dilemma is the likely outcome. Oliver (1997: 706) derives a similar proposition from strategic management theory: 'Firms will be more likely to make optimal use of accumulated resources when manager–employee relations are characterised by trust.' Thus, we hypothesize that inter-firm variations in the pace of innovation and productivity growth are related to inter-firm differences in the degree of consensus in firm culture.

In our model, the location of the firm's feedback curve is determined by corporate culture: lower consensus and trust shifts the whole feedback curve to the left; higher consensus and trust shifts it to the right. At any given rate of productivity growth, low-consensus, low-trust firms can maintain only relatively low levels of internal pressure and effort, whereas high-consensus, high-trust firms can maintain higher levels of internal pressure. Accordingly, relatively low-consensus firms are represented by feedback curve 0. Here, because employees do not trust managers to respond with commensurate rewards, or to demonstrate confidence in and commitment to them, the internal pressure and employee effort that managers can generate is relatively low, which reduces innovation and productivity growth. The lower consensus firm can attain the relatively high-productivity growth at E_1 only *intermittently*, because low-pressure feedback moves the firm towards the lower-pressure, lower-productivity growth equilibrium at E_0 in Quadrant 4. Firms relatively strong in consensus are located closer to feedback curve 1. These can maintain *continuously* higher-pressure, higher-productivity growth equilibrium at E_1 in Quadrant 4, together with a corresponding growth in reward. Clearly, we identify the typical German firm with the higher feedback curve 1, consistent with Streeck's observation (1997b: 41) that the 'pattern of innovation' in German industry is one in which '[a]verages are typically high, coefficients of variation low, and extreme cases are rare at both ends'.

Consensus culture and path dependency

We have seen that consensus culture provides for a high and stable rate of productivity growth in German firms and that this has positive consequences for the economy as a whole. In addition, it can be argued that interconnectedness of consensus-building institutions forms a system – the German Model – whose success is dependent upon the reinforcing nature of its constituent parts (Harding, 1999; Soskice, 1999). The institutionalist approach, as Coates (2000: 164) notes, claims that institutional practices lock economies into certain paths of growth arguing that:

> Economic performance is affected by institutional practices. Institutional practices vary between economies. Those variations are systematic and mutually reinforcing. They are also socially rooted and nationally constrained. Collectively they constitute a social system of production. And that social system holds the key to why growth rates differ.

The suggestion that the interconnectedness of the institutions of the German Model locks the German economy into a certain of path of growth has several implications for the debate about its future.

The consensual institutions of the German Model erect barriers to imitation by firms from outside that culture, because non-consensus cultures will find it difficult to imitate innovations that are either culture dependent or path dependent. Lower consensus firms may attempt to imitate innovations, but some may prove inimitable. For example, certain types of organizational arrangement may only be operable in a consensus culture. Hence, a culture of consensus can provide an institutional 'isolating mechanism' (Oliver, 1997: 704), which prevents other firms from appropriating strategic resources derived from innovation (Teece, 1987). Lower consensus firms may seek to change their culture in the direction of greater consensus. However, organizational theorists agree that culture is resistant to change, adapts only slowly and is not wholly under managerial control (Meyerson and Martin, 1987; Meek, 1988; Pettigrew, 1990).

According to Hofstede (1994) national cultures operate at a more fundamental level than corporate culture. Geletkanycz (1997: 630) agrees that 'the influence of (national) cultural values surmounts that of either firm or industry' on managerial decision-making. Thus 'at the inter-organisational level, pressure emerging from ... societal expectations (i.e., national culture) define socially acceptable firm conduct, and ... cause firms to exhibit similar structures and activities' (Oliver, 1997: 700). Such homogeneity has a beneficial effect on German firms' productivity, since typically they operate with a higher degree of consensus and cooperation than do firms located in less consensual cultures.

Path dependency suggests that the growth, stability and productivity which mark the postwar German economy are the outcome of the consensual institutional framework of the German Model and that a dismantling of this model would undermine the features which led to postwar economic success. This is of central importance in debates about the ability of models of capitalism to respond to changing economic circumstances. It is to this issue that we now turn.

The crisis of consensus, German unemployment and the need for reform

During the 1990s the German Model appeared to struggle to sustain high levels of economic growth, productivity growth and employment. Unemployment rose to historically high levels in the 1990s, as Table 5.1 shows. As a consequence of the shift in economic fortunes, the viability of the consensual German Model, and other trust-based models of capitalism, has been called into question. Within the well-rehearsed debates about the crisis and future of consensus culture and institutions, three distinct themes can be identified. The first issue is whether the advantages of the consensus based German Model are sustainable in the open global economy. Second, a wide range of literature has emerged that deals with the impact of German unification on the consensus-building institutions of the German Model. Finally, it is contested whether the German Model is appropriate to the new technological paradigm of the post-industrial economy. These are now addressed in turn.

Table 5.1 German unemployment, 1993–99. Percentage of the workforce unemployed (standardized definition)

Year	Percentage
1993	7.9
1994	8.5
1995	8.2
1996	8.9
1997	9.9
1998	9.4
1999	8.8

Source: OECD, *Economic Outlook*, 2000d: 232.

Globalization

The first issue is a familiar one: consensual or negotiated versions of capitalism are supposed to be less efficient than liberal capitalist models given the open structures and rapid pace of the global economy. For globalization theorists, as Coates (2000: 251) notes:

the arrival of globalization has awesome consequences for trust-based capitalist models. It has simply destroyed the space previously enjoyed by growth strategies based on state direction or extensive welfare provision, by restricting successful growth strategies to those which are purely market driven and entirely under the control of private capital.

Streeck argues that globalization favours 'national systems like those of the USA and Britain that have historically relied less on public–political and more on private–contractual economic governance, making them more structurally compatible with the emerging global system' (1997b: 53). Furthermore, he notes that globalization undermines negotiated, 'traditionalist' German culture because, compared with the American economic culture, it appears 'slow-moving, conservative, collectivistic … and utterly devoid of "fun"' (ibid: 53).

Such arguments met with a high degree of resonance in Germany in the 1990s, as they appeared to offer explanations for both the stalling economic growth and soaring unemployment as well for the inability of consensual solutions to solve these problems. In response to the globalization thesis, a debate emerged in German political and economic circles about the future of Germany as an industrial location (*Standort*) in the global economy. This debate – the so-called *Standortdebatte* – concerned the view that the German industrial location was disadvantaged on account of, among other things, the culture of consensus inherent in the German Model. The argument against the consensual German Model was led by the business right. Hans-Olaf Henkel, president of the BDI, for example, argued for a 'reengineering of political culture' in order to reestablish Germany's position in the global economic order (Henkel, 1997: 90). Such arguments were not contested by the conservative–liberal (CDU–FDP) government. Helmut Kohl made few political efforts to reassert the importance of consensus culture for Germany's economic success, democracy and political stability. Towards the end of his period in office, Kohl declared that unemployment should be halved by the year 2000. Yet, this rhetoric was not matched by any successful policy initiatives. Indeed one effort to solve the problem of unemployment through a social partner initiative – the *Bundnis für Arbeit* – failed, thus appearing to confirm the widespread view in Germany that consensus was no longer a successful economic strategy.

Arguments about the failure of the German Model under conditions of globalization have, however, been widely contested. Rebecca Harding (1999) argues that the focus of 'crisis writers' on macroeconomic failures, notably unemployment and the growth rate, paints a misleading picture of the German economy. Unemployment, which we examine in more detail below, cannot simply be attributed to globalization. Harding emphasizes the need to adopt a systemic approach that focuses on the structure created by the institutional interrelationships of the German Model, which allows for adaptive rather than dynamic change. From this perspective, it is suggested that there is 'no intrinsic reason why the German system should be any less competitive than its American or British counterparts in the long term. ... Actors within the German economy are interrelated and interdependent through a system that has evolved and shown itself capable of incremental adaptation to exogenous radical change over centuries' (Harding, 1999: 81). At the firm level, German companies continue to be innovative and there Germany's competitive trade position has not been eroded (cf. also Manow and Seils, 2000).

A reassertion of the suitability of the German Model of capitalism in the global era has also been made by leading figures in German business, trade unions, employers associations, politics and the academic world. The 1998 report of the Commission on Codetermination (*Kommission Mitbestimmung*) concluded that 'the experience of the 1990s has shown that true codetermination can be developed to the advantage for the *Standort*' (Bertlesmann Stiftung and Hans-Böckler-Stiftung, 1998: 1). Unlike employers in Sweden, German employers have not clearly rejected current arrangements in favour of more liberal models (Thelen, 2000). Indeed, it can be argued that the economic advantage deriving from cooperation and consensus becomes more crucial in a global economic order. Where all other factors of production are interchangeable, the added value of a skilled workforce and the advantages brought about by institutions of consensus becomes the only variable for national economic advantage in the global economy. From this perspective it appears less likely that globalization will eradicate the consensual institutions of the German economy.

Consensus in post-unification Germany

The future viability of consensus in the German Model has been questioned by the consequences of German unification. Following the events of 1989, and even before legal unification of the FRG and GDR in 1990, the institutions of the German Model were transferred wholesale from the West to the East. Many have argued that the transfer of the institutions of social partnership was undertaken remarkably successfully (e.g. Turner, 1998). However, subsequently it has become clear that the process of transfer has not been matched by a perfect operationalization of the consensus-building institutions of the German Model (French, 2000).

There are a number of ways of accounting for the imperfect operationalization of West German consensus in the new *Länder* of unified Germany. The first concerns the fact that the deindustrialization of the East German economy removed the large autarkic firms, which in terms of scale were most similar to the large West German firms in which institutions of consensus have operated most effectively. New economic activity in the East has increasingly involved the establishment of new firms and the institutions which promote consensus are being bypassed: not all firms are signing up to employers' associations, a decreasing number of new firms are establishing works councils and there is a trend of wage agreements being undercut.

Due in part to both unification and the growth of small firms in the new economy, considered below, the traditional (West) German patterns of centralized industrial relations have declined. The proportion of employees in workplaces without works councils rose from 37 per cent in 1981 to 45 per cent in 1994 and amongst private sector employees from 49 to 61 per cent in the same period (Hassel, 1999: 489). Decentralization of wage bargaining is suggested by the rise in the proportion of company-based agreements from 27 per cent in 1990 to 35 per cent in 1997 (Hassel, 1999: 494). Interestingly, this suggests convergence between the Western and Eastern *Länder* with company-based agreements rising in the former and falling (from a higher level) in the latter.

This is not to say that there is a complete absence of institutions of consensus in the East. Rather it is the case that these are less formalized than in the conventional German Model. There is a fear in the West that the different, less formal form of consensus practiced in the East will undermine the carefully constructed formal culture of consensus in the West.

A second possible explanation for the imperfect operationalization of consensus-promoting institutions in the new *Länder* is that the template of consensus imposed is not appropriate given the economic conditions of the economy in eastern Germany. This problem was most clearly illustrated by the failure of the policy to equalize wage levels in the East and West (French, 2000). If one follows the line of argument of path dependency then it can indeed be argued that it is hard to embed institutions of consensus where they did not exist before and that an attempt to do so might not have the desired effect. However, as noted above, national culture operates at more fundamental level than corporate culture. Firms that operate in a national culture of consensus have a chance to take advantage of the comparative advantage these institutions convey. Thus it is important that the national culture promotes consensus and that the eastern part of unified Germany feels part of this national culture.

The new economy

Consensus culture and consensus-building institutions were developed during the 'economic miracle' of West German industrialism. The crisis of the culture of consensus coincides with the decline of this industrial economic paradigm. It has been asserted that the culture of consensus was unique to the industrial conditions of West Germany but that it is not suited to the new technological paradigm. It has been widely claimed that unified Germany is lagging behind in the information technology revolution and that this is illustrated by the inability to create jobs in the new technology and services industries. The high levels of unemployment appeared to demonstrate that the consensual nature of the German Model, specifically its high-skill and high-wage features, were detrimental to the development of employment especially in new areas of economic activity. Such arguments draw on evidence that liberal economies, particularly the United States and United Kingdom, have attained high levels of employment during the 1990s that the German economy has been unable to replicate.

There is evidence however to suggest that, where they already exist, consensus-promoting institutions can play a constructive and central role in processes of technological transformation (Soskice, 1999). Furthermore, there is evidence that the existence of consensus and consensus-building institutions and highly skilled labour in the German economy is an advantage when negotiating the effective implementation of new technologies (Bertlesmann Stiftung and Hans-Böckler-Stiftung, 1998). However, there is less evidence to support the proposition that consensus institutions are positive for new firms or for creating new jobs. The risk therefore is that consensus will only predominate in traditional, transformed industrial sectors. In other areas there is a danger that consensus is detrimental to the creation of new employment.

Indeed, even in traditional, transformed industrial sectors insider–outsider theory suggests that consensus may not only offer the prospect of productivity growth but also carries the risk of unemployment. The starting point of insider–outsider theory is labour turnover costs to firms. These refer to the costs of recruiting and training employees, as well as to dismissal costs. Labour turnover costs give market power to experienced, incumbent employees – insiders – because they know that their employers find it costly to replace them. Insiders use their power to improve their wages. Employers concede wages above market-clearing rates, because the costs of dismissing and replacing existing workers – even if this were legally possible – make it unprofitable to hire outsiders. This wage benefit for insiders imposes a corresponding employment cost on outsiders – the unemployed, new entrants onto the labour market (e.g. young people, women returnees) and the unskilled.

In Germany, the employment consequences of insider power may be particularly severe for two reasons. First, insider power is enhanced by the consensual system that promotes innovation and productivity growth. Labour turnover costs are compounded by employment protection legislation, strong trade unions and works councils, which constitute much of the formal institutional structure of the consensus culture. Second, employers also benefit from insider power. The rewards that motivate workers to maximum cooperation, effort and innovation embrace both pay and job security, because these together determine the expected utility of wealth. Accordingly, from the employer's perspective, higher wages and certain inflexibilities – particularly those regarding hiring and firing – are not only costs but also workforce incentives.[9] Innovation and productivity growth are maximized when workers trust employers to deliver well-paid, secure jobs over the long term. In this case, workers invest in firm-specific skills. In turn, employers are more likely to undertake investment in equipment, R&D and training because they trust their workers to stay with the firm and make the most productive use of investments, which includes ongoing benefits from learning-by-doing. The loop is closed as the process of consensus, workforce commitment and employer investment generates high productivity growth, high reward and renewed trust. This cumulative causation process supports the productivity performance of German firms (Lange and Pugh, 1998: 124–6). Consequently, in Germany, to the extent that consensus and trust are associated with stability of employment, labour turnover costs are multiplied by the cost of undermining this virtuous circle.

Insider power increases incentives for employers to substitute capital for labour, which is expensive and inflexible. Consequently, insider power tends to promote productivity growth at the expense of employment growth. This link between the (un)employment effects and the productivity effect of insider power is explicit in a recent IMF study:

> In [Germany], investment was capital deepening as indicated by the sharp rise in the capital–labour ratio. With more capital for each worker, the increase in output came about primarily through higher labour

productivity rather than through higher employment. In this sense, investment appears to have been primarily directed towards substituting increases in capital for increases in employment. (IMF, 1997: 32; cited in Funk, 2000)

Moreover, according to Assar Lindbeck (1996: 618–19):

The rapid rise in real product wages has also forced low-productivity plants and firms out of business – indeed, faster than other firms have been able to reemploy 'redundant' workers ... these developments have not only boosted aggregate productivity growth, but also contributed to the slow expansion of aggregate employment.

Thus, insofar as consensus promotes insider power it may be an obstacle to full employment. Consensus and consensus-building institutions help insiders to resist the downward pressure on wages that in a free market economy would result from unemployed outsiders competing for jobs. Wage moderation is possible under the threat of unemployment for employed workers (insiders), but not to the extent necessary to allow net job creation. Unemployment persists even during cyclical upturn, because insiders cease fearing job loss and their pressure causes upward wage adjustment. Firms will not hire outsiders whose marginal product would have a greater value than their reservation wage when this value is less than the actual – insider-determined – wage. This is consistent with the phenomenon of 'jobless growth'. In Germany, therefore, it will be difficult to reduce unemployment as long as insiders determine wage demands in their own interests. Similar analysis informs the majority view in Germany's Council of Economics Experts on the causes and cure of mass unemployment:

The structure of the labour market is in urgent need of reform. In its present form it is focused on the relationship between employers and workers. It protects the interests of those who have jobs to the detriment of the unemployed, whose chances of gaining employment are reduced and whose interests do not receive due consideration in wage negotiations. ... Wage rises in line with productivity can do no more than secure the existing level of employment; if unemployment is to be reduced, there must be a mark-down from the increase in productivity adjusted for any changes in employment. Long-term wage policy must target a higher level of employment. (JG, 1999: 10–11)

The Council majority ranges in attitude from scepticism to hostility towards corporatist means of achieving employment-oriented wage policy: it is 'an illusion to believe that the pressing problems of the labour market can be resolved by means of a corporatist approach'. Rather, labour market reform 'is the government's responsibility' (JG, 1999: 8). Nevertheless, unemployment cannot simply be attributed to corporatist structures. In particular, the low rate of job creation in the services sector may partly reflect the effectively high rates of marginal taxation at the bottom end of pay scales (Manow and Seils, 2000). Reform of the tax and benefit system may be at least as important in job creation as reforming insider–outsider structures.

The crisis of consensus and implications for reform

In this chapter, we have argued that postwar Germany's high employment rate, growth and productivity have derived from consensus and consensus-building institutions. We have also seen that the challenges of globalization, a new technological paradigm and German unification have placed the culture of consensus under pressure and scrutiny. In the new phase of German capitalism it no longer appears possible to sustain full employment, growth and productivity through these institutions. As we have seen, it has been questioned whether it is possible to sustain such a national and corporate culture now and in the future and, should it be possible, whether consensus culture will guarantee the same competitive advantages as in the past. In this concluding section, we argue that these issues highlight not so much the necessity to abandon consensual practices as the imperative to reform.

The pressure to reform

Given the conditions of the new capitalist phase and the apparent success of the liberal Anglo-American paradigm, there has been pressure on consensus-based models of capitalism to reform through liberalization. Pressure to reform in this direction was heightened by the apparent ineffectiveness of consensual approaches in forging successful strategies for reform. For example, the first tripartite Alliance for Jobs in 1996 failed because of the inability of the social partners to reach a consensus. Similarly, as we have illustrated above, the consensus approach tends to deliver unequal gains that favour predominantly, or exclusively, *insiders*. However, this need not be the case.

The social market economy is not just a source of the problems routinely cited by its critics. Cost-increasing inflexibilities are matched by productivity-enhancing benefits. High labour costs, inflexible wages and working practices, as well as cumbersome business decision-making associated with participation and consultation, are all aspects of a system that yields commitment and high productivity. According to Oliver (1997: 709), 'firms need both resource capital and institutional capital for longer-run competitive advantage'. Our conclusion is that these are inter-related phenomena. There is still a future for consensus in Germany and, furthermore, reform that conforms with, rather than goes against, the consensual social market will provide preferable outcomes. The possibilities for reform and their outcomes

Table 5.2   The reform process and its outcomes

Implementation procedure	Outcomes	
	Reform	No Reform
Top-down: i.e., in conflict with social market culture and institutions	*Uncertain:* • Benefit of reform offset by productivity costs	
Corporatist: i.e., through social market culture and institutions	*Positive:* • Cost benefits plus continued productivity benefits	*Negative:* • Productivity benefits eroded by competitive disadvantages

are set out in Table 5.2. If reforms are introduced, they may be introduced either through the social market institutions or 'top-down' in conflict with them (styled 'liberalization').

There are reasons to resist pressure to abandon corporatism and embrace a radical, top-down Anglo-American approach to labour market reform. The process of reform is likely to have a clear influence on the outcome. An Anglo-American approach to the reform process could disrupt the virtuous circle of consensus and productivity growth, thereby offsetting the benefit of change. Accordingly, necessary reforms carried out in conflict with the social market (liberalization) will at best have uncertain results. Market-conforming reforms that undermine and overthrow social market institutions will undermine and overthrow social norms that secure high productivity. In this case, gains from market-conforming reforms (including cost reductions) will be offset by productivity losses, and may even cause German competitiveness to deteriorate.

If social market institutions block reform then corresponding competitive disadvantages are likely to erode the benefits of the unreformed system. In contrast, necessary market-conforming reforms agreed within and implemented on the basis of consensus secured by the institutions of Germany's social market will reinforce this productivity advantage. Reform carried out through the social market will have positive results in terms of both new sources of cost reduction and continuing productivity benefits.

Reform with consensus

Reform of the German Model should be carried out on the basis of consensus. In a corporate strategy context, Nelson (1991) points out that 'there is reason to believe that firms have greater ability to [develop] ... in a way that preserves their strength, than to comprehend and adopt what gives their rivals strength'. Similarly, at a national level, Hollingsworth (1997a: 265–6) holds that 'there are serious limitations in the extent to which a society may mimic the forms of economic governance and performance of other societies'. Putting it differently, both Germany and German firms would be better advised to develop based upon their social market strengths, than to try to adopt free-market approaches more suited to their rivals' national culture.

We conclude that reform of the German Model will have maximum benefit and minimum risk if carried out through rather than against the social market. We draw this conclusion with a note of caution though. First of all, consensus culture has not been fully operationalized in the new *Länder*. We have also argued that a national culture of consensus can promote consensus at the corporate level. Therefore, it is important that a national culture of consensus is nurtured in order to offer a framework within which business can develop in the eastern part of Germany. Furthermore, reform through consensus must be designed to suit contrasting conditions in the East and West, and in the old and new areas of economic activity as well as to obviate insider–outsider rifts. Again, there is a degree of hope that the political conditions since 1998 will promote this.

The attitude towards unemployment changed in 1998, when Germany's new federal government under Schröder declared unemployment to be its highest priority.

Moreover, in December 1998 the Federal Government, unions and employers' associations founded a second Alliance for Employment, Training and Competitiveness to institutionalize dialogue around aims that included reduction of non-wage labour costs, improvement of enterprise capacity for innovation and growth, flexible working time, and employment-creating wage policy. In July 1999, this corporatist approach was confirmed by a joint declaration of the National Confederation of German Employers' Associations (BDA) and the German Trade Union Federation (DGB) that a medium- to long-term wage policy was necessary for a lasting reduction of unemployment. Accordingly, productivity increase is to be dedicated above all to employment creation (JG, 1999: 157–8). These developments have given rise to sharply differing judgements. The Council of Economic Experts has condemned the results as 'pathetic' (JG, 1999: 157–8). Yet the German Institute for Economic Research takes a more optimistic view on the results and prospects for employment-creating wage policy (DIW, 2000: 1 and 14) and recent wage settlements have at least kept wage growth in line with productivity (*Economist*, 1 April 2000: 34).

Notes

1. We are indebted to Peter Matheson of HM Treasury for data, to Lother Funk of the Institute for German Studies for the discussion of insider outsider theory, and to fellow participants at the Political Economy Research Centre conference 'Where Are National Capitalisms Now?' for their many helpful suggestions.

2. These are 'quasi' because state participation is arms length. The state does not participate directly but does exert influence (Streeck, 1997b: 39 and 52).
3. See Pugh and Tyrrall (2000) for empirical evidence that the OECD countries with the most consensual cultures – Austria, Germany, Switzerland and Japan – have had the highest and most stable rates of both innovation and productivity growth.
4. Output per hour worked in the market economy (i.e. the aggregate economy excluding health, education and the government sectors). This is O'Mahoney's 'preferred measure' (1999: 4).
5. In both strategy literature (Porter, 1990a: 6 and 773) and in applied economics (O'Mahony, 1999: 4) labour productivity is measured as the *value* of output produced by an hour of labour.
6. Pugh and Tyrrall (2000) derive and discuss the formal conditions for equilibrium.
7. 'Reward' includes both income and security. Both workers and managers attempt to maximize *their expected utility of wealth*, where the expected utility of wealth is measured by the size of a future return multiplied by the probability of receiving the return (Copeland and Weston, 1992: 86).
8. In both high- and low-consensus firms, market forces enforce at least a rough coordination of reward and effort conventions (Leibenstein, 1987: 92).
9. What matters for an employer is the productivity of its own workforce (insiders), rather than the employment of outsiders or the output per potential employee in the whole economy.

6
The French Model of Capitalism: *Still* Exceptional?

Ben Clift

Introduction

We begin by setting out the core post-war features of the French model of capitalism, with a view to establishing whether recent developments have undermined or reinforced the distinctiveness of the French 'model' of capitalism. We focus first on radical changes to the financial system and the privatization programme, which facilitated a restructuring of French capitalism and changed the relationship between state and industry. Second, we explore the changing size and scope of the public sector in France, noting the importance of the supranational (EU) level regulatory framework. Third, we examine developments in industrial relations and in French labour market and welfare institutions. This provides a backdrop to consideration of state policies aimed at resolving the enduring structural unemployment problem.

Several themes emerge. First, the enduring and enduringly significant role of the state in each area studied. Second, the integral role of elitist networks interlinking industrial and financial capital within France's 'financial network economy' (Morin, 2000), which 'enable profit-seeking companies to co-operate, with co-operation requiring only limited recourse to the sort of state action that is often considered indispensable for collective goods production' (Crouch and Streeck, 1997: 4). Third, the process of restructuring is unfinished, and the likely direction of future developments remains contentious. Finally, a fascination with other 'models' of capitalism – Rhinish as well as Anglo-Saxon – persists, and public debate surrounds desirable institutional 'transplants'. However, there is rather less *evidence* of such transplants. Despite the existence of powerful forces inducing convergence in some areas, the French model continues – and is likely to continue – to display a strong national distinctiveness *in some respects*.

The French model – core features

Levy's comment about the French welfare state – that it 'is a social scientist's worst nightmare... [which] tended to be passed over completely in comparative studies or else appended to a welfare model that it did not fit' (Levy, 2000: 315 and 308) – could be applied to the French model of capitalism generally. The traditional post-war French model was captured in Zysman's account of France's state-led industrial development (Zysman, 1983), portraying an actively interventionist, *dirigiste*, 'player' state using its key agencies to steer the nation's economic development, in keeping with France's *etatiste* tradition (cf. Shonfield, 1969: ch. 5; Hall, 1986). Capital allocation in France in the 1970s did not always display the logic and virtues highlighted by Zysman. An extensive literature questions the *coherence* Zysman attributed to French capitalism, and how much 'glorious' growth was really down to indicative economic planning and strategic interventionism in industry creating 'national champions' (see e.g. Hencké, 2001: 309–12; Guyomarch *et al.*, 1998: 161–8). Often state funds did not feed a dynamic industrial core,[1] but delayed layoffs and restructuring in industries whose collapse was deemed too politically costly in the short term (Levy, 2000: 321).

Nevertheless, more consensus surrounds the four key features of the postwar French model. First, the *dirigiste* tradition of an expansive role for the French state in directive intervention in economic activity is perhaps the diagnostic characteristic of France's 'state-led variant' of Fordism (Boyer, 1997). The coordinating and steering mechanisms of *dirigisme* have been a core feature of the French model: first, a battery of price, credit and exchange controls established after the war, although of decreasing importance from the 1970s. Second, state *tutelle* (or guidance) of some basic nationalized industries, which was combined, in the private sector, with, 'an intricate network of commitments on the part of private firms... all in return for favours from the state... [and] the habit of the exercise of power by public officials over the private sector of the economy' (Shonfield, 1965: 86 and 128). This *tutelle* also extended to much of the financial sector. The third feature at the heart of France's traditional interventionism was the state's central role in providing funds for industrial investment (Zysman, 1983). The state's centrality to the system of 'institutionally allocated credit' (as opposed to 'asset-based credit') from private and public banks gave the French state extraordinary leverage (Loriaux, 1991). The bottom line was that, 'capital would be strategic and cheap' (ibid.: 113). State loans tended to be conditional upon meeting specific restructuring targets, incorporating subsidiaries into parent companies, or merging with other big firms. After 1971, the French government's credit rationing scheme (*encadrement du credit*) controlled the direction of financial flows, but left many areas of the French economy undercapitalized. The problem became acute in the wake of the 1974 industrial crisis. This reliance on institutionally allocated credit explains the chronic lack of investment in many areas which led the French economy to be caricatured as 'capitalism without capital' (Stoffaes, 1989: 122). The final distinguishing feature of

French *dirigisme*, bringing the rest together, was the Plan (Shonfield, 1965; Stoffaes, 1989).

The second element of the French model of capitalism is the coordinating role played by 'an interpenetration of state and business elites' (Maclean, 1999: 101). Their schooling within the *Grands Ecoles*, creating a relatively homogenous elite, has long been noted as a distinguishing factor of French capitalism. Top civil servants, politicians and bosses follow a similar educational path in France and become part of the French *Grand Corps*, an informal community that operates as a coordinating mechanism of French capitalism, in part through *pantouflage*, or the smooth passage, from higher civil service to the boards of major enterprises – public or private. The institutions and practices of elitism in the recruitment and promotion of top managers remain intact today; so rife is it that top business graduates enter the higher echelons of the civil service as a means to rise up the corporate ladder.

A third element of the traditional French 'model' is a distinctive set of corporate governance arrangements, characterized by Napoleonic boardroom power relations. Boards are characterized by the exorbitant powers resting with their PDG, 'in French law, executive authority vests in the PDG and he has the sole right to "represent" the company, a power which only he can delegate' (Charkham, 1995: 131). Boards tend to be rubber stamps for the largely autonomous PDG. In a system characterized as 'capital without sanction' company bosses are not only autonomous, but also insulated from takeover or shareholder pressure by what Schmidt (1996, 1999) has called 'protected capitalism', where small groups of investors, drawn from the same elite, control one another through interlocking shareholding. Building upon the elite's informal networks, such close relations between firms, boards and large shareholders provide a degree of coherence and direction to France's 'financial network economy' (Morin, 2000: 38).

Conflictual and fragmented industrial relations constitute the fourth element of the French Model. The context of French industrial relations is a highly regulated labour market, but formal associations, both trade unions and employer associations, have low membership, few resources and are poorly coordinated. Despite this, both employers and employees play a central role in the (patchy but generous) French 'social wage'-based welfare system – electing representatives to the boards of the *caisses*, the non-state agencies governing France's generous system of welfare provision. Although trade union membership is low, coverage by collective agreements is very high – rising from 85 per cent to 95 per cent between 1980 and 1995 (OECD, 1997d: 71). French unions are not as weak is often portrayed. Workers feel an affinity with unions and feel represented by them, even if they are not members. Furthermore, unions have considerable assets, not least the French *penchant* for protest. Nevertheless, state-led orchestration of collective bargaining has traditionally compensated for the fragmentation of French industrial relations (Howell, 1996).

Financial deregulation and privatization

The fate of the early 1980s Mitterand programme is well known. The 1981–83 period saw a 'redistributive Keynesian' reflation of the economy, through social and economic policies including generous welfare expansion, a minimum wage hike and a nationalization programme, particularly of key banks (Hall, 1986). Downward pressure on the Franc ensued and the Bourse fell sharply. The expansionary Keynesian policies – although more modest than often supposed (Muet and Fonteneau, 1990) – were abandoned as they became incompatible with continued membership of the European Monetary System (EMS). This was widely interpreted as the key turning point in French political economy (Halimi *et al.*, 1994; Cameron, 1996; Levy, 2000), marking the end of France's *dirigisme*, and indicating that radical programmes are no longer operable in the global economy.

The shifts in macroeconomic policy after abandoning reflation were accompanied by financial deregulation and privatization, detailed below. The '*Franc fort*' or 'competitive disinflation' policy of maintaining a high value for the Franc aimed at promoting long-run competitiveness by achieving a stable low inflation rate. With competitive devaluation, and its attendant 'moral hazard' problems, removed, 'the publicly known restrictive orientations of monetary policy, which ceased to be accommodating … worked as a strong incentive on all social groups to radically change their price setting behaviour' (Lordon, 1998: 106). Restructuring and adjustment was achieved through market mechanisms, with firms obliged to pay close attention to their costs and prices. Labour costs, the 'social wage' and unemployment became the adjustment mechanisms. The policy achieved bipartisan consensus and was maintained even after the 1993 EMS crisis. This was an attempt to import *both* Germany's anti-inflationary credibility *and* its 'Ordo-liberal' (Dyson, 2002: 176–80) norms of 'sound' money, wage and budget discipline (Howarth, 2002: 147), leading, it was hoped, to industrial success through macroeconomic stability. The policy was successful at reducing inflation and restoring competitiveness, but singularly failed to tackle unemployment (Blanchard and Muet, 1993; Lordon, 1998).

The mid-1980s saw a marked shift away from institutionally allocated credit, through state-orchestrated deregulation of the French financial system (Cerny, 1989; Loriaux, 1991: ch. 8; Schmidt, 1996). The process of liberalization began in 1983 with the issuing non-voting shares (*titres participatifs*) and preferred stock (*certificats d'investissement*) and the creation of a *Second Marché* of unlisted securities. The development of a commercial paper market allowed companies to raise capital directly from public through private bond issues. The French futures market – the *Marché à terme des instruments financiers* (MATIF) was opened in February 1986. The 180-year monopoly of the *agents de change* or 'artisanal' state stock brokers was ended. As in other countries (cf. Vogel, 1996), reform paradoxically also saw an extension of the powers of the regulatory body (*Commission des Opérations de la Bourse*).

International financial liberalization rendered the *dirigiste* approach (*encadrement du credit*) increasingly unworkable (Cohen, 1996: 351). This was further underlined by domestic deregulation, freeing up the securities, futures and foreign exchange markets and facilitating the decompartmentalization of markets. As Howarth notes, 'the object of opening access to foreign capital to finance French debt was to control inflation and lower interest rates' (2002: 148). This culminated in the monetary policy-making system being overhauled, phasing out of the *encadrement du credit*, in favour of open market operations, and *Banque de France* manipulation of interest rates as a means of controlling the money supply. The Chirac government's deregulation also facilitated stock issues, leveraged management buyouts and employee stock ownership plans (Schmidt, 1996: 140). The effects on the liquidity of French financial markets were dramatic and the CAC index rose from 100 in 1982 to 460.4 in March 1987. Share prices quadrupled in five years, with total transactions of shares leaping from 26 billion francs in 1976 to 411.2 billion in 1986 (Cerny, 1989: 175).

Financial deregulation led to significant shifts in the financing of French enterprises to patterns that are much more 'Anglo-Saxon'. Internal sources of funds and equity have become proportionately more important and bank loans proportionately less important; of the funds available to enterprises, they now spend a smaller proportion on new investment in the firm and a higher proportion on purchasing financial assets, particularly equities (Schaberg, 1999: ch. 2). In these respects industry finance relations became similar to the United States and United Kingdom, having previously been characterized by ratios similar to those in Germany and Japan. The shift away from bank financing was also reflected in the fall in intermediated finance (raised externally by non-financial institutions and intermediated by a financial institution, rather than raised directly). The proportion of such indirect financing fell from 57 per cent in 1985 to only 18.7 per cent a decade later (OECD, 1997b: 166).

Financial deregulation provided the context for Chirac's privatization programme. The July 1986 law anticipated the privatization of 65 industries. The law also legitimized 'respiration' for public firms, namely the sale of subsidiaries. 'Unofficial' privatization (the sale of non-voting shares since 1983) continued apace, but was if anything outstripped by the privatizations themselves. This rolling back of the state reflected fascination with neo-liberal ideology (the so-called *pensée unique*).[2] However, Finance Minister Balladur's privatization programme retained a peculiarly *dirigiste* air. The government decided, through shareholder selection (*gré-à-gré*), the proportion of stock given to the *noyau dur* – or small group of hard-core investors. Such handpicking ensured that the controlling interest fell into friendly hands (Schmidt, 1996: 133).

Following the rash of privatizations, the demands of capital-starved public corporations were met on a piecemeal basis by the Rocard government by allowing them to trade shares in one another, and with foreign companies. After 1991, public corporations could trade shares with the private sector, facilitating the intermixing of public and private share ownership (Schmidt, 1996: 187). Privatizations continued apace under Governments of Right and Left, with state's residual role in managing the privatized firms affirmed (Szij, 1998), although *dirigisme* became more circumscribed and market oriented (Schmidt, 1999: 446). The need to fund social programmes despite budgetary retrenchment provided the rationale for many privatizations. Indeed, the Jospin government (1997–2002) privatized more state assets than all previous conservative governments put together.

The restructuring of French capitalism

This progressive intermixing of public and private sectors has amounted to a restructuring of French capitalism. Schmidt (1996: 369) sees the emergent 'dynamic capitalism', likening the cross-shareholdings and interlocking directorships to German-style banking–industrial partnerships, and even Japanese *keiretsu*. Boyer is sceptical (1997) about the prognosis for the transplant. Indeed, the networks and coordinating linkages of the French state/industry/finance nexus retain distinctively French qualities (Szarka, 1998; Morin, 2000). The state–firm relationship, however, is becoming more arms-length, involving the state inducing change through its enduring influence.

The *noyaux durs* – hard cores of interlinked financial and industrial interests – were principal organizing features of the restructuring of France's 'financial network economy'. These networks, according to a 1994 parliamentary report, 'alleviate the risks which too great a dispersion of capital may represent, and ensure strategic continuity within the enterprise in the years following privatization' (quoted in Szij, 1998: 20). The restructuring partially resembled French 'protected capitalism' of the 1960s and 1970s. The *noyaux durs* offered protection against predation through inside control, involving subsidiary share ownership in the parent company to help protect management teams, or shares assigned to organizations friendly to PDGs. The recreation of old 'strategic' alliances (e.g. Alcatel-Alsthom and Société Générale; Suez and Saint Gobain); and the anti-predatory logic of the system were all familiar (Schmidt, 1999: 455–6; Morin, 2000).

There were, however, novel aspects to the restructuring of the *noyaux durs* in the 1980s and 1990s. Through cross-cutting nationalized and newly privatized shareholdings, financial and industrial concerns became intermingled for the first time, the banks (nationalized or privatized) being particularly active in acquiring industrial interests. These links were cemented through reciprocal share ownership, and interlocking directorships, 'where CEOs sat on one another's boards (whether they held shares or not in one anothers' companies)' (Schmidt, 1999: 460, 1996: 370–7) A final novelty was the entry into the *noyaux durs* of foreign capital on a larger scale (see below).

The result of these interlocking directorships, the intermingling of financial and industrial concerns and reciprocal share ownership was a 'spider's web' of interdependence between financial and industrial concerns. The new hardcores established a distinctive French model of financial and industrial linkages, with networks of capital cohering around 'spheres of influence'. Three 'poles' emerged, around Paribas-AGF-Crédit Lyonnais, around Suez-BNP-UAP and finally around Société Générale-Alcatel-Alsthom (Schmidt; 1996: 384; Szarka, 1998: 159; figure 13.3).

However, the stability of these 'poles' is questionable. Indeed, Morin (2000: 38) charts a decline in the size of the *noyaux durs*, and a growing presence of foreign investors. The *noyau dur* as an organizing mechanism has drawbacks, divorcing capital investment from the importance of financial return, and tying up large amounts of capital, reducing productive investment. It thus, 'immobilizes capital stocks in circular interlocking stakes, so creating a fictitious capital that cannot be called up by the concern' (Morin, 2000: 38). By 1993, between 15 and 18 billion francs of Paribas' capital was 'immobilized' in this way.

The internationalization of French capitalism?

For much of the postwar era, foreign investment was discouraged, even opposed by the French state (Michalet, 1997). However, in the 1990s, acquisitions, joint ventures and participation in the capital of foreign firms all increased. 'Strategic' European allegiances, for example, with the 'opening up' of Air France, Thomson-CSF and Aerospatiale to better equip them for the global marketplace (Clift, 2001b) further augmented the internationalization of French capital. Foreign direct investment (FDI) into France boomed after 1980, but this largely reflects the global boom in FDI and France's share of the world total stocks has remained roughly constant at around 4.5 per cent (estimated from UNCTAD, 1999: 489). Nevertheless, France remains a major recipient country and vied with the United Kingdom over the 1990s as leading recipient of inward FDI flows into the EU. Over the same period France's FDI overseas has grown faster from a 3.5 per cent share of the global total stocks in 1980 to a 5.9 per cent share in 1998 (estimated from ibid.: 495).

The recent expansion in foreign holdings on the French stock exchange is remarkable. Between 1985 and 1997, foreign owners increased their share of stock exchange capitalization from 10 per cent to 35 per cent (compared to 9 per cent in Britain, and 6 per cent in the United States). The Allianz – AGF buyout represented a partial unravelling of the *noyaux durs*. Morin (2000) charts a 'highly significant trend' of the increasing purchase by North American pension funds and fund managers of the stakes in French firms relinquished by the *noyaux durs*. The scale of the holdings is such that, 'in some cases, such as Alcatel, the foreign mutual funds alone hold a greater proportion of the capital than is controlled by the group of committed shareholders' (ibid.: 43). This may presage a sea change in French capitalism, away from the protective logic of unrelated cross-shareholdings and towards a concentration on Anglo-Saxon profitability norms. Morin sees the 'dominant strategic model' of American institutional investors as a growing influence, demanding concentration of ownership, defence of 'core business', breaking up of conglomerates and externalizing 'non-strategic' activities (cf. Morin, 2000: 48–9; Maclean, 1999: 104–5).

It is too early to draw firm conclusions about the impact of these recent changes, but the extent of change should not be overstated. The *noyaux durs* are still predominant. That said, the close-knit and previously relatively impervious networks are being partially opened up by the influx of both foreign investors, and more importantly foreign investment and corporate governance norms. Yet, whilst 'hyperglobal' accounts would see in this development a teleological process of convergence towards the Anglo-Saxon model of capitalism, this oversimplifies and misconceives the probable impact on French capitalism. Hostile takeovers, for example, remain extremely rare in France, and one cannot talk of a genuine 'market for corporate control' in France (Sauviat and Montagne, 2001).

Morin's qualitative analysis of the relationship between American institutional investors and French bosses uncovers a number of instructive developments. First, shared pedagogy has characterized relations between French managers and fund managers, with bosses adapting to the demands of shareholder value, and fund managers, for their part, adapting their expectations to take account of the French social model (Morin, 2000: 48). Second, company bosses were still able to choose their strategy, and respond actively to the changing needs of their investors, indicating enduring autonomy. Furthermore, given *internal* calls for reform to French corporate governance (see below), evolutions should not be seen as externally imposed. Rather, changes result from interaction, characterized by mutual learning. Third, contrary to popular belief, the timescale of these Anglo-Saxon institutional investors is *not* particularly short term – retaining their holding for on average 2–4 years, with bigger funds retaining for longer still. Furthermore, investment decisions are increasingly based on long-term company strategy, and, given the scale of influx, bosses do not see 'exit' by such investors as a manifest constraint, since they are confident that a new investor will be quickly found (Morin, 2000: 47). This all tells against a 'one way traffic' convergence upon Anglo-Saxon norms. That said, such a major evolution in France's industrial/financial nexus would clearly have some impact, not least on the traditional norms of French corporate governance.

Corporate governance – still capital without sanction?

The traditional French problems of overpowerful and undersupervised PDGs, are exacerbated by the inherently elitist *noyaux durs*.[3] Maclean (1999: 104) characterizes French board members as 'overwhelmingly compliant to the wishes of the PDG, especially since he is in turn normally a board member of their own organisation, this incestuousness breeding cosy complacency'. The privatization programme and the state orchestration of the *noyaux durs* have been termed 'the acme of *pantouflage*' – with top *fonctionnaires* simply entering top posts in the newly privatized concerns (Szarka, 1998: 161). Some question the ensuing calibre of management. One senior French Civil Servant put it bluntly, 'the French *patronat* is among the most useless in the World. They are useless because they all come from the same elite.'[4]

Crédit Lyonnais, GAN and Crédit Foncier are but three of numerous examples of the absolutism of French corporate governance ending in disaster (Schmidt, 1999: 458). The tradition of autonomy for the heads of public sector enterprises only aggravates the problem. The parliamentary enquiry into the collapse of Crédit Lyonnais in 1994 found that chairmen of the large state-owned banks regularly colluding to agree their results, plucking numbers such as the birth date of Henri IV from the air and entering them as annual returns (Maclean, 1999: 103). Such high-profile failures have generated pressures for reform of French board behaviour and structures, away from shareholder passivity and the mutual protection of PDGs. These endogenous pressures are compounded, as we saw above, by exogenous pressures (Morin, 2000). The path corporate governance reform should take is disputed. Advocates of the German Vorstand/Aufsichtsrat model were encouraged when AXA-UAP, a key player in the new configuration of French capitalism, restructured its board along German lines after their merger in November 1996 (Schmidt, 1999: 459). Whilst an option in law since 1966 (Charkham, 1995: 130–7), only 2 per cent of firms have taken the opportunity (Maclean, 1999: 103). Morin (2000: 50–1) sees emulation of the Anglo-Saxon 'shareholder value-oriented' model, advocated by American institutional investors, as a more likely outcome.

Overall, the evolution of the managerial and financial structure of French capitalism should not be exaggerated. The role of elite networks, and the state, continues in the orchestration of *noyaux durs* which, despite evolution, still predominate. As Morin (2000: 39) concedes, 'interlocking shareholdings continue to have a role, even if they have recently declined in number…these quite specific financial relations continue to articulate the configuration of the French financial network'. Maclean (1999: 106) concurs, observing that, 'a convergence with Anglo-Saxon financial capitalism is unlikely to be in the offing'. However, the means by which the state exercises its interventionist role, are changing. This is particularly the case in the restructuring of former nationalized utilities.

The European regulatory framework and *le service publique*

French *dirigiste* industrial policy mechanisms were at odds with the neo-liberalism of the Single European Act, predicated upon Anglo-Saxon norms of capitalist organization. This was perhaps most evident in anti-trust directives, based on US anti-trust legislation. The monopolistic, protectionist and *dirigiste* norms of the French industrial policy, particularly in the public sector, were at odds with EU rules on unfair competition, liberalization and deregulation. Another powerful pressure on French industrial policy has been budgetary retrenchment, increasing the need for privatization receipts. Thus radical changes in the public sector brought about by privatization, and radical changes in the European regulatory framework, rendered *dirigiste* instruments (state aid, 'assisted sectors', public procurement and state orchestrated mergers and acquisitions) largely inoperable (Guyomarch *et al.*, 1998, 161–8, 172–6).

However, high-profile instances of European directives ordering repayment of subsidies (Renault), blocked mergers (de Havilland), or enforced opening of markets (Air Inter) are not necessarily representative of wider trends. Air France and Crédit Lyonnais continued to receive sizeable state subsidies, and 'certain nationalized industries continued to receive large infusions of capital while others were encouraged to merge, regardless of their anti-competitive effects' (Schmidt, 1996: 176 and 230). As for French public procurement norms, by 1996, 90 per cent of state contracts *still* went to French firms. Furthermore, as Guyomarch *et al.* note 'theory has changed more than practice' (1998: 176). That said, interventionist industrial policy appears increasingly viable, given the weakening of traditional policy instruments and advancing Europeanization.

French Governments adapted their interventionist strategies to suit the new environment, and developed new means to pursue familiar ends. France has the highest share of government expenditure and employment amongst European countries outside Scandinavia (OECD, 2000b: 62), and the public sector enjoys a peculiar importance within the French constitutional nexus (Cole, 1999). The tension between EU-driven liberalization and deregulation and French *dirigisme* is resolved by two means. First, by including the notion of social cohesion and *le service publique* in the Treaty of Amsterdam, the Jospin Government used subsidiarity to justify interventionist industrial policy and preserve the public sector's peculiar attributes (cf. Cole and Drake, 2000). *Le service publique* (or the public service mission) is a more encompassing concept than the public sector (Cole, 1999), embodying values of citizenship and equality, the Republican state's role as guarantor of these values, and the public-spirited ethos of the *fonction publique*. It thus serves as a justification for quasi-*dirigiste* interventionism. Second, the Jospin Government exploited the opportunity presented by EU pressures to open up state-owned energy, transport and communication monopolies to competition to engage in strategic restructuring of these sectors, thus pursuing industrial policy by another means. Partial privatization of France Télécom involved, in familiar *noyau dur* style, 'the main institutional shareholders in France-Télécom were traditionally close to the French government: Bouygues and Compagnie Générale des Eaux were two of the most important' (Cole, 1999: 176). The sell-off also served to consolidate cross-shareholdings with Deutsche Telekom & Sprint, whilst France Télécom retained its public service mission, becoming *both* as the operator of the public network *and* a telecommunications operator in the competitive sector (Szij, 1998).

EU liberalization and deregulation, opening up markets and in particular public sector monopoly utility providers, to competition, threatens the complexion of state/economy relations in France. Yet, exploiting such *service publique* constitutional prerogatives, the Jospin Government 'defended' the EDF-GDF against liberalization. The public service employment status of EDF-GDF workers was retained, only one-third of the market was opened up, with the state choosing which clients could shop around, and the state imposing public service conditions on its competitors (ibid.: 173). Such pursuit of industrial policy by other means is characterized by Cole as, 'strengthening the strategic role of the French state (or of firms close to the French state) in an age of economic interdependence and globalisation' (Cole, 1999: 175). Thus, despite considerable upheavals within French capitalism, the state's role as a strategic 'player' endures, albeit by different means, and with reduced direct control.

Industrial relations and labour market reform

The post-war state played a primordial role in shaping French industrial relations, compensating for the weakness of unions and employer associations (Milner, 1998). Not only did the state set the benchmark wage agreements in the form of the public sector pay round – which defines the 'social wage' that plays a central role in a French welfare system formally managed by the 'social partners' – it also used the minimum wage to increase the incomes of the lowest paid by indexing it to the median hourly wage. French industrial relations recently entered a period of upheaval and transformation after, in November 1999, the French Patronat peak organization (Mouvement des entreprises de France, MEDEF) called for a 'new social constitution', and French Unions gave a cautious welcome the 'social refoundation' process. An early concrete outcome of this wide-ranging renegotiation was the introducing of a back-to-work assistance plan (*Plan d'aide au retour à l'emploi*, PARE), requiring all unemployment benefit recipients to sign on to a personalized job-seeking contract. MEDEF's aim was to challenge state encroachment into the social protection regime under the *status quo ante*, yet the state continues to play a key brokering role, notably requiring the signatories to revise the content several times and resolving the dispute over funding between UNEDIC and the government (Palier, 2002: 224–5, 378–85).

In the 1980s, unexpected consequences of the Auroux Laws saw a proliferation of company level agreements, at the expense of wider accords whose scope was progressively reduced (Boyer, 1997). Decentralized company-level bargaining rose sharply.[5] Two significant laws underpinned the shift in the locus of activity; The 1995 Accord National Inter-professionnel and more recently the 1998 Loi Aubry concerning the 35-hour week (see later) shifted the centre of gravity from the branch to the firm level. Branch agreements have now become 'additional' (and by implication subordinate) to firm-level agreements, continuing to define the 'space' of the agreement – establishing the walls, but no longer the ceiling (Silhol, 1997). This has taken allowance of company-level derogation (exemption) from wider sectoral agreements onto a new legal basis.

Contemporaneous to this shift in the locus of activity was a shift in priorities in labour market, towards a concern for lightening tax burdens on business, and encouraging labour market flexibility. In 1986, the requirement to notify the labour inspectorate of planned mass redundancies was abolished, marking a significant withdrawal of the state's regulatory role in the labour market. In the late 1980s and 1990s, laws on working time enhanced temporal flexibility through company-level negotiation. Increased flexibility of work contracts have been differentiated considerably (with the introduction of fixed-term, part-time and temporary contracts), increasing quantitative flexibility (the range of number of hours worked), although not necessarily qualitative flexibility (the nature of work).

A series of laws allowed employers to make greater use of short-term contracts (*contrats de durée determinée* – CDD), used as a structural adjustment mechanism by firms, who hire short-term labour in upswings, only to release them when the boom ends. Despite concerns to limit the abuse of CDDs, their number tripled between 1982 and 1997 to 850 000 employees in the private sector (6 per cent of the total). The majority cover the least qualified employees (L'Horty, 1999).[6] The legal framework for temporary work was expanded between 1982 and 1986. Temporary employment increased fourfold between 1985 and 1998, reaching 413 000. As with CDDs, their expansion followed improvements in the economic conjuncture, but they remained stable during the slowdown in economic activity. Temporary work is concentrated in industry and construction, and 86 per cent of such contracts concern manual workers (L'Horty, 1999).

A further change has been the increase in part-time working. A 1992 law offering reductions in employer's social contributions for permanent part-time contracts saw part-time work contracts increase by over a million between 1992 and 1997 to reach 3.7 million. There has been a marked increase in 'forced' part-time working. In 1997, 40 per cent of those on part-time contracts said they wanted to work longer hours, as against 30 per cent in 1990. Indeed, France has the highest level of 'forced' part-time work in Europe (L'Horty, 1999). Another growth area has been 'partial unemployment', where employers can reduce the hours of some or all of their workforce, and 'compensate' them with roughly half their regular salary, with a top-up coming from a state entitlement. Predictably, this too is very sensitive to the economic cycle, with 24 million compensated days in 1993, reducing to 7.4 million in 1997. Three quarters of such 'partial unemployment' is in industry, the rest being in construction and the tertiary sector. All these mechanisms have been exploited by French firms, who, 'react to salarial rigidities and regulations affecting the labour market by modifying their employee selection mechanisms, notably through an ever increasing recourse to shorter term jobs' (Fougère and Kramarz, 1997: 9).

The inexorable road to flexibility?

There has been increased *internal* flexibility – through measures such as partial unemployment, overtime and part-time working, as well as increased *external* flexibility – through temporary work and CDDs, in France in the late 1980s and 1990s. These increases in flexibility have been key adjustment mechanisms by which the labour market adjusts to changes in the economic cycle. This at first glance appears to be the kind of 'normalization' of labour market practices that convergence theorists would predict. However, closer inspection reveals significant degrees of enduring distinctiveness.

First, wage distribution inequality has decreased markedly in France since the 1960s, and shows no sign of growing again (Fitoussi, 1994: 60; Fougère and Kramarz, 2001: 339–42). The ratio of the minimum wage to the average wage has increased consistently and this has the effect of compressing the lower end of the wage distribution. Differentials between the top and bottom 10 per cent earnings groups, and those between the top and middle 10 per cent groups, have changed little since the early 1980s in France (OECD, 1996: 61). As Card *et al.* (1999) have shown, wage differentials between different levels of education have remained constant, or even diminished slightly in the 1980s and 1990s. *Wage flexibility*, then, has not been prevalent in France, in contradistinction to Anglo-Saxon manifestations of labour market flexibility. A more egalitarian society, France resisted the widening labour market inequalities witnessed in the United Kingdom and the United States.

Second, orthodox assumptions about labour market institutions effect on employment assert that unemployment is due to excessive rigidities, causing the labour market to stagnate. However, the French labour market is far from stagnant. For young workers at least, both hiring as well as separation rates are quite high (Cohen *et al.*, 1997: 273; Fougère and Kramarz, 1997: 9). However, the degree of hiring and firing activity is *not* as high as flexibility-enhancing reforms allow. CCDs make it virtually 'costless' to fire young French workers, yet separation rates are only half US levels. The difference is traceable, Cohen *et al.* (1997: 274) argue, 'to irreducible cultural differences...an "implicit contract" that makes it difficult for a firm to fire a worker'. The 'implicit contract' (D'Iribarne, 1990, 1992) is predicated upon the social norms underpinning the labour market.

The third point, which again rests on the social norms and social context within which the labour market is embedded, relates to the welfare provision system, which, Boyer (1997: 81) argues, 'sustained an ever-growing source of redistribution in terms of social welfare'. Replacement rates in terms of unemployment benefits, and early retirement pensions remain quite generous. As Boyer notes of the 1983 U-turn, it was, 'tempered by the promise to uphold a fundamental welfare provision'. Indeed, the changes in what Boyer terms the 'wage relation' have on the whole been achieved whilst maintaining general welfare cover (1997: 86 and 96). According to UNEDIC (the unemployment insurance body) the replacement rate in France reduced slightly from 53.6 per cent in 1989 to 49 per cent by the end of 1996, yet this remains fairly generous.

The public attachment to generous welfare provision was graphically demonstrated in winter 1995, when a massive protest movement, led by rail-workers strikes, which enjoyed widespread popular support, crippled the country for three weeks. The *Plan Juppé*, justified as essential belt-tightening to meet the Maastricht convergence criteria, involved austerity-oriented reductions in French welfare provision, covering, amongst others, social security and health entitlements, public sector pension privileges, and SNCF working practices and benefits.[7] This united normally divided unions behind cherished welfare provision, or *droits acquis*, seen as an integral part of French citizenship. Attacks on the railway system were seen as an assault on *le service publique*. The demonstrations and strikes cohered around issues of 'defence', 'protection' and 'maintenance' of Republican values. This episode made welfare reform almost untouchable.

The distinctiveness and generosity of French welfare provision, however, should not be overstated. Coverage under the French welfare system is patchy. For example, the link between work and entitlement means those not finding work find their benefits diminishing over time. Furthermore, the unemployment insurance system has not adjusted to take account of the new forms of work, leaving many without any entitlements (L'Horty, 1999). The Jospin Government, whose victory in 1997 many attribute to the political aftermath of 1995 (Howard, 1998), attempted to break the link between contribution and entitlement, moving towards citizen-based social rights. This is the rationale behind the *Contribution Sociale Généralisée*, and the universalization of health cover (Palier, 2002: 337–51). However, such tax-financed welfare could lead to a two-tier welfare system as macroeconomic constraints bite. These 'universal means-tested' benefits could, Palier argues, 'progressively lose their universality, in order to make budgetary savings, and to concentrate public money on those in real need' (Palier, 2002: 402–3).

State-led responses to unemployment

Youth employment creation

Analysts of French public policy distinguish between 'heroic' policies, formulated by government elites and imposed on French society (Schmidt, 1996: 50–5), and 'everyday' policy-making. Arguably, the 35-hour week, and the youth employment creation scheme – the *Plan Aubry* of the Jospin Government marked a slight return for heroic policy-making. Both were testaments to the enduringly 'statist' character of the French model (Clift, 2003). The problem both these policies set out to solve was the chronic unemployment record of the French economy since the early 1980s (see Table 6.1).

State-led employment creation and protection schemes have become a structuring feature of the French model (OFCE, 1999: 58, 68, Figure VII.3; Levy, 2001: 195–6). Ministry of Employment figures show that over 2 million people were on state-initiated employment policy schemes in 1996 (Benhayoun and Lazzeri, 1998: 48). 'Active' employment policy takes a number of forms, from apprenticeships, and work placements, to state-subsidized jobs, and employers' social security exemptions, often aimed at 'making work pay' for lower earners and reducing disincentives to hire. These policies increasingly target particular groups 'excluded' from the labour market, notably the long-term unemployed, the uneducated and young people. These groups have borne the brunt of increased labour market flexibility in France. All the new, flexible forms of employment outlined above are relatively overpopulated with young workers (nearly all on short-term contracts). Thus, 'French society puts nearly all the burden of flexibility upon these workers' (Cohen *et al.*, 1997: 272).

After 1997, the Socialist-led government used public sector job creation to tackle unemployment. The resources devoted to employment policy increased markedly, reaching 4.5 per cent of GDP in 2000 (Ministère des Finances, 2001: 15).[8] The *Plan Aubry* pledged to create 350 000 public sector jobs, to be matched by 350 000 new private sector posts. The results were encouraging, with 274 900 jobs created in the public sector by March 2001, and a total of 308 000 private sector jobs under the Plan Aubry framework,[9] and further expansion in the 2001 Budget (Ministère des Finances, 2001: 9).

Table 6.1   French unemployment, 1981–99. Percentage of the workforce unemployed (standardized definition)

Year	Percentage
1982	7.7
1983	8.1
1984	9.7
1985	10.2
1986	10.3
1987	10.5
1988	10.0
1989	9.4
1990	9.0
1991	9.5
1992	10.4
1993	11.7
1994	12.3
1995	11.7
1996	12.4
1997	12.3
1998	11.8
1999	11.3

Source: OECD, *Economic Outlook*, 2000d.

The Jospin Government introduced other anti-exclusion employment measures, 50 000 *Contrats emploi-solidarité* (a Youth employment subsidy scheme) in 2001. Nearly a million young people came under the auspices of the *Nouveau Départ* scheme each year, Meanwhile the number of people covered by the TRACE scheme was set to increase by 50 per cent in 2002 (Ministère des Finances, 2001: 9). As Milner notes, overall these 'anti-exclusion' employment measures cost '50 billion francs over two and a half years, with around 200 million francs coming from the European Social Fund' (2001: 333). The role of the state as guarantor of the job creation programme thus remains a central feature of France's 'model' of capitalism.

The 35-hour working week

The issue of reducing the length of the working week has long been of central importance for the French Left (Muet and Fonteneau, 1990: 190–213). More recently, the right-wing Juppé Government introduced the *Loi Robien*, establishing financial inducements for reductions in working time. Within public discourse, the 35-hour week is an integral part of France's 'model' of capitalism, ripe for export.

The aim of the reduction of the working week was primarily to reduce unemployment, in part by making growth more 'job-rich'. A further aspiration, given the progressive increase in capital returns since the 1980s, whilst wage earners suffered diminishing returns, was a redistributive boost wage earners purchasing power. However, salaries in the private sector are outside the government's jurisdiction, and thus the law makes no legal provision for wages levels (Gubian, 1998: 25). The French law emphasizes job creation, with state aid in the form of reductions in social security contributions offered to firms creating new jobs as a result of the reduction of the working week. The fixed levels of these state financial aids means that they will be relatively more generous for lower earners (Gubian, 1998; Milner, 2002).

The law also reflected enduring 'neo-corporatist' aspirations within the PS (Jefferys, 2000). The national conference on salaries, attended by government, unions and *Patronat* in September 1997 was testament to the PS's faith in the ability of consensual labour-capital relations to alleviate unemployment pressures. Negotiation was predominantly at firm level, and often involved a wider reorganization of work, conditions and pay. 'The spirit of the law', according to Gubian, put 'negotiation at the centre of the process of reduction in working time' (1998: 20).

Such negotiating, as we have seen, goes against the confrontational grain of French industrial relations. The law highlighted certain structural problems, such as the lack of union representation structures to orchestrate the negotiating process in many firms, particularly smaller ones. The 'statist' nature of the negotiation process was a response to the low density and fragmentation of French unions (Muet, 1998: 73, 85). Here again we see the enduring 'statist' nature of the French model of capitalism, in which the state continues to be of central importance to France's economic development, even if its *modus operandi* has evolved.

The law is justified in economic efficiency terms by anticipated gains in productivity. Lower fatigue levels of workers, a lesser instance of absenteeism and a more efficient organization of working time will, it is argued, all improve productivity and reduce production costs (Gubian, 1998). Indeed, the premise of the law is that the burden of cost arising from the transition must be shouldered by state and employees, but *not* by firms (Gubian, 1998: 29). The law also implicitly recognized the need for employees to shoulder the burden of transition costs through wage moderation, for example, with the 35 hours being paid at 38, not 39 hours, so that firms could stabilize their wage costs (OFCE, 2001: 103, 106; Milner, 2002: 345). In terms reminiscent of Glyn (1995), the 35-hour week involves negotiated redistribution amongst workers as a means of furthering full employment objectives. As Fitoussi puts it, 'workers have to agree to share both their jobs and their salaries with the unemployed' (1998: 81).

The Second Aubry law (19 January 2000) involved reducing employers' social contributions, made contingent upon reduction of working time. In keeping with the wider employment strategy, the reductions in social costs were most accentuated at and just above minimum wage, furthering the aim of reducing the costs for firms of hiring low- and medium-wage workers (Gubian, 2000: 15–16). The Second Aubry law relieved the pressure for wage restraint, but this was achieved not by redistribution from capital to labour, but through increased state expenditure. In ideological terms, the 35-hour week is also as a rejection of neo-liberal interpretation of globalization, and its implications for structural reform of labour market institutions. Although labour market flexibility has increased in France in the 1980s and 1990s, the path is not an inexorable road towards an Anglo-Saxon 'model', but retains a significant state role, which seeks to secure equitable social norms.

Conclusion

The traditional means of French *dirigiste* have largely been rendered ineffective by Europeanization, privatization and deregulation. However, the resilience of the French state tradition was paradoxically demonstrated in the *dirigiste* approach to financial liberalization and the privatization programme, where the state was instrumental in shaping the financial and industrial restructuring process. Yet, the French state does not retain the same privileged position it once enjoyed. The ongoing privatization process has permanently reduced the size and scope of public sector, and financial liberalization has allowed an internationalization of French capitalism. In particular, with the influx of North American institutional investors, previously relatively impervious *noyaux durs* have partially opened up to both foreign investors, and foreign investment and corporate governance norms. The implication of this recent shift remain unclear, but predictions of a shift from a 'financial network economy' to a financial market economy appear premature given the process of *interaction* between French institutions and 'Anglo-Saxon' influences, the enduring autonomy of French bosses, and the process of 'shared pedagogy' which the changes have heralded. The limited nature of change is illustrated by examples of novel forms and means of *dirigisme* in recent state-orchestrated restructuring of the *service publique*, where the strategic 'player' state remains in partially evidence.

French capitalism's traditional, hermetically sealed elitism has been penetrated as a result of the internationalization of French capitalism. Despite this, the interlocking of industrial and financial capital and the nature of the inter-relationships remain of a peculiarly French nature, both in the extent to which they are state induced, and in the way they are predicated on the intermingling of French administrative, political and business elites within the *Grands corps*, the alumni of the *Grandes Ecoles*. France financial network economy continues to be built on elitist foundations. The traditional 'Napoleonic' approach to corporate governance has been undermined by serious failures and scandals in recent years. This has led to calls for reform within France. This internal impetus for change dovetails with the growing influence of foreign corporate governance norms – both German and American, which has resulted from the increasing participation of large-scale foreign shareholders in major French industrial and financial concerns.

As for French industrial relations, the state's orchestrating role continues undiminished, as demonstrated by the 35-hour week legislation, where the government brought employees and employers together to negotiate the transition. The context of the shift to a 35-hour week is a labour market which has undergone a significant degree of flexibilization since the mid-1980s. However, whilst short-term, temporary, and part-time contracts have expanded temporal flexibility, the minimum wage and bargaining norms have prevented greater salarial inequalities emerging. Furthermore, cultural norms seem to have prevented the hiring and firing at the 'bottom end' of the French labour market reaching the scale that the legal framework permits. 'Heroic' policy-making, in the form of the 35-hour week and the *Plan Aubry*, combined with a favourable macroeconomic context and economic growth looked to be tackling unemployment, reducing it below 3 million. Here again, a distinguishing characteristic has been their nature. However, subsequent lapses in the growth rate have made such achievements appear ephemeral, and France's structural unemployment problem has stubbornly remained.

For all the 'Anglo-Saxon' influences, be they from the EU regulatory framework, or US institutional investors, the French model continues (and is likely to continue) to display a strong *etatiste* national distinctiveness.

Notes

1. According to Levy (2000, 321), more than 75 per cent of public aid went to fewer than half a dozen firms, most of whom were uncompetitive and many in declining sectors.
2. Nowhere was this more apparent than within the Ministry of Industry, where Alain Madelin halved his own budget, and abolished a series of R&D and infrastructural grants such as the Fonds Industriel de Modernisation (worth 9 billion francs), on the assumption that, 'from now on ... this ministry must adopt, and no longer orient, much less direct, the life of companies' (Schmidt, 1996: 139, 142).
3. In 1995, the 300 board seats on France's top 40 companies were held by just 75 individuals (Maclean, 1999: 102).
4. Interview with the author 22/9/97.
5. From 1477 such agreement in 1981, the number leapt to 6750 by 1990, and by 1994, 7450 agreements were signed – a 14 per cent increase on the previous year (Milner, 1998: 175). The trend towards decentralized agreements was further encouraged by a 1984 law stipulating that all negotiations on training take place at industry or company level.
6. According to L'Horty (1999) 340000 CDDs concern manual labourers, in 1997, and 435000 blue-collar workers.

7. Juppé's bull in a china shop tactics, moving on so many fronts at once, were *very* ill-thought out. As Ross asks, 'what *do* they teach at ENA?' (1996).
8. Spending on employment policy increased by 13 per cent between 1997 and 2002.
9. Labour Ministry figures, see the website, *www.nsej.travail.gouv.fr/actualite/bilan*. Such results, however, must be placed in the context of a wider economic upturn, making the precise impact of the *Plan Aubry* difficult to discern.

7
Scandinavian Capitalism at the Turn of the Century
Juhana Vartiainen

Introduction

The Nordic countries have often been singled out for a social democratic version of capitalism, the characteristics of which include a large welfare state, a high average tax rate, strongly unionized labour markets and relatively narrow income differentials. Although the 'Nordic model' is often characterized directly in terms of these policies and institutions, at a deeper level they are a reflection of mutually reinforcing political values and political and historical traditions. The main content of these values and traditions can be summarized as follows:

(1) A communitarian emphasis on citizens' universal participation via democratic political movements and trade union activity;
(2) Egalitarian political preferences which translate into an aversion towards large income differentials and a consequent acceptance of high tax rates and a large amount of redistribution and public services within the market economy;
(3) Active macroeconomic management to sustain a high rate of employment.

As to the economic management of capitalism, such traditions have generated three powerful collectivist interventions into the market economy; first, a large welfare state and a high level of collectively organized, compulsory social insurance; second, a large coverage of collective agreements in the labour market; and, third, Keynesian demand management to stabilize the economy.

Such a general characterization, while broadly true, is insensitive to inter-country differences. The above caricature applies best to Sweden, whereas the other Nordic countries deviate from that model in different respects.

The main question we discuss in this chapter is to what extent these collectivist interventions prove to be feasible even in an increasingly market-driven, globalized economic environment. Now it is certainly a prevalent view among scholars and politicians that a number of factors have been undermining and go on to undermine the social democratic model of economic management. The factors and trends most often discussed include:

(a) The evolution of productive techniques away from industrial mass production towards a larger share of service jobs; this undermines the traditional institutions and working class culture of social democratic societies;
(b) The liberalization of financial markets and the abolition of credit rationing restrain the toolkit of economic management and the scope for intervening into the economy; this trend is exacerbated by eventual participation in EMU.
(c) European integration and economic globalization will, through increasing competition, in any case make it impossible for small European economies like the Nordic ones to sustain their original social and political institutions.

In the light of such developments, the eventual erosion of the Nordic social democratic welfare state is often depicted as a constrained process in which the traditional solutions have become unfeasible even if the original political preferences were intact.

This chapter makes a short tour of Nordic economics and politics, with special emphasis on the welfare state, labour market corporatism and macroeconomic management. We focus on Sweden, Denmark and Finland in particular. Norway is to some extent left out of the description, partly because the looser fiscal constraints allowed by oil revenue have rendered the political and economic trade-offs of that country less stringent than those of other Nordic countries.

Without adopting any strong programmatic position, this chapter challenges the above view. We argue that the political choice set of the Nordic societies still includes outcomes which are in accordance both with social democratic values and the market economy's incentive compatibility condition. This is especially true of both labour market arrangements and the welfare state. The policies of the 'Nordic model' should ultimately be seen in instrumental terms as devices designed to realize a set of underlying preferences.

These arguments notwithstanding, the eventual erosion of the Nordic model cannot be ruled out. Yet, if it happens, it will be the result of changing political attitudes and lack of political legitimacy and not of external constraints forced on the economy. We will in the concluding section try to pinpoint the most important challenges facing the social democratic regimes. On the plan of employment and macroeconomic management, the key challenge is to coordinate wage bargaining and economic policy in a way that supports full employment. On the plan of microeconomics, the interesting question is whether full employment can be accommodated with a distribution of income that is compatible with Nordic egalitarian political preferences.

Thus, in a debate often dominated by attempts to characterize change, we try to outline possible elements of continuity. Of course, the scholarly debate on different versions of capitalism shows that continuity and change are two largely complementary views on such complex entities as societies. Societies are in constant transformation, but there are, as well, fundamental institutions that persist through change.[1] Hypotheses which claim that the Nordic welfare state would be undermined by the processes of economic integration and globalization should be treated with scepticism, since the most convincing economic explanations of the welfare state in fact relate the rise of the public sector to a need to tackle the economic uncertainty inherent in the participation of small economies to global markets.

The public sector and the welfare state

Although many commentators both on the Left and the Right of the political spectrum speak of the crisis of the welfare state, it is still undoubtedly true that the Nordic countries can be singled out as ones with a relatively large public involvement in the economy. This usually turns out to be true whatever one's measure of the share of the public sector. Table 7.1 depicts the share of public expenditure in total GDP in various OECD countries. Table 7.2, replicated from Iversen (1998) depicts the relative shares of public employment and private service sector employment as per cent of adult population in six OECD countries in different periods.

The data of these tables suggest several things. First, there is a consistent differential between the Nordic countries and the EU average as to the relative role of the public sector. Second, even in Scandinavia, the public economy has matured in the sense that the continuous expansion of the public sector seems to be over. In none of the countries has the public sector exhibited any significant growth since the mid-1980s. This statement seems to be superficially false for Finland, but the sudden surge in the public expenditure share in that country can be accounted for by the exceptionally harsh recession of the early 1990s; thus it has more to do with a shrinking denominator than an expanding nominator.

Third, however, in none of the Nordic countries (nor, for that matter, in major European countries), has there been any significant decline in the share of the public economy. An economist's natural interpretation of this is that the welfare state has matured: given the set of political preferences, the tax burden that the electorate is willing to sustain in exchange for public services and social security has more or less been reached.[2]

The data in Table 7.2 also reveal an interesting structural trend, linking the debate on the public sector and the labour market model to the topical

Table 7.1   Government expenditure as per cent of GDP

Country	1965	1970	1980	1990	1999
Denmark	29.9	40.2	56.2	56.0	54.3
Finland	30.8	30.5	36.6	44.5	47.1
Sweden	36.1	43.3	61.6	60.5	55.9
Norway	34.2	41.0	48.3	52.3	46.1
OECD	30.6	32.3	39.4	35.5	37.8
OECD small countries	28.8	32.6	44.8	37.9	40.3
Euro area	—	—	—	—	45.9
Australia	25.6	26.8	33.8	33.0	31.8
Austria	37.8	39.2	48.9	48.5	49.8
Belgium	32.3	36.5	50.7	50.8	47.9
Canada	29.1	34.8	40.5	46.0	38.8
France	38.4	38.5	46.1	49.6	52.1
Germany	36.6	38.6	48.3	43.8	45.9
Ireland	33.1	39.6	50.8	39.5	30.9
Italy	34.3	34.2	41.7	53.1	48.3
Japan	—	19.4	32.6	31.3	38.1
Netherlands	38.7	43.9	57.5	49.4	42.7
Spain	19.6	22.2	32.9	41.4	39.6
United Kingdom	36.1	38.8	44.8	41.9	39.1
United States	27.9	31.6	33.7	33.6	30.0

General government total outlays as a percentage of nominal GDP in years 1965, 1970, 1980, 1990, 1999.

Source: OECD *Economic Outlook* from years 1986, 1988, 1991, 2000d. The OECD member country set and small member country set has changed in the time period spanned by the table.

Table 7.2   Public and private sector service employment

Year	Denmark		Sweden		UK		USA		Germany		Netherlands	
1970–73	14	20	17	19	13	20	10	26	8	17	7	21
1974–77	17	20	20	20	15	22	10	26	9	17	7	21
1978–81	20	20	24	20	15	23	11	29	10	18	8	21
1982–85	22	20	26	20	14	24	10	31	10	18	8	20
1986–89	22	21	26	22	14	28	11	35	10	19	7	22
1990–92	22	21	26	23	14	31	11	36	10	17	7	24
Change	8	1	9	3	0	11	1	11	2	0	0	3

Public employment and private service-sector employment in six OECD countries, 1970–92, percentage of adult population. The first column for each country depicts total general government employment as percentage of adult population; the second column is total private service sector employment as a percentage of adult population, excluding transport and communication.

Source: Iversen (1998), original data from the OECD Sectoral Data Base.

unemployment problem discussed below. In both Denmark and Sweden, private service sector employment stagnated during the period 1970–92, whereas it grew strongly in the United Kingdom and United States. Many researchers have associated this with the solidaristic wage policies typical for Sweden in particular; as wage differentials are compressed, those potential private service sector jobs that would generate low-wage streams are prevented from being created (Iversen, 1998). While that explanation probably puts too much of the blame on wage bargaining only, it seems true that the Nordic economies, with their relatively high level of social security and low level of wage differentials, have been less able to generate low-paid private service sector jobs.

Again, Sweden is an extreme example, since all net employment growth since the 1960s has in that country occurred in the public sector (see Figure 7.1). This may put the Nordic countries in a disadvantaged position as to job creation. Not surprisingly, the labour market policy debate of all these countries strongly emphasizes the need to increase investment into training, as an alternative to letting wages shrink in the service sector.

The growth of the public sector in the Nordic countries has generated a fierce academic debate on the merits and demerits of a large public involvement in the economy (e.g. Freeman *et al.*, 1997). Critics of the Nordic welfare state have pointed out potential adverse effects on productivity and economic growth, but there are hardly any robust econometric results on the relationship between economic growth and the size of the public sector.

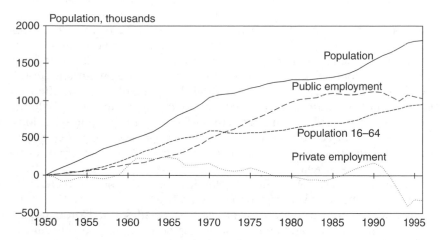

Figure 7.1 Population and public and private employment in Sweden, 1950–95, thousands

Source: Vartiainen (1998).

The growth performance of the Nordic countries does not allow any straightforward characterization of the area as a 'low growth' or 'high growth' area. Even for Sweden, the country most often singled out as 'sclerotic', the evaluation of growth performance remains quite controversial. Furthermore, the Nordic countries have since the late 1990s been able to take advantage of the technological breakthroughs associated with digital information technology; in all of these countries, the IT sector has generated a large part of new value added growth, with firms like Nokia (Finland) and Ericsson (Sweden) at the lead.

From the 1980s onwards, there arose an increasingly critical political discussion on the welfare state, especially in Sweden and Finland. However, systematic studies of the political support for welfare state arrangements have not been able to detect any significant ruptures in political preferences. Most studies of political attitudes show that the Nordic welfare state enjoys quite a robust political support. Regular questionnaires in Finland and Sweden show that popular support for the welfare state remains robust (Svallfors, 1995; Svallfors and Taylor-Gooby, 1999). Even in Denmark, in which there arose, in the 1970s, a populist anti-tax revolt, the support for the expansion of the welfare state rallied during the 1980s.

In the economic literature, the size of the public sector has been scrutinized from a variety of theoretical standpoints. The most convincing general hypothesis on the size of the public sector has been suggested by Rodrik (1997, 1998), who shows that the best predictor of the growth of the public sector is the economy's exposure to external uncertainty. Thus, the more open the economy and the more volatile are its terms of trade, the larger, on average, is the volume of publicly provided goods and social security. There is a simple rationale for this: the public sector acts as a buffer against uncertainty. For a small economy, openness and participation to international trade via specialization is not only a source of wealth but also a source of volatility. The rational political solution is to use the public economy as a buffer. Macroeconomically, the state is able sustain demand and absorb external shocks; ideally, this also has a stabilizing microeconomic effect on individual consumption, since social security transfers can compensate the loss of income during unemployment spells due to economic recessions. When the Nordic countries are looked at in this perspective, a large part of their particular 'social-democratic' characteristics can be accounted for by their smallness and relative openness.

On top of the openness argument, Nordic egalitarian political preferences favour redistribution via a large public sector. The 'crisis of the welfare state' is, therefore, a premature diagnosis of Nordic societies. The Nordic welfare state is firmly in place and enjoys continuing political support. Although a period of fiscal consolidation and welfare spending cuts has occurred in all Nordic countries with the exception of Norway, this reflected fiscal pressure in times of low growth rather than a weakening of the commitment to a generous welfare state.[3] In Finland in particular, the deep recession of the 1990s may even have strengthened that commitment, since the welfare state more or less played out its role in that crisis: although average income shrank significantly in the 1990s, there was no noticeable effect on relative income differentials (Kosonen, 1998). European integration may put pressures on the tax base, but it is in principle economically feasible to go on taxing low-mobility assets and activities like labour and real estate.

Unemployment and labour market institutions

A lacklustre unemployment record

The unemployment problem probably poses the greatest challenge to Nordic societies at the turn of the century. Three Nordic countries – Sweden, Finland and Denmark – have since the 1980s suffered an unemployment rate that would have been regarded as outrageous earlier, and no other economic problem has contributed as much to the general disillusionment with the Nordic model.

Table 7.3 depicts some unemployment data for Finland, Norway, Sweden and Denmark. As far as employment is concerned, the 'full employment' Nordic model has genuinely lost its particular character. Finland's unemployment is still very high at the turn of the century and even Swedish unemployment rose to 'European' levels in the recession of the 1990s. In Denmark and Norway, however, the unemployment problem is less severe. In Denmark, unemployment increased in the 1980s already and unemployment has declined gently but consistently since then, so that Denmark is as of now reckoned to be one of the European success stories. That notwithstanding, Nordic capitalism cannot any more be singled out for its exceptionally and consistently good employment performance.

The Nordic countries have preserved their *high participation rates*. This is largely due to the high participation rate of women, as appears from

Table 7.3 Unemployment in Scandinavian countries

Country	1979–87	1990	1991	1993	1995	1997	1999
Denmark	8.6	7.7	8.4	10.1	7.3	5.6	5.2
Finland	5.2	3.2	6.7	16.4	15.3	12.7	10.3
Norway	2.4	5.3	5.6	6.1	5.0	4.1	3.3
Sweden	2.2	1.7	3.1	9.1	8.8	9.9	7.2
EU		8.2	10.7	10.7	10.6	9.2

Standardized unemployment rates in the Nordic countries.

Source: OECD (1990, 2000d). The definition of unemployment rates for 1979–87 differs somewhat from those of the 1990s.

Table 7.4 Labour force participation rates in Scandinavian countries

Country	1990		1999	
	all	women	all	women
Denmark	82.4	77.6	80.6	76.1
Finland	76.6	73.5	73.6	71.2
Sweden	84.6	82.5	78.5	76.0
Norway	77.1	70.7	80.6	76.1
EU	67.3	54.6	69.0	59.5
OECD Europe	66.6	52.7	67.5	56.6

Source: OECD (2000d)

Table 7.4. Second, all of the Nordic countries have traditions of more or less *corporatist industrial relations*. According to most indices of centralization of wage bargaining, the Nordic countries usually emerge as the ones having the largest degree of coordination in wage bargaining. Such a regime for wage setting has been a staple ingredient in the Nordic countries' economic policy strategy since the 1950s. Although strains have appeared at times, in Sweden in particular, the wage bargain has remained a central element in the national policy agenda.

From the 1970s onwards, such corporatist institutions have attracted considerable attention in theoretical and empirical economic research. Starting with the seminal contribution of Calmfors and Driffill (1988), this literature has concluded that coordination of unions' wage claims benefits employment and leads to lower unemployment in comprehensively organized corporatist economies (Calmfors and Driffill, 1988; Soskice, 1990). A newer literature, based mainly on the writings of Teulings and Hartog (1998) has emphasized the positive aspects of coordinated corporatism even in terms of real wage flexibility. The point of corporatism, that is, encompassing collective agreements, is to allow rapid adjustment to macroeconomic and sectoral shocks without having to renege individual (local) wage agreements. Thus, at least in theory, coordinated corporatism is a viable way of organizing labour market bargains.

Although national characteristics differ, that tradition has not been abandoned and in none of the Nordic countries has economic policy been comprehensively reoriented according to Anglo-Saxon neo-liberal lines. In this respect, however, the current state of labour market policy and labour market politics is very different from country to country and we will analyze each country in more detail. Somewhat surprisingly, it is in Sweden that there is the greatest disarray concerning the future of the wage bargaining system whereas both Finland and Denmark have without much ado been reforming and streamlining their labour market institutions.

Mainstream view: high NAIRU levels

The mainstream OECD view interprets the current high unemployment rates as largely structural and puts the blame on labour market institutions. To get unemployment down, according to the OECD, labour market flexibility should be enhanced by weakening the role of encompassing collective agreements and by increasing incentives to seek work. The mainstream policy framework is based on estimates of the structural unemployment rate or NAIRU (non-accelerating inflation rate of unemployment) which show a very significant increase in structural unemployment since the 1980s.

Yet, the interpretation of the evidence is controversial and many economists do not take the mainstream view seriously. As shown by Holden and Nymoen (2002), the method used to calculate NAIRU estimates is based on dubious assumptions and does not meet normal econometric standards. The high NAIRU estimates are also difficult to reconcile with the fact that the fundamental institutions of the labour market such as the strength of the unions, the stringency of job protection laws or the replacement ratio in unemployment benefits have not changed in the way implied by the assumption of a sharp rise in equilibrium unemployment rates. In practice, OECD estimates of the NAIRU usually track actual unemployment quite closely.

A closer look on the empirical studies on NAIRU confirms the difficulty of explaining the rise in NAIRUs in a satisfactory way. For example, Elmeskov *et al.* (1998) presents a regression analysis, based on a panel of countries, that explains the increase in NAIRU as measured by the OECD. Saliently, it is just Sweden and Finland that exhibit the largest increases in NAIRU between 1983/85 and 1993/95, but, for both countries, the increase remains largely unaccounted for by changes in the regressors.[4]

Yet, it is undeniably true that unemployment has increased in all Nordic countries and, with exception of Norway, has decreased quite slowly. A first step in the evaluation of the Nordic countries' economic performance should be an assessment of why unemployment went up in the first place. Thus, the assessment of Nordic labour market models hinges closely on whether we believe the current unemployment problem in those countries is structural or not.

This issue, in turn, is part of the more general question on the nature of European unemployment. On this issue, economists are quite divided, and empirical studies do not provide a clear-cut picture. The most convincing recent econometric analyses lend support to a mixed view according to which the original increase in unemployment has been due to transient one-off shocks – such as the slowdown in productivity growth in the 1970s, oil price increases and, in particular, the determinate disinflation of the 1980s and 1990s that was part of the single currency project but also a more general phenomenon – but the speed at which economies recover from shocks depends closely on the flexibility of their labour market and the functioning of the welfare arrangements. For example, the analysis of Blanchard and Wolfers (2000) suggests that structural unemployment rates have not necessarily gone up by any large amount, but those countries that have more flexible labour markets are able to manage a quicker return to full employment than those with less flexibility.

Whatever the final truth on this, it is useful to look at country experiences to understand the nature of the unemployment problem.

Verdict on labour market corporatism: thumbs down or up?

In both Sweden and Finland, unemployment soared during the deep recession of the 1990s. Thus, at first sight it is fairly easy to ascribe the rise in unemployment to serious macroeconomic policy failures. In both countries, deregulation of financial markets had led to a serious overheating of the economy in the late 1980s. That was associated with asset price inflation, unemployment rates clearly below any reasonable guess of the NAIRU and a serious current account deficit. In both countries, the economy plunged into a deep recession in the 1990s (Vartiainen, 1998; Honkapohja and Koskela, 1999); in Sweden, unemployment increased from 2 to 8 per cent and in Finland from 3 to even over 16 per cent.

Thus, on the one hand, the growth of unemployment can be attributed to outright macroeconomic policy mistakes and unique shocks emanating from systemic changes. It is also undeniable that the poor employment outcome was associated with a sharp deceleration of inflation; this also became the period in which these countries definitely distanced themselves from their inflation-devaluation-prone past. As in many other countries, even Finland and Sweden had bouts of high and accelerating inflation before the monetary disciplining that took place in the 1980s. The employment record as well as indicators of real wage flexibility was traditionally reasonably good for both countries, but they were achieved in an environment of high and at times accelerating inflation.

Thus, the historical record of Swedish and Finnish labour market corporatism allows for two interpretations. According to the 'nasty' interpretation, the high employment performance only was possible because of high and often *accelerating* inflation, which, in the course of the 1980s, became impossible to sustain (e.g. Calmfors, 1993). Once the 'moment of truth' came in the form of disinflation, unemployment rose to European levels. According to the 'sympathetic' interpretation, the rise in unemployment was mainly due to the harshness of monetary disciplining. If the new inflation targets had been less ambitious and disinflation had taken place less rapidly and in better coordination with fiscal authorities, employment would have dropped less sharply.

There is no quantitative way of assessing these completing interpretations and both may contain grains of truth. In favour of the 'nasty' interpretation it can be said that the traditional economic management of both countries had relied fairly heavily on devaluations which were used to improve competitiveness and accommodate past wage increases. From the 1950s through the 1970s, that *modus vivendi* was feasible without accelerating inflation, since the public had not yet fully learned to incorporate anticipated devaluations into their price and wage claims, and, furthermore, the authorities could control the economy in many other ways; centralized wage agreements were implemented and credit as well as capital movements were controlled. This implied that it was easier to sustain high real wage flexibility: with a quasi-administrative control of wage bargains and some flexibility in the nominal exchange rate, it became possible to implement real wage restraint when needed. With liberalized financial markets and a less complete control of the wage bargaining process (in Sweden in particular), the soft monetary regime was bound to lead to accelerating inflation and there was no alternative to sharp disinflation, even without any eventual European single currency project.

On the other hand, sympathizers of the Nordic labour market model can point out that fatal macroeconomic policy failures took place in the late 1980 and early 1990s, and it would have been an impossible task even for the most flexible of labour markets to accommodate such shocks without a steep rise in unemployment. Indeed a similar pattern of excessive boom followed by recession was experienced in Britain at the same time. First, the overheating of the 1980s was not met with a sufficiently restrictive fiscal policy. Second, the monetary disciplining objective was first interpreted as an *exchange rate target*, with the result that Sweden and Finland attempted, in the early 1990s, to sustain an absurdly uncompetitive and non-credible exchange rate with interest rates of over 10 or even 15 per cent at a time when the economy was already plunging into recession. Eventually, the central banks in both countries had to relinquish the exchange rate targets, but high interest rates had by then destroyed hundreds of thousands of jobs in both countries.

In Denmark, the unemployment crisis was of earlier origin, having started in the late 1970s and continued in the 1980s. At that time, Denmark, too, had to cope with a large external deficit and a large public sector deficit. These twin problems required a restrictive policy stance throughout the 1970s and 1980s. By the same token, Denmark had already started to adapt to German monetary policy and low inflation in the 1980s. This led to contradictions between the government and central bank on the one side and the unions on the other and contributed to a prolonged unemployment problem. These contradictions, associated with a period of monetary disciplining, in many ways resemble those experienced by Sweden in the 1990s.

Thus, although less dramatic in character, the macroeconomic-monetary experiences of Denmark foreshadowed those of Sweden and Finland by about 10 years. Piecemeal reforms of labour market institutions have been taking place in Denmark since the 1980s; they have partly decentralized the wage process of wage formation without questioning the basic Nordic principles of industrial relations.

Labour market strategies in three countries

The employment crisis of the 1980s to 1990s has led to rather different responses in all of our three country cases. In Finland, interestingly, the crisis has reinforced a consensual view of the labour market and centralization of wage bargaining. This is due to many reasons. Finnish corporatism has always been characterized by a high degree of consensual decision-making. Such cooperation has deep historical roots (Vartiainen, 1999). As early as the 1930s, the management of monetary policy had already acquired corporatist characteristics and these were reinforced by the management of the war economy. The postwar period saw a programme of state-sponsored industrialization and the build-up of a corporatist structure that was actively encouraged by the state. In a political climate such as this, the political decision-makers sought to integrate trade union organizations with governmental decision-making. It was also thought that the trade unions would moderate their wage claims if a larger share of savings and investment were undertaken by the state. The comprehensive unionization of Finnish workers was not resisted by the state. On the contrary, it was actively encouraged by the authorities in the 1960s, when the unionization rate increased from under 40 per cent to almost 80 per cent. From the point of view of the state authorities and the employers, the inclusion of workers in a corporatist structure was a safeguard against Communist influence. In economic terms, it was a means of controlling wage inflation and distributive shares and of minimizing industrial disputes. In the 1990s, as Finland has entered EMU and the loss of monetary sovereignty has emphasized the need to keep costs down by direct incomes policies, the country again resorted to coordinated wage settlements and dialogus between government officials and labour market parties as the economy has been in the process of recovering from depression.

In Sweden, by contrast, there is more uncertainty on the future of the labour market regime (Vartiainen, 1998). The traditional Rehn–Meidner model that took shape in the 1950s had relied on centralized and encompassing wage bargains in order to contain inflation and encourage structural change: as wage levels in similar jobs would be equalized across firms, the most productive firms would expand their activity while the less productive ones would have to reorganize their activity or close down.

The coordinated wage bargaining system was plagued by internal and political contradictions from its very beginning, but by and large it worked until the 1970s. The radicalized solidaristic policies of the blue-collar trade union central LO in the 1970s, however, led to accentuated contradictions that finally brought down peak-level wage negotiations (Flanagan *et al.*, 1983; Vartiainen, 1998; Swenson and Pontusson, 2000). The decisive offensive against peak-level bargaining arose from the employers, however, spearheaded by the influential Verkstadsföreningen, the metal industry's employer confederation. Engineering employers began to call into question the system as early as in the early 1970s. From the point of view of technically advanced open sector firms, the radical version of the centralized model had many flaws. First, the centralized system provided these firms with little discretion on wage differentials and incentive pay systems. Second, the levelling of all wages started to decrease the supply of skilled workers to technologically advanced tasks within manufacturing. And, finally, there was the question of the relative wage increases in the open and sheltered sectors of the economy, which also for a long time divided the employers' position. The open sector employers felt that the centralized agreements reflected too much the capacity to pay of the sheltered sector firms and employees, especially retailing, a sector in which it is easier to pass increased costs to product prices.[5]

The centralized bargaining system finally broke down in 1983, when the Swedish Metal Industry's employer association was able to conclude a separate agreement with its workers. That reflected the employers' disillusionment with the centralized and solidaristic wage setting practice. Since then, wage setting has been characterized by varying arrangements and a seesaw between peak-level and industry-level negotiations. The central employers' confederation, SAF, effectively dismantled its negotiating organization in 1992. Since then, Swedish industrial relations are in a state of flux. Central coordination of wage settlements is rejected by employers and many unions as well, although for opposite reasons. The authority of the LO and other central trade union organizations does not suffice to coordinate the claims of their member unions. Since it is part of the Swedish political rules of the game that the government does not interfere with wage bargains, there is no effective political power centre which would take care of the coordinating function. After the so-called Rehnberg wage contract of 1992, wage bargaining has been conducted on a decentralized basis, resulting in with uncomfortably high nominal wage increases. A government committee report has since then analyzed the wage bargaining process, but it is too early to see whether that will lead to a new working model (SOU, 1998).

The Swedish and Finnish experiences are illustrated in Figures 7.2 and 7.3, which show the unemployment rate together with the rate of nominal wage increases in the 1990s in both countries. In Finland, the wage settlements of 1995 were a clear failure, partly based on an opposition between the trade unions and a right-wing government that sat in office from 1991 to 1995. Since then, coordinated wage settlements have damped wage inflation and have undoubtedly contributed to the relatively good employment performance. As is apparent from Figure 7.3, wage pressure has been higher in Sweden, and that may be one factor behind a rather poor employment growth even after the recession of the early 1990s was over.[6]

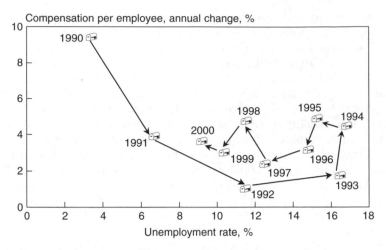

Figure 7.2   Wage increases and unemployment, Finland, 1990–2000

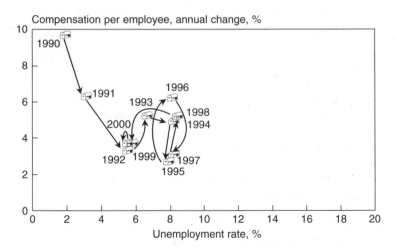

Figure 7.3   Wage increases and unemployment, Sweden, 1990–2000

In Denmark, by contrast, reforms of the wage bargaining system have been going on for a long time and are still going on. The Danish system of industrial relations is also highly institutionalized. However, since the 1980s, the Danes have sought a middle way between decentralization and centralization of wage bargaining. At first sight, that goes against the grain of recent labour market theories which consider the 'middle' alternative as the worst one, but the Danish reforms are in fact quite intricate and not easy to interpret in a simple Calmfors–Driffill framework. It appears that wage bargaining has in fact been decentralized to a large extent and even to the enterprise level, while the central organizations retain instruments which enable them to control average wage inflation. For example, they have the right to veto firm-level or sectoral collective agreements. The unemployment-wage inflation outcome of Denmark is depicted in Figure 7.4.

Thus, all of our three country cases have in their own ways sought a new *modus vivendi* in industrial relations: this new model does not represent an abrupt rupture with the past but is an attempt to accommodate low inflation and a fair degree of local flexibility with formal or informal coordination of wage increases. Contrary to many commentators' views, it seems that a radical individualization of pay bargaining is unlikely, and many factors such as the importance of public sector employment and the aspirations of women work in the opposite direction. Moreover, eligibility for unemployment benefits has in the Nordic countries traditionally been associated with membership in an unemployment insurance fund, and as these funds are to a large extent administered by the unions, union membership is a natural choice for the bulk of wage earners in Scandinavia.

One conclusion of the Nordic coordinated wage bargaining experiences, however, is that *ambitious solidaristic wage bargaining* has been on the retreat since the 1980s. It is important to note that collectivization of wage bargaining has always had two dimensions. First, coordination may be useful to limit the average rate of wage increases and thus to make the level of wage costs compatible with full employment. Second, coordination of wage bargaining can be used to influence *relative* wage differentials. Ambitions of the latter kind have been particularly pronounced in Sweden (Vartiainen, 1998),

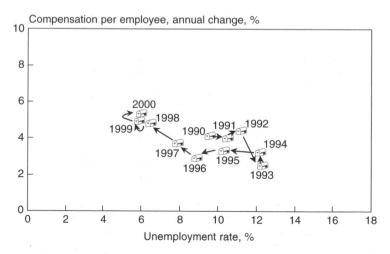

Figure 7.4 Wage increases and unemployment, Denmark, 1990–2000

but they have figured prominently on the political agenda of Denmark as well, in the 1960s and 1970s in particular (Iversen, 1998). Since then, however, it has turned out increasingly difficult to implement solidaristic wage bargaining, for a variety of reasons. Indeed, as argued in Vartiainen (1998), it is doubtful whether income redistribution via wage setting ever could be a long-lasting arrangement; as the redistributive role of the public sector has increased, it is natural that there is less political need nor acceptance for solidaristic pay bargains. The situation was different in the 1950s, when the state was less engaged in public services and redistribution.

This need not imply, however, that coordination of wage setting in order to induce overall wage moderation will or should be abolished. This seems to be the lesson of Swedish, Danish and Finnish experiences. Sweden and Denmark experimented with fairly ambitious solidaristic wage bargaining, but that attempt has been thwarted and reversed in both countries. Finnish trade unions have from the outset been less ambitious in wage compression, and have thereby been able to preserve a more cooperative relationship with employers (Vartiainen, 1998). Note that earnings differentials still remain fairly low in international comparison (see Table 7.5). Indeed, as shown by Teulings and Hartog (1998), Nordic (and, to some extent, European) industrial relations systems that rely on corporatist collective agreements usually

Table 7.5 Measures of earnings dispersion in selected countries, 1994

Country	D9/D5	D5/D1	D9/D1
Japan	1.85	1.63	3.02
Netherlands	1.66	1.56	2.59
New Zealand	1.76	1.73	3.04
Portugal	2.47	1.64	4.05
Sweden	1.59	1.34	2.13
Switzerland	1.68	1.58	2.65
United Kingdom	1.86	1.78	3.31
United States	2.07	2.10	4.35
Australia	1.75	1.64	2.87
Austria	1.82	2.01	3.66
Belgium	1.57	1.43	2.25
Canada	1.84	2.28	4.20
Finland	1.70	1.40	2.38
France	1.99	1.65	3.28
Germany	1.61	1.44	2.32
Italy	1.60	1.75	2.80

The numbers indicate ratios of average wage earnings of different deciles.

Source: OECD, *Employment Outlook*, 1996.

generate a lesser amount of unexplained wage variability and, hence, less overall wage inequality even if the trade unions do not explicitly push for wage compression.

Microeconomics of unemployment: mixed picture

We have so far discussed the macroeconomics of wage determination and the need for comprehensive wage moderation. Another major focus of the contemporary discussion on unemployment is the microeconomic and structural basis of unemployment problems. Much attention has been devoted to such issues as employment protection and the generosity of employment benefit schemes. It is a common perception that there exists some kind of trade-off between 'employment' and 'equality', so that the policy-makers in the Nordic countries should, supposedly, make concessions on their egalitarian objectives in order to increase labour supply and work incentives and foster new employment in low-productivity work.

However, even in the light of mainstream economic theory, it is not obvious that the emergence of a large number of new *low-paid* service sector jobs should represent an optimal response to supposed productivity increases in manufacturing and increased global competition in core manufacturing industries. If manufacturing productivity increases, that should not prima facie imply a decrease in manufacturing employment in small countries like the Nordic ones which can in principle sell as much as they want to the world market provided their competitiveness remains good enough.

A closer look at labour market legislation and other structural characteristics reveals an ambiguous picture. Piecemeal reforms to increase flexibility of the labour market have been going on in all the Nordic countries since the mid-1990s. In general, eligibility conditions for unemployment benefits have been tightened and replacement ratios have decreased (OECD, 1998b, 1999d, 2000d). Furthermore, a closer look at variables like the relative size of minimum social security transfers and unemployment benefits does not confirm the characterization of the Nordic countries as extremely generous in such safety net procurements even in the early 1990s. As an example, look at Table 7.6 which depicts replacement ratios of unemployment compensation in a number of countries in 1991; the Nordic countries cannot be singled out as especially generous in that respect. Since the early 1990s, the replacement ratios have declined slightly in most countries but the overall picture has not changed dramatically.

The same conclusion applies to strictness of employment protection. OECD (2000d) comparisons of employment legislation indicate that the Nordic countries do not have stricter employment protection legislation than European countries on average. Furthermore, the relationship between unemployment and employment protection legislation is theoretically ambiguous.

To sum up, inasmuch as various institutional rigidities are concerned, the Nordic countries can hardly be regarded as especially 'rigid' ones.

Table 7.6   Replacement ratios of unemployment compensation, 1991

Country	% of mean wage	% of 2/3 of mean wage
Austria	42	45
Belgium	34	52
Canada	19	30
Denmark	38	58
Finland	24	36
France	23	34
Germany	35	37
Greece	30	30
Ireland	31	46
Netherlands	39	59
Portugal	34	52
Sweden	29	44
United Kingdom	22	41
Average	31	43

The replacement ratio of unemployment assistance in selected countries (gross benefit as a percentage of mean wage and 2/3 of mean wage) in 1991.

Source: Vartiainen (1998).

This suggests that the final conclusions on the current unemployment problems are not all that dramatic. The high unemployment of the 1990s (1980s and 1990s in Denmark) was a result of the disinflation policy and other large economic shocks of the 1980s and 1990s. Restructuring of activities will take time, so that unemployment will probably shrink slowly and a part of the current older generation of poorly educated long-term unemployed will retreat out of the labour force without finding new employment.

There is one respect, however, in which the high-tax-wedge Nordic societies may be at disadvantage as economic activity is restructured towards service activities. Demand elasticities for many services exceed those for manufacturing products, and services that compete with households' own production (say, restaurants, catering, laundries, etc.) may be at disadvantage in high tax economies. Thus, the growth of private sector service employment in the Nordic countries may continue to lag behind that of other comparable countries, as already indicated by Table 7.2. As to aggregate service sector employment, however, it is in general not low in the Nordic economies, since public services are a big employer and one of women in particular.

Macroeconomic management

The introduction to this chapter took up active macroeconomic management as a third peculiar characteristic of the Nordic countries. During the

Keynesian era, a commitment to full employment was traditionally singled out as the main inspiration of macroeconomic management and fiscal policy in Sweden in particular. To some extent, the same applied to Denmark and Norway, too, whereas Finland has always practised a more conservative and at times clearly procyclical budgeting strategy. In monetary policy, there was also a clear commitment in all the Nordic countries to sustain open sector employment by a soft exchange rate.

It is in this respect that any eventual 'Nordic' characteristic has been most clearly diluted. This has to a large extent been due to the general and encompassing revolution in economists' attitudes. It is by now generally agreed that sustaining a high rate of employment cannot be the primary responsibility of monetary and fiscal policy. At best, these policy tools can be used avoid excessive economic shocks, whereas unemployment is in the long run seen as a structural phenomenon. This new orthodoxy, prompted by the inflationary experiences of the 1970s and the rational expectations literature in economics, has completely permeated the economic policy doctrines of most countries as well as those of international institutions like the OECD or the European Commission.

The conduct of monetary and fiscal policy in the Nordic countries will be conditioned by the same factors and the same debate that inform EU and OECD discussions. As to fiscal policy, the mainstream policy strategies are as of now suspicious of active countercyclical measures, but the use of automatic stabilizers in the face of shocks is not ruled out. In monetary policy, members of the euro area (including Finland) have to do with European Central Bank interest rate policy, whereas those left outside (Sweden, Denmark, Norway) have some more scope for autonomous interest rate decisions. Even the latter group, however, has adopted a low inflation strategy implemented by an independent central bank.

Thus, one cannot now speak of a peculiar 'Nordic' model of macroeconomic management. All the Nordic countries have to operate their demand management policies in the mainstream framework. Furthermore, it is striking that the choices of monetary framework have been very different for the Nordic countries. Finland is a full member of the single currency area. Sweden and Denmark are EU members, but Denmark has explicitly opted out of the single currency project. Sweden has remained outside of the euro area even though its commitment to the Maastricht Treaty did not explicitly allow that option, while Norway has remained outside EU.

Inasmuch as the choice of monetary regime has repercussions for other policy areas, such as labour markets in particular, each country has to address them in its specific policy framework. Yet the change of environment encountered by the labour market agents is similar in all countries as far as it compels the unions and firms to adapt their behaviour to an environment in which inflation is low and monetary policy is not willing to accommodate adverse economic shocks that increase unemployment.

That much is common to all the Nordic as well as European countries. In principle, if wage bargaining institutions reflect rational choices of the different actors, moving from an accommodating and devaluationary monetary policy regime to a regime of low inflation should not entail any real economic loss. However, it is an open question whether Nordic pay bargaining can be swiftly adapted to an environment of low inflation. Some theorists (see Holden, 1990, 1991) have argued that there is a nominal high-inflation bias inherent in the multilayered bargaining systems of the Nordic countries. It is also a real stylized fact that wage drift has traditionally provided a safety valve for relative wage adjustments. With very low inflation, preserving the former level of real wage flexibility requires increasing flexibility even in nominal wages, something that is perhaps not easy to incorporate into collective agreements.

However, it is unlikely that a general decentralization of pay bargaining will occur because of the change in monetary policy regime only. This is a large issue best treated in a more focused paper (see Vartiainen, 1997), but it is not obvious that the commonplace view of a gradual individualization of pay bargaining is right. First, adapting the economy to low inflation and eventual single currency will emphasize the need for coordinating pay increases. As accommodating monetary policy is ruled out, it becomes even more important to contain inflationary pressures and implement wage moderation by using direct incomes policies.

Second, even if workers' individual talents will, as is often supposed, play a greater role in pay determination, that trend may in such egalitarian societies as the Nordic ones emphasize the need for general pay guidelines provided by encompassing collective agreements. Finally, women's equal pay aspirations as well as the prominent role of the public sector as an employer all keep the pay bargain on the political agenda.

Summing up: the Nordic model survives but in diluted form

The above *tour d'horizon* of the Nordic-social–democratic way of managing capitalism has hopefully suggested that at least some of the elements needed to put into question the mainstream view according to which the Nordic model has no future. We will conclude by summing up the main points and by speculating on future trends.

- The welfare state as measured by the size of the public sector still distinguishes the Nordic countries from EU and OECD averages. There is no apparent problem of political legitimacy for Nordic welfare state arrangements; opinion polls suggest that the political support for public services and redistributive transfers remains strong. The *expansion* of the public sector is over, however.
- High labour force participation rates for women remain a Nordic characteristic that distinguishes the Nordic countries from EU and OECD

averages. Thus, provided the Nordic countries can return to low unemployment rates, one of their main distinguishing characteristics, namely a high employment/population ratio, will remain intact.

• Since the 1980s, however, the Nordic countries have not been able to sustain their previously exceptionally good record in maintaining full employment. Unemployment went up in Denmark in the 1980s and in Finland and Sweden in the 1990s. The recovery of employment is still under way in Finland, and the employment performance of the Nordic countries does not single them out in any positive way from other European countries. The increase in unemployment was largely associated with the abolition of an earlier, accommodating monetary policy regime.

• As to the other aspect of coordinated pay bargaining, the implementation of overall wage moderation, the issue remains extremely topical in all Nordic countries, but the future of the rules of the game is somewhat uncertain. Finland seems to be closest to practising the traditional, Swedish-type 'centralized' model. Swedish wage bargaining institutions are in a state of flux while Denmark seeks an ingenious compromise between local flexibility and overall wage moderation.

• As to the general management of the economy, the traditional tool kit of instruments has to be revised to adapt the economy to integration and globally free financial markets and capital markets. Low inflation and credibility of monetary policy present a challenge of adjustment for pay bargaining systems; nominal pay flexibility must be increased if only to preserve the former degree of real wage flexibility.

• We noted in the Introduction that the Nordic economic and social policy model should ultimately be seen as an expression of underlying, egalitarian political valuations. Consequently, it is also important to look at the 'end product', namely the distribution of income. A recent analysis of Nordic income differentials (Aaberge et al., 2000) concludes that income differentials have remained remarkably stable in the Nordic countries, even in times of economic shocks and rising unemployment. Although the underlying mechanisms are difficult to fully account for, it seems clear that the redistributive system of transfers did its job of preventing widespread poverty in Sweden, Finland and Denmark even in times of economic turbulence. This data is from 1994; more recent data indicates that income differentials have increased in Sweden and, even more strongly, in Finland, but it is too early to tell if this is a clear trend.

Notes

1. Furthermore, unsystematic but comprehensive observations on scholars of different disciplines suggest that different disciplines are biased towards different views: on the one hand, sociologists and political scientists often see nothing but an overwhelming and ongoing structural change ('crisis of Taylorism'; 'crisis of the

welfare state'; 'transition to the information society') in whatever snapshot picture in societies' development, whereas, on the other hand, the apparatus of economists is extremely ill-suited to detect large structural transformations; after all, to most economists, such phenomena as globalization, the growth of the service economy or the industrial revolution can all be accommodated within the fundamental theory of rational choice and competitive markets.

2. Indeed, it is not unreasonable to think that the marginal cost of increasing taxation is an increasing function whereas the marginal utility of extra government outlays and services is a decreasing function. If that is true, then a rational political system will end up with a unique political equilibrium.

3. Thus, in both Sweden and Finland, budget cuts of the order of 6 to 8% of GDP were carried out in the aftermath of the depression of the 1990s. In Denmark, a similar fiscal consolidation had occurred 10 years earlier.

4. The set of regressors includes such natural factors as unemployment benefit levels, the tax wedge and other institutional characteristics.

5. The question of price competitiveness of exports and the traded–nontraded sector relative price was addressed by a joint expert group of the employers and the trade unions. The outcome was the well-known EFO-model which in principle could be used to generate an estimate of a rational pay norm associated with full employment and price stability. The EFO model is described in the next section of this chapter.

6. However, employment growth has since Summer 1998 been rather good in Sweden as well, but the rate of wage increases is still uncomfortably high with respect to productivity growth. For example, in a comparison of real wage growth minus productivity growth across OECD member countries in years 1996–99, Sweden emerges with the highest digit of all, 6% (OECD, *Economic Outlook*, 2000d: 221).

8
Institutional Restructuring in the Japanese Economy since 1985[1]

Kazuyoshi Matsuura, Michael Pollitt, Ryoji Takada and Satoru Tanaka

The Japanese economy has experienced an unprecedented period of macroeconomic turbulence over recent years.[2] Even before the 1997 Asian crisis, this had led to a sharp rise in the number of financial institutions experiencing bankruptcy, including a number of large regional banks and an international stockbroking firm.

The question we seek to address is, what effect has this economic turbulence since 1985 had on the four institutional foundations of post-Second World War Japanese industrial success?[3] First, we examine the Japanese 'main bank' system whereby a 'main' bank is involved in a special type of long-term relationship with the non-financial firms that it lends to (Corbett, 1987). Second, we review the Japanese employment system characterized by lifetime employment, a seniority wage system and enterprise unionism (Itoh, 1992). Third, we look at the inter-corporate relationships between main firms and their suppliers (Aoki, 1988). And, fourth, we consider the nature of Japanese industrial policy, the interventionist role of the Ministry of International Trade and Industry (MITI) and the relatively weak role of Japanese competition policy under the authority of the Japan Fair Trade Commission (JFTC) (see Boltho, 1985). In each case we present evidence that suggests that these institutional foundations of the Japanese 'economic success story' have been weakened over the period we look at. Before turning to the institutions, we sketch the wider macroeconomic, political and supply-side situation of the Japanese economy.

The Japanese economic system

Morishima asked the question 'Why has Japan "succeeded"?' in 1982. The answer that he gave suggested that there was a distinctive set of institutional characteristics present in Japan that significantly contributed to Japanese economic success. The interesting thing for Morishima was that although many of the elements of the Japanese system were present elsewhere, it was only in Japan that they were combined in the particular way that fuelled the rapid growth of the postwar Japanese economy. In this chapter, we have picked out four of the most obvious institutions that were part of this Japanese economic system.

The Japanese main bank system successfully recycled domestic savings into manufacturing investment at a time when the stock market was underdeveloped. The *keiretsu* relationships between main firms and their suppliers in the manufacturing sector provided a combination of knowledge sharing, quality control and flexibility for export-oriented firms. The lifetime employment system for workers in exporting firms reduced competition for scarce skilled labour while motivating workers with the threat of being fired and losing future earnings.

These first three institutional arrangements fostered highly cooperative, non-confrontational relationships between related groups in society at a time when economic policy was focused on the stated goal of catching up with western levels of productivity. These private sector aspects of the economic system were supported by the cooperative environment which the Japanese government promoted via MITI. MITI bureaucrats sought to guide the private sector's efforts to catch up with the West. They did this by subjugating competition policy (under the control of the JFTC) to their own industrial policy. Under this arrangement there was legislative underpinning for domestic cartels, aimed at supporting international competitiveness, and government-supported coordination of domestic private sector investment activity.

The system successfully managed to promote cooperation in a way which reduced the transaction costs of competition while maintaining its incentive properties. Masahiko Aoki pointed out that this cooperation and its underlying incentive structures were consistent with rational profit-maximizing behaviour (1988).

As in the nature of successful systems, all the elements of this system are consistent with one another. If one or more of them were to be undermined, it is not at all clear that the other elements would have a rationale and could survive. For instance, if firms were to start competing for all employees on the basis of salary alone, rather than a job for life, this could undermine the *keiretsu* structure. Firms would be unwilling to send employees in to help supplier firms if the latter might be tempted to make them a competitive job offer on the basis of current pay. Higher worker mobility, which is a feature of a more competitive labour market, discourages firm cooperation of this type.

Recent trends in the Japanese economy

The beginning of this recent period of macroeconomic instability can be dated from the September 1985 Plaza Accord, when the United States and Japan reached an agreement aimed at reducing the value of the dollar–yen exchange rate. The Plaza Accord began a period of rapid yen appreciation

(40 per cent increase in real value in two years). This appreciation was accompanied by only a small reduction in the volume of Japanese exports and was not offset by increasing volumes of imports. The result was a substantial increase in the dollar value of the current account surplus. Following the 1987 stock market crash, looser monetary policy worldwide saw the Japanese discount rate fall to a period low of 2.5 per cent in June 1989. Low interest rates prompted a stock and land market boom as lending to financial and property companies rose rapidly in the so-called 'bubble economy' (see e.g. Noguchi, 1993). Rising interest rates from June 1989 led to sharp falls in asset prices in 1990. This put pressure on the financial system as the value of assets used as collateral for bank lending declined, leaving a large number of major financial institutions technically bankrupt. Declining financial wealth contributed to falls in consumption and a recession from 1991 to 1993. From November 1993 to 1997 there was a modest economic recovery.

In tandem with the financial instability initiated by the Plaza Accord, there developed growing political pressure on Japan from the United States at the industry level. The appreciation of the dollar in the early 1980s had sharply worsened the US trade deficit with Japan. Not only did the United States seek and get agreement on macroeconomic policy to reduce the value of the dollar and improve the competitiveness of US exports but it also fought for industry-level agreements aimed at restricting Japanese exports to the United States and at increasing the sales of US components to Japanese firms. Under the Structural Impediments Initiative (SII), beginning in 1987, Japan agreed to maintain and promote competition in its domestic markets with transparent administrative guidance which did not discriminate between domestic and non-domestic firms. It also agreed to deregulate its distribution sector and make more effective use of land. By 1996, continuing rounds of negotiations involved pressure to liberate insurance markets which were closed to foreign insurance firms.

These policies contributed to the trend towards a significant internationalization of the Japanese economy as import volumes rose and Japanese manufacturing firms shifted lower technology production offshore and improved the productivity of high technology production (cf. Yoshitomi, 1996). Japanese firms have invested heavily in manufacturing plants overseas. The production of these plants has often substituted directly for exports from Japan. It is calculated that by 2000 Japanese manufacturing firms had the equivalent of around 20 per cent of their domestic employees overseas, up from 5 per cent in 1985 (Cowling and Tomlinson, 2000: F372).

The other major trend affecting the Japanese economy was the aging of the workforce. The birth rate in Japan is 1.4 children per family unit. However, the life expectancy of the average Japanese has increased to 80.1 years. This implies that the dependency ratio has been increasing and is now one of the highest in the world. The implications of this trend are wide ranging. There are implications for the mix of consumption, the tax burden posed by public pensions and the strain that this puts on company pension schemes and age-related promotion structures. Highly skilled young workers are at a premium, whereas there is a relative abundance of senior employees.

Recent Japanese political economy

Japanese macroeconomic policy has had little impact on the underlying rate of economic growth. This is due to the stop-go nature of the government's fiscal stance against a background of deteriorating revenues. A large stimulus package was adopted in 1994, but the reductions were reversed and taxes increased in 1996. In 1998, another attempt was made to stimulate the economy, but this was reversed in 2001. The policy of low interest rates did not stimulate investment or an increase in the money supply. Banks were unwilling to increase their loans to already financially embarrassed companies and instead absorbed government attempts to increase the money supply by buying government bonds.

In parallel with the economic turbulence that Japan was experiencing, there was considerable political upheaval. A series of corporate scandals involving agreements between politicians and firms were exposed along with the worsening financial situation of companies. In one, the chief of the LDP – the political party that had governed Japan since 1955 – was arrested. This gave rise to widespread public support for reform, leading to a vote of no confidence in the cabinet, a general election and the return of a coalition government without the LDP in 1993. The new administration was, however, short lived, and a new coalition involving the LDP took power in 1994. In 1996, a reformed LDP regained majority control and took sole power again but with a mandate to carry out further political reforms.

Bureaucrats, too, came under public scrutiny for their perceived role in neglecting to monitor failing banks. This culminated in the arrest of officials from the Ministry of Finance and the Bank of Japan in March 1998. The Ministry of Finance officials had allegedly been bribed by officers of several major banks to reveal the timing of ministry inspections. A Bank of Japan official was accused of selling information about the Bank of Japan's economic analysis to private banks in advance of its official publication date. These scandals severely undermined public trust in civil servants responsible for overseeing the banking system.

There is a widespread recognition among the general public, the political elite and the bureaucracy that institutional reform is necessary and desirable. However, the current system seems to be struggling to deliver a coherent and sustained reform package in the face of macroeconomic uncertainty and political instability. It is against this background that we investigate the extent to which the major institutions of the Japanese economic system have actually changed since 1985.

Long-term bank–firm relationships in Japan

The Japanese main bank system

The main bank of a particular industrial company is defined as the bank which has the largest share of bank loans to the company, holds the settlement account of the firm and has a role in dispatching managers from the bank to the firm. In addition, main banks usually have significant share holdings in the industrial company (OECD, 1996a: 161). The main bank has two roles: the provision of corporate finance and the provision of corporate governance.[4]

In the postwar high growth period, a principal feature of the main bank system was the stabilized supply of funds to firms based on long-term bank–firm relationships.[5] Besides bank lending, banks strengthen their ties with firms through holding stocks and by dispatching managers to firms.[6] Japanese cross-share holding makes stockowners' monitoring role rather vague, since it is difficult to understand who is responsible for governing firms and hostile takeovers are extremely rare (see OECD, 1996a). Thus, the main bank replaces large stockowners as the principal monitor of firms.

The main bank's monitoring function has three elements. First, main banks lower agency costs which arise from the asymmetry of information between owners of capital and managers.[7] The second function of main banks is to organize loan syndicates among financial institutions (Horiuchi and Sui, 1992: 15). The third function is the ex-post monitoring role of the main bank, in addition to its ex-ante monitoring (Corbett, 1987: 36; Aoki, 1988: 113–22; Sheard, 1994: 195–210). The main bank plays an important role as a coordinator during periods when the firm is going through financial difficulties involving financial restructuring or merger. The banks' willingness to bear the risks associated with client firms' insolvency can be seen as part of an implicit contract between the bank and the firm which involves the firms' paying higher interest rates when profits recover.

The changing environment surrounding the main bank

Since the early 1980s, there have been a number of changes in the circumstances surrounding the main bank system. Following the era of cheap money which began in 1987, firms have had easy access to the capital market. Financial liberalization and internationalization have increased the number of possible sources of finance for firms, and larger firms have had easy access to overseas financial markets. Therefore corporate firms have gradually gained increased bargaining power in their negotiations with the banks.

The number of firm bankruptcies has dramatically increased since the collapse of the bubble economy at the beginning of the 1990s. The resultant large accumulation of bad debts by financial institutions has become a serious issue.[8] A number of bankruptcies of large banks have shocked the Japanese financial market since 1997, following a major deregulation in 1998. In an environment of financial crisis, banks feared systemic risks and became more prudent about lending to firms.

A change in long-term bank–firm relationships?

Our question is, how have circumstances changed the traditional roles of the main bank with respect to corporate finance and corporate governance? To answer this question, it is appropriate to see how the connection between banks and firms changed during the bubble economy and its aftermath.

With regard to corporate finance, bank lending increased sharply in the bubble of the late 1980s and decreased rapidly in its aftermath.[9] In the 1980s, larger firms were able to utilize internal funds and the external capital market, but smaller firms continued to be dependent on bank borrowing up until the latter half of the 1980s.[10] Many of these small firms were engaged in real estate and stock market speculation in the bubble period. Since the bubble collapse, banks have had a large percentage of bad loans because of falling stock and land prices. In addition, falling bank stock prices have shrunk the value of bank reserves. As the banks tried to write down bad loans in the 1990s, they became cautious in selecting firms to lend to and risk averse towards the small business sector. Moreover, highly rated firms raised funds to repay their bank loans by issuing bonds. As a result, the growth of bank loans to smaller firms slowed down in the first half of the 1990s, and the amount of bank loans showed little change.[11] In the second half of the 1990s, bank loans to smaller firms decreased and loans to bigger firms did not significantly change, leading to a decrease in the total bank loans outstanding.[12] This means that banks' role in corporate finance has decreased.

To think about the corporate governance role of the main bank, it is useful to trace banks' share holding in industrial firms and the scale of dispatching of managers to firms. Measures of these are indicators (albeit imperfect) of banks' ability to influence firm behaviour.

Banks exercise control as main banks or sub-main banks, as indicated by the size of their shareholdings. Figure 8.1 shows the breakdown of the change of firm numbers associated with main banks in terms of owned stock. The number of both main firms and sub-main firms associated with a main bank substantially increased in the late 1980s. However, since the collapse of the bubble, city banks, trust banks and long-term banks show different trends. On the one hand the number of both main firms and sub-main firms associated with a main bank decreased in the 1990s in the case of long-term banks and trust banks. On the other hand, the number of main firms increased in the case of city banks during the same period, while that of sub-main firms has decreased. This indicates that city banks focused their stockholding more onto main firms than onto sub-main firms. As Figure 8.1

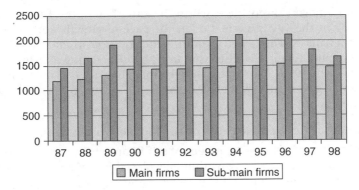

Figure 8.1 Number of firms associated with a main bank through stock ownership

Main firms: bank owns more than 3 per cent of the firm stocks and is the biggest stock owner among the banks. Sub-main firms: the main bank owns more than 3 per cent of the firm stocks and is the second biggest stock owner among banks.

Source: *Kigyo Keiretsu Soran*, Toyo Keizai Shinposha, 1990, p. 96,1991, p. 74,1992, p. 78,1994, 1995, p. 70,1996, p. 70,1999, p. 82,2000, p. 56.

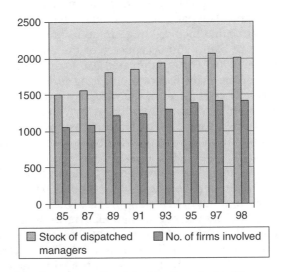

Figure 8.2 Number of managers dispatched to firms by banks

Source: *Kigyo Keiretsu Soran*, Toyo Keizai. Shinposha, 1987, 9.51, 1989, p. 72, 1991, p. 86, 1993, p. 86, 1995, p. 83, 1997, p. 69, 1999, p. 95, 2000, p. 69.

shows, overall there is a significant reversal of previous trends between the bubble period and the post-bubble period.

Figure 8.2 shows the number of managers who were dispatched by banks to client firms and the number of firms to which banks dispatch managers.

The two numbers sharply increased in the latter half of the 1980s and kept increasing in the 1990s, even though the pace of growth slowed. We can guess that banks strengthened their influence in firms in the late 1980s and tried to rebuild financially distressed firms by dispatching managers in the first half of the 1990s. We suspect that the main banks have kept their power of corporate governance over existing large firm clients in the 1990s via this method of control.

Evaluation of the changing role of the Japanese main bank

We find that due to the development of self-finance for large firms and easy access to capital market bank lending has played less of a role in corporate finance in the late 1980s and the 1990s compared with the high growth period.

Judging from the actual state of the financial economy in the bubble and its aftermath, the effectiveness of the main bank's monitoring function deteriorated significantly in the 1980s. Banks responded to increasing competition among financial institutions with offers of easy monitoring that relied on the collateral value of the company's assets (i.e. its stock market valuation) rather than the prospects of the firm. This effectively reduced the control exerted by the main bank and exposed the bank to greater risk.[13] As a result of this, main banks incurred huge amounts of bad loans. This led to some bankruptcies of banks and acceptance of the public funds from the government in the 1990s. The accumulated bad loans are not only due to the deterioration of the main bank's monitoring function but also to the substantial decrease of asset prices in the wake of depression.

The traditional 'implicit contract hypothesis' by which banks rescued distressed firms in return for long-term credit relationships appears to have broken down following the collapse of the bubble. *The Economic Survey of Japan* reports evidence that implies that main banks have become much more cautious in lending and unwilling to provide rescue loans to distressed firms.[14]

In conclusion, the aftermath of the bubble economy has further weakened bank–firm relations in terms of bank lending by highlighting the huge sums in bad loans made during the bubble period. The seeds of the weakening were present in the pre-bubble period, as the banks lost many of their prime borrowers to international competition and internally generated funds (Ozawa, 1999: 356). Although banks have continued to increase the number of managers they dispatch to industrial firms, this seems to reflect a desire to protect their existing loans rather than to strengthen the traditional bank–firm relationship and facilitate rescue lending or new loans. The decline in bank lending and shareholding seems to reflect a desire on the part of banks for greater distance between them and their client firms. Old style bank–firm relations, which expose banks to higher risks, no longer seem appropriate for the new conditions under which banks are operating (Ozawa, 1999: 357).

The Japanese employment system

There are three main features that characterize the Japanese labour market. Not all employees are employed in this way; however, compared with other advanced countries, notably the United Kingdom and the United States, the percentage of workers enjoying these characteristics of their employment is high.[15]

The first feature is a system of lifetime employment. A worker in a Japanese corporation is typically employed immediately after graduation from school. He is expected to stay with the same firm until mandatory retirement. There is a long-term implicit labour contract between the worker and the corporation in Japan (Aoki, 1988). The second feature is a seniority system: wage strongly depends on age and/or the length of service within the same firm. The wage profile strongly relates wage to age or the length of service. Wages tend to start well below average and then rise over 20 years to a relative peak when employees are in their late forties (Tsuru, 1994). The third feature is enterprise unionism: a labour union is organized within each firm. Workers within the same firm (except employees in managerial positions above a certain rank) become members of the same labour union, and there are no industry-wide trade unions as in the United Kingdom or the United States.

The above characteristics can be rationalized by economic theory.[16] Labour skills generally consist of the following two types: (1) general labour skills (which are applicable to all firms) and (2) firm-specific labour skills. When the latter are relatively important, a long-term implicit labour contract between workers (employees) and firms may be an advantageous institutional instrument. Investments in firm-specific labour skills are sunk: neither workers nor firms invest in this type of skill without a long-term contract. The combination of lifetime employment and a seniority wage system provides the incentives by which both workers and firms are willing to accumulate firm-specific labour skills. By paying relatively low wages (less than marginal productivity) to the younger workers and high wages (more than marginal productivity) to the aged workers, firms are able to take the workers as 'hostages'. Using these 'hostages', firms are able to accumulate firm-specific labour skills while paying the total sum of wages to a worker equal to the discounted total sum of his productivity over his length of service within this firm. On the other hand, workers are willing to accept the twin instruments of lifetime employment and the seniority system, because in this system they can 'invest' in their firm while young and recoup their investment when older. Enterprise unionism also supports the accumulation of firm-specific labour skills stimulated by lifetime employment and the seniority system. The accumulation of firm-specific labour skills often requires the rotation of jobs. Enterprise unionism contributes to this by reducing the transactions costs that are brought about by this. Therefore, the above three characteristics which constitute Japanese employment system have a mutually complementary nature. In addition to this, we should note that this system is stronger when more firms adopt it, as this reduces free riding by firms in the provision of training.

The Japanese employment system under pressure

The above employment system was supported by a number of general features of the Japanese economy in the postwar period.[17] First, a high rate of economic growth: this allows most firms to grow. Growing firms are not burdened by the cost of older workers, as general productivity is rising. Workers are more willing to commit to firms because they have a strong expectation that firms will repay their investment in them when they are older and will honour their implicit contract. However, when growth slows and bankruptcies rise, the system comes under pressure: firms will have strong incentives to renege on their implicit contracts and save costs on expensive older workers. Meanwhile, younger workers will realize this and will demand higher wages than in the past. Second, population composition is important. The more younger workers there are in the economy relative to older workers, the less of a strain paying high wages to older workers is for companies, and the cheaper it is to incentivize younger workers with the prospect of higher wages in the future. As the population ages, firms find paying older workers expensive. The labour market for younger workers tightens and puts pressure on firms to compete with one another by raising the wages of the young to attract workers. Third, the importance of firm-specific rather than transferable skills is a crucial underpinning of the employment system. The Japanese employment system works best when firm-specific skills are important: this is important in team production where it is difficult to assess the contribution of individuals. Team production requires firm-specific skills. However, as new technologies, which make use of transferable skills, become more important, workers' productivities are not a function of firm-specific knowledge but of transferable technical skill and training.

The above discussion suggests why the Japanese employment system might have come under pressure since 1985. Japanese economic growth has faltered with the collapse of the bubble economy, and the economy grew very slowly in the 1990s. The population has aged rapidly. Team production based on firm-specific skills has become less important. Japanese firms have had to innovate to grow, and the economy has had to move into new science-driven industries. The skills demanded have been more transferable, and younger workers with the relevant skills have been in demand relative to older workers without technical training.

The evidence is that relative wages are becoming less of a function of age than they were in the past. Figure 8.3 indicates a sharp decline in the ratio of the relative salary of 50–54-year olds to that of 20–24-year olds since 1985 for male university graduates in manufacturing.[18] The ratio declines

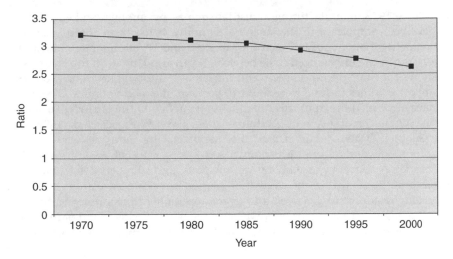

Figure 8.3   The ratio of the relative salary of 50–54-year olds to 20–24-year olds (male university graduates)

Source: Basic Survey on Wage Structure, Ministry of Labour (Ministry of Health, Labour and Welfare since 2001).

gradually from 3.2 to 3.1 between 1970 and 1985 but declines to 2.7 by 1998. The labour force also appears to be becoming more mobile, though this may be masked by the negative effect of unemployment on mobility. For certain categories of workers, job tenure has fallen sharply. For instance, for all male high school graduates in the 35–39 age group job tenure rose marginally from 13.0 years in 1978 to 13.3 years in 1988 but then declined sharply to 12.2 years in 1998 (Ministry of Labour, 1999). Meanwhile part-time working among all male Japanese employees (excluding students) in the 15–24 age group rose from 4.7 per cent of the full time figure in 1985 to 16.1 per cent in 1999 (Ministry of Labour, 1999). In addition, many employers and employees report that they are considering abandoning seniority wages and moving to personal contracts.[19] Although the traditional Japanese employment system still survives for a large number of workers, it has come under significant pressure.

Japanese inter-corporate relationships

Inter-corporate relationships in Japan are very distinctive. We inquire into the nature of recent changes in the structure of the Japanese economy and its inter-corporate relationships, especially those changes associated with the 'production *keiretsu*'. Much of our discussion is with reference to the automobile industry, a typical example of an industry exhibiting Japanese inter-corporate relationships (cf. Aoki, 1988).

Since 1973, manufacturing industries such as automobiles and electronics have been important in the Japanese economy. It has been argued that the competitive difference between the Japanese and US automobile industry is a factor in the unbalanced trade between Japan and United States. Figure 8.4 shows the statistics on exports and imports of automobiles from 1980–98: import volumes in 1998 were about 10 per cent of export volumes. Observers have attributed much of this superior performance to the Japanese automobile subcontracting system (Dertouzos *et al.*, 1989; Wormack *et al.*, 1990).

Supplier systems exist in machine manufacturing industries such as the automobile and electronics industries. Customer (purchaser) firms make finished products by assembling various parts, and suppliers deliver parts to customer firms within the context of a long-term business relationship. The trading relationships between the buyer and supplier firms cannot be characterized as either market or internal exchange but rather as a kind of intermediate or quasi-integrated organization. The *keiretsu* structure is hierarchical,

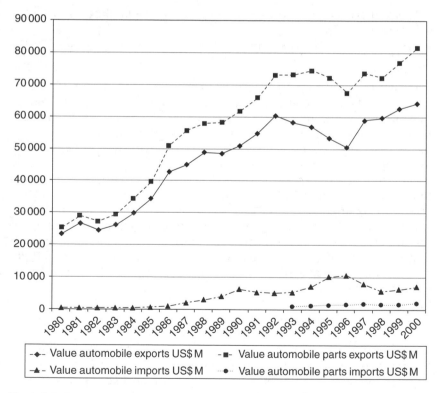

Figure 8.4   Export and import of automobile and automobile parts in Japan
Note: Imports of automobile parts to Japan are not recorded prior to 1992.
Source: Ministry of Finance, *Japanese Trade Statistics*, Ministry of Finance, each year.

having primary subcontractors, secondary subcontractors and tertiary subcontractors.

As the supplier system is the most important system, we will concentrate our discussion on this system. The supplier system, such as at the carmaker Toyota, is the origin of the 'just in time' production system. At the stage of development of new products–the so-called 'design in' stage–buyer and supplier firms work together. At the stage of mass production, subcontractors supply their parts to customers, satisfying the quality, quantity, delivery time and place of delivery criteria specified by the customers.

The features of Japanese inter-corporate relationships

The main function of the supplier system is to overcome asymmetric information. By maintaining continuous business relationships with suppliers, a customer company can maintain good quality information about the ability of the supplier to meet quality and delivery time standards. This enables a customer company to reduce production and transactions costs. On the part of suppliers, investments to meet the need of a particular customer make it possible to lower costs. As these investments do not always meet the needs of other customers, they involve sunk costs. Therefore, long-term trade relationships are individually and collectively rational for both the customer and the supplier and allow technology transfer between each party through the mutual exchange of a wide range of information.[20]

The above inter-firm relations imply good information, long-term sharing and economy-wide information flows between large and small companies. Thus, the features of Japanese inter-corporate relationships, characterized as vertically quasi-integrated *keiretsu*, can be summed up as follows. The ratio of value added in-house to total sales is low, but the numbers of outside makers (subcontractors) per enterprise (purchaser) are small. The structure is hierarchical. The inter-corporate relationships are continuous and long term, depending on an obligational contractual relationship (Sako, 1992).

The advantages of Japanese-type inter-corporate relationships for the customer firm and its supplier are reduced supply- and demand-side risk; shared information about manufacturing technology and R&D; improved investment incentives for relationship-specific assets; increased flexibility of response to changing design and delivery specifications; improved internal efficiency through the ability to exploit high-powered incentives in supplier firms; and technological advance and cost reduction via learning effects, based on a continuous long-term transaction relationship facilitated by the development of relation-specific skills (Asanuma, 1989).

Structural change in the Japanese economy and inter-corporate relationships

In the 1980s, the Japanese economy underwent structural adjustment. The internationalization of the economy, an aging population, technological innovation, the emergence of an information-oriented society, the growing importance of soft and service sectors and deregulation have all put pressure on the economy for structural adjustment. Of all these factors, the internationalization of the economy has most affected inter-corporate relationships. Japanese firms have had to re-examine their supplier system, which has been criticized as an exclusive system. However, even though imports have grown rapidly (as Figure 8.4 illustrates), import penetration remains low.

The Japanese car industry has lost competitiveness since the beginning of the 1990s. This is due to the improving relative productivity of the US automobile industry, which has introduced 'Japanese' production methods and improved US competitiveness via the depreciation of the dollar. The Japanese car industry recovered competitiveness again in 1996 as prior relative productivity and currency trends were reversed. Japanese firms have made efforts to cut down on numbers of parts, improve standardization, streamline the R&D process and use computer-aided design and manufacturing (CAD/CAM) to save design costs. Purchasers have begun to cooperate with suppliers from the beginning of the design stage, in 'simultaneous' engineering. They have begun cooperative relationships earlier (Shimokawa, 1997: 31). They have shortened the lead time between the product planning stage and the stage of mass production. For instance, Japanese automobile makers have recently developed new cars with a lead time of just 20 months, compared with previous lead times in the industry of 36–40 months (Shimokawa, 1997: 31).

These changes have involved severe competition between parts makers, not only between primary subcontractors but also between secondary/tertiary subcontractors. They seem to have occurred because the cost advantages of switching suppliers have begun to outweigh the transaction cost advantages of long-term buyer–supplier relationships. Meanwhile, imports have become cheaper and rapid technical progress has widened the differences in efficiency between the best and the worst firms.[21]

The changing nature of Japanese inter-corporate relationships

Modern Japanese economic structure has fine gradational stratification and hierarchy (see e.g. Takada, 1989: 90–101; 1990: 23–35). These continuous long-term and mutual trust-based buyer–supplier relationships tend to disproportionately favour the party with superior management resources. Japanese inter-corporate relationships are under increasing pressure. First, companies holding a dominant position are likely to abuse their power. This is more likely in an international context, where offshore suppliers compete with traditional domestic suppliers. In this case, traditional Japanese trust norms do not apply. Second, relations based on close negotiation and information exchange involve high communication costs, such as those arising from long working hours. Third, potentially qualified suppliers will need to invest in specific assets in order to enter new markets. These sunk costs create entry barriers. Fourth, Japanese-type inter-corporate relationships need multilateral competition in order to facilitate price competition. Nowadays the business activities of Japanese companies must be open to international competition and be seen to be open to such competition.

The evidence seems to be that there has been a significant hollowing out of Japanese manufacturing since 1985 (Cowling and Tomlinson, 2000). Japanese multinationals have created over two million manufacturing jobs outside Japan. This is thought to have led directly to the loss of one million jobs inside Japan. The transfer of primary firm jobs has particularly affected the small and medium enterprises that supply the larger multinationals. These firms' share of intermediate supplies to foreign affiliates of Japanese firms fell from 55 per cent to 37 per cent between 1986 and 1996. They also suffered from a sharp decline in their average profitability over this period. There is a pressing need for such small firms to de-couple their own futures from that of large-scale manufacturing in Japan and develop the type of diversified markets and products characteristic of successful industrial districts in Germany, Italy and the United States.

It is difficult for Japanese firms to maintain their traditional inter-corporate relationships in an environment of increasing internationalization, where modern innovation requires increasing flexibility. Internationalization is slowly forcing the opening of the supply chain to foreign competition. The aging of the population results in greater competition for skilled labour, making it difficult to maintain continuous long-term employment relationships. Flexible labour markets are being developed where there were once differences in the operation of the labour market for employees of small- and medium-sized enterprises and those of large companies. These trends mean that traditional Japanese inter-corporate relationships are likely to continue to decline in importance.

Japanese industrial policy: towards 'strong JFTC, weak MITI'?

It is well known that industrial policy has been proactive in most manufacturing industries in Japan during the postwar period. In fact, the MITI was given broad authority to intervene in various business activities. It could control business activities directly through import quotas and managing foreign capital flows during the high-growth era.[22] Moreover, it has been able to control firms indirectly by giving pecuniary incentives and undertaking administrative guidance. Although Japan had a superficially tough anti-monopoly law, MITI could pursue these policy instruments because of the existence of various special laws and crippling amendments to the 1947 Japanese anti-monopoly law. As a result the competition authority, the JFTC was forced to accept a weak position.[23] Therefore, 'strong MITI, weak JFTC' has been the common perception in postwar Japan.

The consistency between the weak legal position of the JFTC and the regulatory intervention of MITI enabled a proactive industrial policy to be feasible.[24] Under a situation of weak competition policy enforcement, both MITI and industrial firms could act without considering anti-monopoly law. MITI intervened in industries in accordance with policy goals and in order to raise the probability of *amakudari*.[25] Meanwhile, industrial firms had an incentive to accept the intervention of MITI. Sometimes this was because of the prospect of subsidies and tax reductions. At other times, firms accepted government guidance because of the fear of future retaliation by MITI. In this environment, industrial firms undertook enormous investment programmes in the high-growth period. This has caused 'excessive competition' in many industries during the catching-up period which fuelled Japanese postwar growth.[26]

This picture is no longer sustainable. Japan has been forced to increase the power of the JFTC relative to MITI under the twin shocks of the completion of the catching-up with other advanced economies and growing internationalization. This has resulted in a reduction of MITI's ability to coordinate industry behaviour. As part of a wider reform of government departments MITI was reorganized in 2001 into the new Ministry of Economy, Trade and Industry (METI).

Although it has been pointed out that catching-up with Western countries had been largely achieved by the 1970s, MITI supported joint research in the computer industry in order to catch up with the technological level of IBM during the 1970s. In addition, the Economic Planning Agency (1996) insisted that the Japanese catching-up process was complete by 1990, based on annual per capita GDP. Therefore, we can deduce that Japan's technological catching-up process was nearly completed by the 1980s. As a result of this success in achieving its primary policy objective, MITI has been forced to diversify its policy goals, in order to give itself a rationale.[27]

The second 'shock', internationalization, weakened the strength of MITI's role via two mechanisms. First, internationalization of the Japanese economy has arisen as a result of the increasing share of exports and imports in GDP, the business activities of domestic firms active in foreign direct investment, and the entry of foreign firms into the Japanese market. Because MITI's policy instruments mainly targeted domestic industrial firms, internationalization reduced the strength of these policy instruments, in particular because Japanese transnationals have been able to circumvent MITI control through overseas expansion.[28] Second, internationalization has led to trade disputes between Japan and Western countries (Itoh *et al.*, 1991: 26). Trade disputes have entailed not only opposition to the rapid expansion of exports by Japanese firms but also the requirement for the reformation of Japanese industrial structure. This requirement has substantially weakened MITI's willingness to use its policy instruments.

The changing nature of industrial policy

MITI's changing role in industrial policy is represented by the decline of its ability to exercise control over industries. Figure 8.5 shows the number of cartels permitted as exemptions from anti-monopoly law. After the late 1970s, the number of cartels decreased drastically, reflecting the decline of MITI's role. As a result, the number of manufacturing industries regulated by special law is also decreasing. Anti-monopoly law was also considerably strengthened in 1977. One result of this amendment was that industrial firms may be fined proportionally to profit in the case of unreasonable restraint of trade, and hence be deterred from anti-competitive behaviours (Martin, 1994: 61–5; Kisugi, 1995: 386–8). In addition to this, there is increasing foreign pressure to strengthen the enforcement of Japanese anti-monopoly law. The number of legal actions by JFTC, though it fluctuates sharply, shows an increasing trend (Figure 8.6). The real value of fines in the case of unreasonable restraint of trade increased drastically after 1990 (Matsuura *et al.*, 1999: 29). The anti-monopoly law was further strengthened in 1999 and 2000. Therefore, the role of the JFTC has increased since the 1980s. OECD (1997) also reported further moves to increase the effectiveness of the JFTC. Meanwhile the number of *amakudari* from MITI declined from 36 in 1985 to 17 in 1997 to 2 in 2000.[29]

As a result of the inconsistency between competition and traditional industrial policy and the lack of support MITI is giving to industry, information exchange between MITI and business has become more costly and

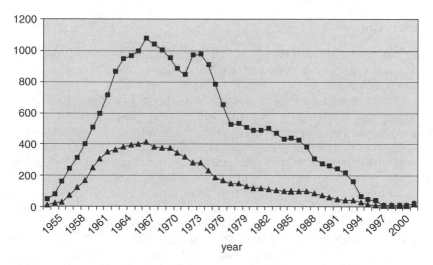

Figure 8.5 The number of cartels permitted as exemptions from anti-monopoly law (upper curve; lower curve is number of industries included in these exemptions)

Source: Japan Fair Trade Commission, *Japan Fair Trade Commission Annual Reports*.

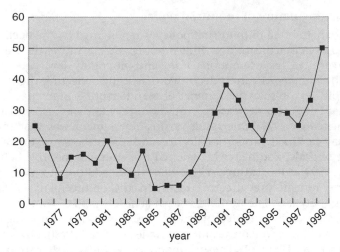

Figure 8.6   The number of legal actions brought by the JFTC

Source: Japan Fair Trade Commission, *Japan Fair Trade Commission Annual Reports*.

less beneficial since the late 1970s. The reason for this is that the weakening of MITI (now METI) means that firms are less willing to cooperate with it and so Japanese industrial policy has become much weaker than in the past. The above factors have promoted the breakdown of the 'strong MITI, weak JFTC' rule in the Japanese economy.

Conclusion

Even before the onset of the Asian economic crisis of 1997, the years since 1985 had witnessed a period of significant institutional pressure in the Japanese economy.

A number of factors have coincided to cause this change. First, the Japanese economy has substantially caught up with Western economies, thus reducing the scope for 'easy' growth. Second, the 1980s were a time of global macroeconomic instability, emanating initially from US domestic economic policy, which eventually led to the emergence of a persistent United States–Japan trade deficit and a sharp appreciation of the yen against the dollar. This macroeconomic stability led to two recessions within six years in the Japanese economy. Third, macroeconomic instability was associated with growing political pressure on Japan from the United States to liberalize its domestic markets in order to facilitate imports. Finally, an aging population and changes in industrial structure increased competition between firms for skilled labour within the Japanese economy. These last two factors have put pressure on the system of stable inter-corporate relationships along the industrial supply chain and on the Japanese employment system.

In our discussion, the above factors were seen to have important implications for the four institutions we examined. First, mutually beneficial long-term relations between banks and firms are increasingly fragile, ineffective and difficult to sustain. The huge amount of bad debt in the financial system suggests a failure of the banks' monitoring function. While banks will undoubtedly continue to be significant lenders to industrial companies, it is already apparent that a move towards a more Anglo-American (arm's length) sort of bank–firm relationship is necessary. Second, the aging population, slow macroeconomic growth and widespread corporate distress have put the implicit contract between workers and companies that is the heart of the Japanese employment system under severe strain. Companies have had to downsize by firing relatively expensive older workers. Third, inter-corporate relations within the production *keiretsu* are being undermined by competition for resources, internationalization and external pressure to liberalize markets for components. If Japan is to respond to international political and economic pressure and the hollowing out of its traditional manufacturing industries, it will have to develop more flexible forms of purchaser–supplier relations and genuine industrial districts of small firms. Fourth, industrial policy has undergone a marked shift as MITI and its bureaucrats have declined in importance and influence and the JFTC has undertaken a more extensive and proactive role in enforcing competition. This switch in the stance of government policy towards industry seems to be an irreversible trend in a world moving towards an ever-freer trade between developed countries.

The evidence is that while change has begun for Japan's economic institutions, it still has some way to go. Banks remain locked into previous relationships with firms by their past debts, and the government is unwilling to initiate full-scale financial restructuring. The Japanese employment system has been changing, but much of the previous system remains intact for current workers. The *keiretsu* structure has seen significant job losses but only slow changes in the nature of continuing relationships. MITI is weak but has yet to find a viable new industrial strategy. It seems self-evident that the former institutional arrangements are no longer delivering sustained economic growth with full employment. However, it is also clear that new, more appropriate, institutional arrangements are emerging only slowly.

Notes

1. The authors acknowledge the very helpful comments of Bill Russell, Yvonne Pollitt and three anonymous referees. All remaining errors are their own.
2. Nominal asset prices have fluctuated wildly: taking a base of 100 for both stock and Tokyo land prices in 1985, stock prices reached 260 in 1989 before falling to below 140 in 1992, while land prices in Tokyo reached 220 in 1990 before falling to 180 in 1992. The external sector saw the value of the yen–dollar exchange rate drop from 250 Y/$ in 1985 to around 100 Y/$ in 1996 while a persistent current

account surplus emerged, accompanied by a sustained growth in the dollar value of net overseas assets. Between 1985 and 1996, Japanese GNP growth fluctuated sharply and unemployment rose to a record postwar high. Since 1996, the economy has stagnated and unemployment has continued to rise (Economic Planning Agency, *Economic Survey of Japan 1992–93* and *1996–97*).

3. In the five decades since the end of the Second World War, the Japanese economy has developed rapidly. Part of this was a catch-up phase of economic development which took place within the framework of unique systems and practices which have come to be known as 'the Japanese economic system'. The chief features of this system are a financial intermediation system centred around 'main' banks and lead underwriters, seniority-based pay and long-term employment, inter-corporate relationships involving a closely linked group of firms known as *keiretsu* and minute government regulation covering a wide range of economic sectors (Economic Planning Agency, *Economic Survey of Japan* 1996).

4. This idea is based on Takeda and Schoenholtz (1985). In observing the key features of the main bank system, Takeda and Schoenholz paid attention to the main bank monitoring of its client firms and stressed the bank's characteristic as a producer of information relevant to a profitable bank–firm relationship.

5. The annual rate of growth of lending by all the banks between 1960 and 1975 varied between 11 per cent and 27 per cent per annum (Economic Planning Agency, *Economic Survey of Japan* 1993: 75).

6. See Kigyo Keiretsu Soran, *Tokyo Keizai Shinposha* (1996: 96). The share of stocks owned by financial institutions increased rapidly during the high growth period.

7. It is hypothesized that such a reduction of the agency cost makes it possible to borrow from banks on easier terms in order to finance equipment investment.

8. The annual rate of change in the number of insolvencies was 10 per cent to 20 per cent in the late 1980s but rose to 65.8 per cent in 1991, followed by 32.1 per cent in 1992 (Bank of Japan, 1995a: 138). Officially announced bad debts, that is, debts of insolvent firms and overdue debts of city banks, long-term credit banks, and trust banks, were about 14 trillion yen in 1995. Adding this figure to an estimate of the value of both overdue debts of local banks and debts of interest reduction or exemption incurred by non-banks, all bad debts amounted to 38 trillion yen (*Economist*, Toyo Keizei Shinposha, 8 May 1995: 80).

9. The average annual rate of change of bank lending (real loans outstanding) was 1.8 per cent between 1981 and 1985, 13.6 per cent between 1986 and 1990, 1.8 per cent between 1991 and 1995 (Bank of Japan, 1995b: 65) and 1.02 per cent between 1995 and 1998 (Bank of Japan, 1999: 2 geppou).

10. Source: Economic Planning Agency, *Economic Survey of Japan* (1999: 205). During the late 1980s loans outstanding to larger firms did not change, and those of smaller firms gradually increased.

11. Source: Economic Planning Agency, *Economic Survey of Japan* (1999: 205).

12. Nihon Keizai Shinbun, 26 December 2001.

13. Evidence of the main banks' monitoring function is provided by *Economic Survey of Japan*. This shows that firms which sharply increased bank borrowing during the bubble period were largely dependent on other banks and not on the main bank for the additional borrowing (Economic Planning Agency, 1996: 305).

14. Source: Economic Planning Agency, *Economic Survey of Japan* (1996: 305–6). In addition the numbers of smaller firms that borrowed from banks decreased rapidly in the 1990s. A questionnaire by MITI analyzed the reasons for the reduction of bank lending as follows: banks raised interest rates (70.2 per cent), banks rejected a renewal of loan contract with firms (50.7 per cent) (Economic Planning

Agency, *Economic Survey of Japan*, 1999: 211–12). The main banks have recently rejected significant rescue loans to firms, precipitating bankruptcy. Recent cases of companies which were not rescued include Sogo (July 2000, total debt 1 trillion 800 billion yen), Marutomi (December 2000, 76.1 billion yen), Fujiko (March 2001, 83.1 billion yen) and Mical (September 2001, 1388.1 billion yen).

15. For details on the Japanese employment system, see Abegglen (1958), Koike (1999), Odagiri (1994) and Itoh (1992).
16. See Aoki (1988) and Aoki and Okuno (1996) for theoretical explanations.
17. See Koike (1994), Yashiro (1996) and Economic Planning Agency, *Economic Survey of Japan*, 1994, 1996 and 1999.
18. There is similar, but not quite as sharp, change at the whole economy level.
19. According to a questionnaire to new employees, the ratio of the number of the employees who wish to work within the same firm until their mandatory retirement to the total number of the employees has fallen since 1985 (see Ministry of Labour, 1999: 35).
20. Source: Economic Planning Agency, *Economic Survey of Japan* (1996).
21. For example, there were 141 primary suppliers to Toyota in 1990. The members of this group were fixed in the 1980s. However, 6 suppliers were dropped in the 1990s and 14 new companies become suppliers (see The Association of Japan Automobile Parts Industry, 1990; 1998).
22. This authority was supported by the Foreign Exchange and Foreign Trade Control Law (1949) and the Law Concerning Foreign Capital (1950).
23. See Best (1990) for an account of the early development of MITI and the JFTC.
24. For detailed discussions, see Okuno-Fujiwara (1996), Okuno-Fujiwara and Sekiguchi (1996) and Matsuura, Pollitt, Takada and Tanaka (1999).
25. By this unique custom, retired civil servants can often find important positions in business firms and/or public-service corporations. OECD (1997: 103) notes that the number of *amakudari* peaked at 318 in 1985 and has fallen to 134 in 1996.
26. According to this view, as Boltho (1985) pointed out, it is very important that MITI preserved competition among a few big firms in most industries.
27. According to MITI (1990), its industrial policy goals in 1990s were the following: (1) international harmonization; (2) improvement of quality of life and (3) preparedness of infrastructure for economic growth.
28. See Cowling and Tomlinson (2000), who stress that MITI lost its ability to direct Japanese industry as overseas investment by Japanese industry became more significant. They suggest that this process has led to national industrial strategy being led by transnational companies rather than the Japanese state.
29. Source: National Personnel Authority, Tokyo.

9
Developmental States Before and After the Asian Crisis
Linda Weiss

Introduction

A familiar litany has taken hold at century's end: capitalist diversity is doomed. It is a luxury that global markets are less and less inclined to tolerate. No matter the form of that diversity – whether it is the welfare statist model of Sweden, the labour-market protection of Germany, the credit activism of France or the state-guided production system of Japan – all such deviations from the neo-liberal or 'Anglo-American' 'norm' are destined, sooner or later, to perish. Politics will retreat from markets as business systems – no longer sheltered from foreign markets – lose their distinctive characteristics, and as national capital becomes disembedded from domestic institutional arrangements. In short, the world is moving towards a new convergence and its mechanism is economic integration, driven not only by trade and investment, but above all by the liberalization of capital markets.[1]

Assuming that liberalization involves similar policies leading to similar institutional outcomes has led many to expect ever-greater conformity with Anglo-American norms and arrangements (so-called 'normalization' or convergence, terms used interchangeably here). This chapter challenges that assumption by focusing on the experience of Korea and Taiwan, two East Asian countries which have spawned 'developmental states' and coordinated market economies. Their fate is therefore of central significance in the 'end of national capitalisms' debate, especially in the light of the 1997 financial crisis.

The analysis points up the weaknesses of convergence thinking by focusing on the different ways in which Korea and Taiwan went about opening their financial systems before the 1997 crisis; the differential importance of domestic and international pressures in shaping the divergent approaches to liberalization; and finally, the enhancement (Taiwan) and unanticipated recomposition (Korea) of core capacities in the aftermath of the crisis.

The key questions are: to what extent have the ideological and institutional 'fundamentals' of the developmental state (discussed later) been eroded; and in what measure, if any, are so-called global economic processes (e.g. liberalization of capital markets and capital mobility) the driving force behind such erosion? This chapter argues that, with some exceptions and in spite of some significant changes over the past decade or so, the tenacity and adaptivity of national institutional arrangements are more impressive than their purported erosion or normalization. The hypothesis of an underlying external-economic logic driving change in a neo-liberal direction lacks convincing evidence. In pre-crisis Korea, where financial reforms appear to have taken a more neo-liberal direction and where some significant state trans-formation occurred, the momentum for change was generated in the first place by domestic power imbalances which preceded external pressures for financial liberalization in the 1990s. Second, notwithstanding significant liberalization of capital markets, these changes have been neither unidirectional nor irre-versible, sometimes suggesting a neo-liberal direction, sometimes strengthen-ing or creatively recomposing familiar institutional arrangements.

Identifying developmental states

Nowadays, the term 'developmental state' is so loosely applied that it has become virtually synonymous with 'the state in East Asia'. This misconception[2] can be found in much recent commentary on the Asian financial crisis. It posits the idea that the crisis-stricken countries have been punished for following the Japanese model of state-guided development and thus deviating too far from free-market logic.

We will be more rigorous in our use of the developmental state concept. Though definitions tend to vary in inclusiveness, most authorities on the region would have little difficulty in accepting the following statement. Developmental states of the kind found in Northeast Asia during their high-growth period could be distinguished by at least three criteria:

(1) their *priorities* (aimed at enhancing the productive powers of the nation, raising the investable surplus, and ultimately closing the technology gap between themselves and the industrialized countries);
(2) their *organizational arrangements* (embodying a relatively insulated pilot agency in charge of that transformative project, which in turn presup-poses both an elite bureaucracy staffed by the best managerial talent available, who are highly committed to the organization's objectives, and a supportive political system); and
(3) their *institutional links with organized economic actors* (privileging cooper-ative rather than arms-length relations, and sectors or industry associa-tions rather than individual firms) as the locus of policy input, negotiation and implementation.

Thus, transformative goals, a pilot agency and institutionalized government–business cooperation form the three essential ingredients of any developmental state (Pempel, 1999). In the absence of the first two criteria, the state lacks an insulated coordinating intelligence and is vulnerable to capture by special interests.[3] In the absence of the third, the state lacks the embedded (quasi-corporatist) quality of effective policy design and implementation, and is vulnerable to information blockage and policy failure. I call this institutional set up 'governed interdependence', which in its most evolved form involves negotiated policy-making under government sponsorship.[4]

Control over key resources such as finance is also very important, but the significance of specific policy tools should not be overstated. For as the relevant tasks of economic transformation have evolved so have the instruments for achieving them. This evolution is clearly illustrated in Taiwan where the strong postwar emphasis of its industrial bureaucracy on enhancing investment and exports has given way to promoting technological diffusion and continuous upgrading. The success of that shift has been much less marked in Korea, where the state has moved between two extremes: on one hand, total reliance on financial control in the 1960s and 1970s to achieve its objectives of creating a Korean presence in all the major export industries and, on the other hand, substantial relinquishment of control over financial institutions and state-guided investment in the late 1980s and 1990s. The politics of that change and its larger consequences are discussed below.

In addition to the three fundamentals outlined earlier, one should note the importance of a political system which supports a shared project of economic transformation, where there is elite cohesion over core national goals, and where the economic bureaucracy is given sufficient scope to take initiatives and act effectively (Pempel and Muramatsu, 1995).

If we apply these criteria to the state structures of Southeast Asia, it becomes immediately apparent that we are dealing with something quite different from developmental states – a patchwork of highly interventionist, yet relatively porous, states whose policies have been less guided by a consistent developmental project than the promotion of ethnic, patrimonial or other particularistic interests. Thus, the constellation of political priorities, state structures and government–business relations that prevailed in Thailand, Malaysia and Indonesia during their high-growth phase has differed significantly from the pattern typically found in Korea and Taiwan in a similar phase. What stands out is the inconsistency, weakness or absence of their developmental priorities and arrangements and thus their *relatively* low transformative capacities. In the Southeast Asian countries, the absence of a consistent developmental project and thus of a sustained effort to transform the industrial structure underpinned loose regulatory control of financial flows. In turn, the availability of easy money through short-term inflows paved the way for massive speculative bubbles and, by 1997, left these countries enormously vulnerable to the shock of sudden investor pullout (Weiss, 1999).

When we turn to Korea and Taiwan, our task is to assess how liberalization has impacted on the goals and institutions of governance, before and since the financial crisis and how these mesh with expectations about closer alignment of East Asian systems with neo-liberal arrangements. As we shall see, Korea underwent more substantial change than Taiwan in the pre-crisis phase. Moreover, in both settings, domestic politics and changing power relations in the domestic arena have tended to produce a more testing environment for the developmental model than changes in the international economy. Why did the developmental state model (or at least a 1990s version of it) begin to unravel in Korea but remain more or less intact in Taiwan, and what light might this difference shed on their differential involvement in the 1997 financial crisis? Finally, how far is unravelling likely to proceed as the Koreans take remedial action and institute wide-ranging reforms?

The argument is developed by way of three propositions. The first outlines flaws in convergence thinking – whereby increasing economic openness, pressures for liberalization and deregulation drive national systems along similar paths, eroding distinctive national styles of capitalism.[5] I examine this thesis against the recent evolution of East Asia's developmental states. The second proposition addresses the sources of developmental state dismantling, showing how in the Korean case liberalization was a consequence rather than a cause of that process. The final proposition centres on the impact of increased pressures for economic opening in the aftermath of the Asian crisis. It challenges the expectation that the post-crisis financial reforms will be more likely to break with developmental patterns than to recompose them in new ways.

Divergent approaches to liberalization

Proposition (1):
Financial liberalization is not unidirectional: it does not lead uniformly to state disengagement. Rather, the course liberalization takes depends upon the prior constellation of regime goals and institutional arrangements.

Whereas commentators earlier emphasized either technological catch up, the growth of big business, or the introduction of competitive politics (democratization), nowadays they invoke financial liberalization in particular and economic openness more generally as the driving force of normalization. Globalization theory anticipates that as firms internationalize their operations and as capital markets are opened, national business systems lose their embedded character and turn away from – or even against – the state (for a critique see Whitley, 1998). Liberalization means that firms in the developmental market economy can now raise funds independently of the state, thus the more financial liberalization proceeds, the more likely dismantling will gather force.

However, as Steven Vogel (1996) has shown in his study of regulatory reform in Britain, France and Japan, financial liberalization leads to different outcomes, depending on pre-existing institutional arrangements and regime orientations. Thus, taking into account the domestic arrangements that differentiate a particular regime can help to predict reform outcomes, that is, whether they will seek primarily to enhance market efficiency or to complement and enhance national governance.

The divergent approaches to liberalization of Taiwan and Korea offer a fruitful application of this idea (Thurbon, 2001). Understanding how and why they diverged on this issue is essential to an explanation of why Korea became directly engulfed in the 1997 financial crisis while Taiwan did not (Weiss, 1999).

The Taiwanese approach

It is widely reported that the Taiwanese were more 'cautious' than the Koreans in the way they set about opening up the capital account, especially in the first half of the 1990s. However, in what ways they have been 'more cautious' and for what reasons are issues which have yet to be analyzed in depth. The Central Bank of China (CBC) on the island of Taiwan appears to be the embodiment of financial caution, keeping a vigilant eye on the disruptive potential of capital flows, insisting on 'emergency powers' of intervention as a *quid pro quo* for opening up the currency and stock markets, and intervening before and after the Asian crisis to prevent currency speculation and stock market manipulation. Such vigilance, moreover, is inseparable from a perceived threat to national security, a point we return to later.

A telling illustration of the two countries' divergent approaches can be seen in the way Ministry of Finance (MOF) officials in each country opened up the corporate bond market. Whereas the Koreans significantly relaxed controls over short-term inflows in the first half of the 1990s, the Taiwanese attached stringent new conditions to capital opening. Thus, when Taiwan began deregulating the corporate bond market in 1989, its companies had to raise funds abroad by issuing bonds overseas, the CBC feared that domestic remittances would disrupt domestic money markets. It therefore limited the proceeds of such overseas issuances to the support of offshore investment and the purchase of raw materials. However, in 1993, the CBC changed the rules, allowing companies to remit the proceeds of overseas bond issues for domestic use.[6] However, in striking contrast to the Koreans, this was accompanied by new rules that all domestic remittances had to be invested in plant expansion. Moreover, the total or national aggregate for all such inflows was not to exceed $3 billion. In specifying that inflows be directed to production, the Taiwanese authorities were perhaps seeking to guard against the sort of speculative investment that fed stock and property bubbles earlier in Taiwan and more recently in Southeast Asia. Whatever the precise intent, the CBC has demonstrated both purpose and capacity in the way it monitors compliance, intervening under emergency powers when it suspects foreign inflows are not being used for designated purposes.thus, the very process of opening up Taiwan's capital markets in the 1990s has brought with it new regulatory controls which have preserved and at times strengthened coordination powers. Financial liberalization in the hands of the Taiwanese has thereby become much more an instrument for complementing and enhancing state capacities than for relinquishing them.

The Korean approach

Turning to the Korean setting, the key difference that leaps to the eye is the large inflow of portfolio investment, taking off in the first half of the 1990s. In the debate on the Asian crisis, these short-term inflows are often attributed to 'poor supervision' and 'ineffective regulatory control'. There is some evidence, however, that the removal of reporting requirements on dollar loans of short-term maturity (less than one year) was the result of a calculated choice. For Ministry of Finance officials, allowing ready access to short-term money markets, including the corporate bond market, was a way of enabling the *chaebol* to gain access to an alternative source of funding at a critical moment. It was critical in two senses. This was a period in which the state – responding primarily to domestic issues – was on the retreat from its traditional forms of industrial governance. (By the early 1990s, under the Kim Young-Sam administration, the state had substantially withdrawn from credit markets and from industry policy.) It was also at a time when Korea's economic performance was deteriorating as a result of rising wages and diminishing productivity. Though partly due to cyclical causes, this deterioration was reflected in a net outflow of long-term capital in the first half of the 1990s. Deteriorating economic performance in this period appears to have diminished Korea's attractiveness to foreign investors. As a result, long-term foreign loans became more expensive, harder to obtain and recorded a net outflow as loan repayments continued. This meant that Korean firms had to turn more to the short-term portfolio capital market for their investment funds, including the overseas bond markets. This was the context in which MOF officials decided to relax controls. The result was a surge in the inflow of portfolio investment in the 1990s. During 1990–94 alone, the total net inflow of foreign capital, reaching some $32 billion, was more than 10 times the total for the 1980s. Most of this was short-term portfolio investment, exceeding $27 billion in the 1991–94 period alone.

The more general point that this episode illustrates is the way in which the *prior weakening of transformative capacity* in Korea (retreat from industry policy and credit activism, and dismantling of the developmental pilot agency, the Economic Planning Board) *paved the way for loose regulatory control*. For in striking contrast to Taiwan, as we have seen, the deregulation of the corporate bond market was undertaken as the complement to state *retreat* from credit allocation and industrial policy (though not from *all* forms of industrial governance: namely, right up until the Asian crisis, the state still undertook to limit certain forms of capital inflow, notably FDI).

In sum, what set Taiwan apart from Korea was the fact that the state centred on Taipei (for reasons outlined in the following section) held fast to its developmental project and thereby approached financial market opening with a view to maintaining state control. Thus the process of liberalizing capital inflows involved reregulation to enhance existing capabilities. Consequently, in the political bargaining that preceded capital account opening in the early 1990s, the CBC held out for a 'safety blanket', insisting on guaranteed emergency powers of intervention in the event of market volatility. Korea on the other hand used liberalization as a means of complementing the larger goal of dismantling the structures of credit activism and industrial policy.

Sources of state dismantling: domestic versus international politics

Proposition (2):
The partial dismantling of core capacities has been a condition, not a consequence, of the way Korea approached financial liberalization. Dismantling, in turn, was primarily a response to domestic tensions, and only secondarily to international pressures.

My second proposition addresses the sources of developmental state dismantling. Globalization theory predicts that dismantling is driven by liberalization. However, evidence from the Korean case suggests that this logic needs to be reversed. As indicated in the previous section, the dismantling of the state's transformative capacities paves the way for a particular kind of liberalization (which may then be the stimulus for further dismantling), and not the other way around. Regulatory reform, as the Koreans undertook it in the five years prior to the Asian crisis (in a quasi-neo-liberal direction) was partly a consequence of the prior unravelling of core capacities and, in part, a means of extending the process of state retreat. Financial reform – as it was executed in Korea, in distinction to Japan and Taiwan – did not *lead to* developmental state dismantling. Rather, it was an *outcome* of that process, namely, of the substantial – though not complete – *unravelling of core capacities which preceded it.*

This of course raises the issue of why state dismantling may occur in the first place. While this topic forms the subject of a separate study of regime shift and cannot be dealt with adequately in this context, nonetheless, two interim conclusions may be offered. One is that the actions which led the Korean state down a neo-liberal path of reform – of which more detail is provided below – were primarily responses to domestic political pressures. Only in a subsidiary way, and at a later stage, were they responses *also* to international economic (and political) pressures. The other conclusion is that, within the category of 'domestic' political pressures, a confluence of three such pressures seems important. First came a multilayered crisis in the 1979–82 period (raising questions of the state's economic management and political legitimacy). In this context, the Korean government took its first steps towards financial liberalization. State actors began to perceive 'liberalization' as a means of untying and eventually severing the financial knot between state and *chaebol*, gradually reducing state control of financial institutions, privatizing banks, developing a stock market and more generally relinquishing the capacity to coordinate investment through control of credit.

Domestic political pressures in the Korean context

Domestic politics provided the initial stimulus pulling apart the government–business relationship and weakening the state's transformative capacity: the massive protest and popular uprising against the authoritarian regime of President Chun Doo Hwan as Korea confronted in 1979–80 its worst economic crisis since the Korean War. In order to shore up legitimacy, Chun undertook to distance the regime from the increasingly unpopular *chaebol* by paring back state-sponsored loans, and by stimulating the development of the stock market to wean these mammoth enterprises off bank credit.[7] Thus began the first step in a lengthy and sometimes ambiguous series of manoeuvres aimed at encouraging financial autonomy for the *chaebol*.

A second source of domestic pressure involved a conflict over fundamental ideological orientations, precipitated by the empowerment of a new kind of bureaucrat. As Meredith Woo-Cumings writes of the 1980s:

> The quest to liberalize Korean finance was carried out by transnational elites now ensconced as economic technocrats … all experts on finance, all with American Ph.Ds, and all professing allegiance to the goal of liberalization, as well as the entire panoply of thirty-five men at the Korea Development Institute, every last one of them a Ph.D from American universities. Ideological osmosis could not have been more complete. (Woo, 1991: 191–2)

The newly empowered neo-liberal bureaucrats spearheaded a battle to dismantle the Korean model that became conjoined with the aims of financial liberalization. This was the first phase of the dismantling process, best described in Woo's terms as a process of 'ideological osmosis'.

Third, there were deep tensions arising from interactions between, on the one hand, a strong state given to top-down, often repressive, control and on the other, huge concentrations of industrial power based on family-centred conglomerates (*chaebol*). In their continuing quest for diversification and expansion, the Korean *chaebol* had become financially overenmeshed in the developmental state, while in their structure and ambition had, in the course of the 1980s, grown more and more independent of it. Herein lies the fundamental contradiction of the Korean model, a contradiction expressed in the form of an entrenched power-standoff between government and business, and ultimately developmental blockage.

One response to this systemic tension was to restructure the *chaebol*, but official efforts proved ineffectual, at least until after the 1997 crisis. The other response was to reform the financial system by creating alternative sources of corporate funding, first domestically then internationally.

In this first phase then, *the developmental state presided over its own dismantling* – first by purposefully giving the *chaebol* the wherewithal (such as securities and bond markets) to get the state out of their hair, then by turning in on itself ideologically, and ultimately by cannibalizing its own coordination powers. The ultimate symbol of cannibalization came with the marginalization and eventually complete dismantling of the Economic Planning Board, absorbed in 1993 within the MOF.

International pressures

To these more directly domestic pressures, one can add, much later, those stemming from the international arena. They concern the ability of outsiders (and insiders) to leverage the Korean desire for international recognition as an advanced country – symbolized by accession to the OECD – by pressing for further opening of Korea's capital account and financial markets. In this second phase of the dismantling process, from 1993 to 1996, Korea's pilot agency (the EPB, which oversaw the country's rapid industrial transformation), by now marginalized, is finally abolished in 1994, prior to a further bout of capital market opening. The liberalization enthusiasts at home could of course offset the vague promise of increased efficiency with the obvious reward of international 'glory' (particularly OECD membership, finally achieved in 1996). Indeed enthusiasts could point to capital market opening as a condition of American support for Korea's entry to the OECD – and thus turn 'external pressure' from the United States to their own ends.

However, international pressures for financial opening were effective to the extent that they piggybacked on domestic ones, and thus followed rather than initiated a lengthy process of revising and reorienting developmental purpose. The Taiwanese case was very different. International pressures were primary, not in reorienting but in sustaining developmental capacity. As interviews with CBC and MOF officials in Taiwan confirm, national security issues remain paramount in state calculations about most aspects of regulatory reform, especially finance. In contrast to South Korea, Taiwan has had to confront a growing power imbalance in favour of its mainland neighbour. Unlike North Korea, China has become increasingly strong economically and assertive diplomatically. Moreover, there is no US commitment to match the South Korean experience, given the absence of US troops on Taiwanese soil. Feeling far less secure from military threat than the Koreans, the Taiwanese authorities have maintained a posture highly sensitive to the disruptive potential of short-term money markets.

How does the conclusion that there is no inherent global economic logic driving 'normalization' of the developmental state stand up to the recent vicissitudes of the Asian crisis and IMF intervention? They surely offer a strong test of viability. So, can we go further and conclude that transformative states are still viable in conditions of increasing economic openness?

The Asian crisis as the final blow to developmental states?

Proposition (3):
The Asian crisis has confirmed rather than undermined the importance and viability of effective national governance in an era of global financial markets. Thus, Korea, where the developmental model had been substantially dismantled, remained more deeply exposed than Taiwan to financial upheaval. However, in the post-crisis cleanup it is the Korean legacy of developmentalism rather than neo-liberalism that is likely to refashion core capacities to meet the new tasks.

When the East Asian economies went into a deflationary tailspin in late 1997, many commentators hailed the Asian financial crisis as confirmation of the superiority of the 'Anglo-American' model of capitalism. They argued that the 'Asian model' was unsustainable, because it ignored the realities of globalization – that is, the power of international markets to punish policies and arrangements that deviated too far from the neo-liberal norm. The IMF message was that the Asian economies had deviated too far and got punished.

There are at several problems with this perception of what went wrong, which cannot be detailed here (see Weiss, 2000). Indeed Korea had undergone such a substantial institutional makeover by the time the crisis struck, that one might plausibly argue that it was Korea's creeping *neo-liberalism* rather than its legacy of *statism* that made it more vulnerable to a financial shakedown.

One can turn the IMF argument on its head: Korea was pulled into the financial maelstrom not because it deviated too far from the free-market norm but because it had abandoned too much of its transformative capacity. This argument gains in plausibility when we reflect on the differential involvement of Taiwan and Korea in the events of 1997.

Unlike Korea, Taiwan maintained a firm grip on core capacities throughout the 1990s, especially in the all-important sphere of industrial upgrading. This contributed to export strength. On the eve of the crisis, Taiwan thus enjoyed strong trade surpluses rather than current account deficits (and, consequently, large international reserves). For geopolitical reasons, the Taiwanese authorities remained more united on fundamental goals and the means of achieving them, and thus more sceptical of the benefits of opening the door wide to volatile capital flows.

On the other hand, by the time President Kim took office in 1993, the Korean government had virtually 'abandoned its traditional role of coordinating investments in large-scale industries'.[8] Policy instead focused on encouraging the *chaebol* to divest themselves of non-core business, to reduce indebtedness, and to concentrate on upgrading. However, in the absence of new instruments to replace credit control, such policies lacked clout. Mostly, the *chaebol* simply chose to expand capacity or to diversify, rather than to upgrade; diversification meant expansion into each other's areas. This exacerbated cyclical problems of excess capacity, dragging down prices, profits and ultimately debt repayment capability. All this left Korean industry highly vulnerable to investor pullout, once perceptions of the region (precipitated by the Thai crisis) began to shift (Weiss, 1999).

Oversupply had certainly occurred several times in the past, notably in the 1979–80 recession. Korean companies responded to that crisis exactly as they have always done – by waiting out the slump, borrowing madly and investing for the recovery.[9] This bold strategy of toughing it out had yielded results in the past and should have worked again, but by mid-1997 the critical ingredient of a steady stream of (state-guided) capital was missing.[10] This was one important outcome of Korean-style liberalization.

The other outcome, the institutional configuration that confronted the Korean collapse of 1997, represented a dangerous half-way house – a corporate body still firmly anchored in the old high-debt system, yet with a political head increasingly unwilling and unable to provide the requisite regulation of that system. As Wade and Veneroso (1998) have argued, this combination makes a highly volatile and ultimately unworkable mix.

Whither Korea?

While developmental purpose and capacity continue to inform state involvement in Taiwan's financial and industrial system, the big question for many observers is 'whither the Korean model?' Has the unravelling of the transformative state in Korea reached a point of no return? In the world of human affairs, the historical record suggests that few trends are irreversible. This applies as much to the process of global integration as it does to the decomposition of state capacity.

Several years on from the turbulence, there would seem to be more factors favouring a reconfigured transformative state in Korea than those pushing against it. On the negative side, there are at least two strong countertendencies: the absence of a clear consensus within the governing elite (political and administrative) over the scope and direction that national economic management should take; and the continuing efforts of the *chaebol* to resist restructuring, making the process, slow, difficult and conflict-ridden.

On the favourable side, three features stand out: a strong social constituency for economic recovery and renewal and for national economic independence (galvanized in the late 1990s by almost universal antipathy to the current IMF regime); a domestic and international situation favouring the curtailment of *chaebol* power and realignment of the government–business relationship; and not least, a reorganization within the state itself which has resulted in the reinvigoration of independent state agencies, insulating them from the political process.

State restructuring is evident in the creation of the new Office of Planning and Budget controlled by the Office of the President, hence independent of the neo-liberal warriors in the Ministry of Finance and Economics (MOFE); the powerful Financial Supervisory Commission (FSC) which now closely regulates financial institutions (and through them, the *chaebol*), independent of the Bank of Korea and the MOFE; and the National Audit Office responsible for monitoring the use of public moneys and investigating issues of corruption (see further Weiss, 2003).

Corporate restructuring is also moving ahead. Under the FSC's tough regulatory stance, Korea's family-centred industrial empires are slowly but gradually being transformed. Measures to modernize their management structures, reduce their indebtedness, clip their expansionist wings and ultimately contain their domestic market power are now being implemented, often with a degree of success that was hard to envision even a year after the crisis. Moreover, an important point often overlooked is that these policies for corporate reform have long been sought by Korean governments. By having them inscribed in the IMF agreements, the Korean state is effectively utilizing the authority of an international organization to drive through its domestic objectives.

One of these objectives is to maintain Korean ownership of Korean assets. It was widely anticipated that whilst Korea remained an IMF patient, it would be powerless to prevent a significant increase in foreign ownership of its assets – especially its financial institutions. Such a shift would in turn compromise any future efforts on the part of the Korean authorities to strengthen core capacities. While foreign ownership of Korean industrial firms and financial institutions has increased somewhat under the recent IMF agreement, it is not nearly as much as Western observers anticipated. In a telling statement, the IMF complained that more than two years after the crisis there was still very little foreign involvement in Korea's banking sector, thus little likelihood of the wholesale changes that it favoured. Most foreign involvement has been in the form of minority stakeholdings. The fact is that, for historical reasons (associated with Japanese colonialism), foreign ownership remains highly unpopular and is not likely to be tolerated to any significant degree in the long term.[11]

Nonetheless, in tandem with reforms to the corporate and public sectors, the state has overhauled the financial system and, through the newly empowered FSC, tightened its control over finance and industry. Through the mechanisms of credit refusal and withdrawal (and not least, the threat of tax investigation), the state has once again adopted a guiding role in the process of change (this time aimed at corporate restructuring). Moreover, through new regulatory measures, the financial authorities are balancing increased openness of the financial system with greater control of outcomes. Thus, for instance, through three measures – a redefinition of bank capital, revised credit ceilings and new monitoring mechanisms – the Koreans have effectively reregulated foreign bank operations and set prudential limits to the *chaebol*'s foreign debt exposure.

While too soon to discern a clear pattern emerging from this array of forces, it is likely that the hybrid nature of the current Korean setup will lead to a more managed and selective liberalization. Korea appears paradoxically now both more nationalistic and more open to American ways than Taiwan. However, while this means a greater openness to international trade and financial markets, it remains a selective openness. Thus, even in Korea, where neo-liberal ideology has a much stronger institutional foothold than in Taiwan or Japan, it is premature to write off the possibility of a revised, globally oriented version of the developmental model. It will not be based on the old system of state-controlled finance. The key test is whether, in the longer run, Korea can renew transformative capacity – as both Taiwan and Japan have done – with 'softer' and subtler forms of government–business interaction and reciprocity, including risk-sharing arrangements, collaborative innovation consortia, and private-sector governance (Weiss, 1998: ch. 3).[12] Such renewal remains of course highly dependent upon the effective transformation of the *chaebol* now under way.

Conclusion

The Asian crisis is not the last chapter in the story of developmental capitalism. But it may be the beginning of a new sequel in which we see developmental states (or, rather their updated, globally oriented version) spearheading the adoption of forms of governance that balance developmental norms with economic openness. One such form will very likely include increasing regional cooperation over financial matters aimed at building regional capacity to prevent crisis deepening in the future.[13] Another may involve strengthening mechanisms for cooperation between government and business in order to manage openness more effectively.

Indeed, if current developments in the region offer any guide to future trends in the region, we should expect to find that states with developmental histories are becoming more active in using regulatory reforms to manage the outcomes of economic openness. This is already evident in Korea and

Taiwan across a range of policy areas – from prudential regulations that constrain currency speculation and limit exposure to short-term money markets, to tax reforms that encourage mergers and acquisitions in order to strengthen national firms in finance and industry, to the redesign of institutions able to regulate and monitor the behaviour of domestic and foreign institutions within the national domain.

Thus, whether one looks to Korea or Taiwan prior to the 1997 financial crisis, or in the most recent period, the conclusion is one at odds with a picture of international convergence. Instead, one finds evidence in both cases of a more mature version of developmentalism – one that is now less propelled by 'catch up' than by an emphasis on policies and institutions aimed at managing economic openness – whether by setting prudential limits to capital flows, sponsoring home-grown mergers or promoting continuous upgrading of the industrial economy. While the reinvigoration of transformative capacity better describes Taiwanese developments (where liberalization of finance was consistently accompanied by reregulation to enhance state capacity), it is the partial unravelling of state capacity – followed by recomposition in the post-crisis phase – which better captures the Korean experience. Here there is evidence of state restructuring as well as the changes implemented in the financial and corporate sectors in response to the IMF-agreed reforms, we should not be surprised to find its resurrection in a new form. If this is an outcome that few commentators have anticipated (including this author), it is because we have too often underestimated the power of path dependency, and thus the legacy bequeathed by pre-existing norms and institutions, a legacy through which the latter help to recast the old.

Notes

1. This chapter is a substantially revised version of Weiss (2000).
2. Ironically, in talking about an 'East Asian miracle' involving Southeast and Northeast Asian countries alike, the World Bank's much-cited 1993 report (World Bank, 1993) may have helped to implant the idea of an institutionally undifferentiated North and South East Asia. (Most of the time of course the World Bank has dismissed the importance of institutions, emphasizing the fundamental role of macroeconomic policies.)
3. Developmental states have been relatively adept at promoting structural change in the industrial economy because not only have they governed through participatory structures and negotiated major decisions, but they have also established agencies responsible for critical parts of decision-making, which operate at some distance from the political scene. Ultimately there is political responsibility for performance of these agencies, but there is also a consensus that certain things are done at some remove from the political process. Civil servants can nonetheless be impeached or prosecuted for mismanagement or breach of their duty.
4. The most evolved form can be found in Japan, for which Richard Samuels coined the term 'reciprocal consent'. My own term 'governed interdependence'

is designed to cover a larger number of cases, hence a broader spectrum of government–business interactions and their evolution over time. On the forms of GI applied to East Asia, see Weiss (1998: ch. 3; on Germany, see ch. 5).

5. The other major strand of the 'normalization' argument is the 'catch-up thesis'. Once catchup is achieved, it is anticipated by proponents of this thesis that the rationale for a production-enhancing project must collapse and, along with it, the underlying state machinery established to promote the catch-up process. For an elaboration and critique see Weiss (2000).

6. The changes occurred in conjunction with a larger government initiative to establish Taiwan as a leading financial centre for the region; all capital controls were to be removed by 2000. Since the 1997 crisis, however, this so-called APROC initiative has been placed on the backburner.

7. Woo argues that the move to liberalize finance was also impelled by the desire to avoid default and this became increasingly imperative as nonperforming loans soared in the 1980s (1991: 192).

8. Chang (1998) argues that the retreat of the state from investment coordination (i.e. industry policy) allowed 'excess capacities to emerge in industries like automobiles, ship-building, steel, petrochemicals and semiconductors, which eventually led to a fall in export prices and the accumulation of non-performing loans'.

9. Korea's external debt leapt from US$20.3 billion in 1979 to $40 billion in 1983. Already at the end of 1980, it ranked second after Brazil, the developing world's largest borrower (Woo, 1991: 181).

10. The relative weakening of the United States–Korea security relationship (see Note 12) was also a new element in the equation and goes some why to explaining why the United States did so little so late in meeting Korean cries for help in their efforts at crisis management. For an argument emphasizing the importance of changes in the United States–Korea security relationship, see Woo-Cumings (1998).

11. After Japan, South Korea rates second lowest in the world in attracting foreign investment. As a share of GDP, the figure for 1992–97 was 0.9 per cent (compared with Japan 0.1, China 12, Singapore 25.4 and the United States 4 per cent) (Myers, 1998: 5).

12. Weiss (1998: ch. 3); for the argument that core capacities can be recomposed, even after a lengthy period of submergence, see the analysis of postwar Germany (ch. 5).

13. On the range of measures being implemented to advance regionalism in East Asia since the financial crisis, see Fred Bergsten (2000).

10
Globalization and 'National Capitalism' in South Korea: Reconfiguring State–Capital–Labour Relations

Barry Gills and Dong-Sook Gills

Introduction

This chapter addresses the relationship between 'globalization', 'national capitalism', reform and democratization in South Korea. The focus of the analysis is on the changing configuration of state–capital–labour relationships in the dual transition from authoritarianism to democracy and from a developmental to a (neo)liberal state.

We adopt a neo-structuralist approach which places analytical emphasis on conjunctural moments where domestic class coalition and state form are transformed in response to key moments of change or 'structural opportunity' in the international political economic environment (see further Gills, 1994; Gills and Palan, 1994). Rather than adopting a 'country by country' approach which analyses a case study as if there were no external environment, we situate domestic change within a regional/international political economy setting to assess their co-determination.

In this framework, therefore, national capitalism is something of an illusion, if detached from a systemic or international context. To insist on the inseparability of any national variant of capitalism from the context of systemic international capitalism is not, however, to deny the existence of important national institutional variants in class and state configuration and concomitant national economic strategy. There are certainly important and distinctive characteristics which apply to the South Korean case, including: the developmental state; authoritarian political system; the political exclusion of organized labour and capital concentration in the form of the family empires or oligopolists known universally as the *chaebol* (loosely translated as 'financial clique').

Just as the origins of South Korean export-oriented industrialization, its developmental state and authoritarian military government arose in a conjunctural moment in the 1960s when the world economy was still expanding but undergoing restructuring towards a new international division of labour, so the emergence of the (neo)liberal and democratic state arises in the 1990s when the global economy has been undergoing further restructuring emphasizing far greater openness, understood under the rubric of 'globalization'.

Both 'transitions' imply important changes in state–capital–labour relations and in the ensemble of institutions and ideology that constitute the state form. However, this is a historically open and intensely political process, the outcome of which depends centrally on the course of class politics and the nature of the new dominant class coalition that emerges, if any.

The present government in South Korea represents a consolidation of the democratic reform impetus initiated by dissident social forces in the 1980s, bent on making a radical departure from the traditional power relationships of the developmental state era. President Kim Dae Jung aims to abandon the traditional state–capital alliance and replace the monopoly capitalism model of the developmental state with a competitive capitalism model aligned to the current global neo-liberal impetus. He seeks labour's incorporation and their support in his effort to use 'globalization' and the inherited economic crisis situation to force liberalization and restructuring on the powerful and reluctant *chaebol* empires.

To do this, he has deployed a hybridized mixture of democratic, neo-liberal, social-democratic and corporatist ideological elements. Kim Dae Jung's economic programme has led to a redeployment of state power towards re-regulation with the aim of fostering market competition and undermining traditional oligopolistic practices. The government has strengthened regulatory agencies such as the Financial Supervisory Commission, the Fair Trade Commission, the Economic Restructuring Agency, as well as the 'Tripartite Commission' which includes representatives of government, business and labour. The aim is to turn the old developmental state model on its head and foster a political economy characterized by domestic and international competition, openness and flexibility.

However, no element of the triad of state–capital–labour appears to be strong enough to go its own way and impose its will on the others. This situation of impasse, which has characterized South Korean internal social relations since the end of the 1980s, continues to hamper the prospects for further meaningful democratization and reform. The *chaebol* have resisted Kim Dae Jung's radical project of restructuring and continually sought to reconfigure the state–capital alliance in order to flexibilize labour domestically, while establishing freedom of manoeuvre to relocate production processes according to a global logic of profitability. Labour, on the other hand, has been both sceptical and receptive to the new government and its strategy of 'tripartism'. The labour movement is torn between the impulse to cooperate with government and business and seize the opportunity for political inclusion on the one hand, and the impulse to resist co-optation into neo-liberal globalization and the continuing mass lay-offs resulting from restructuring on the other. The fight for the rights of labour spills back onto the streets.

The impetus for change

While the *chaebol* had once been considered an asset for the disciplining of industrial investment and pursuit of international export advantages, by the mid-1990s they increasingly became a liability. The litany of *chaebol* sins included their ambitious but reckless investment strategies; antiquated management structures; confrontational industrial relations; private family financial control (albeit reduced to 15 per cent of total equities in the top 30 companies); risky financial practices; hidden debt structure and rent-seeking behaviour.[1]

Long-term national industrial health and economic growth were in question as capital fled from productive industrial investment into so-called '*Jai tech*', 'financialization' or speculation. Employment was threatened as companies increasingly sought to re-locate the production process abroad. The traditional strategy of growth first pursued by the government–*chaebol* alliance, which had involved government financial support for business, was plagued by increasing corruption and concomitant corporate debt, creating fundamental weaknesses in the national financial system.

Some South Korean economists have long argued that both constraints on the *chaebol* and the promotion of small- and medium-size enterprises were indispensable to establishing a pluralistic and competitive national economic structure. The precondition to achieve vigorous domestic competition and fair trade was the implementation of effective regulation to control monopolistic business behaviour. However, despite the existence of rules governing the establishment of cartels, many loopholes in the regulatory system allowed the *chaebol* to circumvent restrictions, especially in the finance and insurance sectors.[2] Furthermore, despite the regulatory focus on prevention of concentration, Korea lacked a direct and enforceable anti-monopoly or anti-trust law.

The impetus for change was not merely internal but involved a significant external influence. The post-Cold War era in Asia has been characterized by continuous pressure from the United States for accelerated market opening and economic liberalization (see Gills and Rocamora, 1992; Gills *et al.*, 1993; Gills, 1996, 1997, 2000). This pressure extended from industrial to financial liberalization and eventual full capital market opening. By the mid-1990s, South Korean economic officials routinely cited US demands as a key factor for the acceleration of economic liberalization.[3]

In an environment characterized by increasing emphasis on market opening, technological innovation and greater capital mobility, the strategic priority of 'growth first' demanded adjustments in order to sustain international competitiveness. In the case of South Korea, this implied moving towards a market-regulated economy rather than a state-regulated one. The renewed emphasis on international competitiveness also included a preference by capital for the flexibilization of labour. At the same time, with aspirations to join the WTO and OECD placed high on the agenda by the Kim Young Sam government (in the mid-1990s), the need to conform to prevailing international norms became much more urgent. However, serious social, economic and political problems have persisted which emanate from the legacy of decades of military rule.

Breaking the mould of the old state form would also imply breaking with its authoritarian power structures. Democratization is therefore a central aspect of the past decade of change in South Korea. Democratization in the South Korean context implies that the traditional 'growth first' model should be abandoned, accepting lower rates of growth in order to achieve other social goals. This is certainly not incompatible with the goal of business deconcentration, albeit that its goals are much broader than achievement of a competitive capitalism and may imply a social democratic model and an expansion of welfare spending by the state.

In South Korea's case, democratization also requires a new democratic industrial relations system. Labour–management relations under the prevailing *chaebol* system have been often characterized by hostility and confrontation. Government–business relations, though close in the past, have been marked by increasing pressure from business on the government to influence economic policy, posing problems of corruption and political paralysis. The weakening or breaking of the government–*chaebol* alliance should provide the political space for a new social alliance between government and labour in pursuit of broad reform and a new economic model. Did 'globalization' provide such an opportunity?

Segyehwa – globalization Korean style

In December 1994, the Kim Young Sam government announced the formal establishment of the Globalization Commission (*Segyehwa Ch'ujin Wiwonhoe*) Presidential order (no. 14504), and the commission was formed by 21 January 1995. President Kim Young Sam described globalization as a 'global trend' and an era characterized by 'a borderless global economy' in which 'room for asserting national sovereignty in economic affairs is sharply diminishing'.[4] He defined *Segyehwa* (globalization) to include: (1) economic reform to meet global standards of practice including transparency of all transactions, fair competition, deregulation of the financial sector and a fairer tax system; (2) industrial relations reform; (3) expansion of the social security system; (4) political reform towards a more open competitive system and (5) administrative reform.

Economic reform

The Kim Young Sam government rejected old principles of state regulation of the economy on the basis that they facilitated concentration and thereby hampered market competition, technological innovation and productivity gains.[5] His first policy initiatives focused on de-concentration, for example, the Real Name financial disclosure system (a reform which his predecessor Roh Tae Woo had abandoned), was based upon the view that 'insufficient controls on monopoly not only prevents successful anti-concentration policy, but limits the competitiveness of Korean enterprise against giant MNCs'.[6] The 1996 Globalization Commission report included measures for de-concentration, and acknowledged the 'need to prepare a legal foundation to prevent monopoly behaviour'.[7]

The initial anti-*chaebol* or deconcentration programme was met by a 'strike by capital'[8] which created a fear in the government of increased unemployment. It was clear that the business community sided with the argument of growth first rather than a priority on welfare, and they had supporters in the bureaucracy and even in the Presidential Secretariat.[9] The growth first camp favoured accession to the OECD in anticipation of enhancing competitiveness and absorbing foreign technologies. However, the idea of joining the OECD, which required acceptance of additional ILO conventions, promised an element of labour relations reform. While some understood this primarily as a matter of improving workers' welfare, others, especially *chaebol* elements, believed the key goal was to enhance Korea's international competitiveness by giving management increased power to discipline and flexibilize labour. Faced with strong resistance by the *chaebol*, President Kim Young Sam chose to restore business confidence and revive the investment climate.

This 'reverse course' demonstrated the increased power of business. This was further illustrated in business's impact on government policy regarding industrial relations reform. The price demanded by the *chaebol* for their cooperation with government included the removal of the Labour Minister, who was regarded as too 'liberal'. Thus, revision of the old authoritarian labour law, promised by the new government and demanded by labour, was deferred.

Industrial relations reform

The issue of labour reform has been a central part of the globalization agenda in Korea. From the government's point of view, there were two goals of labour reform: (1) to reduce the rigidity of the labour market, and (2) to bring Korea's labour practices up to international norms and ILO standards in preparation for OECD membership.[10] On 9 May 1996, a Presidential Commission on Industrial Relations Reform (PCIR) was established, including representatives from the two main Korean trade union federations, the FKTU and KCTU.[11]

However, as *segyehwa* policy reversed back to emphasis on growth first and flexibilization of labour, thus reactivating the government–*chaebol* alliance, organized labour, led by the KCTU, responded with a strong defence. The attempt to legislate flexibilization of labour further threatened the job security of a wide section of the working population, already made uneasy by lay-offs and downsizing, and a trend to impose early retirement or involuntary dismissal had reached even into the white collar and professional sectors of the economy. The KCTU declared a national strike in January 1997, mobilizing both unions and wide sections of civil society. A central goal of the KCTU was recognition of the right of full freedom of association for unions. The two-month period of the national strike was remarkable not only for the extent to which it sustained coordinated nationwide strike activity, but also for the amount of public sympathy it gathered, despite decades of anti-union sentiment in South Korean society.[12] This was possible through growing public awareness of the issues on which the strike was being fought.

The government, facing such a scale of public mobilization, agreed on 21 January to reopen debate on the revision of the labour law. The successful organization of such a prolonged and large-scale action itself was more significant than the outcome of reform of the labour law *per se*. Furthermore, it laid the foundation for organized labour to reconfigure the political terrain so that the role of labour as a partner in social reform is recognized.[13]

Expansion of social security

The substance of *segyehwa* in terms of expansion of social security was quite limited, and primarily oriented to achieving greater productivity in the private sector. For example, the promised extension of the social insurance and welfare system consisted of a modest expansion of coverage for the indigent.[14] The plan to increase public support for the socially marginalized relied largely on appeals for private sector involvement or self-help programmes.

The reforms in welfare and attempts to achieve social justice were insufficient in scope, depth and speed. The general failure of Kim Young Sam's social and welfare policy was related to the government's return to the policy of growth first. No consequential measures followed to support the announcement of the welfare state. ROK social welfare spending remained the lowest in the OECD except on education.[15] The failure to sufficiently expand the social safety net during the Kim Young Sam period left Korean workers badly exposed when the subsequent economic crisis in 1997/98 brought about high unemployment.

Kim Young Sam's *segyehwa* policy failed to make a clear strategic choice and therefore lost the opportunity for effective sequential reforms, such as deconcentration first (Gills and Gills, 1999, 2000). This exacerbated the fundamental structural weaknesses of the Korean economy. On the whole, *segyehwa* policy was more rhetorical than substantive, more of a slogan than a coherent policy. In hindsight, it resulted in missing the window of opportunity for timely reform at less cost to the Korean economy and society. The weakening of the state apparatus and the Presidency facilitated an increase in the power of capital, resulting in business overexpansion and eventual economic crisis.

From 'Segyehwa' to 'The Age of IMF'

In the autumn of 1997, there was an abrupt change in the national economic situation, turning sharply from growth to crisis. After a series of major Korean corporate bankruptcies and currency crises in Southeast Asia, South Korea entered a full scale financial crisis, revealing deep structural problems in the banking and corporate sectors. The crisis was suddenly exacerbated by an acute short-term credit crunch, as mobile capital fled from Korea, and by attacks on the value of the *won*.

In response, the government of South Korea struck a historic agreement with the International Monetary Fund (IMF) on 3 December 1997, on a $55 billion rescue package. The agreement stipulated far-reaching reforms in the financial sector, accelerated liberalization of trade and investment and radical corporate restructuring measures.[16] The IMF rescue package initially entailed sharp budget cuts, higher interest rates and taxation and reduced growth. Such deflationary measures set off economic contraction and a national unemployment crisis. The recessionary tendency was intensified by the consequent fall in domestic demand and the general economic downturn throughout Asia.

The dawning of the 'IMF *shidae*' (The Age of IMF) coincided with a historic political transition. Kim Dae Jung was the first opposition party candidate to be elected President of the Republic since its founding in 1948. He identified the source of the national crisis in the corrupt relationship between the government–*chaebol*–banking triad and the failure of the old state-led development model.[17] The Kim Dae Jung administration took the view that the IMF prescriptions for Korea were basically sound, but that there was a need to negotiate on certain parameters, such as the interest rate and the fiscal deficit.[18] The government embraced a neo-liberal free market philosophy in the area of finance and foreign investment. By shifting from heavy reliance on foreign debt to more foreign direct investment, South Korea would reduce its vulnerability to external shocks, ease the pressures of debt servicing, lower the domestic interest rate and the exchange rate, stimulate new corporate governance norms and attract new technology.[19]

In early 1998, Korea opened its capital market and real estate markets to foreign investment, and allowed mergers and even hostile takeovers by foreign firms, including in the financial sector. The successful renegotiation of short-term domestic banking debts of US$21.8 billion into long-term government-guaranteed loans in April 1998, alongside significant improvement in the current account balance and substantial increase in foreign reserves all contributed to a stabilization of the financial crisis by the end of May 1998. The exchange rate, which also stabilized, was now fully determined by the market.

The unemployment rate for the first quarter of 1999 was approximately 8.5 per cent, up from a mere 2 per cent prior to the crisis. Real wages had dropped by as much as 10 per cent by the end of 1998 compared to the previous year. Labour costs were reduced during the restructuring process, while in some cases, profits were up. This process extended even to the public sector, where, for example, as in the case of Korea Telecom (71 per cent government owned) the workforce was cut by 11 per cent in 1998 while operating profits jumped by 43 per cent.[20]

By late 1998, the government belatedly shifted to a somewhat more expansionary fiscal policy in an effort to stimulate domestic recovery and economic recovery began during the first half of 1999 (OECD, 2000c). The new government used the acute short-term financial crisis to bring about a radical deepening of economic liberalization. The combination of internal intervention via corporate reforms and restructuring and external intervention via market forces and foreign investment constitute the twin pillars of the new government's approach to economic reform.

Ending labour's alienation to the neo-liberal impetus of reforms, however, has proved far more problematic for the government. The key points of reform under Kim Dae Jung are 'to terminate government–business collusion, restructure the *chaebol*, recognize labour as a key factor in production, and bring labour into the policy making process'.[21] The public exposure of colossal corporate debts and mismanagement along with the critical attitude of the IMF towards Korea's major corporations and banks contributed to a weakening of the *chaebol*'s socio-political position. However, as in the past, the resistance of the *chaebol* to pressure for change remains considerable. They have a tendency to invoke economic nationalism to resist the forces of structural reform, especially when that pressure is perceived to come from abroad. In this nationalist stance, they have 'natural allies' in the economic bureaucracy, whose job it has been for several decades to pursue the goals of the developmental state.

With economic recovery the ability of the *chaebol* to resist restructuring has increased. They once again strengthened their centrality by buying up assets on a large scale.[22] Furthermore, the government's strategy of outflanking the *chaebol* via increased inward investment is only tentatively succeeding whilst inward flows remain low after the crisis. Further, where foreign interests threaten to acquire major companies, there is both a popular backlash and government reluctance to see this happen.

The IMF crisis presented South Korea with both a challenge and an opportunity. The national economic crisis made it explicit that cooperation between business, labour and government is an objective necessity. Kim Dae Jung's basic strategy, going under the slogan of 'Parallel Development of Democracy and Market Economy' is to combine accelerating market liberalization, deepening structural reforms and extending the democratization process. However, it has not been entirely clear what model the new government is attempting to follow; since it combines elements of neo-liberal market ideology, liberal democracy and corporatism.

Tripartite commission: the new Korean corporatism?

A central aspect of President Kim Dae Jung's reforms is the creation of a new national system of mediation and policy-making involving government, business and labour. Although there have been recent precedents such as the PCIR and the Labour Relations Commission (LRC), the Tripartite Commission (*No-Sa-Jong Wiwonhoe*), initiated by the new government on 15 January 1998, represents an attempt to bring labour into formal consultations and a further movement in the direction of abandoning the exclusion and subordination of labour. Based on the idea of an equal trilateral representation between government, business and organized labour, the Tripartite Commission embodies ideas of corporatism.

The tripartite system was contingent on certain expectations by each major party to the agreement. Unions aim to ensure that the adjustment to the national crisis occurs on the principle of 'fair burden sharing', requiring the corporate sector to make radical changes and accept responsibility for past mismanagement. It also seeks to establish its influence at national policy-making levels and win acceptance as a legitimate social partner.[23] The *chaebol*, on the other hand, seek to avoid social isolation and punitive government action, while pressing the case for business autonomy in the restructuring process and further flexibilization of the labour market. Government wants to construct a non-confrontational industrial relations system to protect the national interest and to use this as a vehicle to implement structural reforms throughout the economic system.

The issue of redundancy dismissals and unemployment quickly became and still remains at the heart of the confrontation. The companies' plans for massive redundancies for reasons of restructuring have been perceived by labour and business in diametrically opposed ways. Labour has viewed these measures as a one-sided shifting of the costs of adjustment onto workers and their families, without the restraint that both business and government had promised. Business has regarded these measures as both absolutely necessary on financial grounds and a matter for autonomous management decision-making without government interference. Government has accepted that redundancies are an inevitable aspect of economic restructuring, but emphasizes the need not only for economic restructuring but also for unemployment relief and increased public expenditure on the social safety net.

As the government pursues restructuring in order to discipline the *chaebol*, and public sector downsizing and privatization to achieve 'efficient' government, it exacerbates unemployment, thus undermining the basis for a new social and political coalition with labour. For example, the 'first phase' of financial restructuring in 1997–98, which involved extensive merger and downsizing, cost some 40000 jobs in the financial sector alone. 'Phase Two' of this process in 2000 threatens to cost thousands of further redundancies and has provoked resistance by the principal financial services union.

In the case of the industrial sector, the dismantling of Daewoo demonstrated the renewed power of government *vis-à-vis* the *chaebol* and the use of strong interventionist state policy to bring about a liberal economic order. Kim Dae Jung used the financial weakness of the Daewoo group (i.e. its huge private debts and impending threat of bankruptcy) to force negotiation with Daewoo's creditors under the direct arbitration of the FSC. The profound reorganization of Daewoo through leaner firms and allowing foreign acquisition of some elements inevitably induced job losses. The alienation of labour from economic restructuring undermines the basis of the tripartite formula.

The advent of the IMF crisis and its consequent high unemployment threatened to restore the power of business and the state over the unions. The first round of tripartite talks, which were conducted in the context of the initial national financial crisis, congealed with agreement on a trade-off between the interests of labour and business; bringing about revision of the labour laws in an extraordinary session of the National Assembly in February 1998. Organized labour reluctantly accepted legislation permitting redundancy dismissal for reasons of economic restructuring, but did so in exchange for an agreement that the *chaebol* would abide by the 'fair burden sharing' principle. Another way of saying this is that labour accepted reversal of a key gain made in the 1997 national strike (i.e. the moratorium on redundancy dismissals) in order to assist the new government of Kim Dae Jung in overcoming the financial crisis.

Throughout 1998 and early 1999, both labour and *chaebol* moved in and out of the Tripartite Commission. Both were dissatisfied with the progress of negotiations and looked to the government to take their side. By mid-March 1999, KCTU had taken the view that the Tripartite Commission had lost its function as a tool of social negotiation. In the spring of 1999, KCTU returned to militant tactics and initiated major strike and protest actions aimed at government restructuring policies and *chaebol* self-interest. Both FKTU and KCTU had earlier announced their intention to permanently abandon the Tripartite Commission framework if government and *chaebol* promises to labour were not kept. Labour demanded that the government punish business for 'unfair labour practices', as promised in the first round. Unions felt that the government had failed to carry out its promise and the Ministry of Labour was perceived to be indifferent.[24] Business, on the other hand, demanded punishment of labour for illegal strikes. In a bid to mollify labour, the government initiated special legislation which provided the Tripartite Commission with a firm legal basis. Nevertheless, by the end of 1999, organized labour warned the government that they would actively resist the drive to restructure public enterprises and the Daewoo corporate group. Labour lost much of its earlier enthusiasm for the new corporatism and shifted to direct political action. Besides strikes, the labour movement's most significant political effort has been the founding of a new labour-based political party and the fielding of labour candidates in the National Assembly elections in spring 2000.

Certainly, the pursuit of industrial restructuring by the government, in both the private and the public sector, has increased the level of antagonism between government and labour and therefore weakened the social base for the success of the new corporatism. There remains a profound conflict of interests between capital and labour at the very heart of the restructuring process. Without the *chaebol's* cooperation, the transition in South Korea, that is, the perceived transformation of the previous developmentalist variant of Asian capitalism and national capitalism may not be nearly as radical or complete as either labour or the government want it to be. Both labour and *chaebol* are alienated from the government and its neo-liberal economic policy. This impasse cannot be broken unless the state repositions itself in relation to one or both of the antagonists.

Conclusions

Globalization combines two contradictory tendencies. On the one hand it fosters increased competition, fragmentation and destabilization. On the other hand, these very same forces stimulate an opposite socio-political response, one that emphasizes social stability and cohesion, and perhaps democracy and welfare provision. The paradox of globalization is that it tends to weaken organized labour while at the same time strengthening labour's resistance and activism.

South Korea remains mired in the maelstrom of the politics of globalization. President Kim Dae Jung seized the opportunity of the financial crisis to redeploy state power towards the goals of corporate deconcentration, financial reform and economic restructuring. However, while these policies have been fairly successful to date in economic terms they are not fully supported by either big business or organized labour. The reforms undertaken by the Kim Dae Jung government during the two-year economic crisis of 1997/99 were significant enough to weaken the basis of the old state–capital alliance, but not robust enough, nor sufficiently supported by labour, to truly break the mould of the old system. In other words, it is indeed a breaking of the mould of the old developmental state to pursue corporate deconcentration, but this brings mass lay-offs and thus prevents the formation of a new government–labour alliance.

National consensus was short-lived during the height of the financial crisis and entrenched conflicts of interest between business, labour and government soon reasserted themselves. Kim Dae Jung's reassertion of state power puts the government on collision course with both *chaebol* and labour unions, thus alienating both. Therefore, the political position of the Kim Dae Jung government and its neo-liberal reforms is a weak one. The popular impression of the reform process is likewise fairly negative as the general public perceives that there is a lack of substantive political change.

The pursuit of neo-liberal globalization seems to be in conflict with the simultaneous pursuit of democratic deepening and greater social inclusion. The contradiction between neo-liberal globalization and democratization is thus a central aspect of the new 'national capitalism' in South Korea. In South Korea, much remains to be done to overcome this conflict between economic globalization and democratic consolidation. In particular, it requires providing social justice for labour as well as establishing new regulations for capital. Nevertheless, the advent of the IMF crisis and its consequent high unemployment threatened to restore the power of business and the state over the unions.

The Kim Young Sam government's failure to tackle Korea's deep structural problems in good time revealed the underlying vulnerability of the economy, exposing it to increased external risk. The failure to sufficiently prepare the social safety net left workers and society in a very exposed position when the economic system entered full-scale crisis in late 1997. The direct intervention of outside actors such as the IMF set a new agenda which has resulted in rapid rather than gradual adjustment, in a context of serious economic contraction and spiralling unemployment. The two-year 1997–99 economic crisis brought about a situation in which the state and society could no longer ignore the need for reform, including the inclusion of labour in the policy-making process and the expansion of the social safety net. By mobilizing such social opposition globalization may undermine the basis for its own expanded reproduction in social relations.

Notes

1. Personal interview with Kim Jun II, Senior Counsellor to the Deputy PM, Minister of Finance and Economy, Kwachon, Korea, 26 August 1997.
2. Personal interview with You Jong Keun, Economic Adviser to the President, Seoul, 14 August 1998.
3. Personal interviews, various ministries of the government of the Republic of Korea, summer 1994.
4. 'Explanatory notes on President Kim Young Sam's Blueprint for the *Segyehwa* Policy, in *The Segyehwa Policy of Korea under President Kim Young Sam*, Korean Overseas Information Service, Seoul, Korea July 1995, pp. 7–16, p. 7 and see also the Globalisation Commission Report, 1995, pp. 3–19.

5. *Segyehwa chujin chonghap bogoso* (Globalisation Commission Comprehensive Report) Globalisation Commission, 1997, Seoul, p. 345.
6. Ibid., p. 346.
7. It cited evidence that 'Until 1994, 117 cases which breached the controls on economic concentration, and 76 cases of improper internal trade, contrasted to only three cases of industrial combination. *Kyongjaeng chokjin ul wihan Kongjong korae jedo kaeson bang-an* (Improvement plan for the fair trade system for promotion of competition), 1996, *Segyehwa chujin chonghap bogoso* (Globalisation Commission Comprehensive Report) Globalisation Commission, 1997, Seoul, p. 345.
8. In the first quarter of 1993 investment in machine facility dropped by 12.4 per cent, following a drop in the previous quarter of 10.2 per cent, the lowest levels in three decades. This situation continued into the second quarter of 1993 and overall economic growth fell to 3.4 per cent, the lowest since the severe recession of 1980–81.
9. Personal interview with Park Jin, Political Adviser to the President, Blue House, Seoul, 22 August 1997.
10. Personal interview with Cho Won Dong, Policy Planning Staff, Blue House, Seoul, 28 August 1997.
11. The Federation of Korean Trade Unions is the officially recognized peak organization. It has a reputation for moderation and 'bread and butter' unionism. The Korean Confederation of Trade Unions was formed in November 1995, as an illegal rival national confederation, composed of 'democratic' trade unions espousing a broad social agenda.
12. Personal interview with Kwon Young Gil, President of KCTU, Seoul, 22 August 1997.
13. Ibid.
14. The Globalisation Commission Report 1996, p. 536, provides figures on extension of coverage for minimum income support to the indigent from 70 per cent to 80 per cent by 1996, and 90 per cent by 1997 and 100 per cent by 1998.
15. Ibid.
16. 'Seoul, IMF Agree on $55 billion in Bailout Loans' Newsreview, 26(49), 6 December 1997, pp. 12–15.
17. Challenge and Chance: Korea's Response to the New Economic Reality', Ministry of Finance and Economy, Overall Economic Policy Division, ROK, June 1998, pp. 1–2.
18. Personal interview with You Jong Keun, Seoul, Korea, 14 August 1998; Personal interview with Kim Tae Dong, Chief Secretary to the President for Policy Planning, Chongwadae, Seoul, Korea, 12 August 1998.
19. Personal interview with Kim Tae Dong.
20. 'Korea Telecom's Profit Soars After Cost-Cutting Moves', International Herald Tribune, 5 March 1999, p. 17.
21. Choi Jang Jip, 'Korea's Political Economy: Search for a Solution', Korea Focus, 6(2), March–April 1998, Korea Foundation, pp. 1–20, p. 15.
22. Don Kirk 'Korean Companies Cooling to Foreign Investors', *International Herald Tribune*, 3–4 July 1999, p. 9. Investment trust companies owned by *chaebol* have been 'powering the market' in Korea, where stock market prices have been soaring and trading has reached record levels. In June 1999, the *chaebol* funds were net buyers of 2.58 trillion won of stock on the Seoul exchange. All other major categories of players, including securities firms, corporations and individuals were net sellers. The market had one of its heaviest trading days in history on 2 July,

reaching $4.25 billion in a single day. Foreign players are also poised to rush back into Asian stock markets (including 'emerging' ones) just as rashly and heavily as they left them precisely two years ago as this is written. Indeed, they are over-valuing these assets as the rush sets in. See Philip Segal, 'Asian Tigers Bare Their Claws Again: Stocks Are at Pre-Crisis Levels, but Rally's Strength Questioned', *International Herald Tribune*, 8 July 1999, p. 1.

23. Personal interview with Ahn Pong Sul, International Relations Bureau, FKTU, Seoul, 3 August 1998.
24. KBS Report, statement by Lee Yong Bom, spokesman for the Tripartite Commission, 31 July 1998.

11
Comparing National Capitalisms[1]
Hugo Radice

Introduction

Amid the strong continuing interest in comparing national capitalisms, there has been little reflection by 'comparativist' writers on the concepts, theories and methods that they deploy.[2] The aim of the present chapter is to open up a debate on these matters. The chapter looks first at the analytical approaches that underlie the specification of national models of capitalism, and the purposes with which such comparisons are made. Second, it examines the varieties of institutionalist thinking that have been prominent in the analysis of different models of capitalism and goes on to examine in particular the analysis of institutional change. Finally, it focuses on two particular potential sources of institutional change that are highlighted by current debates, globalization and the reorganization of production.

National models of capitalism

The delineation of distinct national models of capitalism is basically a taxonomic approach, in which a generic model of capitalism is refined by further specification of particular features. These features are usually defined in terms of the embodiment of generic concepts such as 'property' or 'labour' in particular organizations and practices.[3] While taxonomic approaches may sometimes purport to be atheoretical and descriptive, the choice of which features are subject to further specification is itself informed by the particular theoretical framework underlying the taxonomy. Thus, the traditional Marxist–Leninist distinction between the competitive, monopoly and (for some analysts) state-monopoly stages of capitalism (see e.g. Baran and Sweezy, 1966; Mandel, 1968; Palloix, 1971) singles out the nature of market competition and price formation as the chief *differentia specifica* of the capitalist mode of production as a whole, and has focused on the ways in which changes in the nature of capitalist markets lead to far-reaching changes in the overall political economy, including accumulation patterns, crises, the state and the world economy. This particular Marxist approach is also explicitly historicist, in that the identified variants are seen as a historical sequence.

However, many institutionalist economists and economic sociologists have presented very different taxonomies, centering on the mechanisms which govern individual economic transactions; for example, the distinction between market and hierarchy[4] (Williamson, 1975) abstracts from historical context and makes patterns of economic behaviour the central differentiated feature, rather than the 'macro' political economy. A third approach is the related but more structural distinction between 'Anglo-Saxon' and 'Rhineland' or 'organized' capitalisms (Albert, 1993; see also the more complex classification of 'business systems' offered by Whitley, 1994; Hutton, 1995). However, it should be noted that many of the key themes of capitalist structures and processes that are studied in the various taxonomic frameworks are still studied far more often without such a framework (see e.g. Zukin and DiMaggio, 1990).

Our present concern is with the identification and comparison of national models of capitalism. In many respects, this is closely related to the identification of generic models such as Anglo-Saxon capitalism, because these are usually illustrated by specific national cases (in this case Britain, the United States, New Zealand, etc.). The great advantage of using nationality as the focus of differentiation is precisely that it permits hypotheses of difference to be 'proved' by the existence of concrete national cases; the approach thereby conforms to the dominant empiricist tradition in English-language social sciences. The capitalist world is self-evidently divided into territorially separated units which exhibit specificities of location, resources, culture and history. The Westphalian principles of sovereign statehood have led to differences in economic and political practice being encased in constitutional and legal differences centred on the modern nation state, and many aspects of the interstate system have evolved precisely to deal with the resulting separations and differentiations. Most quantitative economic and social data are collected and aggregated on a national basis, so that nations appear to be automatically endowed with those system features and performance characteristics that are susceptible to numerical expression: for example, data on market structure, occupational patterns, forms of financial intermediation or economic growth rates. In addition, policy debates on questions of international economic integration, competition for world markets and the regulation of the world economy provide further emphasis on the political economy of the nation state. In short, the principle of sovereign statehood underpins an implicit definition of capitalism as a system divided into distinct national capitalisms, or what may be termed the 'billiard-ball' model of global capitalism.

It is clearly possible to study the comparative performance of national capitalisms without reference to national differences in institutions and practices. Most economists, especially econometricians, either implicitly or explicitly adopt the 'black box' approach in which firms, households, governments and other 'economic actors' are treated as mechanisms for transforming inputs into outputs in accordance with given behavioural principles. Poor performance in a particular observed variable, for example, slow growth or excessive inflation, is attributed through multivariate statistical analysis to one or more other observed variables, such as the savings ratio or wage increases. Non-quantifiable institutional or behavioural differences can be crudely included as dummy variables, or brought in as supplementary causes in a discursive analysis of unexplained variance. However, half a century of econometric work seems to have done little to resolve fundamental disagreements about how the mechanisms connecting economic variables are specified, as Ormerod (1994) among many others has made clear. Hence, just as economic analysts of the firm went 'inside the black box' in developing behavioural and managerial theories in the 1960s, so analysts of the macroeconomy turned to more sociological and historical approaches, a classic example being Shonfield (1965).[5]

More recently, the comparison of national capitalisms has typically entailed judgements about the consequences of different models, especially in synchronic comparisons. A normative dimension characterizes not only the more popular interventions of Reich (1992), Albert (1993) or Hutton (1995) but also much of the more academic research literature. While US academics looked enviously at Japanese success in the 1980s, their British counterparts looked more often at Germany: all sought to identify the causes of superior performance with the aim of learning lessons that could then be applied 'at home'. Although some social science traditions differentiate sharply between 'positive' or 'scientific' analysis and normative analysis, this is a rule which is often either honoured in the breach, or explicitly dismissed because it makes impossible demands on the practitioner as human subject.[6] If a normative project is recognized as legitimate, however, there are still formidable obstacles to its full implementation, for in so far as the causes of performance differences are identified as institutional, it is then necessary to find ways in which institutional change can be promoted and achieved. While the simple answer to this is that in a liberal democratic political system, proposals for institutional change can be adopted in the electoral and legislative programmes of political parties, it is evident that such proposals in practice have to be recognized and accepted within the existing institutions themselves. In order to explore more fully the question of continuity and change in national models, it is clearly necessary to look at how institutions are analyzed in the comparative literatures.

Varieties of institutionalism

It is commonly agreed among those who compare national capitalisms that institutional differences are persistent as well as pervasive. In contrast to the individualist assumptions that have dominated conventional economics, most traditions in social science hold that the patterns of thought and action that are present in the behaviour of individuals are social in nature. In this view, institutions are fields of human action where structure and agents interact: realms of immediate context in which individual behaviour is 'embedded', but which, taken together, form the building-blocks of broader social structures and social forces.[7]

Within economics, the term 'institutionalism' is hotly contested. The 'new institutionalists' acknowledge as their founder Coase (1937), who famously asked why, if markets were so efficient at coordinating the economic behaviour of individuals, we needed to have firms at all. From this insight stemmed the modern transactions–costs approach, whose leading practitioner has been Oliver Williamson (e.g. 1975), in which individuals are viewed as choosing the most resource-efficient coordination mechanism, which *ceteris paribus* means the one that minimizes the cost of transactions. Closely related to this approach, especially in its individualist methodology, is agency theory, which focuses on the difficulty that principals have in ensuring contractual compliance by their agents (e.g. employers seeking extract the work effort they expect from employees). For new institutionalists, economic behaviour in the real world has intrinsic features that are absent in the theoretical abstractions of neoclassical economics, notably incomplete information, bounded rationality and irreversibility. Institutions such as capitalist firms, trade unions, central banks or the IMF arise because of these deficiencies: they represent, in a sense, the outcome of the efforts of rational economic (wo)man to pursue self-interest in a world that is ill-suited to the purpose.

The transactions–cost and principal–agent approaches to institutions have been subject to severe criticisms, perhaps most fully by Dietrich (1994). From our point of view, the principal weakness is that they are 'micro-institutionalist', ahistorical and methodologically individualist. They focus on individual decisions that shape institutional forms, rather than on the overall 'macro'-institutional configurations that constitute national capitalisms; they treat the parameters of institutional choice as unchanging; and they take as given the motivational basis of these decisions. The rise and fall of institutions is seen in terms of a crude model of natural selection, in which a meta-market in institutions ensures the elimination of inefficient ones and the survival of those that are most compatible with the efficient pursuit of individual economic self-interest.

The economic historian Douglass North has struggled hard to escape from these limitations. Agreeing (notably in North, 1990) that institutions exist to economize on transactions costs, and that they have a fundamental determining effect on the economic performance of societies, he accepts that, in a given society, institutions that hold back economic performance may embody constraints on behaviour which block institutional change: in other words, there is path-dependence, and there is no guarantee that more efficient institutions will 'naturally' emerge. Nevertheless, this is history written by the victorious, for throughout the work, it is clear that for North, efficient institutions are those which most clearly define and enforce individual property rights, and that modern 'Western' societies have risen to economic pre-eminence on the basis of continuous improvements in this regard. The eventual outcome seems to offer little advance on the congratulatory pronouncements of earlier modernization theorists such as Rostow (1960).

Overall, the strength of new institutionalist economics is that it provides a framework within which differences in particular institutions, such as those providing corporate governance or national monetary regulation, can be studied. But the narrow economism of this framework, and the limitations of methodological individualism, render it inadequate from the standpoint of a more complete comparative analysis. In contrast, the 'old institutionalist' economists form a heterodox tradition going back to Veblen and Commons, which has always challenged the individualism and reductionism of the orthodoxy. Alongside a self-defined group of mainly American economists who publish the *Journal of Economic Issues*, others acknowledging this tradition, to a greater or lesser degree, include Hodgson (e.g. 1988) and Nelson and Winter (e.g. 1982). In this approach, the pursuit of economic self-interest is only one element in the relation between the individual and society, and its role within society is properly to be regarded as historically and politically contingent. The importance of institutions for these writers is that they embody continuities, including values and routines, that provide necessary context and meaning to economic action; and whereas for their new institutionalist adversaries institutional change is ultimately at the service of a preordained economic rationality, for 'old' institutionalists the dominance of this economic rationality is itself the outcome of a clash of social interests.

The collection edited by Zukin and DiMaggio (1990) demonstrates that economic sociology also offers a rich tradition of institutional analysis.[8] They identify a 'paradigm crisis of neoclassical economics' (1990, p. 3) arising from critiques of its concept of rational behaviour, its theory of the firm and its equilibrium models of the macroeconomy, which has led to increasing interest in organizations, institutions and social structures as keys to understanding the realities of economic life. They place particular importance on the idea of embeddedness, which in the case of economic actions has four distinct dimensions. First, it is *cognitive* in the sense that 'the structured regularities of mental processes limit the exercise of economic reasoning' (ibid., pp. 15–16): this underlies key concepts such as 'bounded' and 'procedural' rationality. Second, it is *cultural*, which refers to 'the role of shared collective understandings in shaping economic strategies and goals' (ibid., p. 17). Third, it is *structural*, meaning 'the contextualization of economic exchange in patterns of ongoing interpersonal relations': in this context 'structure' refers to 'the manner in which dyadic relations are articulated with one another' (ibid., p. 18), and it is implied that economic behaviour varies significantly according to its social or structural context. Finally, embeddedness is *political*, in that 'economic institutions and decisions are shaped by a struggle for power that involves economic actors and nonmarket institutions, particularly the state and social classes' (ibid., p. 20). According to Zukin and DiMaggio, this many-sided concept of embeddedness allows the integration of political-economic approaches rooted in structural determinations, with social-organizational approaches that allow the full appreciation of how these determinations are realized in the concrete outcomes of economic behaviour. In particular, they claim that the approach exemplified in the essays in their volume is much better suited than that of neoclassical economics for the analysis not only of variety in economic organization, but also of change.

In political science too, varieties of institutionalist thinking have come to the fore in recent years, fully surveyed by Peters (1999). According to Peters, in the 1950s and 1960s, older traditions that could be described as institutionalist – in particular, legalist and historicist traditions – were widely supplanted in political science by the behavioural and rational choice approaches, which shared the theoretical foundations of positivism and methodological individualism (Peters, 1999: ch. 1). The various new institutionalisms all see institutions as structural features of society that transcend and shape individual political behaviour, providing continuities and transmitting shared norms and values. Peters identifies seven types of institutionalism in political science, many of them closely related to elements of the economics and sociology literatures discussed already. Of particular interest is the school of 'historical institutionalism', which emphasizes the path-dependent nature of institutions, and thereby focuses attention on why and how institutions evolve and change; and 'international institutionalism', by which Peters means the delineation and analysis of structural constraints upon the international behaviour of both state and non-state actors (as in regime theory).

From the standpoint of comparing national capitalisms, the extent of an institutionalist common ground within the social sciences is striking. Institutionalist arguments validate the identification of distinct varieties of capitalism, and provide a powerful rationale for seeking to relate economic performance to the identified national (or generic) differences in institutions. However, the logical consequence of such analyses – to plan and implement institutional change in order to improve some aspect or aspects of economic performance – is rendered problematic, because in these diverse literatures, the stress on institutional embeddedness and path-dependence makes it hard to theorize institutional change.

Principles of institutional change

How then do models of capitalism change? Do they change from without or within and if the latter, how do particular individuals or groups surmount the path-dependence and 'lock-ins' of 'institutionalized' societies? From a historical point of view, it seems clear that many discontinuities in what would otherwise be incremental change (or none at all) arise from exogenous forces. Conquest typically entails the imposition of institutions and practices transferred from the victors: for example, the transfer of British legal and administrative systems to the colonies, or the deliberate reconstruction of economic, political and social institutions in the Axis powers by the victorious Allies after 1945. More recently, the Bretton Woods institutions were restructured in the 1980s in pursuit of solutions to the debt crisis of less-developed countries; within little more than a decade, this had led in turn to the imposition of new policy priorities, instruments and outcomes on governments all over the world, and thereby to significant institutional change. The problem is that, as the 'international institutionalists' discussed by Peters (1999) would put it, these processes of change that are exogenous to most individual national capitalisms, are *endogenous* to world capitalism as a whole, and have their real origin in specific countries (in this case, the United States and to a lesser extent Britain).

In so far as institutional change is endogenous to a particular national model, one general source of change – and one that appeals especially to those who favour a 'biological' approach to social analysis – is the institutional variety that often lies concealed behind such models. For example, British trade unionism remains characterized by considerable variety even today in fundamental features such as membership criteria, in strong contrast to the institutional simplicity of the German union system. Even institutional sub-systems that are strongly prescribed by formal legal rules, like fiscal systems or corporate governance, are often differentiated in their application. If our definition of institutions includes informal practices and 'routines', norms and values, variety will be still more in evidence. In this case, it is possible to argue that broader institutional change may result from a shift in the balance between sub-national variants: for example, the weakening of national collective bargaining in many countries is seen in part as linked to a continuing shift in employment patterns from manufacturing towards service sectors which have traditionally been characterized by different forms of labour management. In this case the ultimate source of change is exogenous not to the country, but to the institutional system as such: the implication is that technological or social changes require institutional adaptation, analogous to the crude Darwinian model of species adaptation to environmental change. The difficulty here (which parallels the objections of holistic ecologists to crude Darwinism) is that it is very hard to set boundaries between 'the institutions' and 'the environment'.[9]

A further source of change results from interactions between national models of capitalism, or their interpenetration. In so far as companies, for example, conform to the institutional matrix of their country of origin, foreign direct investments (or indeed international trade) will bring them face to face with different institutions and require a measure of adaptive behaviour; in addition, observation of institutional differences that seem to explain superior performance may lead to emulation by companies elsewhere. The recent literature on 'Japanization' illustrates both routes, with the transmission, *mutatis mutandis*, of Japanese methods of organizing production to other countries both through Japanese outward FDI and through deliberate innovation in other countries.[10]

While it is one thing to model the *process* of change, it is however quite another to understand or predict its direction. Historical-institutionalist approaches seek to explain institutional changes (and continuities) by identifying causal sequences. These sequences can be cut short at decisive moments of discontinuity, identifying, for example, a decisive political response to a new and unexpected event or trend. This response in turn typically results from the mobilization of specific social interests, which draws many social scientists towards broadly social-structural explanations of change. This is clearly the position shared by most of the sociologists contributing to Zukin and DiMaggio (1990), and many of the 'historical institutionalists' surveyed by Peters (1999); it is also perfectly compatible with the depiction of actual moments of change in terms of transactions–costs or rational–choice institutionalism. But if they are to provide the basis for predictive modelling, such 'social-structural' explanations have to be rooted in a social theory that accounts consistently for the most far-reaching historical transformations – the Braudelian *longue durée*.[11] As Cammack (1992) argues in his critical review of institutionalism in comparative politics, institutionalism '... cannot of itself provide the basis for a theory of long-run social change' (1992, p. 398).

What this points to is the need for those making comparisons between national capitalisms, with a view to promoting institutional change, to make more explicit their understanding of 'historical capitalism' as a system. Maier (1987) has suggested that only a 'historical political economy' can provide an effective framework for analyzing changes in such key aspects of capitalism as the scope and role of the state. In that vein, we now turn to examine two major social trends that have been widely promoted as sources of institutional change: globalization and changes in production systems.

Sources of change: globalization and the reorganization of production

Globalization may be defined as the expansion and deepening of cross-border economic, political, social and cultural transactions. Whether these very diverse and unevenly developed phenomena deserve to be recognized as a coherent and fundamental change in the nature of capitalism remains a matter of fierce dispute, but there is no doubting the growing importance since the 1960s of international trade, foreign investments, global finance, regional integrations, transnational organizations both inter-governmental and non-governmental, global communications systems and so on.[12] Since these cross-border transactions typically connect institutions that have evolved to varying degrees within distinct national capitalisms, it is natural to expect a progression from the mutual recognition of differences to the identification of potential gains from institutional adaptation.

Drawing on arguments in the previous section, the natural selection approach offers the most forthright argument in this respect: interaction sets in train competition between institutional forms at the global level, and successful forms replace unsuccessful ones leading to a trend of institutional convergence. The (re)imposition of political or economic hegemony, as in restoration of capitalism in the former Soviet bloc, offers a 'macro' example of this, while the recent spread of Anglo-Saxon practices of corporate governance in continental Europe is a more 'micro' case. Considerable efforts have been devoted to charting the origins and evolution of national differences across a great variety of institutional subsystems, such as training and education, finance, innovation, industrial relations, legal and governmental systems, and many authors have identified aspects of globalization as a force for convergence. The introductions to collections such as Hollingsworth et al. (1994), Berger and Dore (1996), Crouch and Streeck (1997) and Hollingsworth and Boyer (1997) all comment on this issue, while Kenworthy (1997) makes a brave attempt to review a wide range of economic data for evidence of convergence.[13]

However, debates on this question are marred by the lack of a shared understanding of the relation between national capitalisms and the world economy as a whole – that is, about the nature and meaning of globalization.[14] Many writers analyze this relation in terms of structural oppositions between market and state, and between national and global. Globalization is identified, by both supporters and critics, as a neo-liberal project, centred on 'rolling back' the state and restoring the free play of market forces at the global level: if you are opposed to the exploitation and inequality that has historically resulted from unfettered capitalism, then you should defend the sovereign nation state as the main site of resistance. This argument depends, however, on accepting a liberal or pluralist theory of the capitalist state, as either standing outside 'capitalism as such', or as 'holding the ring' between the contending social interests which form the primary structural feature of capitalist economies. It also depends upon accepting the view of the world economy as the aggregation or interrelation of national capitalisms. On the other hand, a class analysis of the state coupled with an understanding of global capitalism as a system in its own right leads to a very different understanding of globalization: as an ideology of the restructuring of the state and of major institutions of capitalism that takes place simultaneously at national and global levels.

From this standpoint, institutional change in particular national capitalisms is not just the outcome of a battle between external social forces and resistance founded on internal state – society linkages; nor is the outcome one of the disappearance or persistence of national specificities. Rather, it is about the reconfiguration of patterns of similarity and difference. Partly, this is because not all sorts of transactions can be freely made across boundaries in our supposedly liberal-globalized world: notably, the movement of people is severely restricted, and as a result institutions based upon citizen participation, such as civic associations of all kinds, trade unions, and so on do not experience the high levels of cross-border contact and influence that we observe, say, in stock markets. Partly, this is also because – as institutionalists have emphasized – path-dependence implies a great deal of institutional inertia and resistance to change, while at the same time there are very diverse and unevenly available opportunities for institutional innovation which may or may not be seized by particular social groups: an example is the way in which religious organizations can exploit changes in circumstances to reconstruct belief-systems around principles of ethnic or national exclusivity. But partly the reconfiguration is complex because global capitalism is founded upon enormous, and in many respects still growing, inequalities between as well as within regions and nations. Greatly different socioeconomic circumstances, for example, in life expectancy, living standards and literacy, are bound to be associated with substantial differences in institutional forms. And last but not least, there are equally great differences in the extent and character of resistance to capitalism's economic, social and environmental depredations.

Turning now to the reorganization of production, the phenomena highlighted by various theses on post-Fordism have been seen as providing a powerful source of institutional change. The collection by Hollingsworth and Boyer (1997) represents the meeting of two distinct schools of thought on these matters, the American 'social structures' approach and the French Regulation School. In Hollingsworth and Boyer's formulation (1997: ch. 1), social structures of production are made up of a range of institutions which cohere at national or regional level as a 'complex social configuration ... which usually exhibits some degree of adaptability to new challenges, but continues to evolve within an existing style' (p. 2). Central to their application of this approach is the view, drawn from the post-Fordism literatures, that there has been a significant shift from mass production systems to flexible ones, and that these flexible production systems – unlike their mass predecessors – require 'an institutional environment in which collective forms of coordination are highly developed' (p. 24), particularly based on the nurturing of trust between economic actors.

Views along these lines have become widespread since the 1980s, when the stronger performance of more corporatist or organized capitalisms in continental Europe and Japan encouraged British and American social scientists to take up such post-Fordist thinking as the basis for challenging neo-liberalism. Whether the ultimate source of such changes towards flexible production systems lies in new technologies, in changes in consumer tastes or in a capitalist offensive against the wage and welfare gains of labour,[15] the response of critics of neo-liberalism has been to look for institutional innovations that could provide an alternative 'social configuration' which would be both more effective in terms of aggregate production and welfare, and more egalitarian and democratic. In the context of Hollingsworth and Boyer's emphasis on national difference in social structures of production, this leads to a research programme aimed at identifying national (or regional) varieties of flexible production systems, uncovering how such differences are related to each national (or regional) social structure of production, and then designing appropriate alternatives centred on a greater role for non-market coordination and on more egalitarian policy objectives.

In the light of earlier discussion on institutional change and on globalization, there are grounds for scepticism about this programme. Empirically, it is difficult to establish the nature of these new flexible production systems as compared to earlier systems, and the extent to which they have been adopted. In so far as they have been *adapted* to fit particular national contexts, the result is a new taxonomic exercise[16] which serves inevitably to demonstrate the continued importance of national differences. But in the political-economic circumstances of globalization, it is highly questionable how far this process of adaptation (whether it is in a more egalitarian/progressive direction or not) is actually directed by national social forces: not only do the interests of capital predominate in the lobbies and legislation of the nation state, but in addition globalization is reflected in a new policy agenda for capital which is intrinsically inimical to coherent national or regional economic development. The clearest example of this concerns the policy programme around the promotion of industrial districts. In Britain, this would require a substantial devolution of fiscal and regulatory powers to the local level, going completely against the grain of economic and political centralization favoured by big business: there is no sign that the political devolution moves of the Blair government are anything more than a minimal response to the modest electoral threat of Celtic nationalism.

Conclusion

This chapter has suggested a number of issues of theory and method that need further exploration if comparative studies of national capitalisms are going to yield analytical insights about processes of change in contemporary capitalism. In particular, I have argued that these studies are founded upon a variety of institutionalist approaches that have developed or redeveloped in the social sciences in recent years. While some of these approaches remain rooted in methodological individualism, others offer fruitful ways of understanding the evolution of national institutions, but still need to be located within a broader framework of the dynamics of historical capitalism. The need for deeper theoretical clarification is demonstrated by the ambiguous results of recent explorations of globalization and the reorganization of production as social trends shaping present-day institutional change.

Notes

1. This chapter is part of an ongoing study on the political economy of globalization. Some aspects of the chapter, particularly of the section, 'Principles of institutional change' are examined at greater length in Radice (2000b). I am grateful to the participants at the PERC Conference for their comments on the original version.
2. For exceptions see Hollingsworth *et al.* (1994: ch. 1), Dore (1996), Wilkinson (1996), Crouch and Streeck (1997) and Strange (1997).
3. As a result, taxonomic analyses might be seen as intrinsically 'institutionalist', but as we will see in the Section, 'Varieties of institutionalism' this term itself needs to be investigated further.
4. Hollingsworth *et al.* (1994: ch. 1) add three more coordination mechanisms: networks, associations and the state.
5. There may of course be some system features that are essentially the same in different models, but which are 'operated' more effectively for non-systemic reasons. A conventional economist might argue that the same monetary policy institutions and instruments would yield superior results if key decision-makers were properly trained in economics. On the other hand, the lack of proper training may itself be traced to national institutional or cultural deficiencies, as exemplified in this case by the timeworn criticisms of Britain's 'amateur' Treasury mandarinate.
6. There has been a lively debate on this issue in the 1990s in the field of international relations, critically reviewed by Smith (1996).
7. The anthropologist Radcliffe-Brown defines an institution as 'an established norm of conduct recognised as such by a distinguishable social group or class of which it is therefore an institution' (1952, p. 10).
8. The fact that they do not explicitly use the term 'institutionalism' perhaps reflects the fact that the dominant traditions in classical sociology (and anthropology) were intrinsically institutionalist.
9. This point is explored in more detail in Radice (2000b), Section III.
10. The diffusion of business practices (in either direction) through foreign direct investment has been researched in the field of human resource management in particular: see Ferner and Quintanilla (1998).
11. An excellent illustration of this is Germain (2000), who offers a Braudelian perspective on globalization.
12. A comprehensive review of both these phenomena and of competing explanations of them is provided by Held *et al.* (1999).
13. Radice (1998) reviewed empirical evidence on finance, innovation and corporate governance.
14. The following points are explored much more fully in Radice (2000a).
15. These three factors form the basis of the three varieties of post-Fordist theory reviewed by Elam (1990).
16. This reaches its most baroque form in Lipietz (1997).

12
So Where are National Capitalisms Now?

Jonathan Perraton and Ben Clift

Let us recall that the stiff task set for contributors to this volume was to consider the following questions:

- How far do existing models of national capitalism (chiefly, Anglo-Saxon, Rhineland, East Asian) remain accurate characterizations of national economies?
- How can we analyze the impact of international integration on national models of capitalism beyond simply asking whether convergence is inevitable?
- How have different countries responded to the ways in which international integration has changed the relative costs of different policy options?

We further asked the contributors to consider which institutional features of their countries were regarded as central around 1980. These questions raise key points for the debates over national capitalisms. First, whilst the institutional differences between national economies are typically identified as being embedded and enduring, many of the features identified as central to national models have changed substantially over the past two decades. Second, it has been claimed that international competition and increased international factor mobility – globalization, for short – will lead to countries converging on a single model. Typically, this is predicted to be to a neo-liberal version of the Anglo-Saxon model, although other putative end-points have been proposed. Third, and related to the second point, whilst globalization may not completely determine policy choice it can substantially alter the costs of particular policy options. Stated as such this may sound reasonable, but it fails to provide much insight. Fourth, it is of little use simply to say that the institutional structures of economies arise slowly from their societies – from decades or even centuries of history – and those lessons are often specific to time and place. We should aim to draw more general conclusions from comparative research.

In the next section, we provide a necessarily brief account of institutionalist accounts and economic performance and the associated accounts of
institutional change. In contrast to many accounts, we do not attempt to
explain differences in national economic performances in terms of institutional differences. Instead, we argue that the evidence amongst developed
countries indicates that the impact of institutions on performance is secondary, but that institutions do have a key impact on distribution of income
and employment. The section, 'Varieties of actually existing capitalism' provides a brief overview of the main features of 'actually existing capitalism'
amongst the developed economies as an introduction to a more detailed
consideration of key elements. Following on from the key institutions identified in the introductory chapter, the section, 'States and markets: public
sector growth, but declining intervention' considers the role of the state, the
next section shows the financial system and corporate governance, the following section discusses the industrial relations systems and the next
section is on wage bargaining systems. The last section concludes with some
general observations on the fate of national capitalisms now and the
research agenda remaining.

Institutions and economic performance

The chapters in this volume share the fundamental assumption that institutions differ between countries and that this matters. As noted in the introductory chapter, many economists now recognize the importance of
embedded institutional arrangements in underwriting the functions of business and the market economy. It is hard to account for the range of levels
of income and productivity observed between countries simply in terms of
human and physical capital stocks and available technology – institutional
differences appear to be important to explaining this (Prescott, 1998; Hall
and Jones, 1999; Aron, 2000). Institutionalist economics has often been
divided into the 'new' and the 'old', where the new institutional economics
largely accepts orthodox economics accounts of individual rationality and
often attempts to theorize equilibrium states whilst the older tradition
emphasizes alternative conceptions of economic agency and is sceptical of
equilibrium reasoning (Rutherford, 1994; Hodgson, 1988, 1999). For our
purposes, although there are important differences between these schools
(particularly in their analysis of the efficacy of government intervention),
their empirical predictions concerning the impact and evolution of institutions overlap considerably (Rutherford, 1994: ch. 6; Hodgson, 1996). From
either a 'new' or 'old' institutionalist perspective, institutional arrangements
are expected to be enduring. We would expect to see a diversity of institutional arrangements across national economies and would not necessarily
predict convergence either in response to common exogenous developments or differences in performance.

National institutional diversity can be interpreted in terms of multiple possible equilibria from repeated game playing or from a more discursive historical perspective (Hodgson, 1988: part 3, 1999: ch. 6; North, 1990; Aoki, 2000). From either perspective, institutions are seen as an example of path dependency where the final institutional arrangements are determined in the long run by both initial conditions and histories of adjustment. This follows from Arthur's work on technological lock-in (Arthur, 1989). At the start, there are multiple possible outcomes which are indeterminate from the initial conditions. Once a particularly path is chosen there are powerful forces for universal adoption and it is difficult to exit from the solution: there is 'lock-in'. This is despite the possibility that the outcome may not be the most efficient. Four self-reinforcing mechanisms are required for lock-in. First, there must be large set-up or fixed costs. Second, there must be learning effects from using the technology. Third, there must be coordination advantages or network effects from widespread adoption of the technology. Fourth, there must be adaptive expectations: full knowledge of the effects of the technology should preclude inefficient outcomes. Recalling North's cogent definition of institutions in the introductory chapter, he argues that Arthur's four self-reinforcing mechanisms apply to institutions:

> In a dynamic world characterized by institutional increasing returns, the imperfect and fumbling efforts of the actors reflect the difficulties of deciphering a complex environment with the available mental constructs – ideas, theories and ideologies. (North, 1990: 96)

Formal legal rules are by definition universal in their application throughout the nation, but there are also powerful reasons for informal institutions to persist in national societies. Widely understood procedures reduce uncertainty and lower the costs of social interaction. One upshot of this is that unsuccessful economies may get locked-in to a low performance equilibrium. Shifting to higher performance institutions may be blocked by the costs of institutional adjustment, the difficulties of organizing collective action to change institutions and powerful interest groups.

Many theorists of national capitalism go further, arguing that institutional relations in each country have evolved to form a mutually reinforcing ensemble. Hollingsworth (1997a: 266–7) states this most explicitly:

> A nation's financial markets, educational system, industrial relations system, and other sociopolitical factors influence sectoral and national economic performance. In order to understand how and why a society's economy performs, it is necessary to understand its entire social system of production. If a society is to improve substantially the performance of its economy, it must be do more than adopt some of the management and work practices of its foreign competitors. It must alter its entire social

system of production.... [I]nstitutions are embedded in a culture in which their logic is symbolically grounded, organizationally structured, technically and materially constrained, politically defended, and historically shaped by specific rules and norms. Though institutions are constantly changing, there are sharp limits to the type and direction of change that any particular institution can undergo because of its linkages with other institutions. Thus, a society's business firms, educational system, capital markets, industrial relations system, etc. can engage in serious restructuring only if the norms and rules, as well as most of the other institutions with which they are linked, also change.... [I]nstitutions making up a social system of production are interdependent, and changes in one institution generally result in changes in other institutions.

More succinctly, Soskice (1999: 109) argues that 'there are strong interlocking complementarities between different parts of the institutional framework. Each system depends on the other systems to function effectively.' Hugo Radice, in his chapter, criticizes this explanation for its functionalism. Further, the emphasis on lock-in means that theory provides little account of institutional change. Once the possibility of change is allowed for one can see path dependence rather than absolute lock-in operating. The upshot is that one expects – and, indeed, finds – national conformity in institutions but global diversity. More controversial is the nature of institutional change. In game theory approaches change occurs with punctuated equilibrium: institutions are stable as long as shocks are small but change irregularly with accumulated shocks (Aoki, 2000). The nature of the game constrains strategic choices, but there are also typically multiple equilibria from the same initial conditions so that different institutions can emerge depending on national historical episodes. This follows from the game theory logic: repeated game playing may lead to stable solutions. There remains, though, an infinite regress problem in explaining institutions in game theory terms, since it pushes back the question of where the game's rules arise from in the first place (Field, 1984; Mirowski, 1986; Hodgson, 2002). More generally, an emphasis on mutually reinforcing aspects leads not only to an emphasis on stability, but also that change in one institution is likely to lead to changes in others. This, too, would imply that institutional change would take place with sharp discontinuity. Conventions, formal and informal, are by their very nature followed by most people; as such, one would expect changes to be radical and discontinuous, typically in periods of crisis. However, the historical record is ambiguous than this allows and others emphasize more gradual, evolutionary change. North, for example, argues that: 'institutions typically change incrementally rather than in discontinuous fashion' (North, 1990: 6). Work in the Austrian economics tradition emphasizes continuous innovation in practices by entrepreneurs over stability with punctuated equilibria.

Developing Hugo Radice's criticisms, there are several difficulties with this approach. The focus of this work is almost bound to be on national differences rather than common trends, on institutional persistence rather than change. Discussions tend to emphasize long-term continuity in institutional structures, often back decades or even centuries. The logic of conceiving of countries as having an ensemble of mutually reinforcing institutions is that change in just one would undermine the whole system. Sometimes analysts of national capitalisms do trace through the unravelling of systems in response to changes in just parts of them; more commonly there is a tendency to downplay the extent and significance of any changes and assert that each national model persists and remains viable. Further, the analytical tools that we have to analyze institutional change are much weaker than those to analyze the effects of institutions. We have more or less good indicators of institutional differences (we discuss the limitations of these indicators below) and can relate these to economic performance. However, both measuring the degree of institutional change and accounting for it pose methodological challenges. Whether inspired from game theory or more discursive historical analysis, accounts of institutional change typically remain at the level of plausible stories: we can produce explanations that fit available evidence, but so do other accounts and few analyses systematically compare possible accounts and evaluate which has greater explanatory power.

Nevertheless, we can conceptualize several different patterns of institutional change. Institutions can mutate through changes in behaviour. In the most extreme cases institutions will simply collapse and be forced to choice of new ones or be subject to external invasion by a group with different conventions. More generally, periods of crisis – typically from an external shock – are more likely to lead to radical change in institutions, often through deliberate government action. Institutional change may occur through more deliberate translation of alternative institutions into a national context. These will differ in their compatibility with existing institutions and it cannot be assumed that the cumulative transformations will evolve towards more compatible solutions now or mimic those countries from which the translation has been taken. Relatedly, within a national economy a demonstration effect may occur if some agents change their practices leading to others following. These approaches have been criticized for being largely reactive and ignoring the potential role of leadership and/or collective agreement in initiating institutional change. Given the difficulties of private collective agreement for change, the standard free rider problems, there may be a key role for the state here.

Institutional change, in this schema, would be expected in response to changes in tastes, technology or relative prices. Analysis of these has often reflected the focus of different disciplines. Changes in tastes have been least considered by economists, partly because these are least amenable to economic

explanation.[1] Nevertheless, North (1990) and others have latterly emphasized the role of ideology in constructing, maintaining and changing institutions. Using this language may seem economistic, but we can interpret
shifts in class politics in this way. Nevertheless, most of these discussions
have focused on relatively narrow electoral politics whilst, as noted in
Juhana Vartiainen's chapter and below, support for institutions like the welfare state remains strong. Nor is a fall in trade union membership a universal trend, as we document below. How far in practice there has been a
decline in class voting and with it a shift in political programmes remains
unclear (see Clift, 2001a and references therein). Cultural explanations of
economic performance face major difficulties, both in establishing that the
claimed norms are widely shared and in specifying the causal relations
between these and economic outcomes (Coates, 2000: ch. 5). For this reason
we largely ignore cultural explanations as, for the most part, do our
contributors.

Changes in technology have often been discussed in this literature. The
chief paradigm here is the post-Fordism/flexible specialization literature
where the shift away from mass production in developed economies undermines the institutional relations of the post-war Golden Age (e.g. Amin,
1994). This is not a simple case of iron technological determinism, indeed
this literature often emphasizes that industrial trajectories involve choice
(Piore and Sabel, 1984). The chief problem here is empirical: it is hard to
account for more than a minority of structural change in developed
economies in these terms (Dietrich, 1999). Nor would such changes imply
that there is only one possible or even optimal institutional response
(cf. Ruigrok and Tulder, 1995).

In some versions this argument shades into a free market critique of state
intervention, Keynesian demand management and trade union activity.
Neo-liberal critiques argue that these will all have detrimental effects on
economies, but even to the extent that their argument holds its universal
claims makes it unsuitable for explaining either why institutions have
changed in this period rather than earlier or why changes have been so
much more pronounced in some countries than others.[2] Audretsch and
Thurik (2001) attempt to tie the new technology literature with a neo-liberal
analysis. New technologies, in this argument, increase the rate of structural
change and raise the importance of small and new firms for growth and
employment. Government intervention and trade union activity are thus
predicted to have a more detrimental on small firms and the creation of new
ones than on large, established concerns.

Changes in relative prices are, not surprisingly, the common focus for economic analysis of institutional change, but this has extended to political scientists with reference to globalization. Thus, Milner and Keohane (1996: 4):

> Internationalization ... refers to the processes generated by underlying
> shifts in transaction costs that produce observable flows of goods, services

and capital.... [I]nternationalization ... involves an exogenous reduction in the costs of international transactions.

Their own analysis indicates that the use of 'exogenous' here is partially misleading, as international economic integration has in part been engineered by nation states – the removal of barriers to cross-border activity has reduced transaction costs but is at least in part endogenous to national polities. Predicting the impact of internationalization on institutions, though, is not straightforward; global market competition would not necessarily force national societies to adopt more efficient institutions. Countries are not competitors in the same way that companies are and will not simply go out of business if they have less efficient institutional arrangements (e.g. Krugman, 1996). Even a nodding acquaintance with trade theory tells us two things here. First, countries of radically different levels of efficiency and productivity can still trade to their mutual advantage provided there are differences in their *relative* efficiency. Second, it is differences between countries that are expected to drive specialization and its associated trade. Thus, there is no reason to think that increased international trade as such will generate convergence. Hall and Soskice (2001) find that institutional differences significantly affect patterns of relative advantage (cf. Crouch *et al.*, 1999: ch. 3). Thus if institutional differences lead to different patterns of specialization increased trade would not necessarily lead to convergence. Naive views that international integration must necessarily lead to convergence on one model do not hold water, but simply pointing this out still begs the question of how international integration does affect institutional structures. Theories of globalization processes suggest that international economic integration will undermine the differences between national economies. A 'hyper-globalization' position predicts convergence on Anglo-Saxon capitalism due to the logic of the market/capitalism (delete according to neo-liberal or Marxist taste) but this position has few academic proponents and is too often used as a 'straw man' argument in institutional accounts.[3] Typically 'tests' of the globalization hypothesis either crudely test for convergence in some variables (sometime this is with reference to formal tests for international income convergence, but a clearly specified model underlies income convergence models). Alternatively, change is related to the degree of integration as measured by the relative size of flows of trade, finance or FDI. Flows are important, particularly compared over time, but economic integration is dependent on converging prices – of goods, financial assets and so on – and there is no straightforward relationships between international price convergence and the size of flows in any one country. Accounts here often blur the distinction between an idealized conception of free market capitalism and the reality of models like the United States and Britain; as Grahame Thompson's and Andrew Gamble's chapters make clear not only are these countries some way from a hypothetical ideal, but many apparent features of these models have emerged over the past 20 years.

We can cut through some of this following Freeman (2000), noting evidence indicates that institutions make little difference to developed countries' economic performance but makes a significant difference to income distribution. Levels of income per head have tended to converge amongst developed countries in the postwar period, although this needs to be qualified particularly in relation to hours worked (Crafts, 1997; see also below). The performance on other indicators, such as unemployment or inflation, typically depends on the period of comparison chosen: different economies have appeared to be top dog at different times which in itself should indicate that there is no one superior model. The evidence on inflation shows clearly that rates were both generally lower and converged in the 1990s compared with the 1980s. The evidence on unemployment shows no clear pattern since the end of the postwar Golden Age, partly due to the worsening unemployment performance of the Scandinavian economies in the 1990s as analyzed by Juhana Vartiainen in his chapter. As we noted in the introductory chapter, one of the problems with the national capitalisms literature is its frequent attempt to use long-run institutional differences to explain performance differences over relatively short-run periods. This is crucial to later arguments: too often national capitalisms theorists attempt to refute hypotheses of convergence towards Anglo-Saxon institutions by showing that these are not necessarily optimal. However, strictly, this is only relevant if convergence is being predicted on performance grounds.

The limited apparent impact of institutions on performance amongst developed countries is less surprising than it might first appear. For the new institutionalist economists, much of the focus has been on property rights. Although there are remaining differences in areas such as protection of minority shareholders, property rights are largely secured in developed economies and the differences between these countries are small. Income convergence processes amongst developed countries are now fairly well understood. For all the talk of differences between Continental European and Anglo-Saxon labour markets leading to divergent unemployment outcomes there is only limited evidence that labour market regulations, trade union activity and minimum wages significantly affect unemployment levels (Crouch *et al.*, 1999: ch. 2; OECD, 1999b: ch. 2).

Nevertheless, it is one thing to argue that there is no simple logic that globalization will lead to convergence to an Anglo-Saxon model; it is quite another to suppose that greater international integration will have little significant impact on domestic institutional arrangements. Even proponents of German and Japanese varieties of capitalism, such as Dore (2000), see integration of capital markets, increased foreign ownership of firms and inward investment as likely to undermine these models and orientate businesses towards maximizing shareholder value in Anglo-Saxon fashion. Streeck (1997a) argues that in the past national stakeholders were compelled to achieve socially beneficial bargains they would not voluntarily have chosen; globalization processes may weaken the basis of such bargains, and the commitment of business to them in particular. Below we attempt to examine the effects of globalization, as well as other trends in contemporary capitalism, on different aspects of national institutional arrangements.

Varieties of actually existing capitalism

The simplest division of types of capitalism is Soskice's binary classification between coordinated and liberal market economies according to their organization of production and market institutions (Soskice, 1999). In his schema, coordinated economies have the following features:

1. *Industrial relations*: Wage determination is formally or informally coordinated with industry-level bargaining important and both unions and employers' organizations playing a key role. Within firms employee-elected bodies play an important role in decision-making.
2. *Education and training*: Vocational education is well established with strong involvement of firms and unions. Higher education provides a strong supply of scientists and engineers.
3. *Company financing*: Publicly quoted companies generally have stable shareholdings where hostile takeovers are rare and difficult. Banks play a key role monitoring companies and are central to financing of smaller companies. This can result in limited investment in new technologies and industries.
4. *Inter-company relations*: Consensus-based relations operate, often through business associations. Although there is typically orientation towards international markets, certain sectors may be protected domestically.

Decentralized or liberal market economies, by contrast, have the following features:

1. *Industrial relations*: Wage bargaining is largely company based, often with little coordination. Employees have few if any rights to workplace representation and the density of unionization is now typically low.
2. *Education and training*: There is limited vocational training and company-based schemes. Higher education may be strong, but is less closely integrated with industry than in coordinated economies.
3. *Company financing*: Higher levels of stock market capitalization than under coordinated economies with the threat of hostile takeovers playing a key role in firm governance. Capital markets for risky finance tend to be better developed than in coordinated economies.
4. *Inter-company relations*: With less developed business associations these are more governed by arms-length legal relations. Competition law tends to be strongly anti-collusion.

This dovetails with other analysis, dividing the major varieties of capitalism into three:

• *Anglo-Saxon*: Exemplified by the United States, United Kingdom, Canada and Ireland, but also includes Australia and New Zealand (at least after economic changes in the 1980s). Essentially these are the liberal market economies. This model is closest to orthodox economics conceptions of market flexibility – particularly in the labour market – and limited state intervention. Its strengths are seen as flowing from this, particularly its apparently superior employment record in the 1990s and, at least in the United States, the ease with which new firms and industries can emerge. Its weaknesses are seen as related to the high value key agents place on exit, which militates against constructing relations of trust; in particular, the premium financial markets place on liquidity is claimed to inhibit the emergence of the long-term relations between finance and industry characteristic of the other models.

- *Continental European or Rhineland*: Exemplified by Germany, Austria, Switzerland and the Benelux countries; the Scandinavian countries are often seen as sharing at least some Rhineland characteristics. These countries are characterized by large scale social bargains struck between well-organized social interest groups on a regularized basis; extensive use of bank finance by industry leading to long-term relations between the two; strong universalist welfare states are the main distinguishing characteristics of the Scandinavian economies. Its strengths believed to flow from consensual nature of economic relations, improving short-run macroeconomic performance and easing investment and the introduction of new technology. Its weaknesses are particularly seen in terms of labour and product market rigidities ratcheting up unemployment and discouraging the emergence of new industries.

- *East Asian*: Exemplified above all by Japan, but followed by the leading newly industrializing economies (NIEs) notably Korea and Taiwan. Extensive state intervention was used to direct industrialization of the economy and encourage upgrading of sectors. Integration between firms at different levels of production entails extensive cooperation between assembly firms and their suppliers. There are strong links between banks and industry, which, together with extensive cross-holding of shares between firms, means that banks have key monitoring functions. Trade union power and workers' rights are limited, but these countries are associated with paternalistic employment patterns, implicit guarantees of long service and pay based on seniority. Consensual industrial relations and cooperation between firms have been seen as central to the Japanese techniques of management that allowed major productivity gains in manufacturing industries.

This finer classification points to the different institutions of coordination between the European and East Asian coordinated market economies. Within the European coordinated market economies a division has also between proposed those with social democratic welfare states (the Scandinavian economies) and those with Christian democratic welfare states (Germany, Austria, Switzerland and the Benelux countries, plus France and Italy) (Boyer, 1997; Kitschelt *et al.*, 1999). This still leaves the poorer Southern European countries of Spain, Portugal and Greece. Indeed the inclusion of France and Italy is questionable here. Boyer (1997) and Rhodes and Apeldoorn (1998), amongst others, point out that relative to the Rhineland countries, these comprise a 'Latin' European group with a more interventionist state which played a key coordinating role, together with lower union density and more fragmented human capital systems. Their welfare states are more variegated – generous in some areas but not in others – with greater reliance on non-state actors and more clientalistic relations (Ferrara, 1996). Consequently these countries are classified here as 'Southern Europe'.

Updated and extended comparative indicators of differences between national capitalisms that Kitschelt *et al.* (1999) provided for 1980 are given in Table 12.1. Figures on social expenditures, trade union density and collective wage agreements are considered in relevant sections below. Given limitations of quality and frequency of data, formal tests for convergence are not carried out on this and subsequent data; however, calculating the coefficient of variation[4] provides some indication of whether differences have increased or decreased since 1980. Government expenditure and revenues are considered in more detail in the next section; overall there is evidence of continued divergence in taxation, but with some evidence of lower dispersion. The relative position of the different groups remains largely unchanged with the Anglo-Saxon and East Asian countries being low tax countries and the Scandinavian countries being the highest tax countries; however, increases in tax levels in the Southern European countries have brought them up to levels close to those of the Rhineland countries.

The welfare state and levels of social security expenditure are also considered in more detail in the section, 'States and markets: public sector growth, but declining intervention'. The figures for social security transfers show some growth relative to GDP, except for the Rhineland group. Patterns are broadly as expected, with the lowest levels in the Anglo-Saxon and East Asian countries; for the 1990s the highest group is the Scandinavian countries although this was not the case in 1980. Nevertheless, variations within the groups are considerable and belie straightforward classification. More precise figures for social security expenditure are considered in the next section.

Given the difficulties of reliably comparing Gini coefficients over time we just report latest figures and indicators for the order of magnitude of changes. The group averages generally conform to expectations: the Scandinavian economies have the lowest levels of inequality, the Rhineland countries are more unequal and the Anglo-Saxon countries more unequal still. Although these indicators give a mixed picture, the indicators of trends in inequality show that inequality has not only risen in the Anglo-Saxon

Table 12.1 Selected indicators of national capitalisms, 1980s and 1990s

	Tax revenues (% GDP)		Transfers (% GDP)		Gini coefficient	Gini change		Female labour force participation		Wage inequality D9/D1 ratios		Theil index	
	1980	1999	1980	1996	1999	1970s–80s	1980s–90s	1980	1999	1980	1994	1980	1994
Australia	27.4	29.9	8.1	11.3	35.2	0	+	49.1	62.5	2.8	2.9	81	145
Canada	32.0	37.4	9.9	11.9	31.5	−	0	57.4	70.5	4.0	4.2	88	134
Ireland	31.5	32.1	12.6	13.8	35.9	−	+	35.2	55.7		4.1	93	248
New Zealand	33.0	35.2	13.4	16.6	37.0	0	+++	45.0	67.5	2.9	3.0	73	169
UK	35.4	36.9	10.0	12.5	36.1	++	++	58.0	68.9	2.8	3.4	90	97
USA	27.0	28.9	10.0	12.1	40.8	++	++	58.9	70.8	3.6	4.4	143	177
Mean	31.1	33.4	10.7	13.0	36.1			50.6	66.0	3.2	4.4		
Austria	39.5	44.4	15.1	17.5	23.1	0	++	50.3	65.5	3.5	3.7	87	64
Belgium	43.1	45.7	21.9	21.2	25.0	0	+	46.3	56.6	2.3	2.2	69	74
Germany	33.1	37.4	14.8	17.1	30.0	−	+	52.2	63.2	2.7	2.4	110	114
Netherlands	43.4	40.7	24.8	22.7	32.6	0	++	33.4	65.7	2.2	2.6	75	76
Switzerland	28.9	35.1	12.7	11.5	33.1	−	+	53.0	73.9		2.7		
Mean	37.6	40.7	17.9	18.0	28.8			47.0	65.0	2.7	2.7		

Denmark	44.0	50.2	16.6	21.5	24.7	—	—	69.9	75.9	2.1	2.2	67	66
Finland	36.2	46.4	10.1	22.1	25.6	—	+	68.9	72.0	2.5	2.4	75	92
Norway	42.7	42.7	14.4	14.8	25.8	0	++	61.7	76.5	2.1	2.0	85	86
Sweden	47.1	52.1	16.9	21.7	25.0	—	+	72.8	76.4	2.0	2.1	66	72
Mean	42.5	47.9	14.5	20.0	25.3			68.3	75.2	2.2	2.2		
France	40.6	45.6	17.3	21.5	32.7	—	—	54.2	61.7	3.3	3.3	150	156
Greece	24.0	36.4	9.2	16.9	32.7			32.8	49.7			130	141
Italy	30.3	42.9	14.1	9.3	27.3	—	++	38.7	46.2	2.6	2.8	62	89
Portugal	24.6	34.4	10.0	13.5	35.6			57.3	63.6	3.6	4.1	49	59
Spain	22.9	34.7	12.7	15.7	32.5			32.6	51.8			102	84
Mean	28.5	38.8	12.7	15.4	32.2			43.1	54.6				
Japan	25.4	28.1	10.1	13.5	24.9	0	++	54.7	59.6	3.0	3.0	89	77
Korea	17.7	22.5	1.3	3.3	31.6			41.6	51.8			60	113
Mean	33.2	38.2	13.0	15.5	30.9			51.1	63.9				
Variation	23.9	19.3	37.7	31.8	16.1			23.5	14.1				

Source: See Appendix.

countries (except Canada) but also in most Rhineland and Scandinavian countries despite their differences. The trend to greater inequality in the United States is discussed in detail in Grahame Thompson's chapter; interestingly the distributional trends in the US 1990s boom show similarities to those in the 1920s boom (Lindert, 2000). A similar picture of variations can be seen with the figures for wage inequality. The D9/D1 ratios (the ratio of earnings in the top decile to the bottom) only provide an indicator of the extremes; the Theil index provides an overall measure of wage inequality (note that since the index is set at 1970 = 100 for all countries it cannot be used for comparison between countries only within countries over time). Both measures point to increases in wage inequality amongst Anglo-Saxon countries but less clear trends elsewhere. This is consistent with more detailed evidence that amongst the coordinated market economies labour market institutions (notably trade union strength and wage bargaining coordination) significantly affect the levels and evolution of wage inequality (Rueda and Pontusson, 2000). However, these figures mask evidence of a general trend towards increased male wage inequality, again most clearly amongst Anglo-Saxon countries (Clayton and Pontusson, 1998). Note that changes in wage inequality are not always clearly related to changes in Gini coefficients (cf. Atkinson, 2001). Changes in the experiences of households cannot simply be read off from the experience of waged individuals.

Although there are continued differences in the levels of female labour force participation, this has risen in all countries – usually substantially – and the dispersion in levels has fallen. The Scandinavian countries, with institutionalized commitments to gender equality, still have the highest levels, but there have also been sharp rises amongst the Anglo-Saxon countries and the Rhineland group, despite historically low female participation rates in Rhineland countries. Although participation has risen in Southern European countries, it remains low and indicative of continued gender inequalities in employment and welfare provision amongst these countries (Trifiletti, 1999). Overall trends in employment are considered in the section, 'States and markets: public sector growth, but declining intervention' and section, 'Wage bargaining: coordinated versus decentralized systems' below.

Below we consider the key features of different varieties of capitalism outlined above in detail, with the exceptions of human capital formation and inter-company relations. Education and training systems may be an important determinant of comparative advantage, but the impact of internationalization on them is likely to be indirect. Recent studies are getting a handle on the complex interactions between national groups in determining systems of human capital generation (e.g. Crouch *et al.*, 1999; Estevez-Abe *et al.*, 2001). On inter-company relations, there are grounds for believing that differences between national capitalisms on this score are less than often supposed. In the section, 'Varieties of capitalism in a global era' we note evidence that close relations between Japanese firms and their suppliers have declined over the 1990s; Burchell and Wilkinson (1997) surveyed firms in Britain, Germany and Italy on levels of trust between businesses and found the similarities more important than differences.

States and markets: public sector growth, but declining intervention

Dividing countries between liberal and coordinated varieties leaves open the role of the state in the latter. In the institutional literature this is often conceived in terms of the state's role in setting the rules and framework for market activity: state intervention is necessary for the governance of markets. This is a useful corrective to the notion that even the Anglo-Saxon states are, have been or even could be reduced to night watchman states. Nevertheless, as an insight it only gets us so far: recognizing the ubiquity of state intervention does not preclude examining changes in its level over time and differences between countries. Further subdivision between Scandinavian/ Social Democratic and Rhineland/Christian Democratic states is largely in terms of differences in their welfare states. As noted above, in some coordinated market economies the state has played a key role in the coordination. Although liberal economies would be expected to largely eschew industrial policy interventions, during the postwar period neither Canada nor the United Kingdom had particularly low shares of government expenditure in GDP (see the chapters by Andrew Gamble and Juhana Vartiainen). In the paradigm case of the United States' limited industrial policy is combined with strong anti-trust policies, but the picture is less clear with other Anglo-Saxon economies. In principle Germany's social market economy eschewed industrial policy, although in practice it was often greater than official pronouncements would suggest (Weiss, 1998: ch. 5); by contrast, Austria had one of the highest levels of state ownership of enterprises amongst developed countries. The high levels of welfare state expenditure amongst Nordic countries are well known. Japan and other East Asian countries combined strong industrial policies with low welfare state provision.

We can make two clear statements about state activity in developed economies now. First, as a share of total economic activity public expenditure has largely stabilized in developed economies, with continued differences in these shares between countries. Hence, it continues to rise in real terms as these economies grow. Second, state intervention in economies as industrial policy has declined. Some qualifications to these statements are necessary.

Welfare state developments[5]

Juhana Vartiainen examines trends in the share of government economic activity in his chapter. One key change from the 1970s and 1980s is that budget deficits have been reduced, partly in European cases from the need to meet the criteria for entering EMU. In the short run global capital markets actually helped governments to run budget deficits as demands for public expenditure outstripped growth in revenues, but ultimately this is unsustainable. Common lazy formulations are confounded here. Although the postwar Golden Age is often characterized as Keynesian, for most countries the major growth in public expenditure took place in the 1970s after the end of the postwar boom. In the 1980s, for all the New Right rhetoric of 'rolling back the frontiers of the state', few governments even of that persuasion actually managed major reductions in the government share of GDP. This should come as no surprise: as Andrew Gamble points out in his chapter and elsewhere (Gamble, 1994b), attempts to pursue neo-liberal policies may increase the demands placed upon certain state agencies. Whilst governments made cuts in particular programmes, even during 1990s EMU candidates largely met the Maastricht fiscal criteria through increasing taxes rather than cutting expenditure (Genschel, 2002). Juhana Vartiainen further argues that the stabilization of these shares can be seen as reflecting citizens' preferences for levels of public expenditure; he finds that support for current levels public expenditure remains in Scandinavian countries and this also seems to be true elsewhere in Europe (Boeri *et al.*, 2001).

Table 12.2 shows that once net social expenditures are considered (allowing for the taxability of certain benefits in some countries) the differences amongst developed economies are considerably smaller with the differences between the Scandinavian economies and the rest becoming less pronounced. Note, too, that only Ireland of the Anglo-Saxon countries saw a reduction in net public social expenditures over this period (partly reflecting falling Irish unemployment). The rankings, though, remain broadly similar. Moreover, these figures also point to some narrowing of differences between countries since the 1980s – this is pronounced if comparison is limited to the 12 countries for which data was available in both years (the coefficient of variation fell from 34.1 to 19.8).

Rather than reflecting a social equilibrium, a less sanguine interpretation is that this represents an unstable compromise, with governments trying to balance both growth in demand for public services with downward pressure on tax revenues (Ganghof, 2000; Genschel, 2002). Swank (2002) refutes any hyperglobalization notion of a race to the bottom in welfare provision or taxation and shows the clear influence of domestic groups on the evolution of national welfare states. Nevertheless, this is not quite the same as concluding that globalization has no significant impact. An ageing population and persistent unemployment places increasing demands on welfare states. Although social expenditure has risen in real terms and usually as a proportion of GDP, increases in social exclusion meant that Clayton and Pontusson (1998) found that in Germany, Sweden, Britain and the United States, real social expenditure per poor person grew slower than GDP: welfare states

Table 12.2 Gross and net public social expenditures

	Public social expenditures as a percentage of GDP		
	1980 Net	1997 Gross	1997 Net
Australia	11.9	17.4	16.6
Austria	—	25.4	20.9
Belgium	—	27.2	23.5
Canada	13.2	17.9	16.2
Denmark	—	30.7	22.9
Finland	18.9	28.7	21.4
France	23.5	—	—
Germany	25.7	26.4	24.6
Ireland	17.6	17.6	15.4
Italy	18.4	26.4	21.6
Japan	10.0	14.2	13.9
Korea	—	4.3	4.4
Netherlands	28.5	24.2	18.2
New Zealand	—	20.7	17.0
Norway	18.8	26.1	21.1
Sweden	29.9	31.8	25.4
Switzerland	16.6	—	—
United Kingdom	18.3	21.2	19.2
United States	13.7	14.7	15.3
Mean	18.9	22.1	18.7
Variation	32.0	32.1	27.1

Sources: Adema (2001), Caminada and Goudswaard (2001).

have become less generous. There is evidence that globalization has reduced effective corporate tax rates (including amongst the Scandinavian countries) and reduced cross-country variance amongst developed economies and shifted the burden towards labour and indirect taxation (Bretschger and Hettich, 2002). In part governments have responded by broadening the corporate tax base but cutting rates on the most mobile capital (Ganghof, 2000; Devereux *et al.*, 2002). It is not simply that the tax burden has shifted towards labour and indirect taxation; globalization would be expected to raise the elasticity of demand for labour so that the incidence of taxes (the real economic burden) would increasingly fall on labour and this would worsen the adverse employment impact of taxation (Rodrik, 1997). Although Rodrik (1997) found that across countries more open developed economies have larger welfare states, as Juhana Vartiainen notes in his chapter, Rodrik also found that over time increased openness was associated with lower expenditure. Arguably globalization constrained governments' ability to raise revenues to levels that they desired and restricted their ability to cut income taxes where they harmed employment (Genschel, 2002). Although downward pressure on corporate tax rates has not led to a race to the bottom as such, arguably it has been a key constraint on expanding welfare provision in line with rising demand.

The fiscal pressures may have led to qualitative convergence between welfare states. Schwartz (1994) found that in Denmark, Sweden and the Antipodean countries reorganization within the state – particularly within welfare state provision – saw operational responsibility increasingly devolved to local levels whilst control over spending became increasingly centralized and strict. Similar remarks could be made about the Netherlands (cf. Kurzer, 1993: ch. 3). Increased use of markets and quasi-markets for provision of welfare services meant that local-level managers had more devolved power, mirroring developments in private corporations. Competition and comparisons ('benchmarking') was encouraged between agencies and sometimes with private sector providers. These processes have the effect of diffusing pressures on the welfare state by limiting the power of interest groups whilst strengthening the power of fiscal bureaucrats. This has continued apace in Denmark and New Zealand (OECD, 2002a: ch. 3; 2002d: ch. 3) and recent reforms in Norway have been along these lines (OECD, 2002e: ch. 2), although attempts to implement them in Italy have been less successful (OECD, 2002c: 79–89). The parallels with British welfare state reform under the 1979–97 Conservative administrations (Clarke and Newman, 1997) – and, arguably, continued under new Labour – are striking.

The notion of trends towards 'decommodification', particularly in Social Democratic welfare states, is complex covering a range of factors determining the degree to which individual welfare (Esping-Anderson, 1990). Nevertheless, here we update and extend Glyn (1992a) who considered two aspects of these trends. The first is 'demarketization', akin to deindustrialization; if the growth of productivity in the market sector exceeds the growth of output then this will lead to a fall in the hours worked in the market sector. This would not necessarily lead to a fall in total employment, but its distribution would depend on the changes in the average hours worked in the market sector and the changes in state employment. Historically productivity growth has not been associated with lower employment due to a combination of shorter working hours (including rises in part-time working), the growth of employment in low productivity services and higher state employment. Private sector workers would gain from higher state employment to the extent that they consumer public services; nevertheless, this does require an acceptance of higher taxes – attempting to pass on higher taxes in higher wage claims would undermine this 'employment spreading' effect.

In Table 12.3, demarketization is indicated by the third column – the change in hours worked in the market sector – which is the first column less the second (productivity is the change in market output per person hour worked in the market sector). As can be seen demarketization is not universal across developed countries since 1986, but is prevalent in the

Table 12.3 Demarketization and employment annual growth rates, 1986–96

	Market output per head	Productivity	Hours in market sector/population	Share of state employment	Fall in average hours worked	Share of part-time work	Employment/ population
Denmark^c	1.3	2.5	-1.2	0.2	0.4	-0.2	-0.8 (-0.7)
Finland	1.5	3.9	-2.4	0.7	-0.2	0.0	-1.7 (-1.8)
Norway^c	2.1	4.1	-2.0	1.1	0.3	0.0	-0.7 (-0.6)
Sweden^a	0.2	1.5	-1.3	0.1	-0.5	-0.1	-1.8 (-1.7)
Austria	2.0	3.0	-1.0	0.6	-0.1	0.2	-0.3 (-0.1)
Belgium^c	2.3	2.2	0.1	-0.3	0.3	0.2	0.3 (0.2)
Netherlands^c	2.1	1.5	0.6	-0.3	0.3	0.2	0.8 (0.7)
West Germany^d	2.3	2.6	-0.3	-0.1	0.7	0.1	0.4 (0.3)
France	1.7	2.6	-0.9	0.4	0.3	0.1	-0.1
Italy	2.2	2.5	-0.3	0.1	0.0	0.1	-0.1
Spain^b	1.7	1.3	0.4	-0.2	0.0	0.1	0.3 (0.4)
Japan	2.8	3.4	-0.6	-0.1	0.7	0.3	0.3 (0.4)
Australia	1.8	1.0	1.0	-0.3	-0.3	0.2	0.4
Canada	1.0	1.2	-0.2	-0.1	0.2	0.1	0.0 (0.1)
Ireland	5.3	4.7	0.6	-0.4	0.2	0.4	0.8 (0.7)
UK^c	2.2	0.8	1.6	-1.1	0.0	0.1	0.4 (0.5)
USA^b	1.8	0.9	0.9	-0.2	0.0	0.0	0.7

Notes: Figures in brackets in the final column are actual changes in employment/population ratio.
[a] 1987–94.
[b] 1987–96.
[c] 1986–95.
[d] 1986–93.

Source: See Appendix.

Scandinavian economies (the low Swedish market output growth figure is partly due the sample period chosen) and Austria – the countries Glyn (1992a) singled out for their strong corporatist relations – plus the former West Germany and the Southern European countries. Both the corporatist and Southern European country groups saw relatively slow rates of growth in low productivity services, often attributed to high wage costs in the corporatist economies (discussed below in the section, 'Wage bargaining: coordinated versus decentralized systems') and to restrictive employment legislation in the Southern European countries. In the latter case this may also be due to demand side factors – particularly in the 1990s these countries pursued deflationary policies to ensure that they met the Maastricht criteria for EMU entry. The 'competitive disinflation' policy in France – discussed in Ben Clift's chapter – combined deflationary policies with active attempts to boost productivity growth.

The experience of the corporatist countries differs somewhat from earlier periods. Whereas Glyn (1992a) found that these countries had lower rates of demarketization over 1979–86 than other West European countries: their strong employment performance reflected high output growth relative to productivity as well as expansion of state employment. The contribution of state employment to total employment growth largely ground to a halt in Denmark and Sweden but not in Austria and Norway (buttressed by oil revenues) and the special case of Finnish recovery from recession. This is consistent with the evidence in Juhana Vartiainen's chapter for the Scandinavian economies: although their labour force participation rates remained high in these economies, whereas in the 1970s and 1980s state employment was often the largest contributor to employment expansion, since then it has not raised employment rates overall. By contrast, the Anglo-Saxon countries saw output growth rise in line with or more rapidly than productivity. As Graham Thompson points out in his chapter even in the late 1990s the United States unlike European economies was able to generate rising employment together with rapid productivity growth.

Amongst the Anglo-Saxon countries the twentieth-century trend towards shorter working hours for full-time workers ground to a halt or even reversed in the 1990s (cf. OECD, 1998b: ch. 5). Legislation and/or trade union bargaining appear to be prerequisites for a continued fall in working hours. The trend towards shorter working hours largely continued elsewhere – and has been strengthened in France by the 35-hour week legislation discussed in detail in Ben Clift's chapter even before this, lower working hours were used as a policy to reduce unemployment (Muet and Fonteneau, 1990: ch. 4). State employment growth remains important. In the West German case this was a deliberate choice by the labour movement as an attempt to redistribute employment (Streeck, 1997b). The sharp decline in Japan should be seen in the context of historically long working days, as noted earlier. The impact of changes in part-time work is smaller than might be expected. It makes the expected positive contribution in Anglo-Saxon economies with the surprising exception of the United States and in the Rhineland countries. Whilst there are clear differences between developed countries in their shares of part-time employment, in most countries these shares did not change much over the period considered; hence, their contribution to employment growth, and accounting for differences between countries' experience, is often relatively small.

Overall, for all the concern in the 1980s with 'jobless growth', it is growth of private sector output that is most strongly related to net employment growth in this period. The employment spreading effects of state employment and changes to working times for full time workers typically contributed little to net employment growth; in the Southern European countries where both these effects were strong they acted to partly offset negative employment trends from sluggish output growth. Rises in part-time working were more clearly related to rising net employment levels than other forms of employment spreading, but this was typically less important than output growth.

Following Glyn (1992a) we can provide some indicators of decommodification by analyzing trends in the growth of consumption out of earnings, property and transfers. In the 1979–86 period Glyn (1992a) observes that consumption out of earnings barely grew in real terms in the Scandinavian countries so that in Sweden virtually all of the net growth in consumption was out of transfers. Table 12.4 provides comparable figures for 1986–96. Consumption from work continued to stagnate in the Scandinavian countries, which (with France) continued to see transfers rise relative to market output. In this sense, the decommodification trends continued in these countries, although overall, all but two countries saw government transfers rise relative to market output over this period.

Industrial policy and the developmental state

Whilst it is hard to provide definitive comparisons of state intervention as industrial policy in national economies, not least because of its multiple aspects, some general trends can be discerned. OECD (1999a: ch. 7) provides an exhaustive survey of state intervention amongst developed economies in the late 1990s. In general the Anglo-Saxon economies typically have the lowest levels of intervention, although Sweden also scores lowly on some dimensions.[6] Juhana Vartiainen notes that both Austria and Finland operated extensive industrial policy in the 1950s and 1960s to boost development, but have retreated from these since with industrial maturity (Vartiainen, 1999); there is no simple association between levels of public expenditure and levels of state intervention. The OECD countries with the highest levels of intervention are typically Greece, Italy, Belgium, France and Italy; Japan still scores relatively high for administrative regulation. Korea was not included in the study, but other work indicates a significant decline

Table 12.4 Sources of real consumption growth, 1986–96

Country	Market output per worker	Consumption from work	Consumption from work per worker	Consumption from government transfers/market output	Consumption from property income
Australia	1.4	3.0	1.2	1.5	1.5
Austria	2.2	1.6	1.2	0.8	5.1
Belgium	2.0	1.1	0.8	−0.2	2.6
Canada	1.0	2.6	1.4	2.0	0.7
Denmark[b]	2.1	−2.4	−1.8	4.2	11.7
Finland	3.4	−1.0	0.6	4.8	0.0
France	1.8	0.0	−0.3	0.6	5.2
Italy	2.3	0.1	0.4	1.0	3.0
Japan	2.4	2.7	1.8	1.4	1.4
Netherlands[c]	1.4	1.6	0.3	−0.8	3.9
New Zealand	0.8	1.3	0.2	0.9	3.9
Norway[c]	2.7	−0.5	−0.5	1.8	−0.1
Spain	1.3	1.2	−0.2	1.5	3.3
Sweden[b]	2.1	−1.1	−0.1	2.6	−4.8
UK	1.4	1.8	1.1	1.0	3.7
USA	1.1	1.9	0.4	1.9	2.9
West Germany[a]	1.8	1.6	0.5	0.8	5.8

Notes
[a] 1986–93.
[b] 1986–94.
[c] 1986–95.

Source: See Appendix.

in state intervention following the 1997 crisis in part from pressure by international agencies (OECD, 2001: ch. 5); Linda Weiss's chapter notes the limits to this process and the contrast with more cautious reform in Taiwan. These patterns are largely in line with expectations. Nevertheless, at least as important are the similarities. In general levels of state intervention amongst developed countries are low and the differences between them are small. Only limited evidence is available over time, but this indicates a decline in state intervention particularly in respect of cross-border trade and capital movements. Declines are evident through privatization, where the share of state-owned enterprises in OECD countries' GDP is estimated to have fallen from about 10 per cent in the late 1970s to less than 5 per cent now (OECD, 2000d: 154). The evidence above from Ben Clift's chapter on France and Chapter 8 on Japan by Matsuura, Pollitt, Takada and Satoru is that even the traditionally most interventionist states have seen significant declines in their industrial policy. Indeed, MITI has moved from strategic industrial policy towards more incremental and less targeted programmes precisely in response to changes in the international environment (Fong, 1998). As Chapter 8 documents, the proportion of the economy under MITI measures has fallen with structural change in the Japanese economy and MITI's power within the government apparatus appears to be diminishing as its budget and personnel fall relative to the rival competition agency, the Japanese Fair Trade Commission (Matsuura *et al.*, 1999). This is hardly surprising given the pressure for external liberalization from global and regional agreements and bilateral pressure from the United States. The Southern European economies have also seen a seismic shift as they have largely abandoned their postwar tools of industrial policy.

State intervention is nevertheless hardly negligible, even in Anglo-Saxon economies. Andrew Gamble notes in his chapter that state support has been important for certain key industries in Britain. In the United States state support, both directly and indirectly through government purchases and universities, has been key to the development of the new industries on which the 1990s expansion was based (cf. Coates, 2000: 201–10; Nelson, 2000: 253). In Canada the patterns of tax incentives towards particular sectors and small enterprises played a key role in its structural change over the past 20 years (Stanford, 1999). For much of the postwar period state intervention to support industry and agriculture was extensive in Australia and New Zealand, although this has been sharply reduced since the 1980s (Quiggin, 1998). In both Anglo-Saxon and continental European economies there has been a shift away from targeted support for large national champions to more general support for smaller firms. This is consistent with flexible specialization trends, although the appropriateness of much of this support is questionable: the contribution of SMEs to innovation is often negligible and their role in promoting sustained employment is overstated (Parker, 1999).

Alice Amsden (2001: 125) summarizes the developmental state thus:

> The developmental state was predicated on performing four functions: developmental banking; local-content management; 'selective seclusion' (opening some markets to foreign transactions and keeping others closed); and national firm formation…. Two principles guided developmentalism: to make manufacturing profitable enough to attract private enterprise through the allocation of 'intermediate assets' (subsidies) and to induce such enterprises to be results-oriented and to redistribute their monopoly profits to the population at large.

The undermining of the developmental state arises from the decline of its policy instruments (Perraton, 2004). Zysman (1983) identified government direction of credit as central to industrial policy; deregulation of the financial system has fundamentally undermined this as discussed in the next section. Direct means of industrial support through trade protections, local content requirements, subsidies and tax breaks are now severely restricted by the WTO and regional trade agreements. *Pace* Ruigrok and Tulder (1995: ch. 9), amongst others, countries do not and cannot systematically use trade policy to promote national industries. Nationalized industries have largely been discredited and sold off. Many of the tools of industrial policy that were used by European and North American economies earlier in their history, and Japan and Korea in the postwar period, are no longer available to developing countries because of global and regional trade rules (Chang, 2002).

There are two qualifications commonly offered to this analysis: one may be tenable, the other is not. The tenable argument is that the nature of deregulation over the past 20 years varied between economies and this reflected different objectives by the nation states some of which are able to pursue their policy goals with new tools; the untenable argument is that increasing global competition induces nation states to put more, not less, effort into supporting national firms.

The argument that global competition actually induces national states to increase support for their firms (e.g. Cerny, 1997; Palan, 1998), is a combination of two claims: states increasingly compete to attract inward foreign investment and states see indigenous firms as needing support to increase market share. States do use incentives to attract inward investment and we note below that this may be exerting downward pressure on corporate tax income; however, the EU has been fairly successful in limiting this (Thomas, 2000). The claim that states are increasingly promoting domestic firms cannot be sustained though. Such policies are increasingly not permitted under regional and global agreements and the available evidence does not bear out claims of increased support. There is no trend for state support to grow amongst developed countries: state support for manufacturing in the 1990s was typically less than 5 per cent of manufacturing value added in EU countries and was falling rather than rising (Thomas, 2000: ch. 6). Moreover, much of this support tends to be concentrated either on particular regions and/or declining industries, notably airlines, steel, shipbuilding and textiles. Government expenditure on public and human capital may aid business, but it is not direct support. Provision of public infrastructure provides a clearer case for government intervention to support industry, but in most developed economies public capital expenditure has declined to historically very low (real) levels to the extent that it may threaten future growth prospects (Sturm, 1998). Overall, advanced states are not systematically using their funds to boost domestic firms.

The more tenable argument here is that deregulation involves not simply removing restrictions but active reregulation: the new regulatory frameworks differ between countries in ways that are designed to promote particular outcomes. If the institutionalist argument is accepted so far then it follows that deregulation has not and could not ever simply be a case of eliminating controls; the huge raft of legislation and directives required to institute the Single European Market is a good example of this. Vogel (1996) argues through case studies of key industries that the nature of post-deregulation regimes differs significantly across countries for this reason. Andrew Gamble's chapter on Britain, Ben Clift's chapter on France and Linda Weiss's chapter contrasting deregulation in Korea and Taiwan all emphasize that deregulation programmes were specifically designed in an attempt to ensure outcomes desired by the government. It is also central to the argument of Linda Weiss's chapter that state intervention remains viable in the global economy. Greater economic integration would not necessarily reduce the market failures and may well increase some (cf. Kitson and Michie, 1999; Stiglitz, 2002). Elsewhere Linda Weiss has argued that 'it is important to distinguish between state capacity for adjustment and the tools or instruments of policy. Economic integration does not so much enfeeble *the state* as weaken the efficacy of specific policy instruments' (Weiss, 1998: 197). Although she argues that globalization may weaken the capacity for Keynesian policies, 'the very opposite is the case with *industrial policy*. In so far as industry itself is constantly changing, "industrial policy" must of necessity be creative. ... It must be stressed ... *that the very capacity for industrial policy is one that requires the state constantly to adopt its tools and tasks*' (ibid., p. 198). A good case in point here is the use of capital controls by several Asian and Latin American states following the 1997 East Asian crisis (Higgott and Phillips, 2000). This was use of a new or modified policy tool for developmental purposes and shows that post-crisis reform does not necessarily or invariably lead to liberalization as the sole policy response. Ben Clift's chapter shows France as an example of this phenomenon: despite abandoning many of its postwar interventionist tools, its deregulation policies meant that the state still retains key powers and has innovated new policy approaches.

Nevertheless, there are three main limitations of this line of argument. First, there is evidence of convergence in business regulation. Braithwaite and Drahos (2000) in their exhaustive study of business regulation find significant similarities between national regimes, attributing this in part to the emergence of an international epistemic community of business regulators leading to global regimes of regulation. Second, it bears repeating that formal international integration, both regionally and globally through the WTO, reduces the scope for state intervention. The Single European Market programme has produced marked convergence in competition policy broadly along Anglo-Saxon lines (Dumez and Jeunemaitre, 1996); policy convergence through APEC and NAFTA has been less strong but still tangible. Finally, it is one thing for states to design deregulation programmes in order to retain certain powers and in an attempt to secure particular outcomes, it is quite another to assume that they will succeed. The case of finance, considered in more detail in the next section, shows that government regulation frequently is playing 'catch-up' with developments in the industry with regulations leading to outcomes not foreseen by the authorities and convergence can be seen. In telecommunications regulation, a key example in Vogel (1996), national institutional differences appear ultimately to have made little difference to the outcome of deregulation (Bartle, 2002; Serot, 2002).

What is driving this reconfiguration of relations between states and markets? An interpretation in the spirit of Polyani might see this as the pendulum swing of contemporary wisdom – just as disappointment with government intervention led to a neo-liberal backlash, in time a disenchantment with the effects that market liberalization may trigger a swing back towards intervention. Economic liberalization does not clearly boost growth in contemporary economies (Mosley, 2000); indeed a general global shift to liberalization has coincided with lower growth rates in the world economy. It is worth noting though that most institutionalist theorists at least from Shonfield (1965) did not predict a shift towards *laissez-faire* policies; on the contrary almost invariably their emphasis on the limitations of markets for solving social problems led to predictions of the *lessening* of the role of markets (Howard and King, 2002). We cannot discount the profound ideological shifts away from faith in state intervention. This is not just on the left, but also amongst European Christian democracy so that Southern European governments of the right are pursuing more clearly *laissez-faire* policies than they did for much of the postwar period. Ideological shifts are less obviously important in explaining shifts in welfare expenditure; although they were important for particular governments. As we noted above welfare states continue to enjoy widespread popular support in Europe.

The chief limitation of explaining these trends in terms of political programmes and processes is that such approaches emphasize the diversity of responses and tend to miss common trends. Thus, for example, King and Wood (1999) argue that the British neo-liberal programme under Thatcher achieved a 'fiscal miracle', with 'marginal reform in the United States [and] substantial restructuring in Britain', arguing that 'it is difficult to see how such policies could have been pursued in political and constitutional systems significantly different from that of the United Kingdom' (ibid.: 383, 393). In other words, the concentration of central government power despite the ruling party winning a minority of the vote enabled decisive reform whereas other systems typically require compromise and negotiation. In this context they also contrast the liberalization programmes in Australia and New Zealand, attributing the more thoroughgoing New Zealand to programme to its electoral system. In the first place, this account underplays the degree of change in the United States over the 1980s noted in Grahame Thompson's chapter. Further, the experience of the 1990s undermines this account. If anything is worthy of being termed a 'fiscal miracle' it is the elimination of the US budget deficit, not cyclical surpluses in the United Kingdom which were replaced with large budget deficits in the early 1990s. Across Europe, governments undertook far-reaching privatization programmes and welfare state retrenchment often, as in France and Spain, by social democratic parties in coalition governments (Smith, 1998). Jospin's French Socialist government privatized more concerns than any of its predecessors.

Flexible specialization explanations are also limited. Post-Fordist arguments often stress state support for the development of firms' competitive advantage (e.g. Ruigrok and Tulder, 1995) and thus fail to account for these developments. The post-Fordist argument for a shift from a welfare state to a 'Schumpetarian workfare state' (Jessop, 1994) exaggerates the generosity of earlier welfare provision and misses the differences in welfare states' responses to persistent unemployment. The more *laissez-faire* 'new economy' versions of this approach appear consistent with these developments, but much of the shift away from state intervention predates the late 1990s investment in new information and communications technology (as Grahame Thompson points out in his chapter).

We should emphasize what we are and what we are not saying here. On the welfare state we are not resurrecting the hyper-globalization claim of a race to the bottom. But that is too easy a hypothesis to refute and should not lead to a downplaying of the constraints that globalization processes do pose. In particular, the expectation that globalization will increase the incidence of the tax burden on labour should be tested further. External pressures on welfare states are refracted through national institutions: different aspects of welfare expenditure face different pressures and have different constituencies of support and more disaggregated testing is likely to be more illuminating than yet more tests of simple convergence stories (Burgoon, 2001).

On state intervention, governments spend large amounts of money and pass laws, they cannot but influence patterns of economic activity for better or worse. Nevertheless, regional and global integration has been identified here as central to undermining state intervention. Crucially new rules of regional and global governance have reduced the scope for industrial policy, whilst increased MNC activity undermines attempts to build national industries. One conclusion that could be drawn from the French experience is that it is those who have most clearly understood and acknowledged the impact of globalization who have also produced the most novel attempts to maintain an active state.

Financial systems and corporate governance

Differences in financial systems are central to the national capitalisms literature. The financial system is not only key to channelling funds for investment; the patterns of ownership and control of firms – corporate governance – are seen as determining social outcomes. Systems of corporate governance not predicated upon maximizing shareholder value are said to permit 'voice' to other stakeholders; with employees this may be formalized through representation on company boards. Authors in this debate often claimed the benefits of 'patient' finance in Continental European and East Asian systems, with banks' close ties to creditor firms, over the 'arms-length' Anglo-Saxon models (Albert, 1993; Hutton, 1995, 2002). However, 1990s crises among European and Japanese banks, and the alleged failure of these systems to support new firms, have led to recent praise for the Anglo-Saxon system. Moreover, trends towards financial globalization are often believed to undermine the basis for alternative systems to Anglo-Saxon finance.

The usual starting point for classifying financial systems is between equity (or capital) market and bank-based systems, divided in terms both of the main source of external finance and the key mechanisms for corporate governance. Extending this, Story and Walter (1997: ch. 5) propose four stylized models: the equity market system; the bank based system; the bank–industrial cross-holding system and the state-centred system.

- The equity or capital market system is exemplified by the Anglo-Saxon economies and is characterized by external funds primarily being raised on equity markets, arms-length relations between firms and banks and monitoring of firms through active trading of equities including the threat of hostile takeover. Individuals own shares in firms and banks both directly and indirectly through investment vehicles, notably pension funds. High external disclosure requirements placed on firms and strong legal protection for minority shareholders (La Porta *et al.*, 1998, 2000) work to ensure the market for corporate control operates effectively. A strong framework of competition law may be instituted to try to ensure that firms' maximization of shareholder value is not at the expense of consumers by exploitation of monopoly power.
- The bank-based system, exemplified in particular by Germany, is characterized by external finance being primarily raised through banks. Equity capitalization and turnover tends to be low. Banks maintain close relations with firms, partly through their significant equity stakes and banks ownership of investment companies – the universal bank system. Banks play a key monitoring role on firms through active membership of boardrooms using their inside knowledge. Financial disclosure requirements tend to be low with regulations providing banks with considerable discretionary powers and legal protection for shareholders tends to be weaker than with equity market systems. Hostile takeovers occur rarely if ever. Similar systems can be observed during the postwar period in other Rhineland countries and Scandinavia.
- The bank–industrial cross-holding system has been best exemplified by Japan where, in addition to extensive recourse to bank loans for external

financing, equities tend to be held by other companies. Firms prefer this pattern of equity holding, believing that other firms share their concerns. Patterns of reciprocal shareholding by firms at different stages of the supply chain help underwrite cooperation between these firms. Hostile takeovers are virtually unknown. The character of relations between firms and banks under the Japanese 'main bank' system is similar to that in bank-based systems.

• The state-led financial system was exemplified in the postwar period by France. Greece, Italy and Portugal all had high levels of state ownership of banks in the postwar period, although with less state direction of credit than in France. State direction of investment funds was also common in East Asia. Belgium also had a significant state-owned banking sector on similar lines to France until the 1980s. The Scandinavian countries also had significant state direction of credit in the postwar period, but this too was largely abandoned under 1980s liberalization and had been directed more towards social housing rather than industrial investment. Firms in state-led financial systems are typically reliant on external finance from banks, with state direction of investment funds through its ownership of banks and other investment institutions. Equity markets tend to be underdeveloped, partly reflecting weak legal protection for minority shareholders (La Porta *et al.*, 1998, 2000).

The 'outside' Anglo-Saxon model puts the emphasis on liquidity, whilst other 'insider' systems have emphasized closer relations between lender and borrower to reduce the information gap between the two. Anglo-Saxon models emphasize discipline by potential exit – selling shares, hostile takeovers, foreclosing on loans and so on – whilst other systems emphasize 'voice', continuous monitoring through relations between lender and borrower. This distinction is central to much of the national capitalisms literature and much is claimed to flow from it (Pollin, 1995; Grabel, 1997). It is not just that investors under capital-market systems are said to have shorter time horizons and demand high hurdle rates of return; the longer term, 'voice' character of bank-based systems permits the development of long-term relations with other stakeholders, including training workers, credible commitment to investment in return for wage restraint and not resorting to hire-and-fire policies over the business cycle. The evidence on post-takeover performance of companies is mixed, to put it mildly (O'Sullivan, 2000; Gugler, 2001b). If takeovers do not improve the performance of firms then higher dividends may be ensured through lower employment, pay and conditions – effectively a transfer from the work force to equity holders – and/or reducing long-term budgets, notably for R&D and training.

The experience of the 1990s has shaken some of the faith in the European and East Asian systems. In France, as Ben Clift notes in his chapter, and East Asia's close relations between lender and borrower have led to serious mismanagement and outright corruption. More widely, debates in Germany and elsewhere suggest that although close bank–industry relations may be useful for established firms, they perform poorly in supplying funds to new firms and as such may limit structural change and the emergence of new industries. In keeping with our general approach, we note that both bank and equity-based systems have strengths and weaknesses and overall the evidence on financial systems and performance is mixed and does not clearly indicate the superiority of any particular system (Allen and Gale, 2000; Beck and Levine, 2002; Coates, 2000: ch. 6). Equity market systems expose investors to greater risk from market fluctuations, whereas banks may act to smooth returns. Given the costs to information gathering, there may be advantages to delegating monitoring of firms to intermediaries like banks. However, when there is a diversity of opinion amongst investors, equity market-based systems facilitate different investors taking different positions; thus, equity-marked systems may have advantages over bank-based systems where returns are relatively uncertain, notably with the financing of new technologies and firms.[7] Whilst the separation of ownership from managerial control does pose a principal–agent problem it may still be optimal to allow some autonomy discretion for managers rather than imposing strict monitoring to maximize shareholder value. Although a firm's stakeholders have an interest in its success it may be necessary to allow managers discretion to achieve cooperation between stakeholders whilst this can help solve the principal–agent problem to the extent that managers' own interests depend on the long-term health of the company (Allen and Gale, 2000: ch. 12).

In this literature the origins of bank-based systems are often seen as arising from latecomer industrialization where banks, sometimes state-owned, would have specific information gathering and processing advantages. A parallel literature stresses the role of legal systems and traditions. La Porta *et al.* (1998, 1999, 2000) argue that common law traditions tend to provide greater protection to investors, particularly minority investors, both in terms of legal rights and their enforcement. This is typically prevalent in the Anglo-Saxon countries. Countries in the civic law tradition tend to provide investors with less protection, although within this countries with civic law in the Germanic and Scandinavian traditions tend to provide more protection than those with civic law in the French tradition. Limited stock market development, concentrated ownership and reliance on bank finance then becomes a defensive measure in response to limited investor protection rather than a reflection of the superiority of bank-based systems. Historically, though, it is not clear that legal differences can account for differences in financial development which may be better located in twentieth-century politics in that on standard indicators many developed countries were more financially developed in 1913 at the end of the pre-First World War globalization phase than around 1980 (Rajan and Zingales, 2003).[8] A coalition of interest groups around labour and entrepreneurs/managers may have a common interest in avoiding hostile takeovers which would lead them to promote a legal framework limiting investor protection but promoting workforce rights; a coalition of interest groups around entrepreneurs and investors would lead instead a strong framework of investor protection but limited labour rights (Fehn and Meier, 2001). Alternatively, where strong labour movements are able to impose formal and/or informal rights on firms, managers face strong pressures to respond to these stakeholders rather than shareholders; this will tend to inhibit stock market development (Roe, 2002). Organization of business interests may be aided through extensive cross-ownership of shares and patterns of interlocking directorships (Scott, 1997). Overall the conclusion of this literature is that formal or informal incorporation of labour rests upon limited investor protection so that managers and workers can share available rents; strengthening investor rights would thus tend to undermine these relationships.

One might conclude that the optimal arrangement is likely to be some combination of bank and equity finance and that countries would tend towards this. Matters may not be so straightforward. Although we may not necessarily expect convergence on efficiency grounds, financial globalization might be expected to lead to convergence towards the capital market system. Financial globalization has the increased possibilities for large firms at least to raise funds on international capital markets as global financial markets have grown exponentially since the 1970s and cross-border barriers have been liberalized (Held *et al.*, 1999: ch. 4). Although share market capitalization varies markedly across countries, as Table 12.5 shows it is rising generally partly from increased investment by private pension funds. Since banks tend to act to smooth returns over time, during equity market boom periods the return on bank deposits will be relatively low: the rational response of savers is to shift funds towards equities during market booms, but over time this would act to undermine bank finance (Allen and Gale, 2000).

Global private financial markets are seen as Anglo-Saxon finance writ (very) large. For some theorists of national financial systems increased flows and convergence in interest rates and asset prices are secondary: provided finance continues to be channelled through different systems then different behavioural relations can still be expected. Grahl (2001) argues that it is not simply the rise in cross-border flows and convergence in returns on financial assets – important as these are – it is that access to international markets for borrowers and savers increasingly set the terms for both savers and borrowers. The depth and breadth of international financial markets makes them attractive to both savers and borrowers, particularly as it tends to raise returns to the former whilst offering keener terms to the latter. The effective processes of cross-subsidization that often operated within bank-based systems – between firms and from savers to borrowers – are undermined by financial globalization which thus undermines a key foundation of cooperative market economies. Globalization can undermine these relations in

Table 12.5   Stock market capitalization, 1980–99.
Per cent of GDP

Country	Year		
	1980	1990	1999
Australia	38	37	113
Austria	3	17	17
Belgium	9	31	82
Canada	46	122	122
Denmark	9	67	67
France	9	24	117
Germany	9	20	67
Italy	7	13	68
Japan	33	164	95
Netherlands	19	50	203
Norway	54	23	70
Spain	17	41	69
Sweden	11	39	177
Switzerland	44	193	323
UK	38	81	225
USA	46	54	152
Mean	24.5	61.0	122.9
Variation	71.6	88.2	62.8

Source: Rajan and Zingales (2003).

other ways. Product market integration through trade will tend to increase the pressure on companies to maximize profits; inward investment tends to exert even more pressure (Baily and Gersbach, 1995). This will act to reduce rents available to insiders, particularly labour. Legal integration may lead to convergence towards Anglo-Saxon norms. For much of the postwar period (and earlier) key industrial markets in continental Europe were cartelized so that established firms were effectively protected not just from foreign competition but from potential new domestic competition (Schroter, 1996). With European and global integration such protection, and the rents it generated, has gone.

The same debates noted in the previous section over whether styles of (de)regulation vary across countries, and whether this matters, recur with financial liberalization. The United States and United Kingdom authorities have promoted patterns of financial regulation both globally, notably through the Bank for International Settlements, and regionally through NAFTA and the EU (Germain, 1997; Story and Walter, 1997: ch. 9; Braithwaite and Drahos, 2000: ch. 8; Simmons, 2001). Arguably the 1988 Basel Capital Accord reflected US lobbying to ensure that capital adequacy regulations aided the competitive advantage of US banks. The United States has successfully applied bilateral pressure to Japan to liberalize its financial markets. The result is that from very different institutional structures, histories and cultures the financial regulatory systems of Japan and Britain have largely converged (Laurence, 2001). IMF restructuring programmes, including in East Asia after the 1997 crisis, have often entailed rewriting financial regulations along Anglo-Saxon lines although progress has been limited and some reintroduced capital controls. Some countries liberalized their financial markets in an active attempt to attract foreign business: this is most clear in the case of France, discussed in Ben Clift's chapter, but can also be seen in Sweden. Overall the evidence points to convergence in financial regulation. Regional integration through the Single European Market has eliminated remaining to barriers to cross-border financial activity in the EU.

How far convergence in regulations has led to convergence in the operation of financial systems is another question. Some indication of diversity and convergence in national financial systems is provided by the sources and uses of funds by non-financial enterprises. For the G5 economies, Schaberg (1999) estimated the proportion of funds raised by firms from different sources – chiefly internal funds, bank borrowing and issuing of bonds and equity – and the relative use of those funds between new investment, bank deposits and purchases of financial assets. Here one can discern clear patterns between the German and Japanese systems of heavier reliance on bank loans to raise finance and a larger proportion of funds used to finance new investment, as against an Anglo-Saxon system of heavy reliance on internal funds to raise finance, as well as equities, with a lower proportion used for new investment and a correspondingly higher proportion used to purchase financial assets, sometimes for speculative purposes. The most interesting case in Schaberg's analysis is that of France: following the financial deregulation of the 1980s (see Ben Clift's chapter), the patterns of sources and uses of funds have shifted from a German/Japan case to an Anglo-Saxon one. There is also evidence of a decline in bank loans as a source of funds for Japanese firms and the decline in the Japanese 'main bank' system, examined in more detail in Chapter 8. This is particularly striking in the case of large firms; as Table 12.6 shows, in the 1990s their financing patterns have come to resemble those of firms in Anglo-Saxon countries at least insofar as they are much less reliant on bank loans.

Available data limits our ability to extend Schaberg's analysis, but recent data for Sweden suggest a transition towards an Anglo-Saxon system following Swedish financial liberalization in the 1980s. Table 12.7 shows that retained income has become much more important in firms' financing and the share of loans has dropped sharply. Other figures also point to Anglo-Saxon financial sources in Sweden (Beck and Levine, 2002). Table 12.8 shows that although, the proportion of investment in uses of funds has risen, so

Table 12.6   Financing of main Japanese enterprises

	Percentages				
	1970–74	1975–79	1980–84	1985–89	1990–94
Retained income	35.1	45.8	55.3	45.2	87.3
Loans	41.6	26.5	16.4	6.4	5.2
Short term	19.3	16.9	9.9	5.3	−2.8
Long term	22.4	9.6	6.5	1.1	8.0
Bonds	5.1	10.6	8.5	17.4	11.1
Capital increase	3.2	8.0	10.4	15.8	4.6
Trade credit	21.9	17.7	9.6	5.0	−7.1

Source: Nabeshima (2000).

Table 12.7   Sources of funds for Swedish enterprises

	1983–89	1990–93
Retained income	44.0	94.4
Loans	16.8	−0.8
Bonds	−2.5	−0.7
Equities	6.8	14.0
Trade credit	7.1	−20.3
Other debt	28.3	13.4
Net capital transfers	−0.5	−0.9

Source: OECD, *Financial Statistics*, various issues.

Table 12.8   Uses of funds by Swedish enterprises

	1983–89	1990–93
Investment	40.3	59.3
Cash and deposits	4.1	−7.1
Bonds	5.9	0.3
Equities	16.2	36.2
Trade credit	8.0	−11.7
Other assets	25.4	24.9
Statistical discrepancy	0.2	−2.0

Source: OECD, *Financial Statistics*, various issues.

too have purchases of equities. Other evidence also points to a shift towards Anglo-Saxon patterns of sources and use of finance amongst Scandinavian economies (Oxelheim, 1996). These examples indicate that financial liberalization can lead to rapid changes in patterns of finance.

Nevertheless, focusing on sources of funds the similarities are at least apparent than the differences. In developed countries, with the exceptions of Japan and Korea (but not Taiwan[9]), internal finance is clearly the most important source of funds (Corbett and Jenkinson, 1997; Allen and Gale, 2000: ch. 3). Bank loans provide a small part of finance for firms in Germany, as well as the United States and United Kingdom; equities play a small role in raising new finance for firms in the United States and United Kingdom. Thus, it is hardly accurate to characterize German industry as 'bank financed' or Anglo-Saxon countries' industry as 'equity financed'. Evidence for EU countries shows no evidence of convergence in the use of bank loans for investment funds but some evidence of convergence in the use of equity funds and thus is consistent with convergence to an Anglo-Saxon system (Murinde *et al.*, 1999). Although Japan appears closer to a bank-based system, bank loans have fluctuated as a share of total funds and tended to decline. The figures show a decline in bank borrowing and a rise in use of internal finance in the 1990s, particularly amongst large firms. Further, from the late 1980s onwards banks increased their loans for speculative purposes.

One clear change is the effective end of state banking, with privatization of state banks across the Southern European countries where they had been strong in the postwar period. This is a key aspect of the demise of postwar state intervention systems in these countries. State banking is also in decline in East Asia, although even in the first half of the 1990s almost half gross capital formation in Taiwan was financed through publicly directed funds, compared with a quarter share in Korea (Amsden, 2001: 23). This may, though, give a misleading impression of the direct involvement of the Tawianese state where specific state direction of finance remained limited, the public banks were risk-averse and did not develop close monitoring relationships with their clients (Fields, 1995: chs 3, 5).

If differences in sources of finance are not great, then the emphasis shifts to forms of corporate governance and particularly governance by an active market for corporate control against governance by a main bank lender. However, even in the paradigm cases of Germany and Japan the corporate governance role of banks appears to be in decline, at least for the larger firms. It is not clear that Germany banks play any greater role in corporate governance of those firms in which they hold equities than other large shareholders (Edwards and Nibler, 2000), although some evidence does point to banks' specific positive role (Gorton and Schmid, 2000). Formal integration tends to strengthen equity market investors and observers have noted an increased emphasis on shareholder value in Germany companies and greater use of international finance by larger German firms (Rhodes and Apeldoorn, 1998; Dore, 2000). There is some evidence that this is already changing the behaviour of large German firms towards a greater focus on maximizing shareholder value (Beyer and Hassel, 2002). There is also evidence that German banks lending policies towards SMEs have shifted so that relations have become more arms-length with banks playing less of a supervisory role and reducing rather than increasing exposure when firms run into difficulties (Lane and Quack, 2001). The transformation amongst Japanese firms has been more dramatic with the decline in bank borrowing by larger firms and the 1990s Japanese banking crisis. For those Japanese firms which have maintained relations with a main bank the main bank has continued to play a key governance role. However, the character of that governance relationship was significantly different from that claimed for the Japanese main bank system. Although the theory of the Japanese main bank system predicts the main bank tends to increase its exposure to firms with falling profits (Sheard, 1994), the reverse happened in the 1990s (Matsuura *et al.*, 1999). In the 1990s Japanese bank-based corporate governance appears to have been a curse than a blessing. Although earlier studies had attempted to test whether main bank relationships increased investment, even after controlling for other factors, Japanese firms whose debt had a higher fraction of bank loans in 1989 performed worse and invested less in the 1990s than other firms did (Kang and Stulz, 2000). Close firm–bank ties tended to raise the cost of capital, so that most of the benefits from these relationships are appropriated by the banks (Weinstein and Yafeh, 1998). This may be related in part to the banks need to repair their balance sheets. The poor corporate governance of Japanese banks in the 1990s also had a detrimental effect on their creditor firms, raising the question of who governs the governors? Cross-shareholding in Japan fell from 55.8 per cent in 1986 to 45.7 per cent in 1997 and continues to fall (Yasui, 2001); much of this is accounted for by non-financial enterprises selling their shares in banks, not least because of the poor performance of those banks (Okabe, 2002).

Elsewhere in Europe although there is no evidence of a shift towards a bank-based system it has been argued that this does not presage a shift towards an Anglo-Saxon system because barriers to a market for corporate control remain in place and thus the insiders retain control (e.g. Deeg and Perez, 2000). This includes both formal legal restrictions but also features including high concentration of share ownership, interlocking share ownership between firms and differential voting rights of shareholders. Indeed, Allen and Gale (2000: ch. 4) find that legal restrictions on takeovers are often weak in countries without effective markets for corporate control and it is these informal barriers that are important. Transformations here are closely related to rising levels of foreign share ownership and multinationalization (the two often being closely associated, since FDI flows between developed countries have mostly been mergers and acquisitions).[10]

The Anglo-Saxon countries conform to expectations with widely dispersed share ownership predominating for United Kingdom, United States and Irish companies. Similar patterns are observed in Australia and New Zealand, although family ownership of these firms remains important and dispersed ownership developed more slowly in the antipodes (Scott, 1997: ch. 4). Rather than being a long-run embedded institutional feature of Anglo-Saxon economies, though, shareholder activism appears thus as the result of recent general changes. Holmstrom and Kaplan (2001) show that shareholder activism as a key element of corporate governance and the consequent pressures to maximize shareholder value only really emerged in the United States in the 1980s. Before that, shareholder activism had been relatively rare in the postwar period. In part a response to poor corporate performance in the 1970s, it also reflected increased power of financial markets with deregulation and globalization. Whilst hostile takeovers and leveraged buy-outs were common in the 1980s, their decline in the 1990s reflects the general shift towards firms maximizing shareholder value. In the United Kingdom dispersed (and often passive) investors have given rise to the standard theoretical problem of insufficient monitoring and the record of hostile takeovers is poor (Goregen and Renneboog, 2001). As Andrew Gamble discusses in his chapter how the apparent inability of British corporate governance systems to deliver has led to widespread debate and proposals for reform. Although he also points to shifts in British class politics that open up space for this, few concrete changes have been instituted. Recent corporate scandals in the United States, following the collapse of the dotcom share boom, have led even a Republican government to propose tightening of corporate regulation. These scandals also weaken the claims of La Porta *et al.* (1998, 2000) for the superiority of Anglo-Saxon common law systems. Although evidence is provisional,[11] these scandals appear to display precisely the phenomena La Porta *et al.* claim is characteristic of other legal systems: expropriation of assets by insiders at the expense of minority shareholders (and other stakeholders), market manipulation and limited transparency and inadequate reporting so that minority shareholders were provided with misleading information (cf. Stiglitz, 2003: chs 5–6).

The ownership patterns of the largest, usually multinational, firms in Germany, Switzerland and the Netherlands show some similarity to the dispersed ownership patterns of the Anglo-Saxon countries, but more generally the Rhineland countries have highly concentrated patterns of share ownership with various formal and informal mechanisms to limit hostile takeovers and the market for corporate control. Versions of the co-determination system with employee representation on company boards are instituted in Austria, Germany and the Netherlands, but not Belgium or Switzerland. The role of co-determination in industrial relations is considered in the next section. In Switzerland, like Germany, not only is bank finance important, banks also play a key corporate governance role with bank ownership of creditor firms' shares and bank representatives on firms' board (Hertig, 1998). Outside these two, though, bank ownership of shares is limited. In key respects Switzerland is closer to the Netherlands with high levels of market capitalization and outward investment; both countries have small open economies with internationally oriented MNCs and banks, sometimes with internationally dispersed ownership. Both Austria and Belgium are classic examples of highly concentrated ownership with a range of mechanisms that effectively block markets for corporate control. In Austria stock market capitalization remains low and the government retains shares in privatized concerns. Nevertheless, outside Austria stock market capitalization has risen to high levels in Rhineland countries and foreign ownership has risen along with this.

The Southern European countries also exhibit concentrated share ownership, share cross-holdings and limited markets for corporate control. The French system of corporate governance is described in detail in Ben Clift's chapter, where share ownership concentration is relatively low albeit higher than in the United Kingdom or United States (Becht and Mayer, 2001: 19). To reiterate, even after privatization of dense interlocking networks of share ownership effectively precluded a market for corporate control. However, recently these networks show signs of breaking up with both increased foreign ownership, but also increased acquisition of foreign shares as French business elites extend their networks abroad. Southern European countries' banks, frequently state-owned until the 1990s, usually had more arms-length relations with their creditor firms and often did a poor job of monitoring firms (as Ben Clift's chapter shows for France). This was largely true of Italy, where until the 1990s banks prohibited from acquiring significant shareholdings in creditor firms. An important exception was the more active role played by some local banks in financing SMEs in Italy's industrial districts. Smaller firms in Spain particularly though often found it difficult to obtain finance and became heavily dependent on retained income (Deeg and Perez, 2000). Foreign ownership still remains limited in Italy and Spain, and concentrated in particular sectors. France thus appears to have changed rather more than other Southern European countries, although Portugal saw rising stock market capitalization (to around 50 per cent of GDP) and capital inflows in the 1990s following financial liberalization (OECD, 1999c: ch. 3).

Until recently the Scandinavian system of corporate governance had similarities with both its Rhineland and Southern European counterparts. This paragraph concentrates on the Swedish case, as the one for which information is most readily available. Share ownership was highly concentrated, partly through the use of dual class shares with superior voting rights. Strong owner groups formed in a climate of social democratic government and powerful labour movements (Agnblad *et al.*, 2001). Ownership concentration appears to have been more the result of disadvantageous tax regimes than lack of legal protection and share market capitalization has risen rapidly since liberalization despite limited changes in legal protection (Agnblad *et al.*, 2001; Henrekson and Jakobsson, 2003). Bank finance was important and for some firms at least close bank–industry relations with main bank-type relations. Governments directed credit and operated extensive systems of controls. In the 1970s the Swedish trade unions proposed a Wage Earner Fund system of using their pension fund share investments to acquire controlling interest in major Swedish companies. In retrospect the business and political opposition to this can be seen as the start of decisive trends towards financial liberalization. As we noted above, since the 1980s the Scandinavian countries have seen a thoroughgoing programme of financial liberalization. Extensive development of new markets has been central to the success of Finnish and Swedish IT firms outside of traditional bank relations. As a result of liberalization stock market capitalization has risen sharply (Table 12.5) and share ownership is now less concentrated than other continental European countries (Faccio and Lang, 2002). More importantly, strong capital inflows have led to foreign ownership of Swedish shares is now over 40 per cent (Henrekson and Jakobsson, 2003; Reiter, 2003) and around 70 per cent in Finland where the leading bank is foreign owned (OECD, 2002b). Major firms have moved away from issuing dual-class shares. This rapid transformation has fundamentally changed Swedish corporate governance so that foreigners have large and increasing stakes in companies that are multinational in their operations anyway. This is likely to weaken their commitment to social relationships in Sweden's political economy (Henrekson and Jakobsson, 2003; Reiter, 2003).

We have noted above the crisis in the Japanese banking system and evidence of a sharp decline in main bank relations and share cross-holdings amongst large companies. It is less clear, though, what new system of corporate governance is emerging. With financial deregulation and openness, some moves towards Anglo-Saxon norms can be seen with a greater emphasis on shareholder value, rising foreign share ownership from a very low base and a few contests for corporate control. Nevertheless, moves in this direction so far have been incremental (Yafeh, 2000). Foreign investment has grown, but from a very low base and remains low. The nature of the new system will probably emerge following the full working out of the Japanese banking and economic crisis; the regulatory and funding conditions for a move towards a more Anglo-Saxon system, though, are evident.

Although ownership of corporations is typically dispersed in Japan, elsewhere in East Asia it is heavily concentrated and dominated by family ownership (Claessens *et al.*, 2000). As noted above, bank finance predominates: in Korea over 1975–90 external sources accounted for a majority of firms' sources of funds, unlike developed countries (Cho, 1996: ch. 3). Within this, firms inside the *chaebol* groups were heavily reliant on external financing and had reached debt–equity ratios several times than those in other developed countries by 1997, but other firms were strongly reliant on internal sources. This is similar to some Southern European countries, where smaller companies find it difficult to access bank finance. The workout of reforms of the *chaebols* in Korea post-crisis has been limited for the reasons outlined in the chapters by Linda Weiss and Barry and Dong-Sook Gills. The IMF East Asian restructuring programmes are predicated upon an analysis of the 1997 crisis in terms of limited investor protection and disclosure rules, weak corporate governance mechanisms and moral hazard from industrial policy (Johnson *et al.*, 2000; Mako, 2002). However, it is far from clear that this is an accurate account of the Korean crisis; as Linda Weiss argues in her chapter it may be better explained in terms of poorly designed financial liberalization in the context of indebted firms (cf. Chang *et al.*, 1998). New regulations on more Anglo-Saxon lines and restructuring of failing banks and corporations has been undertaken, but this still falls short of IMF reformers' aims (Nam *et al.*, 2001; Mako, 2002). The liberalization of the inward investment regime has led to foreign corporations acquiring large stakes, but not control, over several major Korean corporations (Chopra *et al.*, 2002); this still falls short of the 'fire sale' of Korean businesses to foreign corporations some predicted in the aftermath. The limited workout of Korean reform is not surprising in the light of the chapters in this volume. Both Linda Weiss's and Barry and Dong-Sook Gills's chapters point out the challenges this poses not just for the state, but for business groups and organized labour. It is also clear that earlier liberalization in Korea reflected internal political programmes as well as external pressure and there is an important domestic constituency for liberalization. By contrast, there is much less pressure on Taiwan with its gradualist approach to liberalization and more conservative bank lending policies (Fields, 1995: chs 3, 5). Although stock market capitalization is relatively high, concentrated family ownership remains the norm and there is no effective market for corporate control (Ko *et al.*, 2001).

We can now draw the threads together. Returning to the four-way classification scheme above, the Anglo-Saxon systems have not stood still. Rather their financial markets have become more extensive and liquid. Mergers and acquisitions – and, hence, corporate governance by threat of takeover – have tended to grow, especially across borders. Shareholder activism has become more evident and is a more recent phenomenon than commonly supposed. Has the expansion of international banks and cross-border FDI transformed financial relations elsewhere? As noted earlier stock market capitalization has risen sharply in most developed countries over the past 20 years. Coffee (2002) distinguishes between formal and functional convergence here. Although formal rules of corporate governance may not converge, firms can increasingly access foreign financial markets and new classes of investors. The rise in stock market capitalization, Coffee (2002) argues, undermines both the legal investor protection arguments of La Porta *et al.* (1998, 2000) and the political regime approach of Roe (1994, 2002) since capitalization has risen despite limited changes in either legal or political regimes. Although there has been some harmonization of disclosure rules and stock market regulations across Europe, attempts to create a common formal system of corporate governance in the EU have foundered (Berglof, 1997; Hopt, 2002). The cases of the Scandinavian countries and, to some extent, France bear out the Coffee (2002) argument that once embedded systems can change rapidly through financial integration even without major legal or political changes. Increased cross-border flows create pressures for legal harmonization (Hopt, 2002), but note the direction of causality. For political influence over finance, it is the demise of state-directed banking that is most significant. Moreover, bank-based systems in general face major internal and external pressures. Indeed informal rather than formal barriers appear to be more important to limiting convergence in corporate governance regimes. Where major share cross-holdings remain an effective market for corporate controls still seems unlikely to emerge; nevertheless this does not preclude shifts in behaviour towards maximization of shareholder value to the extent that firms wish to attract equity finance. Moreover, although Ben Clift's chapter points to significant networks of shareholding in France, he also notes their tendency towards decline; similar observations can also be made about Germany (Windolf, 2002). Countries have not all converged towards an Anglo-Saxon system, although some have moved a long way in the last 20 years in that direction. How the Anglo-Saxon system itself evolves, with ongoing debates in Britain and the aftermath of corporate scandals in the United States, remains to be seen.

Industrial relations systems

Employment relations are hypothesized as key national institutionalist features. Firm-level employer–employee relations are examined in this section and national wage bargaining systems examined in the next; although they are closely related they are distinct and their trajectories may differ. Marsden (1999) and Whitley (1999), amongst others, make industrial relations systems central to their analysis of different capitalisms and argue that globalization is unlikely to produce convergence in these. Marsden (1999), in particular, argues that norms governing relations within firms over managerial power and job boundaries can evolve through uncoordinated decision-making. However, norms will tend to persist once established and be common across national economies in line with institutionalist theory. This account focuses on employment relations themselves, but Whitley (1999) and others situate employment relations within the wider context of national capitalisms, particularly systems of corporate governance and human capital formation. Again this is in line with the general institutionalist approach of emphasizing the interdependence of institutional arrangements in each national capitalism. Indeed the bifurcation argument goes further, arguing that international market integration is likely to increase the divergence between national capitalisms. In this view, whereas liberal market economies are likely to see an increase in pressure for reducing the power of organized labour, by contrast in coordinated market economies employers need for stability and cooperation at the enterprise level shores up their cooperative relations with the workforce, including unions (Thelen, 2001).

Hypotheses abound in this area; hard evidence does not. Some convergence pressures may emanate from inward investment by foreign multinationals. Global markets may also increase the pressure for flexibility if, by increasing product market competition, they raise the costs of union activity and/or legal protection for workers. The flexible specialization literature sees change in industrial relations as driven by a shift from Fordist mass production towards specialized quality production; the latter requires granting greater autonomy and discretion to the workforce and, hence, greater trust. More broadly, the increased importance of information in economic activity is said to require greater worker autonomy and less hierarchical organization of production (Hodgson, 1999: part III). Depending on the author these trends are seen as common across developed countries or as involving a choice between 'high' and 'low' roads: it is only with national commitment to human capital formation and appropriate management strategies that a high productivity–high wage economy can be achieved. It is hard to assess these claims either across countries or over time. Evidence is often collected through impressionistic surveys whose representativeness and comparability across nations is questionable. Assertions about attitudes of management and workers and the degree of consensus within firms are at least partially subjective. Disproportionately the evidence is drawn from manufacturing. Much of the literature here lives in ignorance of the tertiary sector where most men, and an even higher proportion of women, actually work.

Data is available on union density rates and the proportion of firms with some form of employee representation on their boards. Starting with union density levels, the figures in Table 12.9 provide some support for the bifurcation argument of the emergence of a low union density group of liberal market economies and high union density group of coordinated market economies. Nevertheless, anomalies remain. Density has indeed fallen in the Anglo-Saxon countries, with the exception of Canada, but the evidence for the emergence of a high union density group is weak. The claim that where unions were initially strong that strength has increased only holds for the Scandinavian countries, where the 'Ghent' system of unions providing unemployment insurance operates; elsewhere union density has either shown no trend over the past 40 years or density has fallen.

Of course union density figures are only a crude proxy for the strength of the union movement in any country: in his chapter Ben Clift points out that French unions exercise greater power than these figures suggest and similar remarks could be made about Spanish unions (Royo, 2000: ch. 4). The role of unions in wage bargaining is considered in more detail in the next section.

Table 12.9 Trade union density, 1970–94

Country	Membership of trade unions as percentage of the workforce			
	1970	1980	1990	1994
Australia	45	48	41	35
Austria	58	56	46	42
Belgium	46	56	51	54
Canada	32	36	36	38
Denmark	60	76	71	76
Finland	51	70	72	81
France	22	18	10	9
Germany	33	36	33	29
Italy	36	49	39	39
Japan	35	31	25	24
Netherlands	37	35	26	26
New Zealand	55	56	45	30
Norway	51	57	56	58
Portugal	—	61	32	32
Spain	—	9	13	19
Sweden	68	80	83	91
Switzerland	30	31	27	27
United Kingdom	45	50	39	34
United States	25	22	16	16
Mean	42.9	46.2	40.1	40.0
Variation	30.5	42.1	49.9	56.1

Sources: OECD, *Employment Outlook*, 1997d, p. 71; Traxler *et al.* (2001: 82).

As noted above, formal employee representation is hypothesized as one distinguishing feature of coordinated market capitalism. Mandatory systems of co-determination are essentially a German–Dutch–Austrian system. Gill and Krieger (2000) found that although some form of formal employee workplace representation is common in Western Europe, the German Works Council system is hardly universal amongst these economies: apart from Germany, Spain is the only country here where works councils are the norm on this evidence. Latterly German employers have used works councils to bypass the unions in decision-making (Heinisch, 2000), but in Spain trade union participation in these councils gives unions an influence that belies their low density rates (Royo, 2000: ch. 4).

Overall few patterns emerge: even countries with similar traditions and economic structures – such as Germany and the Netherlands, or Portugal and Spain – still have marked differences in forms and levels of employee representation. Further, as noted in the Annesley, Pugh and Tyroll chapter, the proportion of German workplace operating works councils is falling (Hassel, 1999). Overall formal involvement of employees in company boards is not universal amongst Rhineland countries, let alone coordinated market economies, and may be in decline in those countries where it has been strongest.

One systematic attempt at cross-country comparison of industrial relations is provided by Gordon (1994, 1996). This is a variant of the bifurcation argument: low-trust employers have top-heavy management structures to monitor their workforces. Managerial bureaucracies become multilayered as the monitors must themselves be monitored and so on. One consequence of bloated managerial bureaucracies is that competitiveness can only be maintained through a consequent squeeze on production workers' wages. Such traditions tend to be self-perpetuating: unable to offer the prospect of higher wages or allow workers to develop their skills, low-trust employers continue to rely on monitoring to ensure productivity. By contrast, high-trust employers have more limited monitoring allowing their workers greater autonomy and discretion. This affords workers greater opportunities to develop their skills and may facilitate the introduction and operation of new technology; as such, productivity tends to rise faster and with it wages. Thus, a cooperative high productivity–high wage solution can emerge.

Although low- and high-trust employers coexist in any economy, in line with the institutionalist approach Gordon views the emergence of these practices as largely determined at the national level. As well as the US evidence reviewed by Grahame Thompson in his chapter, some support for this can also be found in an extensive study of the United Kingdom (Gallie *et al.*, 1998: chs 2–4): they found that the introduction of new practices and technologies was associated with an intensification of surveillance and did not lead to greater autonomy for workers. Gordon (1994) compared national levels of the managerial workforce relative to other workers – what he termed the 'intensity of supervision' – and found clear evidence of a division between high- and low-intensity management structures; we update and extend this in Table 12.10. The figures for 1980 and 1999 are not exactly comparable, as there have been small changes in the definitions over this period. Nevertheless, the figures are broadly indicative.

Overall the figures confirm Gordon's thesis that those economies he characterized as 'conflictual' – the Anglo-Saxon countries – have relatively large managerial bureaucracies, the size of which has tended to rise contrary to frequent claims of 'managerial downsizing'. Australia, though, is a clear exception to this. The countries Gordon identified as having cooperative industrial relations – the Rhineland and Scandinavian countries plus Japan – continue to have much smaller managerial bureaucracies. However, even here there are signs of common trends: in all but two countries the relative size of the managerial bureaucracy increased and the relative dispersion fell. The differences between the cooperative European countries Gordon focused on – Germany, the Netherlands, Norway and Sweden – are less pronounced now than they were in 1980 or earlier postwar decades; this is particularly so for the Netherlands.

Table 12.10   Intensity of supervision in developed economies

Country	Ratio of managers/ administrators to clerical, service and production workers	
	1980	1999
Australia	0.100	0.117
Austria	0.078	0.116
Belgium	0.065	0.063[d]
Canada	0.126	0.183
Denmark	0.063	0.119[e]
Finland	0.060	0.111
Germany	0.044	0.100
Greece	0.044[a]	0.217[e]
Ireland	0.058[b]	0.184
Italy	0.037	0.050
Japan	0.063	0.052
Korea	0.029	0.034
Netherlands	0.045	0.235[e]
New Zealand	0.088[c]	0.234
Norway	0.085	0.142[f]
Portugal	0.021	0.107[e]
Spain	0.026	0.124
Sweden	0.040	0.083
Switzerland	0.036	0.111
United Kingdom	0.154	0.253
USA	0.176	0.282
Mean	0.068	0.139
Variation	60.6	51.6

Notes
[a] 1981.
[b] 1983.
[c] 1987.
[d] 1992.
[e] 1998.
[f] 1995.

Sources: International Labour Organisation, *Yearbook of Labour Statistics*, 1989/90, 2000; Gordon (1994). See Appendix for further details.

Gordon (1996: 85) found a significant negative correlation between managers and administrators as percentage of non-farm employment and growth of real hourly wage rates for production workers in manufacturing over 1973–89, consistent with his argument that large managerial work-forces lead to a squeeze on wages for production workers.[12] Estimating this for the larger sample of the countries in Table 12.10 (except Greece) over

1990–2000 produced a correlation coefficient of −0.43, less than for Gordon's sample but still significant at the 5 per cent level. Several countries with low levels of supervisory labour are also relatively low income which might also lead to catch-up effects; however, controlling for this in a regression on real wage growth made the coefficient on managers and administrators as a proportion of the workforce *more* significant (see Appendix). Thus the evidence continues to support Gordon's assertion that burgeoning managerial bureaucracies tend to squeeze production workers' wages.

As with the authors cited at the start of this section, Gordon (1996) maintained that cooperative approaches must be systemic and cannot successfully be implemented piecemeal. As such, although particular firms in any society may attempt to implement cooperative industrial relations this is largely determined at the national level. Here Gordon (1996) places particular emphasis on the cooperative systems of Germany, Japan and Sweden. The analysis in the Annesley, Pugh and Tyroll chapter is broadly consistent with Gordon's approach. In their chapter they show that moves by some German employers to increase the intensity of supervision threaten to upset the basis of the high productivity–high wage system. Overall they describe a system of industrial relations in transition with considerable debate over the appropriate direction. There is evidence of maintenance of the cooperative nature of industrial relations at the firm level even while the macro system of wage bargaining has come under strain since unification. This queries the argument of Thelen (2000) that German employers do not wish to dismantle their national system of industrial relations and see it instead as a key competitive strength. The picture that emerges here instead is that some German employers clearly do wish to retain the West German system of industrial relations – particularly cooperation at the firm level through works councils – others wish to move to more Anglo-Saxon patterns and others remain undecided about the appropriate future course. Whilst cooperative structures with the workforce have been seen as a source of relative advantage in skills-based quality production, the sustainability of this in the face of evolving trade advantage and competition is unclear (Streeck, 1997b). In Sweden there is a clearer trend, but this is of employers scaling back their cooperative industrial relations system (Swenson and Pontusson, 2000). Much of this effort had been to reduce the role of national bargaining systems, considered in more detail in the next section, but it also entails reassertion of managerial authority. More generally in Europe regional and global integration is not leading to any clear pattern in the development of industrial relations for convergence on either model; rather systems are becoming more variegated with trends differing by company and industry as well as between countries (Marginson and Sisson, 2002). As Teague (1999) points out, although European integration has not led to a simple convergence towards Anglo-Saxon norms from product and financial integration, EU policy towards employment and legal integration have reduced the scope for purely national systems of industrial relations. European law does provide for some common framework, although the provisions of the European Works Council Directive only give limited workers' rights (largely to information) and do not enshrine co-determination.

The Japanese system of industrial relations has also been commonly marked out as distinctive, particularly in terms of its consensual nature. Coates (2000: 234–9) rightly warns us against romanticizing Japanese industrial relations. Not only are conditions for the workforce less favourable than often claimed, the key distinctive aspects of the Japanese systems – notably lifetime employment systems with seniority-based pay scales – only ever applied to a minority of the Japanese workforce. As Chapter 8 documents, Japanese employment relations have come under strain, although how far the employers have succeeded in changing the Japanese system has changed remains unclear – recent evidence indicates little actual decline in lifetime employment (Kato, 2001) but does point to a shift away from seniority-based pay scales with increased dispersion of earnings within firms but a flatter age-earnings profile (see also Rebick, 2001). Similar observations could be made about East Asian countries (cf. Deyo, 1989): the consensual nature of industrial relations has sometimes been exaggerated and such lifetime employment relations as did exist in Korea have been undermined since the 1997 crisis. Barry and Dong-Sook Gills's chapter shows the fragility of gains by the Korean labour movement as political struggles have emerged over employers' desire to reverse these gains after the 1997 crisis.

Thus the countries that Gordon (1996) – and others – identified as exemplifying cooperative and consensual industrial relations have each undergone or are undergoing significant changes in their systems. The point here is not that they are converging to some Anglo-Saxon norm, although in these countries at least some employers wish to move in that direction. Instead available evidence increasingly points not to clear national systems of employment relations but to their fragmentation. Katz and Darbishire (2000), for example, discuss a range of employers' workplace strategies. Whilst a low wage strategy, along the lines suggested by Gordon (1996), is a key management approach in countries with weak unions, other companies in these countries pursue human resource management (HRM) strategies aimed at developing employees' skills through programmes that bypass unions. Companies may combine HRM strategies for some workers with low wage strategies for others. This may be done through greater use of outsourcing for low wage products. HRM strategies will typically offer relatively high wages; as such it offers a partial explanation for rising wage inequality particularly in Anglo-Saxon countries. Rory O'Donnell's chapter discusses in detail how inward investment by MNCs has transformed many Irish workplaces using HRM strategies; this may also help explain rising wage inequality and rising returns to education and skills in a centralized wage bargaining economy (Barrett *et al.*, 1999). Direct emulation of Japanese work organization patterns mostly takes place where similar patterns of Japanese enterprise unionism are in place (which is often the case with Japanese transplants in the United Kingdom and elsewhere); where other forms of union organization are dominant joint team working is organized with greater cooperation with unions. Thus, the strength of unionism in Scandinavian countries continues to shape industrial relations practices, but employers in Sweden particularly have moved to decentralize bargaining and reassert managerial authority.

Other evidence points to increasing diversity of industrial relations systems within countries. Appelbaum and Batt (1993) found that US firms increasingly adopt mixed or 'eclectic' industrial relations strategies, drawing on a variety of national and international traditions. Evidence from a major survey of new work practices also indicates few clear national patterns (OECD, 1999b: ch. 4). The prevalence of practices such as job rotation, team working and delegation to groups or individuals varies considerably between firms within a country and between countries. Further, there are often considerable differences between countries with ostensibly similar industrial relations systems. The survey found, for example, noticeably higher group delegation in the Netherlands than in Germany. Some patterns are discernable: where Scandinavian firms use team working membership of these is typically voluntary but this is rarely found elsewhere. However, there are wide variations in these practices amongst Scandinavian countries. For example, group delegation is relatively high in Sweden but low in Denmark; delegation to individuals is high in Denmark, Sweden and Finland but low in Norway. Delegation of tasks to groups or individuals not surprisingly is low in the Southern European countries with their traditions of hierarchical management, but this does not appear to be the case with France despite its similar industrial relations traditions outlined in Ben Clift's chapter. Overall, though, differences between national economies had little explanatory power in accounting for the differences in the preva- lence of these new work practices. Decentralization of bargaining over pay and conditions employers have had greater freedom to tailor their industrial relations strategies. All this indicates that the notion of national industrial relations systems is misleading – developed countries contain a diversity of industrial relations practices. National traditions are not unimportant and trade union strength in particular affects the strategy pursued by firms, but the coherence of industrial relations systems is weakening as bargaining becomes more decentralized. The claim in relation to German and Swedish industrial relations systems that 'now that they [employers] have organized their competitive strategies around these institutions, they find they can scarcely do without them' (Thelen, 2001: 101) is highly questionable. What the evidence points to is a growing diversity of industrial relations practices within each country, which belies notions of national employment systems. Decentralization of bargaining is consistent with a flexible specialization story, but grander claims of greater autonomy for the workforce are not borne out. These developments are more consistent with the globalization story: intensified competition and new practices transferred by MNCs are part of a process whereby employers attempt to evolve more profitable workplace strategies. This also supports a gradualist explanation of institutional change, where different employers experiment with new work practices, over a punctuated equilibria explanation. The latter presupposes a national coherence to industrial relations that no longer appears to apply, even to the extent it ever really did.

Wage bargaining: coordinated versus decentralized systems

Few areas better illustrate the pitfalls of comparative national capitalisms analysis than analysis of wage bargaining systems. Since Calmfors and Driffill (1988) a large literature has developed relating wage bargaining systems to inflation and unemployment performance. The basic hypothesis is well known: a hump-shaped relation between the degree of centralization or coordination of the wage bargaining system and inflation/unemployment performance. In this version, highly decentralized systems which approximate to labour market flexibility or highly centralized systems deliver the best performance. In a market economy there is no intrinsic mechanism for coordinating wage and price setting: workers may bargain for a given money wage only to find the price level rising faster than expected and their real wage expectations thwarted. In a highly decentralized system this may have few inflationary consequences given the limited bargaining power of labour. However, if labour possesses some bargaining power – say, at the level of an industry – it will be able to raise money wages; firms will respond by raising prices but this would still raise the real wages of workers in that industry since the general rise in the price level would be a fraction of the increase in the industry's prices. Of course, if unions in all industries attempted to raise their wages in this way it would become self-defeating. However, it is usually assumed in these cases that there is an insider–outsider split in the labour force, so that organized insider groups are able to pass the costs of inflationary wage claims onto other groups. Similarly, when authorities respond to rising prices with deflationary policies, then it is the outsiders who bear the brunt of the resulting unemployment which would be expected to have persistence effects. However, if unions are all-encompassing, coordinate their wage bargaining and are able to ensure local compliance with negotiated wage settlements then there are effectively no outsiders in a national economy on to whom they could pass the costs of inflationary bargains. In the limit case of completely centralized bargaining even in a closed economy unions could not raise real wages through money wage increases as these would simply be passed on raising the general price level proportionately; in an open economy – and those economies with strong corporatist relations typically have high trade shares – inflationary wage rises would simply worsen the country's external position. Thus, centralized and coordinated wage bargaining systems can ensure that wage and price setting is effectively coordinated in an economy; this can be particularly important when the economy is subject to a negative shock by ensuring that the resulting adjustment minimizes the rise in inflation and/or unemployment. Highly centralized systems may also have certain other advantages: cohesive employer organization can aid the provision of collective goods, particularly training systems (this is discussed further in the next section). The wage bargaining systems also limit employers' ability to pursue low wage strategies and thereby increases the incentives for them to invest in worker training (Streeck, 1997a).

As noted above the Scandinavian countries and Austria have traditionally been noted for their systems of centralized wage bargaining. The apparent superiority of centralized wage bargaining systems seemed to diminish in the 1990s. Any of the main perspectives can in principle explain this. Globalization could act to undermine centralized wage bargaining system in several ways. Economic integration would be expected to generate convergence pressures on wages and there is evidence that this has already happened in the EU (Andersen *et al.*, 2000). Increased elasticity of demand for labour from globalization (Rodrik, 1997) would undermine labour's ability to extract production rents; by shifting power towards capital this may lessen employers' commitment to centralized bargaining system. This would be reinforced by higher capital mobility which increases exit possibilities for capital and thus undermines attempts to bind business to national partnerships with other stakeholders. Corporatist wage bargaining entails workers precommitment to wage moderation in the expectation of future investment by firms ensuring rising incomes; however, this presupposes firms invest at home whereas increased opportunities for foreign direct investment can undermine this. The demise of centralized wage bargaining systems has also been prophesied on flexible specialization and/or 'new economy' grounds. The argument here is that national set pay rates become increasingly inappropriate for firms seeking specific skilled workers and with the shift in work away from occupational specialization towards multitasking – centralized bargaining becomes less efficient by preventing firms from being able to offer adequate incentives to induce workers to perform the optimum combination of tasks (Lindbeck and Snower, 2001). Indeed this does appear to have been a key motivation behind the Swedish engineering employers' efforts to dismantle centralized bargaining (Swenson and Pontusson, 2000). However, centralized bargaining systems have not prevented the emergence of several of the world's leading high-tech firms in Scandinavian countries, as Juhana Vartiainen points out in his chapter. Finally, a decline in class identification may have undermined the social solidarity of a cohesive labour movement. Changing patterns of ownership and increased orientation

Table 12.11 Collective bargaining coverage, 1980–94

Country	Percentage of the workforce covered by collective bargaining agreements		
	1980	1990	1994
Australia	88	80	80
Austria	98	98	98
Belgium	90	90	90
Canada	37	38	36
Denmark	69	69	69
Finland	95	95	95
France	85	92	95
Germany	91	90	92
Italy	85	83	82
Japan	28	23	21
Netherlands	76	71	81
New Zealand	67	67	31
Norway	75	75	74
Portugal	70	79	71
Spain	76	76	78
Sweden	86	86	89
Switzerland	53	53	50
United Kingdom	70	47	47
United States	26	18	18
Mean	71.8	70.0	68.3
Variation	30.1	33.9	38.4

Source: OECD, Employment Outlook, 1997a, p. 71.

to shareholder value may undermine cohesiveness amongst employers as a bargaining group.

We examine the recent performance of corporatist countries below, but first we examine whether bargaining systems have become more similar over time. At first sight the figures for coverage of collective agreements in Table 12.11 appear to support claims of bifurcation between bargaining systems (Freeman, 2000; Thelen, 2001) as divergence appears to have occurred in the percentage of workers covered by collective agreements.

Nevertheless, these figures need to be interpreted with caution and may conceal significant changes in the nature of the wage determination system over time. Assessing change in corporatist systems presents several problems. Accounts typically stress continuity and path-dependence along institutionalist lines in these systems, as either emerging from historical settlements and established norms between employers and organized labour or as the outcome of a repeated bargaining game between the two groups. In the latter case, the cooperative solution to the game will not necessarily be stable; in either case corporatist relations would only be expected to flourish in countries where they have become well established over time. Soskice (1999) emphasizes the importance of collective organization amongst employers, but there is no significant correlation between levels of employee and employer organization across developed economies (Traxler *et al.*, 2001: 95). Assessing changes in the degree of centralization or coordination of wage bargaining is problematic because available indicators use relative rather than absolute and typically averages for lengthy periods; as such they can give few, if any, indications of common trends. For example, Traxler and Kittel (2000), who provide 3–4 year averages for 18 OECD countries over 1970–90, estimate that half of the countries have seen *no* change in the degree of centralization of their bargaining. This includes Austria, Germany, Holland and Japan, which would probably surprise observers of those countries. The most comprehensive comparative indicators from Siaroff (1999) report average values on a 1–5 scale for the degree of 'integration' in a national economy, a broadly similar concept to Soskice's notion of 'coordination' in a market economy and one strongly correlated with narrower indices of coordination of wage bargaining (Iversen, 1999; Traxler and Kittel, 2000). These are reported in Table 12.12.

Table 12.12   Composite index of 'integration'

Country	Late 1960s	Late 1970s	Late 1980s	Mid-1990s
Australia	2.500	2.500	3.375	3.000
Austria	4.625	4.625	4.625	4.625
Belgium	4.125	4.125	3.625	3.750
Canada	1.625	1.625	1.750	1.875
Denmark	4.375	4.375	3.875	4.250
Finland	3.500	4.250	4.250	4.375
France	1.875	1.875	2.250	2.250
Germany	4.125	4.125	4.125	4.125
Greece	—	—	1.625	2.000
Ireland	2.250	2.250	2.375	2.625
Italy	2.000	2.125	2.750	3.000
Japan	3.375	3.375	3.625	3.625
Netherlands	4.250	3.875	4.000	4.000
New Zealand	2.375	2.375	2.125	2.375
Norway	4.625	4.625	4.625	4.625
Portugal	—	—	2.375	2.375
Spain	—	—	1.875	2.000
Sweden	4.750	4.750	4.625	4.625
Switzerland	4.375	4.375	4.375	4.375
United Kingdom	2.000	2.125	1.750	2.000
United States	1.625	1.750	2.215	2.125

Source: Siaroff (1999).

Table 12.13 Standardized unemployment rates, 1980–2000

Country	Per cent of the labour force			
	1980	1990	1995	2000
Australia	6.0	6.7	8.2	6.3
Austria	1.6	4.7	3.9	3.7
Belgium	8.8	6.6	9.7	6.9
Canada	7.4	8.1	9.4	6.8
Denmark	6.9	7.2	6.8	4.4
Finland	4.6	3.2	15.2	9.7
France	6.3	8.6	11.4	9.3
Germany	2.9	4.8	8.2	7.9
Greece	—	—	10.5	8.1
Ireland	7.0	13.4	12.3	4.2
Italy	7.5	8.9	11.5	10.4
Japan	2.0	2.1	3.1	5.0
Netherlands	6.0	5.9	6.6	2.8
New Zealand	2.5	7.8	6.3	6.0
Norway	1.6	5.3	5.0	3.5
Portugal	—	4.8	7.3	4.1
Spain	11.1	16.1	22.7	14.0
Sweden	2.0	1.7	8.8	5.1
Switzerland	0.2	2.0	3.5	2.6
United Kingdom	6.4	6.9	8.5	5.4
United States	7.0	5.6	5.6	4.8

Source: OECD, Employment Outlook, various issues.

Comparing these indices with unemployment and employment suggests that some evidence for Calmfors–Driffill relationship can still be found, even with the deteriorating employment performance of the Scandinavian countries. Table 12.13 provides unemployment figures and Table 12.14 employment/population rates.

Not surprisingly more formal tests find only weak evidence of the standard Calmfors–Driffill relationship and generally find relations between bargaining systems and macroeconomic outcomes are not robust (Traxler et al., 2001: ch. 6). This it to be expected with changes in central bank policies and union objectives. By the end of the 1990s the strongly corporatist countries, with the exception of Finland, had regained relatively good unemployment and participation records. However, the notable performers in terms of employment growth over the 1990s are to be found in the Anglo-Saxon countries and the Netherlands.

The indices in Table 12.12 show, these indices indicate little change in the degree of corporatism amongst most countries. Yet, much of the case study evidence tells a somewhat different story. Earlier we characterized Austria

Table 12.14 Employment–population ratios, 1980–2000

Country	Per cent of the 15–64 age group			
	1980	1990	1995	2000
Australia	66.3	67.9	67.5	69.1
Austria	67.5	64.2	68.4	67.9
Belgium	57.3	54.4	56.3	60.9
Canada	67.5	70.3	67.6	71.1
Denmark	74.8	75.4	73.9	76.4
Finland	72.0	74.1	61.0	67.0
France	64.1	59.9	59.0	61.1
Germany	66.1	64.1	64.7	66.3
Greece	—	54.8	54.5	55.9
Ireland	59.0	52.1	53.8	64.5
Italy	56.8	52.6	50.5	53.9
Japan	70.3	68.6	69.2	68.9
Netherlands	55.4	61.1	64.2	72.9
New Zealand	64.3	67.3	70.0	70.7
Norway	74.0	73.1	73.5	77.9
Portugal	—	67.5	63.2	68.1
Spain	—	51.1	47.4	57.4
Sweden	79.5	83.1	72.2	74.2
Switzerland	74.3	79.7	78.1	78.3
United Kingdom	69.7	72.5	69.3	72.4
United States	65.9	77.2	72.5	74.1

Source: OECD, *Employment Outlook*, various issues.

and the Scandinavian countries as the most corporatist countries, a grouping which would command widespread assent as the figures above suggest. Juhana Vartiainen argues in his chapter that whilst centralized bargaining has declined in Sweden it largely remains intact in the other Scandinavian countries (cf. Wallerstein and Golden, 2000). Nevertheless, there have been some shifts towards bargaining decentralization in the other Scandinavian countries, albeit with continued high levels of coordination between both sides (Jochem, 2000). Arguably the key difference between Sweden and the other Scandinavian countries is that Swedish employers are actively trying to dismantle key aspects of the wage bargaining system whilst bargaining systems still retain employer support elsewhere (cf. Bowman, 2002).

Moving to the next level of corporatism, in both Austria and Germany, whilst many aspects of cooperative relations between employers and unions at the firm level remain, centralized wage bargaining as such has declined (Hassel, 1999; Heinisch, 2000; Kittel, 2000). This state of flux in German corporatism is explored in more detail in the Annesley, Pugh and Tyrrall chapter. Significantly, multinationals appear to be in the vanguard of shifts towards decentralized wage bargaining, although often with the support of works councils and unions given the prospects for higher pay (Kurdelbusch, 2002). Whilst wage bargaining has become somewhat more decentralized in Austria, there has been an enduring strength of Austrian corporatist relations; by bargaining over economic reforms Austrian unions have successfully maintained a key influence over wider economic policy (Heinisch, 2000; Kittel, 2000).

Classifying Switzerland and Japan in these schema is typically problematic. Switzerland has seen decentralizing of wage bargaining in the 1990s with a shift towards the firm level and successful employer pressure to liberalize labour markets (Bonoli and Mach, 2000). It is questionable how far Switzerland could legitimately be characterized as corporatist earlier: coordinated bargaining between employers and labour was limited and outsiders, mostly female and guest workers, bore the brunt of adjustment. It may be more accurate to see Switzerland as a case of the central bank providing effective signalling to which wage and price setters would respond (Lane, 2001). With Japan the classification problems reflect the informal, but well-understood, nature of the wage bargaining system. Under the *Shunto* system wage settlements in key export-oriented firms and industries set industry-wide, and economy-wide, rates for wage increases but these are supplemented enterprise-level bonuses. This system has been effective at achieving low unemployment and inflation, but often informal in its operation (Wakita, 2001). Informal coordination amongst employers plays a key role in disseminating information about how prices and labour costs affect the external competitiveness of leading sectors whilst there is a clear consensus between labour and employers that the export-oriented sectors should set the pattern for wage bargaining. Pay dispersion within firms has risen in the 1990s, as we noted in the previous section, variance between firms of wage settlements remains low (Rebick, 2001).

Whilst most of the core Anglo-Saxon countries – United States, United Kingdom, Canada and New Zealand – continue to have low levels of collective wage bargaining, corporatist relations have strengthened or (re)emerged amongst virtually all other developed economies in the 1990s,[13] including where historically they have not been strong. The Irish and Dutch cases stand out: Rory O'Donnell provides a detailed account of the Irish case in his chapter and we consider the Netherlands further below. Case studies also point to the renewed importance of corporatist bargains in Australia (Archer, 1992), Italy (Regini, 1997; Baccaro, 2002; Perez, 2002), Portugal (Hartog *et al.*, 2000; Royo, 2002) and Spain (Royo, 2000, 2002; Perez, 2002). Even in France, as Ben Clift's chapter shows, although there was some decentralization of wage bargaining there was also macrosocial bargains involving labour over key policies. In their chapter Barry and Dong-Sook Gills note the role of corporatist bargains in Korea following the 1997 crisis. These developments challenge both the reliability of indicators of corporatism – across countries and over time – and, more fundamentally, theories of how and why corporatist relations emerge. It also challenges both globalization and flexible specialization theories which would predict the demise of corporatism. These countries often lacked cohesive employers' organizations and had fragmented trade unions with limited powers to making binding agreements centrally. Indeed, with the Italian unions local-level discussion and democratic consent have been central to their 1990s corporatist relations (Baccaro, 2002). Theories of corporatism have emphasized the theoretical and practical difficulties of aggregating preferences of members and the need for central agreements to be credibly binding. Further, these new corporatist relations have not solely governed wage bargaining, but have often extended to bargaining over fiscal consolidation, particularly welfare state reform, and economic liberalization, particularly labour market reform. In the Irish case particularly, as Rory O'Donnell discusses in his chapter, these relations cover not just bargaining between organized labour and employers, but also a range of stakeholder groups. Some common trends can be discerned. The arrangements arose following a widespread perception of economic crisis within the country even if there was not a consensus over the appropriate reforms. In each of these countries trade unions covered a minority of the workforce and any trend (outside low union density Spain) was towards falling density (see Table 12.9 above). The emergence of corporatist relations in these countries was thus in part a defensive measure, a view that bargaining with government over reform, as well as with employers, would be more effective than simple opposition. Unions typically abandoned any commitment to indexing wages to inflation and their opposition to expanding part-time work. Whilst corporatism has typically been associated with compression of wage differentials these countries have seen widening wage inequalities in Ireland (Barrett *et al.*, 1999), the Netherlands (Jones, 1999; Becker, 2001) and elsewhere (see Table 12.1), although in Portugal they declined from relatively high levels with corporatist bargaining (Hartog *et al.*, 2000). This form of corporatism can therefore be seen as a response to neo-liberal policies as much as an alternative to them. In the Southern European countries particularly the role of political processes has been crucial: organized labour has attempted to trade cooperation in these areas for various concessions, particularly from governments of the left. How successful trade unions have been in extracting such concession is questionable: Royo (2000) attributes the collapse of Spanish centralized bargaining in 1986 to the inability (or, at least, unwillingness) of the Spanish socialist government to provide the social goods the unions desired.

Overall the picture differs from a bifurcation between liberal and coordinated market economies in their wage bargaining systems. As Regini (1997) points out increased wage flexibility has been common to developed countries with increased pressure on wage costs. Where union density was high this has remained so, but unions ability to bargain with the state over social goods and political goals has, in general, declined. Although union power has tended to diminish in the Anglo-Saxon countries (except Australia), where unions had medium strength corporatist relations have tended to emerge despite the absence of conditions typically thought conducive to this. Unions were powerful enough for employers and governments to seek accommodation with them, but this also had advantages in terms of delivering cooperation. In Calmfors–Driffill terms moves towards more coordinated bargaining could produce gains if political authorities were unwilling or unable to shift the economies to Anglo-Saxon levels of flexibility. Perez (2002) argues this holds for Italy and Spain – decentralization of the bargaining system in the 1980s led not to labour market flexibility but a fragmented bargaining system where wages became increasingly set by workers in the sheltered sectors to the detriment of external competitiveness. Italy and Spain shifted towards more coordinated systems so that wage bargains more clearly reflected conditions in the tradable sectors.

These moves towards more coordinated bargaining are explicable in terms of recent modifications to the Calmfors–Driffill model. Iversen (1999) provides a systematic analysis between corporatism and macroeconomic performance in terms of policy shifts towards non-accommodation of inflation and changes in economic structure. If central banks accommodate inflationary wage increases by allowing prices to rise then the costs of inflationary wage bargaining can be partially externalized along Calmfors–Driffill lines. However, if instead central banks place a high weight on controlling inflation they would not accommodate inflationary wage increases leading instead to unemployment. Rational wage setters will incorporate this into their behaviour. This reverses the expected relationship between wage bargaining systems and inflation/unemployment. Ignoring the completely flexible extreme, initially higher levels of bargaining lead to superior outcomes but these now peak at intermediate bargaining levels where labour would not rationally push for inflationary wage increases because of non-accommodation. However, at very high levels of labour organization, if unions use their power to pursue solidaristic wage bargaining in support of equality objectives this is likely to lead to wage inflation pressures. This will particularly be the case if there is wage drift amongst the most productive workers which is anticipated and incorporated into wage claims by low productivity workers. Iversen's analysis overlaps with others who stress the role of public sector unions (Garrett and Way, 2000). Relatively sheltered from competition, public sector unions may push for higher wages and if, by analogy, the fiscal authorities accommodate their demands then this can lead to higher unemployment through higher taxes and/or upward pressure on wage demands.

Iversen (1999) thus offers a coherent account of why strongly corporatist systems have become less successful at delivering low unemployment together with an explanation for shifts away from centralized bargaining systems. Moreover, his account is a cogent synthesis of several points made more widely but in looser formulations. Non-accommodation would be expected to lead to lower inflation and unemployment with less variation across economies, as we have observed amongst most developed economies in the 1990s. The shift to non-accommodation was universal amongst developed economies with the general shift towards independent central banks. Iversen (1999) predicts that solidaristic wage bargaining will now have a greater adverse impact on employment since it will inhibit the growth of relatively low productivity private services jobs that have provided much of the increase of employment in the United States and other Anglo-Saxon economies. Indeed lower wage differentials do appear to be associated with lower private sector service employment and lower employment growth in the 1990s (Iversen, 1999: ch. 6; Scharpf, 2000), but it is unclear that this can account for much of the slower employment growth in these countries (Kenworthy, 2003). Further, solidaristic wage bargaining provides incentives for the most skilled workers to defect from coordinated arrangements to the extent that such arrangements hold back their wage rises by reducing firms' discretion to offer higher wages. Both employers and skilled employees therefore have a common interest in undermining centralized bargaining systems. Thus, this analysis appears to explain both the worsening of strongly corporatist countries' unemployment record in the 1990s and the shifts away from centralized wage bargaining in these countries.

Nevertheless several question marks remain over this analysis. Our starting point here is Juhana Vartiainen's analysis of unemployment trends amongst the Scandinavian countries. As he puts it, there are 'nice' and 'sympathetic' stories here and it is far from clear that the equilibrium level of unemployment has risen in these countries. Although the absolute and relative position of the Scandinavian countries worsened in the 1990s, and their employment growth records were poor, they retained above-average employment–population levels. The first major limitation of Iversen's analysis is that it concentrates almost exclusively on the supply side, but other work points to the importance not just of aggregate demand shocks but also the policy response of the authorities on unemployment rates in the 1990s (Ball, 1999). Specific analysis of the Scandinavian economies also indicates that there is no clear evidence of rising equilibrium unemployment rates and indicates the importance of demand side factors in explaining their unemployment levels over time (Holden and Nymoen, 2002; Nyomen and Rødseth, 2003). There are also questions over why the 1990s should see a regime shift. The relationship between wage inequality and unemployment rates in Europe has fluctuated between being positive and negative over the past 40 years (Galbraith and Berner, 2001: ch. 6). The strongly corporatist economies were operating largely non-accommodating monetary policies in the 1980s from their fixed exchange rate regimes. The emphasis on private sector employment implies major structural change from the 1980s, unless it is being argued that employment levels were sustained by an expansion of public sector employment that has now reached its limit.

Corporatist bargaining in response to earlier shocks was successful, at least according to its proponents, because unions were prepared to accept wage moderation in return for an expectation that this would result in higher investment and hence higher income and employment. Further, this was achieved (outside Austria) on an at least tacit acceptance by both sides of the relatively egalitarian levels of income distribution (Pohjola, 1992; Henley and Tsakalotos, 1993). Thus, egalitarianism was not simply a union objective, but a signal of commitment to national burden sharing in adjustment. Much of the earlier praise for corporatist systems was precisely for their ability to limit the effects of negative shocks and minimize the costs of adjustment. The nature of the early 1990s downturns may be important here. Whereas earlier shocks were largely external, the early 1990s downturns in Scandinavian countries were partly related to the collapse of a financial boom following liberalization. It is not just the direct effects of this, which were particularly severe in Finland (Honkapohja and Koskela, 1999) and would tend to support the 'nice' story, it is also the disruption to corporatist relations caused by the earlier financial boom. Clearly Iversen (1999) argues that economies have changed sufficiently that unions must accept greater inequality in the 1990s than the 1980s if they are to achieve high employment objectives. But this misses the capital side of the bargain (Varghese, 2001). The neglect of corporatism's disciplining effect on business and the investment response in the 1990s is to miss half the story of corporatism. This is particularly important given that the expected negative relationship between wage moderation and unemployment is not found in Europe over the 1990s, if anything the reverse (Varghese, 2001). What role globalization and financial liberalization has played in this shifting investment response is an important question that remains to be answered adequately.

Iversen (1999: ch. 6) points to Germany and the Netherlands as alternatives to the Scandinavian model: by relaxing egalitarian objectives but largely maintaining wage bargaining systems unions (and social democratic parties) would be able to achieve their employment objectives without necessitating a shift to Anglo-Saxon style labour markets or a shrinkage of the welfare state. Indeed, the 1990s Dutch employment 'miracle' is frequently attributed to corporatist bargains since the 1982 Wassenaar Agreement where the unions agreed to cooperate on welfare state and labour market reforms (e.g. Visser and Hamerijck, 1997). Case studies and Table 12.12 indicate that the Netherlands had strong corporatist relations for much of the postwar period; the decade of conflictual industrial relations after 1973 may have been something of an aberration (Hartog, 1999). Nevertheless, the figures in Table 12.14 put the Dutch experience into perspective (Jones, 1999; Becker, 2001). Although employment creation was strong it was from a base of low participation and participation rates remained relatively low until the late 1990s. Participation rates remain low amongst older workers, with many effectively retired from the labour force through sickness and invalidity schemes whilst non-employment rates amongst single parent households remained above the OECD average in 1996 (OECD, 1998b: 18). In general, the lowest income groups have shouldered much of the burden of adjustment. It is not to deny the strength of employment creation to point out that much of it has been in part-time and/or low-paid jobs; the former may reflect life-style choices by female workers (although it may also reflect relatively low state childcare provision), in contrast to the Scandinavian countries. Again, it is the capital side of the story that is missing in many accounts of the Dutch experience – despite the wage restraint there has not been a marked rise in investment.

Turning to decentralized end of the Calmfors–Driffill curve, amongst the Anglo-Saxon countries that have most clearly embraced labour market flexibility and have least centralized bargaining (i.e. United States, United Kingdom, Canada and New Zealand), their performance has largely been above average on unemployment rates and, more clearly, labour force participation rates. Nevertheless, although the differential between these countries and the strong corporatist ones has narrowed since the 1980s, a strong aggregate performance nevertheless conceals important variations for different groups. The US employment boom did generate rising employment amongst the least qualified (Pryor and Schaffer, 1999), but the UK was less successful in this. As Andrew Gamble notes in his chapter, there was an important regional dimension to this – the United Kingdom failed to generate sufficient jobs in the urban areas where the least qualified are concentrated although New Labour policy since 1997 has attempted to tackle this (Gregg *et al.*, 2000; Rowthorn, 2000; Webster, 2000). In part this reflects a European-wide problem of regional unemployment clusters (Overman and Puga, 2002). Employment disadvantage has been concentrated on particular groups of households, so that lone parent households in particular have above-average non-employment levels by OECD standards in Anglo-Saxon countries (OECD, 1998b: 17). This has been a particular problem in Australia (Dawkins *et al.*, 2002). More generally, Glyn notes that in the 1990s the least skilled in developed countries have seen a worsening in both their employment rates and relative wages (Glyn and Salverda, 2000; Glyn, 2001). The position of the least educated men particularly worsened: only Ireland, the Netherlands and the United States saw no fall in employment rates amongst the least educated quartile. The position of the least educated women was stronger, although rises in their employment rates were most pronounced in the Anglo-Saxon countries and the Netherlands. Interestingly there was no significant relationship between wage inequalities and job creation amongst the least skilled. Anglo-Saxon countries' employment performance in the 1990s has undeniably been strong, albeit typically at the expense of widening wage inequality and relatively less generous welfare provision, but some groups remain excluded and labour market flexibility Anglo-Saxon style cannot clearly be said to be the only route to high employment.

That wage bargaining systems have not converged onto one model or become clearly bifurcated between two extremes raises questions for all theoretical approaches. Traxler *et al.* (2001) are right to point out that there has not been clear convergence from globalization or flexible production methods. To reiterate, Finland and Sweden have both established strong positions in emerging high-technology industries, their centralized wage bargaining systems notwithstanding. Nevertheless, case study evidence indicates weakening of the German and Scandinavian bargaining systems, especially in Sweden, that is not always picked up in composite indicators. The continued diversity of bargaining supports the national capitalisms literature view that different systems remain viable and national institutions still matter. However, many of the key cases were established recently despite the absence of favourable institutional conditions, rather than being embedded in established institutions and practice. Moreover, the shift towards more decentralization amongst some strongly corporatist countries and the rise of bargaining relations amongst many others at first seems to run counter to the bifurcation that might be expected along Calmfors–Driffill lines. Iversen's (1999) model may explain this as an appropriate response; an optimistic view of changes in the Scandinavian countries and Japan would be that they combine the coordination advantages of central bargaining with firm-level flexibility. Yet for EU countries, EMU may unbalance this since wage bargaining remains national whilst monetary policy is determined at the Euro-zone level (Hall and Farenzese, 1998).[14] It is unclear where countries are now be on any Calmfors–Driffill curve and there are grounds for pessimism. Unlike Germany under the Bundesbank, there is no means to coordinate bargaining across countries and little information on price setting behaviour elsewhere; this may be aggravated by little knowledge of the ECB's behaviour given its limited history and high secrecy.

The character of recent corporatist relations is typically defensive. Where labour has not been excluded from political processes, it has played some role in negotiating reform. The classic models of corporatism where labour and capital credibly exchange wage restraint for high levels of investment are not typically found here and have been undermined in Scandinavian countries. Paradoxically, national arrangements between social groups may be easier to establish than corporatist theory indicates, but classic corporatist bargains have become harder to sustain.

Varieties of capitalism in a global era

We can now draw our discussion together to see where the varieties of capitalism stand and the implications of this for the national capitalisms research agenda.

We noted in the introductory chapter that at the end of the 1990s a certain triumphalism surrounded some accounts of Anglo-Saxon capitalism.

With the bursting of the dotcom share bubble and the end of the US boom the 1990s experience can be put into perspective, as Grahame Thompson's chapter does for the United States. As he points out, puncturing the hype around the new economy should not detract from the real achievements of the 1990s boom. The varieties of capitalism literature has often argued that the lack of embeddedness in civil society networks of US firms in particular may limit their ability to innovate and introduce new technology success-fully into the workplace (Boyer, 1997; Hollingsworth, 1997b). The success of new technology firms not only points to continuing US dynamism but also reflects their enduring relations with the government and universities. (The British experience, with continued lagging productivity, fits this picture bet-ter.) American capitalism, as Hollingsworth (1997b) recognizes, is variegated with hierarchical firms competing on low wages in some industries coexist-ing with skill-intensive firms following human resource-based strategies in others. This is to return to the point made in section, 'Industrial relations systems' that labour systems vary more within countries than the varieties of capitalism literature often allows.

It might be tempting to see change in the Anglo-Saxon countries as sim-ply reinforcing their pre-existing liberal market economies, but this is to understate the nature of their change over the past 20 years. Andrew Gamble details the shifts in the British model from its version *c.* 1980 and Grahame Thompson notes the rupture with key elements of the postwar (if not post-New Deal) settlement in the United States. Australia and New Zealand have moved from relatively protected economies to wholehearted embrace of world markets. Variations within the Anglo-Saxon group are important too and indicate the viability of cooperative social arrangements. Indeed, Dalziel (2002) shows that New Zealand's more thoroughgoing neo-liberal structural policies relative to Australia led to a poorer productivity performance and lower income per head. Rory O'Donnell's chapter shows the Ireland's recent success owed much to its new-found corporatist relations. The key features typically associated with Anglo-Saxon capitalism are evident, but it is worth reiterating how recent the importance of the markets, particularly the stock market is. It remains to be seen what impact the collapse of the dotcom bubble and corporate scandals will have on this.

Performance of the Rhineland model in its German heartland is bound to have suffered from the shock of German unification; as the Annesley, Pugh and Tyroll chapter discusses this has lead to a wide debate on the future of the German model. In the 1990s the Netherlands can more clearly be held up as a Rhineland model of success. The key feature of the German model was a culture of consensus built around both macro and plant-level cooperative relations between employers and workers, an embedded system of industrial training and research and the bank-based system (cf. Dore, 2000: part III; Lane, 2000). Germany came to financial liberalization and significant FDI relatively late. Most varieties of capitalism accounts see the impact as leaving the German model largely intact as its strengths continue to give it a comparative advantage in key industries and/or leading to incremental change along path-dependent lines. On the latter, Lane (2000: 230) makes the important point of much wider relevance that such an account 'leaves unclear when an instance of transformation conforms to the established path and when it deviates from that path'. The evidence here points to a more varied picture of hybridization. Germany and the other Rhineland countries are not simply converging to an Anglo-Saxon model. The system of industrial training and research appears largely intact. At the macro level there has been a shift away from the wage bargaining system; at the firm level many employers clearly do want to continue the cooperative systems, but this is not universal. Large firms are shifting away from reliance on main banks are becoming more oriented towards shareholder value, but this remains some way short of Anglo-Saxon countries (or Scandinavian ones) and is less true of SMEs.

If the German system is changing and, particularly, moving towards more decentralized wage bargaining what implications does this have for Scandinavian countries positioned as neither neo-liberal nor Germanic (e.g. Pontusson, 1997)? Whilst there is a widespread view that Scandinavian capitalism had reached its limits by the 1990s in terms of decommodification, expansion of public sector employment and wage compression, in an optimistic scenario the problems of these economies in the 1990s were largely cyclical. Their welfare states appear intact, but question marks remain over other aspects of this model. Iversen (1999) though argues that this is a decisive moment where the Scandinavian labour movement must shift away from its equality commitments if it is to achieve its employment objective. If, following Varghese (2001), this misses the capital side of the picture, then the profound changes in the Scandinavian financial system and corporate governance may make it harder to tie firms into national social arrangements.

Although often neglected, the transformations in Southern European countries have also been dramatic over this period with the decline in state activism, particularly through the financial system. Ben Clift shows both the abandonment of key elements of postwar French statism and the attempts of the French state to retain key powers through novel instruments. Elsewhere in Southern Europe the abandonment of traditional interventionist policies has not clearly led to the innovation of new instruments.

A summary of the Japanese model that would gain reasonable assent is given in Chapter 8.

The chief features of this system are: a financial intermediation system centered around 'main' banks and lead underwriters; seniority-based pay and long-term employment; inter-corporate relationships, involving a closely linked group of firms, known as 'Keiretsu'; and minute government regulation covering a wide range of economic sectors.

The evidence indicates that the internationalization of Japanese enterprises and the 1990s crisis have undermined all of these features. Large firms have become less reliant on main banks and the banks themselves have ceased to play their traditional role in the 1990s crisis. So far there has been limited erosion of long-term employment relations amongst those sections of the work force to which this applies; nevertheless, employers wish to change these relations and pay relations do appear to have changed. Chapter 8 found that inter-corporate relationships have tended to decline, partly with increased production overseas and increased competitive pressure to switch suppliers as enterprises have become more profitability focused. Under internal and external pressure Japan has liberalized much of its postwar interventionist regime. Indeed, Porter *et al.* (2000) argue that the postwar regime, especially state intervention, are now key constraints on Japanese growth. It is important to note that even if these arguments were accepted in its entirety – and the foregoing gives reasons not to – deregulation would still be insufficient to solve Japan's economic problems. The basic imbalance between savings and investment requires greater consumption by the Japanese and higher levels of investment. Deregulation would do little to boost consumption and at best would have a modest positive impact on investment.

The recovery of East Asian economies from the 1997 crisis despite limited reform should not be surprising in the light of Linda Weiss's chapter. Further, this may not presage the shift towards Anglo-Saxon capitalism widely expected and advocated in the immediate aftermath of the crisis. Several countries successfully imposed capital controls. The withering critique of IMF intervention in East Asia by, amongst others, former World Bank chief economist Joseph Stiglitz (Stiglitz, 2002) is symptomatic of a deeper unease at the imposition of a particular brand of capitalism that took decades if not centuries to evolve. This is also reflected in debates over the transition economies. It remains to be seen whether this will create space for developmental states to innovate effective policy instruments.

The picture that has emerged here is that though there is considerable continuity in the institutional features of national capitalisms, supposedly key features of these models have changed over the past two decades which call into question to coherence of their institutional systems. Rather than a clear divergence between liberal and coordinated market economies, we observe fragmentation and hybridization. This is particularly so if we move away from focusing on a few exemplary country cases. We have emphasized change over continuity in this chapter and argued that globalization forces are important in explaining these changes. This is not a rejection of the varieties of capitalism literature, but a contribution to its research agenda. We have argued that it is important to move away from simply testing and refuting hyper-globalization theses and/or simple convergence stories. In this respect it is the dynamics of change in national capitalisms that need to be addressed.

Appendix

Table 12. 1. *Sources*: Tax – OECD, *Economic Outlook*, No. 69; Transfers – calculated from United Nations, *National Accounts Statistics*, various issues; Gini – United Nations Development Program, *Human Development Report*, 2001; Female Labour Force Participation – OECD, *Employment Outlook*, various issues. Wage Inequality – D9/D1 ratio, from Kitschelt *et al.* (1999), *Employment Outlook*, 1996, except Ireland (Barrett *et al.*, 1999) and United States (Pollin, 2000); Theil index (1970 = 100) from Galbraith and Berner (2001).

Tables 12.3 and 12.4. These follow Glyn (1992a). Hours worked in the market sector (MH) relative to population of working age (POP) is linked to market output (MO) by the following decomposition:

$$MH/POP = (MO/POP)*(MH/MO)$$

The employment–population ratio (EMP/POP) is given by the following decomposition:

$$EMP/POP = (MH/POP)*(MSH/MH)*(FTE/MSH)*(EMP/FTE)$$

Where MSH is hours worked in the market and state sectors and FTE is full-time equivalent employment (total employment adjusted for part-timers). Thus the growth rate of hours worked in the market per head of population is equal to the growth rate of market output per head less the growth rate of hourly productivity. The growth of the employment–population ratio equals the growth of market hours per head plus the growth of total hours worked to market hours worked (the state employment contribution), less the growth of average hours worked per full time employee (or plus the rate of decline in average hours worked per full time employee) plus the growth rate of the ratio of total employment to full time equivalent employment (the effect of part-time employment).

Market output per head of population is GDP at constant market prices minus the output of producers of government services (Source: OECD, *National Accounts Statistics*, 1998). Population is total population of working age (15–64) (from OECD, *Labour Force Statistics*, various issues). Productivity is market output per hour worked in the market sector. For Canada, Finland, Sweden and United States data for hours worked in state and market sector is available (from OECD, *National Accounts Statistics*), otherwise they are estimated from hours worked per person employed (from OECD, *Economic Outlook*, data CD-Rom, 2003). In Table 12.4 it is assumed transfers are not fixed and entirely spent on consumption. Consumption from work and property is from disposable income from these sources. Full details and estimates are available from the author.

Table 12.10. Under the International Standard Classification of Occupations 1968 the intensity of supervision ratio is Category 2: Categories 3, 5, 7–9; under International Standard Classification of Occupations 1988 the ratio is Category 1: Categories 4, 5, 7–9. The real hourly wage rates for production workers in manufacturing are derived from hourly compensation costs in national currency (United States Department of Labor data available at http://www.bls.gov/news.release/ ichcc.toc.htm), deflated by the consumer price index (from OECD, *Economic Outlook*).

Regressing the real growth of hourly wage rates for production workers in manufacturing as a function of the supervision ratio and the initial wage level produced the following result:

5.95	−0.22 Supervision ratio	−0.026 Initial wage level
(5.44)	(−3.18)	(−3.33)

$R^2 = 0.50$. Adjusted $R^2 = 0.45$, F = 8.66. *t*-statistics in parentheses are significant at the 1 per cent level. This is compared to regressing wage growth as a function of the supervision ratio alone:

2.92	−0.17 Supervision ratio
(3.84)	(−2.00)

$R^2 = 0.18$. Adjusted $R^2 = 0.14$, F = 3.98. Here the coefficient on the supervision ratio is only significant at the 10 per cent level.

Notes

1. This is to adopt a new institutionalist approach of taking agents' preference as exogenous and then explaining institutional development in terms of them. 'Old' institutionalist theorists like Hodgson (2002) emphasize how institutions can partly shape preferences, particularly through desire to conform. However, institutions are often not universally supported and key groups, particularly elites, have actively tried to change national institutions since the 1970s.
2. We define neo-liberalism as the doctrine 'that all, or virtually all, economic and social problems have a market solution, with the corollary that state failure is typically worse than market failure' (Howard and King, 2002: 3). This is to distinguish it from orthodox neo-classical economics. Whilst neo-classical economics may start with models of perfect markets this can be extended to incorporate market imperfections, as recent work on globalization illustrates (Stiglitz, 2002), and has no *a priori* grounds for regarding state failure as being worse than market failure. In inspiration and conclusions, neo-liberal thought is closer to Austrian economics than textbook neo-classical economics.
3. On hyper-globalization and other positions see Held *et al.* (1999: introduction).
4. This is simply the standard deviation divided by the mean (then multiplied by 100) to produce a scale invariant measure of dispersion.
5. We cannot hope to do justice to the voluminous literature on the welfare state. The reader is referred to treatments in Goodin *et al.* (1999), Scharpf (2000), Pierson (2001) and the references cited therein.
6. Parenthetically, this evidence indicates that the McKinsey Management Consultant's attempt to explain Britain's relatively low productivity in terms of the burden of business regulation is unpersuasive.
7. Houben and Kakes (2002) find that countries with equity–finance systems have tended to be more successful in the new information and communications technologies. Even though Finland and Sweden have traditionally had bank-based systems, their successful companies in these industries have by-passed this and raised capital on the new financial markets.

8. Chang (2002) also notes that the legal framework claimed to be necessary to promote financial development was often not present during leading economies' industrialization.
9. Taiwanese firms are much less reliant on bank finance than Korean firms were before the 1997 crisis. At the onset of the crisis the debt–equity ration in Taiwan was similar to the United Kingdom, whilst Korea's was around five times higher (Nam *et al.*, 2001).
10. Unless otherwise stated, details on corporate ownership are from Faccio and Lang (2002), Barca and Brecht (2001), Gugler (2001a) and La Porta *et al.* (1999).
11. Cassidy (2003) provides a good journalistic account.
12. This of course is not real wages since it does not take into account differences in the working week; however, part of Gordon's point is that working weeks tend to be longer in countries with low-trust employers.
13. Belgium may be an exception here. Both Iversen (1999: 7) and Traxler and Kittel (2000) find evidence of a shift towards more decentralized bargaining. Following several legal changes in the 1970s and 1980s a stable bargaining system did not emerge, possibly because of fragmentation amongst employers (Kurzer, 1993). In the absence of voluntary agreements, legislation gives the state power to ensure wage increases are consistent with maintaining external competitiveness (Traxler *et al.*, 2001: ch. 10).
14. At time of writing only two of the five highly corporatist countries, Austria and Finland, participate in EMU. Denmark and Sweden have opted to remain out and Norway remains outside the EU.

References

Aaberge, R., Björklund, A., Jäntti, M., Pedersen, P., Smith, N. and Wennemo, T. (2000) 'Unemployment Shocks and Income Distribution: How did the Nordic Countries Fare during their Crises?', *Scandinavian Journal of Economics*, 102(1), pp. 77–99.

Abegglen, J. (1958) *The Japanese Factory: Aspects of its Social Organization* (Glencoe, Illinois: Free Press).

Adema, W. (2001) Net Social Expenditure. Labour Market and Social Policy Occasional Papers No. 52. Paris: Organisation for Economic Co-operation and Development.

Adnett, N. (1996) *European Labour Markets* (London: Prentice Hall).

Agnblad, J. *et al.* (2001) 'Ownership and Control in Sweden: Strong Owners, Weak Minorities and Social Control', in F. Barca and M. Becht (eds), *The Control of Corporate Europe* (Oxford: Oxford University Press).

Albert, M. (1993) *Capitalism Against Capitalism* (London: Whurr).

Allen, F. and Gale, D. (2000) *Comparing Financial Systems* (Cambridge, MA: The MIT Press).

Amin, A. (ed.) (1994) *Post-Fordism: A Reader* (Oxford: Blackwell).

Amsden, A. (2001) *The Rise of 'the Rest': Challenges to the West from Late-Industrializing Economies* (Oxford: Oxford University Press).

Andersen, T., Haldrup, N. and Sørensen, J. (2000) 'Labour Market Implications of EU Product Market Integration', *Economic Policy*, (30), pp. 105–34.

Anderson, P. (1987) 'The Figures of Descent', *New Left Review*, (161), pp. 20–77.

Aoki, M. (1988) *Information, Incentives, and Bargaining in the Japanese Economy* (Cambridge: Cambridge University Press).

Aoki, M. (2000) *Information, Corporate Governance and Institutional Diversity* (Oxford: Oxford University Press).

Aoki, M. and Dore, R. (eds) (1994) *The Japanese Firm* (Oxford: Oxford University Press).

Aoki, M. and Okuno, M. (1996) *Keizai-Sisutemu no Hikaku-Seido Bunseki (Comparative Institutional Analysis of the Economic System)* (Tokyo: Tokyo University Press).

Aoki, M. and Patrick, H. (1994) *The Japanese Main Bank System* (Oxford: Oxford University Press).

Appelbaum, E. and Batt, R. (1993) 'Policy Levers for High Performance Production Systems', *International Contributions to Labour Studies*, (3), pp. 1–30.

Archer, R. (1992) 'The Unexpected Emergence of Australian Corporatism', in J. Pekkarinen, M. Pohjola and R. Rowthorn (eds), *Social Corporatism: A Superior Economic System?* (Oxford: Oxford University Press).

Aron, J. (2000) 'Growth and Institutions', *World Bank Research Observer*, 15(1), pp. 99–135.

Arrighi, G. (1994) *The Long Twentieth Century: Money, Power, and the Origins of Our Times* (London: Verso).

Arthur, W.B. (1989) 'Competing Technologies, Increasing Returns and Lock-in by Historical Events', *Economic Journal*, 99, pp. 116–31.

Association of Japan Automobile Parts Industry (1990) *The Japanese Automobile Parts Industry. Auto Trade Journal*.

Association of Japan Automobile Parts Industry (1998) *The Japanese Automobile Parts Industry. Auto Trade Journal*.

Asanuma, B. (1987) '*Kankei-rent to sono Bunpai-kousyou*' *Keizai Ronsou (The Economic Review)*, 139(1), pp. 39–60.

Asanuma, B. (1989) 'Manufacturer–Supplier Relationships in Japan and the Concept of Relation-Specific Skill', *Journal of the Japanese and International Economies*, 3(1), pp. 1–30.

Astlay, W.G. and Fombrum, C.J. (1983) 'Technological Innovation and Industrial Structure: The Case of Telecommunications', in R. Lamb (ed.), *Advances in Strategic Management 1* (London: JAI Press).

Atkinson, A. (2001) 'A Critique of the Transatlantic Consensus on Rising Income Inequality', *World Economy*, 24(4), pp. 433–52.

Audretsch, D. and Thurik, A. (2001) 'What's New About the New Economy?', *Industrial and Corporate Change*, 10(1), pp. 267–315.

Augar, P. (2000) *The Death of Gentlemanly Capitalism: The Rise and Fall of London's Investment Banks* (London: Penguin).

Baccaro, L. (2002) 'The Consolidation of "Democratic" Corporatism in Italy', *Politics and Society*, 30(2), pp. 327–57.

Badarraco, J. Jr (1990) *The Knowledge Link* (Harvard: Harvard Business School Press).

Baily, M. and Gersbach, H. (1995) 'Efficiency in Manufacturing and the Need for Global Competition', *Brookings Papers on Economic Activity*, Microeconomics Issue, pp. 307–47.

Ball, L. (1999) 'Aggregate Demand and Long-Run Unemployment', *Brookings Papers on Economic Activity*, (2), pp. 189–236.

Bank of Japan. (1995a) *Comparative Economic and Financial Statistics, Japan and Other Major Countries* (Tokyo: Bank of Japan).

Bank of Japan. (1995b) *Economic Statistics Annual* (Tokyo: Bank of Japan).

Bank of Japan. (1996a) *Nippon Ginko Geppo, July* (Tokyo: Bank of Japan).

Bank of Japan. (1996b) *Economic Statistics Monthly* (Tokyo: Bank of Japan).

Bank of Japan. (Various Years) *Financial Statement of Principal Enterprises* (Tokyo: Bank of Japan).

Bank of Japan. (1999) *Economic Statistics Annual* (Tokyo: Bank of Japan).

Baran, P. and Sweezy, P. (1966) *Monopoly Capitalism* (New York: Monthly Review Press).

Barca, F. and Becht, M. (eds) (2001) *The Control of Corporate Europe* (Oxford: Oxford University Press).

Barrett, A. *et al.* (1999) 'Rising Wage Inequality, Returns to Education and Labour Market Institutions: Evidence from Ireland', *British Journal of Industrial Relations*, 37(1), pp. 77–100.

Bartle, I. (2002) 'When Institutions no Longer Matter: Reform of Telecommunications and Electricity in Germany, France and Britain', *Journal of Public Policy*, 22(1), pp. 1–27.

Becht, M. and Mayer, C. (2001) 'Introduction', in F. Barca and M. Becht (eds), *The Control of Corporate Europe* (Oxford: Oxford University Press).

Beck, T. and Levine, R. (2002) 'Industry Growth and Capital Allocation: Does Having a Market- or Bank-based System Matter?', *Journal of Financial Economics*, 64(2), pp. 147–80.

Becker, U. (2001) 'A "Dutch Model": Employment Growth by Corporatist Consensus and Wage Restraint? A Critical Account of an Idyllic View', *New Political Economy*, 6(1), pp. 19–43.

Benhayoun, G. and Lazzeri, Y. (1998) *L'Evaluation des Politiques Publiques de l'Emploi* (Paris: PUF).

Berger, S. and Dore, R. (eds) (1996) *National Diversity and Global Capitalism* (Ithaca: Cornell University Press).

Berglof, E. (1997) 'Reforming Corporate Governance: Redirecting the European Agenda', *Economic Policy*, (24), pp. 91–117.

Bergsten, F. (2000) 'East Asian Regionalism: Towards a Tripartite World', *The Economist*, 15 July, pp. 23–5.

Bertlesmann Stiftung and Hans-Böckler-Stiftung (eds) (1998) *Mitbestimmung und neue Unternehmenskulturen – Bilanz und Perspectiven* (Güntersloh: Verlag Bertlesmann Stiftung).

Best, M. (1990) *The New Competition – Institutions of Industrial Restructuring* (Cambridge: Polity).

Beyer, J. and Hassel, A. (2002) 'The Effects of Convergence: Internationalization and the Changing Distribution of Net Value Added in Large German Firms', *Economy and Society*, 31(3), pp. 309–32.

Blanchard, O. and Muet, P-A. (1993) 'Competitiveness Through Disinflation: An Assessment of the French Macroeconomic Strategy', *Economic Policy*, (8), pp. 11–56.

Blanchard, O. and Wolfers, J. (2000) 'The Role of Shocks and Institutions in the Rise of European Unemployment: The Aggregate Evidence', *Economic Journal*, 110, pp. C1–33.

Boeri, T., Börsch-Supar, A. and Tabellini, G. (2001) 'Would You Like to Shrink the Welfare State? A Survey of European Citizens', *Economic Policy*, (32), pp. 7–50.

Boltho, A. (1985) 'Was Japan's Industrial Policy Successful?', *Cambridge Journal of Economics*, 9, pp. 187–201.

Bonoli, G. and Mach, A. (2000) 'Switzerland: Adjustment Politics within Institutional Constraints', in F. Scharpf and V. Schmidt (eds), *Welfare and Work in the Open Economy: Volume Two* (Oxford: Oxford University Press).

Borjas, G., Freeman, P. and Katz, L. (1997) 'How Much do Immigration and Trade Affect Labor Market Outcomes?', *Brookings Papers on Economic Activity*, 1, pp. 1–90.

Bowman, J. (2002) 'Employers and the Persistence of Centralized Wage Setting: The Case of Norway', *Comparative Political Studies*, 35(9), pp. 995–1026.

Boyer, R. (1997) 'French Statism at the Crossroads', in C. Crouch and W. Streeck (eds), *The Political Economy of Modern Capitalism: Mapping Convergence and Diversity* (London: Sage).

Braithwaite, J. and Drahos, P. (2000) *Global Business Regulation* (Cambridge: Cambridge University Press).

Breen, R., Hannan, D., Rottman, D. and Whelan, C. (1990) *Understanding Contemporary Ireland: State, Class and Development in the Republic of Ireland* (London: Macmillan).

Bretschger, L. and Hettich, F. (2002) 'Globalisation, Capital Mobility and Tax Competition: Theory and Evidence for OECD Countries', *European Journal of Political Economy*, 18, pp. 695–716.

Brittan, S. (1971) *Steering the Economy* (London: Penguin).

Burchell, B. and Wilkinson, F. (1997) 'Trust, Business Relationships and the Contractual Environment', *Cambridge Journal of Economics*, 21(2), pp. 217–37.

Burgoon, B. (2001) 'Globalization and Welfare Compensation', *International Organization*, 55(3), pp. 509–51.

Cain, P. and Hopkins, A. (1993) *British Imperialism: Vol I Innovation and Expansion 1688–1914; Vol. 2 Crisis and Deconstruction 1914–1990* (London: Longman).

Calmfors, L. (1993) 'Lessons from the Macroeconomic Experience of Sweden', *European Journal of Political Economy*, 9, pp. 25–72.

Calmfors, L. and Driffill, J. (1988) 'Bargaining Structure, Corporatism and Macreconomic Performance', *Economic Policy*, (6), pp. 13–61.

Cameron, D (1996) 'Exchange Rate Politics in France 1981–83: The Regime Defining Choices of the Mitterrand Presidency', in A. Daley (ed.), *The Mitterrand Era: Policy Alternatives and Political Mobilization in France* (Basingstoke: Macmillan).

Caminada, K. and Goudswaard, K. (2001) 'International Trends in Income Inequality and Social Policy', *International Tax and Public Finance*, 8, pp. 395–415.

Cammack, P. (1992) 'The New Institutionalism: Predatory Rule, Institutional Persistence, and Macro-social Change', *Economy and Society*, 21(4), pp. 397–429.

Card, D., Kramarz, F. and Lemieux, T. (1999) 'Changes in the Relative Structure of Wages and Employment: A Comparison of the United States, Canada, and France', *Canadian Journal of Economics*, 32(4), pp. 843–77.

Cassidy, J. (2003) *Dot.Con: The Real Story of Why the Internet Bubble Burst* (London: Penguin Books).

Cawson, A. (1986) *Corporatism and Political Theory* (Oxford: Basil Blackwell).

Cerny, P. (1989) 'The "Little Big Bang" in Paris: Financial Deregulation in a *Dirigiste* System', *European Journal of Political Research*, 17, pp. 169–92.

Cerny, P. (1997) 'Paradoxes of the Competition State', *Government and Opposition*, 32(2), pp. 251–74.

Chandler, A. (1990) *Scale and Scope: The Dynamics of Industrial Capitalism* (Cambridge, MA: Harvard University Press).

Chang, H.-J. (1996) *The Political Economy of Industrial Policy* (London: Macmillan).

Chang, H.-J. (1998) 'Korea: The Misunderstood Crisis', *World Development*, 26(8), pp. 1555–61.

Chang, H.-J. (2002) *Kicking Away the Ladder: Development Strategy in Historical Perspective* (London: Anthem).

Chang, H.-J., Park, H.-J. and Yoo, C.G. (1998) 'Interpreting the Korean Crisis: Financial Liberalisation, Industrial Policy and Corporate Governance', *Cambridge Journal of Economics*, 22(6), pp. 735–46.

Charkham, J. (1995) *Keeping Good Company* (Oxford: Oxford University Press).

Cho, Y.-D. (1996) *Financial Factors and Corporate Investment: An Empirical Analysis of Korean Manufacturing Firms* (Aldershot: Avebury).

Chopra, A. *et al.* (2002) 'From Crisis to Recovery in Korea', in D. Coe and S.-E. Kim (eds), *Korean Crisis and Recovery* (Washington DC: International Monetary Fund).

Claessens, S., Djankov, S. and Lang, L. (2000) 'The Separation of Ownership and Control in East Asian Corporations', *Journal of Financial Economics*, 58(1–2), pp. 81–112.

Clancy, P., O'Connell, L. and Van Egeraat, C. (1998) 'Porter's Clusters: Still the Way to Go', in *Sustaining Competitive Advantage* (Dublin: National Economic and Social Council).

Clarke, J. and Newman, J. (1997) *The Managerial State: Power, Politics and Ideology in the Remaking of Social Welfare* (London: Sage).

Clayton, R. and Pontusson, J. (1998) 'Welfare State Retrenchment Revisited', *World Politics*, 51(1), pp. 67–98.

Clift, B. (2001a) 'Social Democracy in the 21st Century: Still a Class Act?', *Journal of European Area Studies*, 9(2), pp. 191–215.

Clift, B. (2001b) 'The Jospin Way', *The Political Quarterly*, 72(2), pp. 170–9.

Clift, B. (2003) *French Socialism in a Global Era: The Political Economy of the New Social Democracy in France* (London: Continuum).

Clift, B., Gamble, A. and Harris, M. (2000) 'The Labour Party and the Company' in J. Parkinson *et al.* (eds), *The Political Economy of the Company* (London: Hart).

Coase, R. (1937) 'The Nature of the Firm', *Economica*, new series, 4, pp. 386–405.

Coates, D. (1994) *The Question of UK Decline* (London: Harvester Wheatsheaf).

Coates, D. (2000) *Models of Capitalism: Growth and Stagnation in the Modern Era* (Cambridge: Polity Press).

Coffee, J. (2002) 'Convergence and its Critics: What are the Preconditions to the Separation of Ownership and Control?', in J. McCahery *et al.* (eds), *Corporate Governance Regimes: Convergence and Diversity* (Oxford: Oxford University Press).

Cohen, E. (1996) *La Tentation Hexagonale* (Paris: Fayard).

Cohen, D., Lefranc, A. and Saint-Paul, G. (1997) 'French Unemployment: A Transatlantic Perspective', *Economic Policy*, (25), pp. 265–85.

Cole, A. (1999) 'The *Service Publique* Under Stress', *West European Politics*, 22(4), pp. 166–84.

Cole, A. and Drake, H. (2000) 'The Europeanisation of the French Polity: Continuity, Change and Adaptation', *European Journal of Public Policy*, 7(1), pp. 26–43.

Compston, H. and Greenwood, J. (eds) (2001) *Social Partnership in the European Union* (Basingstoke: Palgrave).

Copeland, T. and Weston, J. (1992) *Financial Theory and Corporate Policy*, 3rd ed. (Reading, MA: Addison-Wesley).

Corbett, J. (1987) 'International Perspectives on Financing: Evidence from Japan', *Oxford Review of Economic Policy*, 3(4), pp. 30–55.

Corbett, J. and Jenkinson, T. (1997) 'How is Investment Financed? A Study of Germany, Japan, the United Kingdom and the United States', *Manchester School of Economic and Social Studies*, 65(Supplement), pp. 69–93.

Cowling, K. and Tomlinson, P.R. (June 2000) 'The Japanese Crisis – A Case of Strategic Failure?', *Economic Journal*, 110, F358–F381.

Crafts, N. (1997) *Britain's Relative Economic Decline: 1870–1995* (London: Social Market Foundation).

Crotty, R. (1986) *Ireland in Crisis: A Study of Capitalist Colonial Underdevelopment* (Dingle: Brandon Book Publishers).

Crouch, C. (1994) 'Incomes Policies, Institutions and Markets', in R. Dore *et al.* (eds), *The Return to Incomes Policy* (London: Pinter).

Crouch, C. and Streeck, W. (1997) 'Introduction: The Future of Capitalist Diversity', in C. Crouch and W. Streeck (eds), *The Political Economy of Modern Capitalism: Mapping Convergence and Diversity* (London: Sage).

Crouch, C., Finegold, D. and Sako, M. (1999) *Are Skills the Answer? The Political Economy of Skill Formation in Advanced Industrial Countries* (Oxford: Oxford University Press).

Dalziel, P. (2002) 'New Zealand's Economic Reforms: An Assessment', *Review of Political Economy*, 14(1), pp. 31–46.

Dawkins, P., Gregg, P. and Scutella, R. (2002) 'The Growth of Jobless Households in Australia', *Australian Economic Review*, 35(2), pp. 133–54.

Deeg, R. and Perez, S. (2000) 'International Capital Mobility and Domestic Institutions: Corporate Finance and Governance in Four European Cases', *Governance*, 13(2), pp. 119–53.

Department of Trade and Industry (DTI) (1998) *Fairness at Work* Cmnd 3968 (London: Stationery Office).

Dertouzos, M.L. *et al.* (1989) *Made in America* (Cambridge: MIT Press).

Devereux, M., Griffith, R. and Klemm, A. (2002) 'Corporate Income Tax Reforms and International Tax Competition', *Economic Policy*, (35), pp. 450–88.

Dodwell Marketing Consultants (1994) *Industrial Grouping in Japan*, 11th ed. 1994/95. Dodwell Marketing Consultants.

Deyo, F. (1989) *Beneath the Miracle: Labor Subordination in the New Asian Industrialism* (Berkeley: University of California Press).

Dietrich, M. (1994) *Transactions Cost Economics and Beyond* (London: Routledge).

Dietrich, M. (1999) 'Explaining Economic Restructuring: An Input–Output Analysis of Organisational Change in the European Union', *International Review of Applied Economics*, 13(2), pp. 219–40.

D'Iribane, P. (1990) *Le Chomage Paradoxal* (Paris: PUF).

D'Iribane, P. (1992) 'La Logique de l'Honneur', *Le seuil*.

DIW (2000) German Economic Trends, *Economic Bulletin* 1/2000: *http://www. diw-berlin.de/diwwbe/eb00–01/n00jan_2.html*.

Dore, R. (1987) *Taking Japan Seriously: A Confucian Perspective on Leading Economic Issues* (London: Athlone).

Dore, R. (1996) 'Convergence in Whose Interest?', in S. Berger and R. Dore (eds), *National Diversity and Global Capitalism* (Ithaca: Cornell University Press).

Dore, R. (2000) *Stock Market Capitalism, Welfare Capitalism: Japan and Germany Versus the Anglo-Saxons* (Oxford: Oxford University Press).

Dorf, M. and Sabel, C. (1998) 'A Constitution of Democratic Experimentalism', *Columbia Law Review*, 98(2), pp. 267–473.

Dumez, H. and Jeunemaitre, A. (1996) 'The Convergence of Competition Policies in Europe', in S. Berger and R. Dore (eds), *National Diversity and Global Capitalism* (Ithaca: Cornell University Press).

Durkan, J. (1992) 'Social Consensus and Incomes Policy', *Economic and Social Review*, 23(3), pp. 347–63.

Dyson, K. (2002) 'Germany and the Euro: Redefining EMU, Handling Paradox, and Managing Uncertainty and Contingency', in Dyson, K. (ed.), *European States and the Euro* (Oxford: Oxford University Press).

Economic Planning Agency (Various Years) *Economic Survey of Japan* (Tokyo: Economic Planning Agency).

Economic Planning Agency (Various Years) *Annual Report of National Accounts* (Tokyo: Economic Planning Agency).

Edgerton, D. (1991) *England and the Aeroplane: An Essay on a Militant and Technological Nation* (London: Macmillan).

Edwards, J. and Nibler, M. (2000) 'Corporate Governance in Germany: The Role of Banks and Ownership Concentration', *Economic Policy*, (31), pp. 237–60.

Elam, M. (1990) 'Puzzling Out the Post-Fordist Debate: Technology, Markets and Institutions', *Economic and Industrial Democracy*, 11(1), pp. 9–37.

Elbaum, B. and Lazonick, W. (eds) (1986) *The Decline of the British Economy* (Oxford: Oxford University Press).

Elmeskov, J., Martin, J. and Scarpetta, S. (1998) 'Key Lessons for Labour Market Reforms: Evidence from OECD Countries' Experiences', *Swedish Economic Policy Review*, 5(2), pp. 205–52.

English, R. and Kenny, M. (eds) (2000) *Rethinking British Decline* (London: Macmillan).

Esping-Andersen, G. (1990) *The Three Worlds of Welfare Capitalism* (Cambridge: Polity Press).

Estevez-Abe, M., Iversen, T. and Soskice, D. (2001) 'Social Protection and the Formation of Skills', in P. Hall and D. Soskice (eds), *Varieties of Capitalism: The Institutional Foundations of Comparative Advantage* (Oxford: Oxford University Press).

European Foundation for the Improvement of Living and Working Conditions (1997) *New Forms of Work Organisation: Can Europe Realise its Potential?* (Luxembourg: Office for Official Publications of the European Communities).

Evans, P. (1995) *Embedded Autonomy: States and Industrial Transformation* (Princeton, NJ: Princeton University Press).

Faccio, M. and Lang, L. (2002) 'The Ultimate Ownership of Western European Corporations', *Journal of Financial Economics*, 65, pp. 365–95.

Farber, H. (1997) 'The Changing Face of Job Loss in the United States, 1981–95', *Brookings Papers on Economic Activity* (Microeconomics Issue), pp. 55–142.

Fehn, R. and Meier, C.-P. (2001) 'The Positive Economics of Labour Market Rigidities and Investor Protection', *Kyklos*, 54(1), pp. 557–90.

Ferner, A. and Quintanilla, J. (1998) 'Multinationals, National Business Systems and HRM: The Enduring Influence of National Identity or a Process of "Anglo-Saxonisation"?', *International Journal of Human Resource Management*, 9(4), pp. 710–31.

Ferrara, M. (1996) 'The Southern Model of Welfare in Social Europe', *Journal of European Social Policy*, 6(1), pp. 17–37.

Field, A. (1984) 'Microeconomics, Norms and Rationality', *Economic Development and Cultural Change*, 32, pp. 683–711.

Fields, K. (1995) *Enterprise and the State in Korea and Japan* (Ithaca: Cornell University Press).

Fine, B. and Harris, L. (1985) *The Peculiarities of the British Economy* (London: Lawrence and Wishart).

Fitoussi, J.-P. (1994) 'Wage Distribution and Unemployment: The French Experience', *American Economic Review*, 84(2), pp. 59–64.

Fitoussi, J.-P. (1998) 'Table ronde: Comment appliquer les 35 heures?', *Revue Politique et Parlementaire*.

Fitoussi, J.-P. *et al.* (1993) *Competitive Disinflation* (Oxford: Oxford University Press).

Flanagan, R., Soskice, D. and Ulman, L. (1983) *Unionism, Economic Stabilization and Incomes Policies* (Washington DC: The Brookings Institution).

Fong, G. (1998) 'Follower at the Frontier: International Competition and Japanese Industrial Policy', *International Studies Quarterly*, 42, pp. 339–66.

Fougère, D. and Kramarz, F. (1997) 'Le marché du travail en France: quelques pistes d'analyse' *Problèmes Economiques* No. 2545.

Fougère, D. and Kramarz, F. (2001) 'La mobilité salariale en France de 1967 à 1999', in T. Atkinson *et al.* (eds), *Inégalités économiques*, Paris: La documentation Française, pp. 339–42.

Frantz, R. (1997) *X-Efficiency: Theory, Evidence and Applications* (Boston: Kluwer).

Freeman, R.B. (2000) Single Peaked vs. Diversified Capitalism: The Relation Between Economic Institutions and Outcomes. New York: National Bureau of Economic Research Working Paper No. 7556.

Freeman, R.B., Topel, R. and Swedenborg, B. (eds) (1997) *The Welfare State in Transition* (Chicago: University of Chicago Press).

French, S. (2000) 'The Impact of Unification on German Industrial Relations', *German Politics*, 9(2), pp. 195–216.

Funk, L. (2000) 'The European Unemployment Problem' (Birmingham University, Institute for German Studies; mimeo).

Galbraith, J.K. and Berner, M. (eds) (2001) *Inequality and Industrial Change: A Global View* (Cambridge: Cambridge University Press).

Gallie, D., White, M., Cheng, Y. and Tomlinson, M. (1998) *Restructuring the Employment Relationship* (Oxford: Oxford University Press).

Gamble, A. (1994a) *Britain in Decline: Economic Policy, Political Strategy and the British State* (London: Macmillan).

Gamble, A. (1994b) *The Free Economy and the Strong State: the Politics of Thatcherism* (London: Macmillan).

Gamble, A. and Kelly, G. (2000a) 'The British Labour Party and Monetary Union', *West European Politics*, 23(1), pp. 1–25.

Gamble, A. and Kelly, G. (2000b) 'The Politics of the Company', in J. Parkinson *et al.* (eds), *The Political Economy of the Company* (London: Hart).

Gamble, A. and Kelly, G. (2000c) 'New Labour and the Economy', in S. Ludlam and M. Smith (eds), *New Labour in Power* (London: Macmillan).

Gamble, A. and Payne, A. (eds) (1996) *Regionalism and World Order* (London: Macmillan).

Ganghof, S. (2000) 'Adjusting National Tax Policy to Economic Internationalization', in F. Scharpf and V. Schmidt (eds), *Welfare and Work in the Open Economy: Volume Two* (Oxford: Oxford University Press).

Garrett, G. and Way, C. (2000) 'Public Sector Unions, Corporatism and Wage Determination', in T. Iversen *et al.* (eds), *Unions, Employers and Central Banks* (Cambridge: Cambridge University Press).

Gates, J. (1998) *The Ownership Solution* (London: Allen Lane).

Garvin, T. (1981) *The Evolution of Nationalist Politics* (Dublin: Gill and Macmillan).

Gautié, J. (1997) 'Insertion professionnelle et chomage des jeunes en France', *Regards sur L'Actualité*, July.

Geary, J. (1999) 'The New Workplace: Change at Work in Ireland', *International Journal of Human Resource Management*, 10(5), pp. 870–90.

Geary, J. and Roche, W. (2001) 'Multinationals and Human Resource Practices in Ireland: A Rejection of the "New Conformance Thesis"', *International Journal of Human Resource Management*, 12(1), pp. 109–27.

Geletkanycz, M. (1997) 'The Salience of "Culture's Consequences": The Effects of Cultural Values on Top Executive Commitment to the Status Quo', *Strategic Management Journal*, 18(8), pp. 615–34.

Genschel, P. (2002) 'Globalization, Tax Competition and the Welfare State', *Politics and Society*, 30(2), pp. 245–75.

Georgen, M. and Renneboog, L. (2001) 'Strong Managers and Passive Investors in the United Kingdom', in F. Barca and M. Becht (eds), *The Control of Corporate Europe* (Oxford: Oxford University Press).

Germain, R. (1997) *The International Organization of Credit: States and Global Finance in the World Economy* (Cambridge: Cambridge University Press).

Germain, R. (2000) 'Globalization in Historical Perspective', in R. Germain (ed.), *Globalization and its Critics: Perspectives from Political Economy*, London: Macmillan, 67–90.

Gill, C. and Krieger, H. (2000) 'Recent Survey Evidence on Participation in Europe', *European Journal of Industrial Relations*, 6(1), pp. 109–32.

Gills, B. (1994) 'The International Origins of South Korea's Export Orientation', in R. Palan and B. Gills (eds), *Transcending the State/Global Divide: A Neo-Structuralist Agenda in International Relations* (Boulder Co: Lynne Rienner).

Gills, B. (1996) 'Economic Liberalisation and Reform in South Korea in the 1990s: A "Coming of Age" or a Case of "Graduation Blues"?', *Third World Quarterly*, 17(4), pp. 667–88.

Gills, B. (1997) 'Whither Democracy? Globalization and the "New Hellenism"', in C. Thomas and P. Wilkin (eds), *Globalization and the South* (London: Macmillan).

Gills, B. (2000) 'American Power, Neoliberal Economic Globalisation, and Low Intensity Democracy: An Unstable Trinity', in M. Cox *et al.* (eds), *American*

Democracy Promotion: Impulses, Strategies, and Impacts (Oxford: Oxford University Press).

Gills, B. and Gills, D.-S. (1999) 'South Korea and Globalization: The Rise of Globalism?', *Asian Perspective*, 23(4), pp. 199–228.

Gills, B. and Gills, D.-S. (2000) 'Globalization and Strategic Choice in South Korea', in S. Kim (ed.), *South Korea's Globalization* (Cambridge: Cambridge University Press).

Gills, B. and Palan, R. (1994) 'Introduction', in R. Palan and B. Gills (eds), *Transcending the State/Global Divide: A Neo-Structuralist Agenda in International Relations* (Boulder Co: Lynne Rienner).

Gills, B. and Rocamora, J. (1992) 'Low Intensity Democracy', *Third World Quarterly*, 13(3), pp. 501–23.

Gills, B., Rocamora, J. and Wilson, R. (eds) (1993) *Low Intensity Democracy: Political Power in the New World Order* (London: Pluto Press).

Girvin, B. (1989) *Between Two Worlds: Politics and Economy of Industrial Society in Ireland* (Dublin: Gill and Macmillan).

Glyn, A. (1992a) 'Corporatism, Patterns of Employment and Access to Consumption', in J. Pekkarinen, M. Pohjola and R. Rowthorn (eds), *Social Corporatism: A Superior Economic System?* (Oxford: Oxford University Press).

Glyn, A. (1992b) 'The "Productivity Miracle", Profits and Investment', in J. Michie (ed.), *The Economic Legacy 1979–92* (London: Academic Press).

Glyn, A (1995) 'Social Democracy and Full Employment', *New Left Review*, 211, pp. 33–55.

Glyn, A. (2001) 'Inequalities of Employment and Wages in OECD Countries', *Oxford Bulletin of Economics and Statistics*, 63, pp. 697–713.

Glyn, A. and Salverda, W. (2000) 'Employment Inequalities', in M. Gregory *et al.* (eds), *Labour Market Inequalities* (Oxford: Oxford University Press).

Goodin, R., Headey, B., Muffels, R. and Dirven, H.-J. (1999) *The Real Worlds of Welfare Capitalism* (Cambridge: Cambridge University Press).

Gordon, D.M. (1994) 'Bosses of Different Stripes: A Cross-national Perspective on Monitoring and Supervision', *American Economic Review*, 84(2), pp. 375–9.

Gordon, D.M. (1996) *Fat and Mean: The Corporate Squeeze of Working Americans and the Myth of Managerial 'Downsizing'* (New York: The Free Press).

Gordon, R. (1999) 'Has the "New Economy" Rendered the Productivity Slowdown Obsolete?' unpublished, (*http://www.nwu.edu/economics/gordon*).

Gordon, R. (2000) 'Does the "New Economy" Measure up to the Great Inventions of the Past?' *Journal of Economic Perspectives*, 14(4), pp. 49–74.

Gorton, G. and Schmid, F. (2000) 'Universal Banking and the Performance of German Firms', *Journal of Financial Economics*, 58(1–2), pp. 29–80.

Grabel, I. (1997) 'Savings, Investment, and Functional Efficiency: A Comparative Examination of National Financial Complexes', in R. Pollin (ed.), *The Macroeconomics of Saving, Finance, and Investment* (Ann Arbor: University of Michigan Press).

Grahl, J. (2001) 'Globalized Finance: The Challenge to the Euro', *New Left Review*, Series 2(8), pp. 23–47.

Grant, R. (1991) 'Porter's Competitive Advantage of Nations: An Assessment', *Strategic Management Journal*, 12, pp. 535–48.

Gregg P., Wadsworth, J. and Dickens, R. (2000) 'New Labour and the Labour Market', *Oxford Review of Economic Policy*, 16(1), pp. 95–113.

Grosser, A. (1970) *Germany in Our Time* (Harmondsworth: Penguin).

Gubian, A. (1998) 'Les 35 heures et l'emploi: la loi Aubry de juin 1998', *Regards sur L'Actualité*, November.

Gubian, A. (2000) 'Les 35 heures et l'emploi: d'une loi Aubry à l'autre', *Regards sur L'Actualite*, 259, pp. 3–26.

Gugler, K. (ed.) (2001a) *Corporate Governance and Economic Performance* (Oxford: Oxford University Press).

Gugler, K. (2001b) 'Takeovers and the Market for Corporate Control', in K. Gugler (ed.), *Corporate Governance and Economic Performance* (Oxford: Oxford University Press).

Gust, C. and Marquez, J. (2000) 'Productivity Developments Abroad', *Federal Reserve Bulletin*, October, pp. 665–81.

Guyomarch, A., Machin, H. and Ritchie, E. (1998) *France in the European Union* (Basingstoke: Macmillan).

Halimi, S., Michie, J. and Milne, S. (1994) 'The Mitterand Experience', in J. Michie and J. Grieve Smith (eds), *Unemployment in Europe* (Aldershot: Academic Press).

Hall, P. (1986) *Governing the Economy: The Politics of State Intervention in Britain and France* (Cambridge: Polity Press).

Hall, P.A. and Franzese, R. (1998) 'Mixed Signals: Central Bank Independence, Coordinated Wage Bargaining, and European Monetary Union', *International Organization*, 52(3), pp. 505–35.

Hall, P.A. and Soskice, D. (2001) 'Introduction' in *idem* (eds), *Varieties of Capitalism: The Institutional Foundations of Comparative Advantage* (Oxford: Oxford University Press).

Hall, R. and Jones, C. (1999) 'Why do Some Countries Produce so Much More Output Per Worker than Others?', *Quarterly Journal of Economics*, 114(1), pp. 83–116.

Hardiman, N. (1988) *Pay, Politics and Economic Performance in Ireland 1970–87* (Oxford: Oxford University Press).

Harding, R. (1999) '*Standort Deutschland* in the Globalising Economy: An End to the Economic Miracle?', *German Politics*, 8(1), pp. 66–88.

Hartog, J. (1999) 'Wither Dutch Corporatism? Two Decades of Employment Policies and Welfare Reforms', *Scottish Journal of Political Economy*, 46(4), pp. 458–87.

Hartog, J., Pereira, P. and Vieira, J. (2000) 'Inter-industry Wage Dispersion in Portugal', *Empirica*, 27(4), pp. 353–64.

Hassel, A. (1999) 'The Erosion of the German System of Industrial Relations', *British Journal of Industrial Relations*, 37(3), pp. 483–505.

Hay, C. (1999) *The Political Economy of Labour* (Manchester: Manchester University Press).

Healey, N. (ed.) (1992) *Britain's Economic Miracle: Myth or Reality?* (London: Routledge).

Heinisch, R. (2000) 'Coping with Economic Integration: Corporatist Strategies in Germany and Austria in the 1990s', *West European Politics*, 23(3), pp. 67–96.

Held, D. (1995) *Democracy and the Global Order: From the Nation State to Cosmopolitan Governance* (Cambridge: Polity Press).

Held, D., McGrew, A., Goldblatt, D. and Perraton, J. (1999) *Global Transformations: Politics, Economics and Culture* (Cambridge: Polity Press).

Helleiner, E. (1994) *States and the Reemergence of Global Finance* (Ithaca: Cornell University Press).

Hencké, B. (2001) 'Revisiting the French Model: Coordination and Restructuring in French Industry', in D. Soskice and P. Hall (eds), *Varieties of Capitalism* (Oxford: Oxford University Press).

Henkel, H.-O. (1997) 'Für euie Reform des politischen systems' in M. Bissinger (ed.), *stimmen gegen den stillstand* (Hamburg: Campe 87–90).

Henley, A. and Tsakalotos, E. (1993) *Corporatism and Macroeconomic Performance* (Aldershot: Edward Elgar).

Henrekson, M. and Jakobsson, U. (2003) 'The Transformation of Ownership Policy and Structure in Sweden', *New Political Economy*, 8(3), pp. 73–102.

Hertig, G. (1998) 'Lenders as a Force in Corporate Governance: Criteria and Practical Examples from Switzerland', in K. Hopt *et al.* (eds), *Comparative Corporate Governance* (Oxford: Oxford University Press).

Higgott, R. and Phillips, N. (2000) 'Challenging Triumphalism and Convergence: The Limits of Global Liberalization in Asia and Latin America', *Review of International Studies*, 26, pp. 359–79.

Hirst P. and Thompson, G. (1992) 'The Problem of Globalisation: International Economic Relations, National Economic Management and the Formation of Trading Blocks', *Economy and Society*, 21(4), pp. 357–96.

Hirst, P. and Thompson, G.F. (1999) *Globalization in Question: The International Economy and the Possibilities of Governance*, 2nd ed. (Cambridge: Polity Press).

Hirst, P. and Thompson, G.F. (2000) 'Globalization in One Country? The Peculiarities of the British', *Economy and Society*, 29(3), pp. 335–56.

Hobsbawm, E. (1968) *Industry and Empire* (London: Penguin).

Hodgson, G. (1988) *Economics and Institutions* (Cambridge: Polity Press).

Hodgson, G. (1996) 'An Evolutionary Theory of Long-Term Growth', *International Studies Quarterly*, 40, pp. 391–410.

Hodgson, G. (1999) *Economics and Utopia: Why the Learning Economy is Not the End of History* (London: Routledge).

Hodgson, G. (2002) 'The Evolution of Institutions', *Constitutional Political Economy*, 13, pp. 111–27.

Hofstede, G. (1994) *Cultures and Organisations* (London: Harper-Collins).

Holden, S. (1990) 'Wage Drift in Norway: A Bargaining Approach', in L. Calmfors (ed.), *Wage Formation and Macroeconomic Policy in the Nordic Countries* (Oxford: Oxford University Press).

Holden, S. (1991) 'Economic Policy in an Economy with Local and Central Wage Bargaining', Memorandum from the Department of Economics, University of Oslo, 1991: 8.

Holden, S. and Nymoen, R. (2002) 'Measuring Structural Unemployment: NAWRU Estimates in the Nordic Countries', *Scandinavian Journal of Economics*, 104(1), pp. 87–104.

Holland, S. (1975) *The Socialist Challenge* (London: Quartet).

Hollingsworth, J. (1997a) 'Continuities and Changes in Social Systems of Production: The Cases of Japan, Germany and the United States', in J. Hollingsworth and R. Boyer (eds), *Contemporary Capitalism: The Embededness of Institutions* (Cambridge: Cambridge University Press).

Hollingsworth, J.R. (1997b) 'The Institutional Embeddedness of American Capitalism', in C. Crouch and W. Streeck (eds), *Political Economy of Modern Capitalism* (London: Sage).

Hollingsworth, J.R. and Boyer, R. (eds) (1997) *Contemporary Capitalism: The Embeddedness of Institutions* (Cambridge: Cambridge University Press).

Hollingsworth, J.R., Schmitter, P. and Streeck, W. (eds) (1994) *Governing Capitalist Economies: Performance and Control of Economic Sectors* (Oxford: Oxford University Press).

Holmes, M. (ed.) (1996) *The Eurosceptic Reader* (London: Macmillan).

Holmstrom, B. and Kaplan, S. (2001) 'Corporate Governance and Merger Activity in the United States', *Journal of Economic Perspectives*, 15(2), pp. 121–44.

Honkapohja, S. and Koskela, E. (1999) 'The Economic Crisis of the 1990s in Finland', *Economic Policy*, (29), pp. 399–434.

Hood, S. and Young, S. (1997) 'The United Kingdom', in J. Dunning (ed.), *Governments, Globalization and International Business* (Oxford: Oxford University Press).

Hopt, K. (2002) 'Common Principles of Corporate Governance in Europe?', in J. McCahery *et al.* (eds), *Corporate Governance Regimes: Convergence and Diversity* (Oxford: Oxford University Press).

Houben, A. and Kakes, J. (2002) 'ICT Innovation and Economic Performance: The Role of Financial Intermediation', *Kyklos*, 55(4), pp. 543–62.

Howard, D. (1998) 'The French Strikes of 1995 and their Political Aftermath', *Government and Opposition*, 33(2), pp. 199–220.

Howard, M. and King, J. (2002) 'The Rise of Neoliberalism in Advanced Capitalist Economies', *International Papers in Political Economy*, 9(3).

Howarth, D. (2002) 'The French State in the Euro Zone: "Modernization" and Legitimizing *Dirigisme*', in Dyson, K. (ed.), *European States and the Euro* (Oxford: Oxford University Press).

Howell, C. (1996) 'French Socialism and the Transformation of Industrial Relations Since 1981', in A. Daley (ed.), *The Mitterrand Era* (Basingstoke: Macmillan).

Hutton, W. (1995) *The State We're In* (London: Jonathan Cape).

Hutton, W. (2002) *The World We're In* (London: Little, Brown).

IBEC (1999) *Partnership at Enterprise Level: Survey Results 1999* (Dublin: IBEC Partnership Unit).

Ikeo, K. (September 1991) 'The Financial Liberalization and the Maintenance of Credit Order', *Kinyu (Finance)*.

IMF (1997) *Germany – Selected Issues*, IMF Staff Country Report No. 97/01 (Washington: International Monetary Fund).

Industrial Policy Review Group, (1992) *A Time for Change: Industrial Policy for the 1990s* (Dublin: Government Publications Office).

Ingham, G. (1984) *Capitalism Divided? The City and Industry in British Social Development* (London: Macmillan).

Inglis, T. (1987) *Moral Monopoly: The Catholic Church in Modern Irish Society* (Dublin: Gill and Macmillan).

Itoh, H. (ed.) (1996) *Nihon no Kigyo-Sisutemu (The Corporation System in Japan)* (Tokyo: Tokyo University Press).

Itoh, M., Kazuharu K., Masahiro Okuno-Fujiwara and Kotaro Suzumura (1991) *Economic Analysis of Industrial Policy* (San Francisco: Academic Press).

Itoh, O. (1995) *Nihongata Kinyu no Rekishiteki Kozo* (Tokyo: Tokyo Daigaku Shuppankai).

Itoh, T. (1992) *The Japanese Economy* (Cambridge: MIT Press).

Iversen, T. (1998) 'The Choices for Scandinavian Social Democracy in Comparative Perspective', *Oxford Review of Economic Policy*, 14(1), pp. 59–75.

Iversen, T. (1999) *Contested Economic Institutions: The Politics of Macroeconomics and Wage Bargaining in Advanced Democracies* (Cambridge: Cambridge University Press).

Japan Fair Trade Commission (various years) *Japan Fair Trade Commission Annual Report* (Tokyo: Japan Fair Trade Commission).

Jefferys, S. (2000) 'A "Copernican Revolution" in French Industrial Relations: Are the Times a'Changing?', *British Journal of Industrial Relations*, 38(2), pp. 241–60.

Jessop, B. (1994) 'The Transition to Post-Fordism and the Schumpetarian Workfare State', in R. Burrows and B. Loader (eds), *Towards a Post-Fordist Welfare State* (London: Routledge).

Jessop, B., Bonnett, K., Bromley, S. and Ling, T. (1988) *Thatcherism: A Tale of Two Nations* (Cambridge: Polity Press).

JG (1999) *Jahresgutachten 1999/2000 des Sachverständigenrates zur Begutachtung der gesamtwirtschaflichen Entwicklung* (Bonn: Deutscher Bundestag): *http://www. sachverstaendigenrat-wirtschaft.de/pm/info-e.htm.*

Jochem, S. (2000) 'Nordic Labour Market Policies in Transition', *West European Politics*, 33(3), pp. 115–38.

Johnson, S. *et al.* (2000) 'Corporate Governance in the Asian Financial Crisis', *Journal of Financial Economics*, 58(1–2), pp. 141–86.

Jones, E. (1999) 'Is "Competitive" Corporatism an Adequate Response to Globalisation? Evidence from the Low Countries', *West European Politics*, 22(3), pp. 159–81.

Jorgenson, D. and Stiroh, K. (2000) 'Raising the Speed Limit: US Economic Growth in the Information Age', *Brookings Papers on Economic Activity*, 1, pp. 125–235.

Joseph, K. (1976) *Monetarism is not Enough* (London: Centre for Policy Studies).

Jospin, L. (1991) *L'Invention du Possible* (Paris: Flammarion).

Kang, J-K. and Stulz, R. (2000) 'Do Banking Shocks Affect Borrowing Firm Performance? An Analysis of the Japanese Experience', *Journal of Business*, 73(1), pp. 1–23.

Kato, T. (2001) 'The End of Lifetime Employment in Japan? Evidence from National Surveys and Field Research', *Journal of the Japanese and International Economies*, 15(4), pp. 489–514.

Katz, H. and Darbishire, O. (2000) *Converging Divergences: Worldwide Changes in Employment Systems* (Ithaca: Cornell University Press).

Katz, L. and Krueger, A. (1999) 'The High-Pressure US Labor Market of the 1990s', *Brookings Papers on Economic Activity*, I, pp. 1–87.

Katzenstein, P. (1985) *Small States in World Markets* (Ithaca: Cornell University Press).

Kay, J. (1993) *Foundations of Corporate Success* (Oxford: Oxford University Press).

Kelly, A. and Brannick, T. (1985) 'Industrial Relations Practices in Multinational Companies in Ireland', *Irish Business and Administrative Research*, 7, pp. 98–111.

Kelly, G. (1997) 'Economic Policy', in P. Dunleavy *et al.* (eds), *Developments in British Politics 5* (London: Macmillan).

Kelly, G. (1998) *Regional Finance: History, Theory, Policy* (Sheffield).

Kennedy, K., Giblin, T. and McHugh, D. (1988) *The Economic Development of Ireland in the Twentieth Century* (London: Routledge).

Kennedy, P. (1988) *The Rise and Fall of the Great Powers* (London: Unwin Hyman).

Kenworthy, L. (1997) 'Globalization and Economic Convergence', *Competition and Change*, 2(1), 1–64.

Kenworthy, L. (2003) 'Do Affluent Countries Face an Incomes-Jobs Trade-off', *Comparative Political Studies*, 36(10), pp. 1180–1209.

Kigyo K.S. (1996) *Toyo Keizai Shinposha* (Tokyo).

Kilpatrick, A. and Lawson, T. (1980) 'On the Nature of Industrial Decline in the UK', *Cambridge Journal of Economics*, 4(1), pp. 85–102.

King, D. and Wood, S. (1999) 'The Political Economy of Neoliberalism: Britain and the United States in the 1980s', in H. Kitschelt *et al.* (eds), *Continuity and Change in Contemporary Capitalism* (Cambridge: Cambridge University Press).

Kisugi, S. (1995) 'Dokusen Kinsi Seisaku (Competition Policy)', in M. Uekusa (ed.), *Nihon no Sangyou-sosiki (Industrial Organization in Japan)* (Tokyo: Yuuhikaku).

Kitschelt, H., Lange, P., Marks, G. and Stephens, J. (1999) 'Convergence and Divergence in Advanced Capitalist Economies', in H. Kitschelt *et al.* (eds), *Continuity and Change in Contemporary Capitalism* (Cambridge: Cambridge University Press).

Kitson, M. and Michie, J. (1996) 'Britain's Industrial Performance Since 1960: Underinvestment and Relative Decline', *Economic Journal*, 106, pp. 196–212.

Kitson, M. and Michie, J. (1999) 'The Political Economy of Globalisation', in D. Archibugi *et al.* (eds), *Innovation Policy in a Global Economy* (Cambridge: Cambridge University Press).

Kittel, B. (2000) 'Deaustrification? The Policy-Area-Specific Evolution of Austrian Social Partnership', *West European Politics*, 23(1), pp. 108–29.

Ko, C.-E. *et al.* (2001) 'Corporate Governance in Chinese Taipei', in OECD, *Corporate Governance in Asia* (Paris: Organisation for Economic Co-operation and Development).

Kobayasyi, Y. (ed.) (1958) *Kigyou Keiretsu no Jittai (The Current State of the Keiretsu)* (Tokyo: Toyokeizai Shinposya).

Koike, K. (1994) *Nihon no Koyou-Sisutemu (The Japanese Employment System)* (Toyko: Toyokeizai Shinposya).

Koike, K. (1999) *Shigoto no Keizaigaku (The Economics of Employment)* 2nd ed. (Tokyo: Toyokeizai Shinposya).

Kosai, Y. (1996) 'Competition and Competition Policy in Japan: Foreign Pressures and Domestic Institutions', in S. Berger and R. Dore (eds), *National Diversity and Global Competition* (Ithaca: Cornell University Press).

Kosonen, P. (1998) *Pohjoismaiset mallit murroksessa* 'Nordic Models in Transition'. (Vastapaino Tampere).

Krieger, J. (1999) *British Politics in the Global Age* (Cambridge: Polity Press).

Krugman, P. (1991) *Geography and Trade* (Cambridge, MA: The MIT Press).

Krugman, P. (1996) *Pop Internationalism* (Cambridge, MA: The MIT Press).

Krugman, P. (1998) 'America the Boastful', *Foreign Affairs*, 77(3), pp. 32–45.

Krugman, P. and Lawrence, R. (1994) 'Trade, Jobs and Wages', *Scientific American*, April, pp. 22–6.

Kurdelbusch, A. (2002) 'Multinationals and the Rise of Variable Pay in Germany', *European Journal of Industrial Relations*, 8(3), pp. 325–49.

Kurzer, P. (1993) *Business and Banking: Political Change and Economic Integration in Western Europe* (Ithaca: Cornell University Press).

Labbe, D. (1994) 'Trade Unionism in France since the Second World War', *West European Politics*, 17(1).

Ladrech (1998) '*Towards a Social Europe? Policy Issues and the French Socialist Government*', Paper presented at the PSA conference at Keele.

Landes, D. (1969) *The Unbound Prometheus: Technological Change and Industrial Development in Western Europe from 1750 to the Present* (Cambridge: Cambridge University Press).

Lane, C. (2000) 'Globalization and the German Model of Capitalism: Erosion or Survival?', *British Journal of Sociology*, 51(2), pp. 207–34.

Lane, C. and Quack, S. (2001) How Banks Construct and Manage Risk: A Sociological Study of Small Firm Lending in Britain and Germany. Centre for Business Research, University of Cambridge, Working Paper No. 217.

Lane, J.-E. (2001) 'The Political Economy of Switzerland', *West European Politics*, 24(2), pp. 191–210.

Lange, T. and Pugh, G. (1998) *The Economics of German Unification* (Aldershot: Edward Elgar).

La Porta, R., Lopez-de-Silanes, F., Shleifer, A. and Vishny, R. (1998) 'Law and Finance', *Journal of Political Economy*, 106(6), pp. 1113–55.

La Porta, R., Lopez-de-Silanes, F., Shleifer, A. and Vishny, R. (1999) 'Corporate Ownership around the World', *Journal of Finance*, 54(2), pp. 471–517.

La Porta, R., Lopez-de-Silanes, F., Shleifer, A. and Vishny, R. (2000) 'Investor Protection and Corporate Governance', *Journal of Financial Economics*, 58(1–2), pp. 3–27.

Laurence, H. (2001) *Money Rules: The New Politics of Finance in Britain and Japan* (Ithaca: Cornell University Press).

Lee, J.J. (1989) *Ireland 1912–1985* (Cambridge: Cambridge University Press).

Leibenstein, H. (1978) *General X-efficiency Theory and Economic Development* (New York: Oxford University Press).

Leibenstein, H. (1982) 'The Prisoners' Dilemma in the Invisible Hand: An Analysis of Intrafirm Productivity', *American Economic Review*, 72(2), pp. 92–7.

Leibenstein, H. (1987) *Inside the Firm* (Cambridge, MA: Harvard University Press).

Levy, J. (2000) 'France: Directing Adjustment?', in F. Scharpf and V. Schmidt (eds), *Welfare and Work in the Open Economy: Volume Two* (Oxford: Oxford University Press).

Levy, J. (2001) 'Social Policy in the Age of High Unemployment', in A. Guyo March *et al.* (eds), *Developments in French Politics 2* (Basingstoke: Palgrave).

L'Horty, Y. (1999) 'L'Emploi précaire en France', *Regards sur L'Actualité* March.

Lindbeck, A. (1996) 'The West European Employment Problem', *Weltwirtschaftliches Archiv*, 132(4), pp. 609–37.

Lindbeck, A. and Snower, D. (2001) 'Centralized Bargaining and Reorganized Work: Are they Compatible?', *European Economic Review*, 45, pp. 1851–75.

Lindert, P. (2000) 'When did Inequality Rise in Britain and America?', *Journal of Income Distribution*, 9(1), pp. 11–25.

Lipietz, A. (1997) 'The Post-Fordist World: Labour Relations, International Hierarchy and Global Ecology', *Review of International Political Economy*, 4(1): 1–41.

Lordon, F. (1998) 'The Logic and Limits of Désinflation Competitive', *Oxford Review of Economic Policy*, 14(1), pp. 96–113.

Loriaux, M. (1991) *France after Hegemony* (Ithaca: Cornell University Press).

Loughlin, M. and Scott, C. (1997) 'The Regulatory State', in P. Dunleavy *et al.* (eds), *Developments in British Politics 5* (London: Macmillan).

Maclean, M. (1999) 'Corporate Governance in France and the UK: Long-term Perspectives on Contemporary Institutional Arrangements', *Business History*, 41(1), pp. 88–116.

Maddison, A. (1991) *Dynamic Forces in Capitalist Development* (Oxford: Oxford University Press).

Maddison, A. (2001) *The World Economy: A Millennial Perspective* (Paris: Organisation for Economic Co-operation and Development).

Maier, Charles (1987) *In Search of Stability: Explorations in Historical Political Economy*, (Cambridge: Cambridge University Press).

Majone, G. (1994) 'The Rise of the Regulatory State in Europe', *West European Politics*, 17, pp. 77–101.

Majone, G. (ed.) (1996) *Regulating Europe* (London: Routledge).

Mako, W. (2002) 'Corporate Restructuring and Reform: Lessons from Korea', in D. Coe and S.-E. Kim (eds), *Korean Crisis and Recovery* (Washington DC: International Monetary Fund).

Malcolm, J. (2001) *Financial Globalisation and the Opening of the Japanese Economy*, (London: Curzon).

Mandel, E. (1968) *Marxist Economic Theory* (London: Merlin).

Manow, P. and Seils, E. (2000) 'Adjusting Badly: The German Welfare State, Structural Change, and the Open Economy', in F. Scharpf and V. Schmidt (eds), *Welfare and Work in the Open Economy: Volume Two* (Oxford: Oxford University Press).

Marginson, P. and Sisson, K. (2002) 'European Integration and Industrial Relations', *Journal of Common Market Studies*, 40(4), pp. 671–92.

Marquand, D. (1988) *The Unprincipled Society* (London: Cape).

Marsden, D. (1999) *A Theory of Employment Systems: Micro-Foundations of Societal Diversity* (Oxford: Oxford University Press).

Marsh, D. (1992) *The New Politics of British Trade Unionism* (London: Macmillan).

Marsh, D. and Rhodes, R. (eds) (1992) *Implementing Thatcherite Policies: Audit of an Era* (Milton Keynes: Open University Press).

Martin, R. and Tyler, P. (1992) 'The Regional Legacy', in J. Michie (ed.), *The Economic Legacy 1979–1992* (London: Academic Press).

Martin, S. (1994) *Industrial Economics*. 2d ed. (Englewood Cliffs, N.J.: Prentice Hall).

Matsuura, K., Pollitt, M., Takada, R. and Tanaka, S. (1999) Institutional Restructuring in the Japanese Economy, 1985–1996. Cambridge: Centre for Business Research Working Paper No. 115.

Matsuura, K., Michael Pollitt, Ryoji Takada and Tanaka Saturo. (1999) 'Institutional Restructuring in the Japanese Economy 1985–1996', Working Paper No. 115. ESRC Centre for Business Research (Cambridge: University of Cambridge).

Mayer, C. (1987) 'The Assessment: Financial Systems and Corporate Investment', *Oxford Review of Economic Policy*, 3(4), pp. i–xvi.

McCartney, J. and Teague, P. (1997) 'Workplace Innovations in the Republic of Ireland', *Economic and Social Review*, 28(4), pp. 381–99.

Meek, V. (1988) 'Organisational Culture', *Organisation Studies*, 9(4), pp. 453–73.

Meyerson, D. and Martin, J. (1987) 'Cultural Change', *Journal of Management Studies*, 24, pp. 623–47.

Michalet, C.-A. (1997) 'France', in J. Dunning (ed.), *Governments, Globalization and International Business* (Oxford: Oxford University Press).

Michie, J. (ed.) (1992) *The Economic Legacy 1979–1992* (London: Academic Press).

Middlemas, K. (1979) *Politics in Industrial Society: The Experience of the British System since 1911* (London: Andre Deutsch).

Milgrom, P. and Roberts, J. (1992) *Economics, Organization and Management* (New Jersey: Prentice Hall).

Milner, S. (1998) 'Industrial Relations in France: Towards a New Social Pact?', in M. Maclean (ed.), *The Mitterrand Years* (Basingstoke: Macmillan).

Milner, S. (2001) 'Globalisation and Employment in France: Between flexibility and Protection?', *Modern and Contemporary France*, 9(3), pp. 327–37.

Milner, S. (2002) 'The Jospin Government and the 35-Hour Week', *Modern and Contemporary France*, 10(3), pp. 339–52.

Milner, H. and Keohane, R. (1996) 'Introduction', in R. Keohane and H. Milner (eds), *Internationalization and Domestic Politics* (Cambridge: Cambridge University Press).

Minato, T. (1997) 'Inter-corporate Governance under Innovations of Information Technology', The Japan Association for Small Business Studies: 1996 Conference Proceedings (Tokyo: Doyukan).

Ministère des Finances (2001) 'Projet de loi de finances pour 2002' Les Notes Bleues Hors-śrie, September.

Ministry of Finance (Various Years) *Japanese Trade Statistics* (Tokyo: Ministry of Finance).

Ministry of Finance (Various Years) *Ministry of Finance Statistics Monthly* (Tokyo: Ministry of Finance).

Ministry of International Trade and Industry (MITI) (1990) *90-nenndai no tsuusan siesaku vision (The Vision of Industrial Policy in the 1990s)* (Tokyo: Tsuusyou-sangyou chosa-kai).

Ministry of Labour (1999) *White Paper on Labour 1999* (Tokyo: Ministry of Labour).

Mirowski, P. (1986) 'Institutions as a Solution Concept in a Game Theory Context', reprinted in G. Hodgson (ed.), *The Economics of Institutions* (Aldershot: Elgar, 1993).

Mjoset, L. (1992) *The Irish Economy in a Comparative Institutional Perspective* (Dublin: National Economic and Social Council).

Moran, M. (1991) *The Politics of the Financial Services Revolution: The USA, the UK, and Japan* (London: Macmillan).

Morin, F. (2000) 'A Transformation in the French Model of Shareholding and Management', *Economy and Society*, 29(1), pp. 36–53.

Moscovici P. (1994) *A La Recherche de la Gauche Perdue* (Paris: Calmann-Levy).

Moscovici P. (1997) *L'Urgence: Plaidoyer pour une autre politique* (Paris: Plon).

Mosley, P. (2000) 'Globalisation, Economic Policy and Convergence', *World Economy*, 23(5), pp. 613–34.

Muet, P.-A. (1998) 'Table ronde: Comment appliquer les 35 heures?', *Revue Politique et Parlementaire*.

Muet, P.-A. and Fonteneau, A. (1990) *Reflation and Austerity: Economic Policy under Mitterrand* (Oxford: Berg).

Muller, M. (1998) 'Human Resource and Industrial Relations Practices of UK and US Multinationals in Germany', *International Journal of Human Resource Management*, 9(4), pp. 732–49.

Müller-Armack, A. (1990) 'Das Konzept der Sozialen Marktwirtschaft', in D. Grosser *et al.*, *Soziale Marktwirtschaft* (Stuttgart: Kohlhammer).

Murinde, V., Agung, J., Mullin, A. and Mullineux, A. (1999) 'Convergence of European Financial Systems', in M. Fischer and P. Nijkamp (eds), *Spatial Dynamics of European Integration* (Berlin: Springer-Verlag).

Myers, R. (1998) 'The Faltering Economic Reforms of South Korea', JPRI Working Paper No. 51, November.

Nabeshima, N. (2000) 'The Financial Mode of *Régulation* in Japan and its Demise', in R. Boyer and T. Yamada (eds), *Japanese Capitalism in Crisis* (London: Routledge).

Nairn, T. (1977) *The Breakup of Britain* (London: Verso).

Nakamura, F. (1988) *Nihon keizai (The Japanese Economy)* (Tokyo: Tokyo Daigaku Shppan-kai).

Nakatani, I. (1984) 'The Economic Role of Financial Corporate Grouping', in M. Aoki (ed.), *The Economic Analysis of the Japanese Firm* (North Holland: Elsevier).

Nam, I.C. *et al.* (2001) 'Corporate Governance in Korea', in OECD, *Corporate Governance in Asia* (Paris: Organisation for Economic Co-operation and Development).

National Personnel Authority (Various Years) *Komuin-Hakusyo (Annual Report on Civil Servants)* (Tokyo: National Personnel Authority).

Neary, J.P. and Thom, R. (1997) 'Punts, Pounds and Euros: In Search of an Optimum Currency Area', *Journal of Irish Business and Administrative Research*, 18, pp. 211–25.

Nelson, R. (1991) 'Why Do Firms Differ, and How Does it Matter?', *Strategic Management Journal*, 12 (Winter), pp. 61–74.

Nelson, R. (2000) 'The Sources of Industrial Leadership', in M. Aoki and G. Saxonhouse (eds), *Finance, Governance and Competitiveness in Japan* (Oxford: Oxford University Press).

Nelson, R. and Winter, S. (1982) *An Evolutionary Theory of Economic Change* (Cambridge, MA: Belknap Press).

NESC (1982) *A Review of Industrial Policy* (Dublin: National Economic and Social Council).

NESC (1986) *A Strategy for Development 1986–1990* (Dublin: National Economic and Social Council).

NESC (1989) *Ireland in the European Community: Performance, Prospects and Strategy* (Dublin: National Economic and Social Council).

NESC (1990) *A Strategy for the Nineties: Economic Stability and Structural Change* (Dublin: National Economic and Social Council).

NESC (1993) *A Strategy for Competitiveness, Growth and Employment* (Dublin: National Economic and Social Council).

NESC (1996) *Strategy into the 21st Century* (Dublin: National Economic and Social Council).

NESC (1999) *Opportunities, Challenges and Capacities for Choice* (Dublin: National Economic and Social Council).

NESF (1997) *A Framework for Partnership: Enhancing Strategic Consensus Through Participation* (Dublin: National Economic and Social Forum).

Noguchi, Y. (1993) *Baburu no Keizaigaku (The Bubble Economy)* (Tokyo: Nihon keizai shinbunsha).

North, D.C. (1990) *Institutions, Institutional Change and Economic Performance* (Cambridge: Cambridge University Press).

Nyomen, R. and Rødseth, A. (2003) 'Explaining Unemployment: Lessons from Nordic Wage Formation', *Labour Economics*, 10(1), pp. 1–29.

Odagiri, H. (1994) *Growth through Competition, Competition through Growth* (Oxford: Clarendon Press).

O'Donnell, R. (1993) *Ireland and Europe: Challenges for a New Century* (Dublin: Economic and Social Research Institute).

O'Donnell, R. (1995) 'Irish Policy in a Global Context: From State Autonomy to Social Partnership', in B. Leavy and J. Walsh (eds) *Strategy and General Management* (Dublin: Oak Tree Press).

O'Donnell, R. (1998) 'Post Porter: Devising Policies for the Irish Context', in *Sustaining Competitive Advantage* (Dublin: National Economic and Social Council).

O'Donnell, R. (2000) 'The New Ireland in the New Europe', in R. O'Donnell (ed.), *Europe – the Irish Experience* (Dublin: Institute of European Affairs).

O'Donnell R. and O'Reardon, C. (1997) 'Ireland's Experiment in Social Partnership, 1987–96', in P. Pochet and G. Fajertag (eds), *Social Pacts in Europe* (Brussels: European Trade Union Institute).

O'Donnell R. and O'Reardon, C. (2000) 'Social Partnership in Ireland's Economic Transformation', in P. Pochet and G. Fajertag (eds), *Social Pacts in Europe* (Brussels: European Trade Union Institute).

O'Donnell R. and Teague, P. (2000) *Partnership at Work in Ireland: An Evaluation of Progress under Partnership 2000* (Dublin: Stationery Office).

O'Donnell R. and Thomas, D. (1998) 'Partnership and Policy-making', in S. Healy and B. Reynolds (eds), *Social Policy in Ireland* (Dublin: Oak Tree Press).

OECD (1990) *Employment outlook, 1990* (Paris: Organisation for Economic Co-operation and Development).

OECD (1996) *OECD Economic Surveys Japan 1996* (Paris: Organisation for Economic Co-operation and Development).

OECD (1996a) *Economic Survey: Japan* (Paris: Organisation for Economic Co-operation and Development).

OECD (1996b) *Employment Outlook 1996* (Paris: Organisation for Economic Co-operation and Development).

OECD (1997) *OECD Economic Surveys Japan 1997* (Paris: Organisation for Economic Co-operation and Development).

OECD (1997a) *Employment Outlook 1997* (Paris: Organisation for Economic Co-operation and Development).

OECD (1997b) *OECD Economic Surveys: France* (Paris: Organisation for Economic Co-operation and Development).

OECD (1997c) *OECD Economic Surveys: United States 1997* (Paris: Organisation for Economic Co-operation and Development).

OECD (1997d) *OECD Economic Outlook No. 62* (Paris: Organisation for Economic Co-operation and Development).

OECD (1998a) *OECD Economic Surveys: Japan* (Paris: Organisation for Economic Co-operation and Development).

OECD (1999a) *Economic Outlook No. 66* (Paris: Organisation for Economic Co-operation and Development)

OECD (1999b) *Employment Outlook 1999* (Paris: Organisation for Economic Co-operation and Development).

OECD (1999c) *Economic Survey: Portugal* (Paris: Organisation for Economic Co-operation and Development).

OECD (2000a) *OECD Economic Surveys: France* (Paris: Organisation for Economic Co-operation and Development).

OECD (2000b) *OECD Economic Surveys: Korea* (Paris: Organisation for Economic Co-operation and Development).

OECD (2000c) *OECD Economic Surveys: United States 2000* (Paris: Organisation for Economic Co-operation and Development).

OECD (2000d) *OECD Economic Outlook No. 67* (Paris: Organisation for Economic Co-operation and Development).

OECD (2001) *Economic Surveys: Korea* (Paris: Organisation for Economic Co-operation and Development).

OECD (2002a) *Economic Surveys: Denmark* (Paris: Organisation for Economic Co-operation and Development).

OECD (2002b) *Economic Surveys: Finland* (Paris: Organisation for Economic Co-operation and Development).

OECD (2002c) *Economic Surveys: Italy* (Paris: Organisation for Economic Co-operation and Development).

OECD (2002d) *Economic Surveys: New Zealand* (Paris: Organisation for Economic Co-operation and Development).

OECD (2002e) *Economic Surveys: Norway* (Paris: Organisation for Economic Co-operation and Development).

OECD (1998b) *Employment Outlook 1998* (Paris: Organisation for Economic Co-operation and Development).

OFCE (1999) *L'Economie Francaise 1999*, Paris, La Découverte.

OFCE (2001) *L'Economic Francaise 2001*, Paris, La Découverte.

O'Hearn, D. (1989) 'The Irish Case of Dependency: An Exception to the Exceptions?', *American Sociological Review*, 54, pp. 578–96.

O'Hearn, D. (1998) *Inside the Celtic Tiger: The Irish Economy and the Asian Model* (London: Pluto Press).

O'Hearn, D. (2000) 'Globalisation, "New Tigers", and the End of the Developmental State? The Case of the Celtic Tiger', *Politics and Society*, 28(1), pp. 67–92.

Okabe, M. (2002) *Cross Shareholdings in Japan* (Cheltenham: Edward Elgar).

Okuno-F.M. (1996) 'Toward a Comparative Institutional Analysis of the Government–Business Relationship', in M. Aoki and M.O.-Fujiwara (eds), *The Role of Government in East Asian Economic Development* (Oxford: Clarendon Press).

Okuno-F.M. and Sekiguchi, I. (1996) 'Seihu to Kigyou (Government and Firms)', in M. Aoki and M.O-Fujiwara (eds), *Keizai Sisutemu no Hikaku Seido Bunseki (Comparative Institutional Analysis of the Economic System)* (Tokyo: Tokyo University Press).

O'Leary, J. and Leddin A. (1996) 'Monetary and Exchange Rate Policy', in J. O'Hagan (ed.), *The Economy of Ireland* (Dublin: Gill and Macmillan).

Oliner, S. and Sichel, D. (2000) 'The Resurgence of Growth in the Late 1990s: Is Information Technology the Story?' *Journal of Economic Perspectives*, 14(4), pp. 3–22.

Oliver, C. (1997) 'Sustainable Competitive Advantage: Combining Institutional and Resource-based Views', *Strategic Management Journal*, 18(9), pp. 697–713.

Olson, M. (1982) *The Rise and Decline of Nations: Economic Growth, Stagflation and Social Rigidities* (New Haven: Yale University Press).

O'Mahony, M. (1999) *Britain's Productivity Performance, 1950–1996* (London: National Institute for Economic and Social Research).

O'Malley, E. (1981) *Industrial Policy and Development: A Survey of the Literature from the Early 1960s* (Dublin: National Economic and Social Council).

O'Malley, E. (1986) 'Foreign Owned Industry in Ireland: Performance and Prospects', *Medium Term Outlook No 1* (Dublin: Economic and Social Research Institute).

O'Malley, E. (1989) *Industry and Economic Development: The Challenge for the Latecomer* (Dublin: Gill and Macmillan).

O'Malley, E. (1998) 'The Performance of Indigenous Industry, 1985–98', *Quarterly Economic Commentary* (Dublin: Economic and Social Research Institute).

O'Riain, S. (2000) 'The Flexible Developmental State: Globalisation, Information Technology, and the Celtic Tiger', *Politics and Society*, 28(2), pp. 157–93.

Ormerod, P. (1994) *The Death of Economics* (London: Faber and Faber).

O'Sullivan, M. (2000) *Contests for Corporate Control* (Oxford: Oxford University Press).

Overbeek, H. (1990) *Global Capitalism and National Decline: The Thatcher Decade in Perspective* (London: Unwin).

Overman, H. and Puga, D. (2002) 'Unemployment Clusters Across Europe's Regions and Countries', *Economic Policy*, (34), pp. 115–47.

Owen, G. (1999) *From Empire to Europe: The Decline and Revival of British Industry since the Second World War* (London: HarperCollins).

Owen-Smith, E. (1994) *The German Economy* (London: Routledge).

Oxelheim, L. (1996) *Financial Markets in Transition* (London: Routledge).

Palan, R. (1998) 'Luring Buffaloes and the Game of Industrial Subsidies: A Critique of National Competitive Policies in the Era of the Competition State', *Global Society*, 12(3), pp. 323–42.

Palier, B. (2000) ' "Defrosting" the French Welfare State', *West European Politics*, 23(1), pp. 113–36.

Palier, B. (2002) Gouverner la Sécurité Sociale (Paris: Presse Universitaire Francaise).

Palloix, C. (1971) *L'économie mondiale capitaliste*, Paris, Maspéro (two volumes).

Parker, R. (1999) 'From National Champions to Small and Medium Sized Enterprises: Changing Policy Emphasis in France, Germany and Sweden', *Journal of Public Policy*, 19(1), pp. 63–89.

Parkinson, J. (2000) 'Evolution and Policy in Company Law', in J. Parkinson *et al.*, (eds), *The Political Economy of the Company* (London: Hart).

Pelkmans, J (1982) *Market Integration in the European Community* (The Hague: Martinus Nijhoff).

Pempel, T. (1999) 'The Developmental Regime in a Changing World Economy', in M. Woo-Cumings (ed.), *The Developmental State* (Ithaca: Cornell University Press).

Pempel, T. and Muramatsu, M. (1995) 'The Japanese Bureaucracy and Economic Development: Structuring a Proactive Civil Service', in H.K. Kim, M. Muramatsu, T. Pempel and K. Yamamura (eds), *The Japanese Civil Service and Economic Development* (Oxford: Oxford University Press).

Perez, S. (2002) 'Monetary Union and Wage Bargaining Institutions in the EU', *Comparative Political Studies*, 35(10), pp. 1198–227.

Perraton, J. (2004) 'What's left of "State Capacity"? The Developmental State After Globalisation and the East Asian Crisis' in G. Harrison (ed.), *Global Encounters: International Political Economy, Development and Globalisation* (Basingstoke: Palgrave).

Peters, B.G. (1999) *Institutional Theory in Political Science: The 'New Institutionalism'*, (London: Pinter).

Pettigrew, A. (1990) 'Is Corporate Culture Manageable?', in D. Wilson and R. Rosenfield (eds), *Managing Organizations* (London: McGraw-Hill).

Pierson, P. (ed.) (2001) *The New Politics of the Welfare State* (Oxford: Oxford University Press).

Piore, M. and Sabel, C. (1984) *The Second Industrial Divide* (New York: Basic Books).

Pochet, P. and Fajertag, G. (2000) *Social Pacts in Europe* (Brussels: European Trade Union Institute).

Pohjola, M. (1992) 'Corporatism and Wage Bargaining', in J. Pekkarinen, M. Pohjola and R. Rowthorn (eds), *Social Corporatism: A Superior Economic System?* (Oxford: Oxford University Press).

Polanyi, K. (1944) *The Great Transformation* (New York: Rinehart).

Pollin, R. (1995) 'Financial Structures and Egalitarian Economic Policy', *New Left Review*, Series 1, No. 214, pp. 26–61.

Pollin. R. (2000) 'Anatomy of Clintonomics', *New Left Review*, 2(3), pp. 17–46.

Pontusson, J. (1997) 'Between Neo-Liberalism and the German Model: Swedish Capitalism in Transition', in C. Crouch and W. Streeck (eds), *Political Economy of Modern Capitalism* (London: Sage).

Porter, M.E. (1990a) *The Competitive Advantage of Nations* (London: Macmillan).

Porter, M.E. (1990b) 'The Competitive Advantage of Nations', *Harvard Business Review* (March–April), 73–93.

Porter, M.E., Takeuchi, H. and Sakakibara, M. (2000) *Can Japan Compete?* (London: Palgrave).

Prescott, E. (1998) 'Needed: A Theory of Total Factor Productivity', *International Economic Review*, 39(3), pp. 525–51.

Pryor, F. and Schaffer, D. (1999) *Who's Not Working and Why* (Cambridge: Cambridge University Press).

Pugh, G. and Carr, D. (1993) The Monetary Consequences of German Re-unification, *Economics and Business Education*, 1(1) Part 1, No. 3, pp. 116–23.

Pugh, G. and Tyrrall, D. (2000) Culture, Productivity and Competitive Advantage: The Role of Consensus in Sustaining Innovation, *Economic Issues*, 5(3), pp. 5–25.

Quiggin, J. (1998) 'Social Democracy and Market Reform in Australia and New Zealand', *Oxford Review of Economic Policy*, 14(1), pp. 76–95.

Radcliffe-Brown, A.R. (1952) *Structure and Function in Primitive Society* (London: Cohen and West).

Radelet, S. and Sachs, J. (1998) 'The East Asian Financial Crisis', *Brookings Papers on Economic Activity*, No. 1, pp. 1–74.

Radice, H. (1998) ' "Globalization" and National Differences', *Competition and Change*, 3(4), pp. 263–91.

Radice, H. (2000a) 'Responses to Globalization: A Critique of Progressive Nationalism', *New Political Economy*, 5(1), pp. 5–19.

Radice, H. (2000b) 'Globalization and National Capitalisms: Theorizing Convergence and Differentiation', *Review of International Political Economy*, 7(4), pp. 719–42.

Rajan, R. and Zingales, L. (2003) The Great Reversals: The Politics of Financial Development in the Twentieth Century *Journal of Financial Economics*, 69(1), pp. 5–50.

Rajan, R. and Zingales, L. (2003) 'The Great Reversals: The Politics of Financial Development in the Twentieth Century', *Journal of Financial Economics*, 69(1), pp. 5–50.

Rebick, M. (2001) 'Japanese Labor Markets: Can We Expect Change?', in M. Blomström, B. Gangnes and S. La Croix (eds), *Japan's New Economy* (Oxford: Oxford University Press).

Regini, M. (1997) 'Still Engaging in Corporatism? Recent Italian Experience in Comparative Perspective', *European Journal of Industrial Relations*, 3(3), pp. 259–78.

Reich, R. (1992) *The Work of Nations* (New York: Vintage Books).

Reiter, J. (2003) 'Changing the Microfoundations of Corporatism: The Impact of Financial Globalisation on Swedish Corporate Ownership', *New Political Economy*, 8(1), pp. 103–25.

Rhodes, M. and Apeldoorn, B. van (1998) 'Capital Unbound? The Transformation of European Corporate Governance', *Journal of European Public Policy*, 5(1), pp. 406–27.

Roche, W. (1994) 'Pay Determination, the State and the Politics of Industrial Relations', *Irish Industrial Relations in Practice* (Dublin: Oak Tree Press).

Roche, W. (1998) 'Between Regime Fragmentation and Realignment: Irish Industrial Relations in the 1990s', *Industrial Relations Journal*, 29(2), pp. 112–25.

Roche, W. and Geary, J. (1996) 'Multinational Companies in Ireland: Adapting to or Diverging from National Industrial Relations Practices and Traditions?', *Irish Journal of Business and Administrative Research*, 17, pp. 14–31.

Roche, W. and Geary, J. (2000) 'Collaborative Production and the Irish Boom: Work Organisation, Partnership and Direct Involvement in Irish Workplaces', *Economic and Social Review*, 31(1), pp. 1–36.

Rodrik, D. (1997) *Has Globalization Gone Too Far?* (Washington DC: Institute for International Economics).

Rodrik, D. (1998) 'Why do More Open Economies Have Bigger Governments?', *Journal of Political Economy*, 106, pp. 997–1032.

Roe, M. (1994) *Strong Managers, Weak Owners: The Political Roots of American Corporate Finance* (Princeton, NJ: Princeton University Press).

Roe, M. (2002) *Political Determinants of Corporate Governance* (Oxford: Oxford University Press).

Rostow, W.W. (1960) *The Stages of Growth: A Non-Communist Manifesto* (Cambridge: Cambridge University Press).

Rowthorn, R. (1992) 'Government Spending and Taxation in the Thatcher Era', in J. Michie (ed.), *The Economic Legacy 1979–1992* (London: Academic Press).

Rowthorn, R. (2000) 'The Political Economy of Full Employment in Modern Britain', *Oxford Bulletin of Economics and Statistics*, 62(2), pp. 139–73.

Rowthorn, R. and Wells, J. (1987) *De-industrialisation and Foreign Trade* (Cambridge: Cambridge University Press).

Royo, S. (2000) *From Social Democracy to Neoliberalism: The Consequences of Party Hegemony in Spain, 1982–1996* (Basingstoke: Macmillan).

Royo, S. (2002) ' "A New Century of Corporatism?" Corporatism in Spain and Portugal', *West European Politics*, 25(3), pp. 77–104.

Rubinstein, W. (1993) *Capitalism, Culture, and Decline in Britain* (London: Routledge).

Rueda, D. and Pontusson, J. (2000) 'Wage Inequality and Varieties of Capitalism', *World Politics*, 52(3), pp. 350–83.

Ruigrok, W. and Tulder, R. van (1995) *The Logic of International Restructuring* (London: Routledge).

Rutherford, M. (1994) *Institutions in Economics: The Old and the New Institutionalism* (Cambridge: Cambridge University Press).

Sabel, C. (1996) *Ireland: Local Partnerships and Social Innovation* (Paris: Organisation for Economic Co-operation and Development).

Sauviat, C. and Montagne, S. (2001) 'L'influence des marchés financiers sur les politiques sociales des entreprises: le cas français', *Travail et Emploi*, 87, p. 111.

Schaberg, M. (1999) *Globalization and the Erosion of National Financial Systems* (Cheltenham: Edward Elgar).

Scharpf, F. (2000) 'Economic Changes, Vulnerabilities and Institutional Capabilities', in F. Scharpf and V. Schmidt (eds), *Welfare and Work in the Open Economy: Volume One* (Oxford: Oxford University Press).

Schmidt, V. (1996) *From State to Market? The Transformation of French Business and Government* (Cambridge: Cambridge University Press).

Schmidt, V. (1999) 'Privatisation in France: The Transformation of French Capitalism', *Environment and Planning C*, 17, pp. 445–61.

Schroter, H. (1996) 'Cartelization and Decartelization in Europe, 1870–1995: Rise and Decline of an Economic Institution', *Journal of European Economic History*, 25(1), pp. 129–53.

Schwartz, H. (1994) 'Small States in Big Trouble: State Reorganization in Australia, Denmark, New Zealand and Sweden in the 1980s', *World Politics*, 46(4), pp. 527–55.

Scott, J. (1997) *Corporate Business and Capitalist Classes* (Oxford: Oxford University Press).

Serot, A. (2002) 'When National Institutions Do Not Matter: The Importance of International Factors: Pricing Policies in Telecoms', *Journal of European Public Policy*, 9(6), pp. 973–94.

Sheard, P. (1994) 'Main Banks and the Governance of Financial Distress', in M. Aoki and H. Patrick (eds), *The Japanese Main Bank System* (Oxford: Oxford University Press).

Shimokawa, K. (18 March 1997) 'Jidousha Shinhuhou de Kyousouryoku (Competitiveness by New Technology in Automobile Industry)', *Nihon Keizai Shinbun (Japanese Economic Newspaper)*, p. 31.

Shonfield, A. (1965) *Modern Capitalism: The Changing Balance of Public and Private Power* (Oxford: Oxford University Press).

Siaroff, A. (1999) 'Corporatism in 24 Industrial Democracies: Meaning and Measurement', *European Journal of Political Research*, 36, pp. 175–205.

Silhol, B. (1997) 'Branche et entreprise dans le nouveau droit de la négociation collective', *Droit social*, (11), pp. 931–6.

Simmons, B. (2001) 'The International Politics of Harmonization: The Case of Capital Market Regulation', *International Organization*, 55(3), pp. 589–620.

Smith, H. (1996) 'The Silence of the Academics: International Social Theory, Historical Materialism and Political Values', *Review of International Studies*, 22(2), pp. 191–212.

Smith, W.R. (1998) *The Left's Dirty Job: The Politics of Industrial Restructuring in France and Spain* (Pittsburgh: University of Pittsburgh Press).

Soskice, D. (1990) 'Wage Determination: The Changing Role of Institutions in Advanced Industrialised Countries', *Oxford Review of Economic Policy*, 6(4), pp. 36–61.

Soskice, D. (1999) 'Divergent Production Regimes: Coordinated and Uncoordinated Market Economies in the 1980s and 1990s', in H. Kitschelt *et al.* (eds), *Continuity and Change in Contemporary Capitalism* (Cambridge: Cambridge University Press).

SOU (1998) (Statens offentliga utredningar, 'Government Committee Papers') 141, 1998: *Medling och lönebildning*, Stockholm, 1998.

Stanford, J. (1999) *Paper Boom: Why Real Prosperity Requires a New Approach to Canada's Economy* (Toronto: John Lorimer & Co.).

Stephens, P. (1996) *Politics and the Pound: The Tories, the Economy and Europe* (London: Macmillan).

Stiglitz, J. (2002) *Globalization and its Discontents* (London: Allen Lane).

Stiglitz, J. (2003) *The Roaring Nineties: Seeds of Destruction* (London: Allen Lane).

Stoffaes, C. (1989) 'Industrial Policy and the State: From Industry to Enterprise', in P. Godt (ed.), *Policy-making in France* (London: Pinter).

Story, J. and Walter, I. (1997) *Political Economy of Financial Integration in Europe* (Manchester: Manchester University Press).

Strange, S. (1971) *Sterling and British Policy* (Oxford: Oxford University Press).

Strange, S. (1997) 'The Future of Global Capitalism: Or, will Divergence Persist for Ever?', in C. Crouch and W. Streeck (eds), *Political Economy of Modern Capitalism: Mapping Convergence and Diversity* (London: Sage).

Streeck, W. (1997a) 'Benefical Constraints: On the Economic Limits of Rational Voluntarism', in J.R. Hollingsworth and R. Boyer (eds), *Contemporary Capitalism: The Embeddedness of Institutions* (Cambridge: Cambridge University Press).

Streeck, W. (1997b) 'German Capitalism: Does It Exist? Can It Survive?', in C. Crouch and W. Streeck (eds), *Political Economy of Modern Capitalism* (London: Sage).

Sturm, J.-E. (1998) *Public Capital Expenditure in OECD Countries* (Cheltenham: Edward Elgar).

Svallfors, S. (1995) 'The End of Class Politics? Structural Cleavages and Attitudes to Swedish Welfare Policies', *Acta Sociologica*, 38(1), pp. 53–74.

Svallfors, S. and Taylor-Gooby, P. (1999) *The End of the Welfare State?* (London: Routledge).

Swank, D. (2002) *Global Capital, Political Institutions, and Policy Change in Developed Welfare States* (Cambridge: Cambridge University Press).

Swenson, P. and Pontusson, J. (2000) 'The Swedish Employer Offensive Against Centralized Wage Bargaining', in T. Iversen *et al.* (eds), *Unions, Employers and Central Banks* (Cambridge: Cambridge University Press).

Szarka, J. (1998) 'French Business in the Mitterrand Years: Continuity and Change', in M. Maclean (ed.), *The Mitterrand Years* (Basingstoke: Macmillan).

Szij, E. (1998) 'Les privatisations en France depuis 1993', *Regards sur L'Actualité*, February.

Takada, R. (1989) *Gendai Cyusyo Kigyo no Kozo Bunseki (The Structure of Modern SMEs)* (Tokyo: Shinhyoron).

Takada, R. (1990) 'Small and Medium Enterprises and Subcontracting System in Japan', *Journal of the University of Marketing and Distribution Sciences*, 3(1), pp. 23–35.

Takeda, S. and Schoenholtz, K. (1985) 'Information Activity and the Main Bank System', *Kinyu Kenkyu (Monetary and Financial Studies)*, 4(4), pp. 1–24.

Tansey, P. (1998) *Ireland at Work* (Dublin: Oak Tree Press).

Taylor, G. (1996) 'Labour Market Rigidities, Institutional Impediments and Managerial Constraints: Some Reflections on the Experience of Macro-Political Bargaining in Ireland', *Economic and Social Review*, 27(3), pp. 253–77.

Taylor, R. (1998) 'The Fairness at Work White Paper', *Political Quarterly*, 69(4), pp. 451–7.

Teague, P. (1995) 'Pay Determination in the Republic of Ireland: Towards Social Corporatism?', *British Journal of Industrial Relations*, 33(2), pp. 253–73.

Teague, P. (1999) 'Reshaping Employment Regimes in Europe', *Journal of Public Policy*, 19(1), pp. 33–62.

Teece, D. (1987) *The Competitive Challenge* (Cambridge, MA: Ballinger Publishing).

Teulings, C. and Hartog, J. (1998) *Corporatism or Competition?* (Cambridge: Cambridge University Press).

Thelen, K. (2000) 'Why German Employers Cannot Bring Themselves to Dismantle the German Model', in T. Iversen *et al.* (eds), *Unions, Employers and Central Banks* (Cambridge: Cambridge University Press).

Thelen, K. (2001) 'Varieties of Labor Politics in Developed Democracies', in P. Hall and D. Soskice (eds), *Varieties of Capitalism: The Institutional Foundations of Comparative Advantage* (Oxford: Oxford University Press).

Thomas, K.P. (2000) *Competing for Capital: Europe and North America in a Global Era* (Washington DC: Georgetown University Press).

Thompson, G.F. (1989) (ed.), *Industrial Policy: USA and UK Debates* (London: Routledge).

Thompson, G.F. (1999a) 'From Long-Boom to Recession and Stagnation? The Post-war American Economy to 1990', in G.F. Thompson (ed.), *America in the Twentieth Century – Markets* (London: Hodder and Stoughton).

Thompson, G.F. (1999b) 'The US Economy 1990–1999', in G.F. Thompson, (ed.), *America in the Twentieth Century – Markets* (London: Hodder and Stoughton).

Thompson, H. (1996) *The British Conservative Government and the European Exchange Rate Mechanism, 1979–1994* (London: Pinter).

Thurbon, E. (2001) 'Two Paths to Financial Liberalization: South Korea and Taiwan', *The Pacific Review*, 14(2), pp. 241–67.

Traxler, F. and Kittel, B. (2000) 'The Bargaining System and Performance: A Comparison of 18 OECD Countries', *Comparative Political Studies*, 33(9), pp. 1154–90.

Traxler, F., Blaschke, S. and Kittel, B. (2001) *National Labour Relations in Internationalized Markets* (Oxford: Oxford University Press).

Trifiletti, R. (1999) 'Southern European Welfare Regimes and the Worsening Position of Women', *Journal of European Social Policy*, 9(1), pp. 49–64.

Tsuru, K. (1994) *The Japanese Market System: Its Strengths and Weaknesses.* (Tokyo: LTCB International Library Foundation).

Turner, L. (1998) *Fighting for Partnership: Labor and Politics in Unified Germany* (Ithaca: Cornell University Press).

UNCTAD (1999) *World Investment Report 1999: Foreign Direct Investment and the Challenge of Development.* UN, Geneva and New York.

US Government Printing Office (1998a) *Statistical Abstract of the United States 1998*, US Bureau Census of Statistics, Washington DC.

US Government Printing Office (1998b) *Economic Report of the President 1998*, Washington DC.

US Government Printing Office (1999a) *Economic Report of the President 1999*, Washington DC.

US Government Printing Office (1999b) *Statistical Abstract of the United States 1999*, Washington DC.

US Government Printing Office (2000) *Economic Report of the President 2000*, Washington DC.

Varghese, R. (2001) '"The Operation was a Success...but the Patient is Dead": Theorizing Social Democracy in an Era of Globalization', *Review of International Political Economy*, 8(4), pp. 720–38.

Vartiainen, J. (1997) 'Can Nordic Social Corporatism Survive?', in R. Kindley and D. Good (eds), *The Challenge of Globalization and Institution-Building: Lessons from Small European States* (Boulder, Co: Westview Press).

Vartiainen, J. (1998) 'Understanding Swedish Social Democracy: Victims of Success?', *Oxford Review of Economic Policy*, 14(1), pp. 19–39.

Vartiainen, J. (1999) 'The Economics of Successful State Intervention in Industrial Transformation', in M. Woo-Cumings (ed.), *The Developmental State* (Ithaca: Cornell University Press).

Visser, J. and Hamerijck (1997) *A Dutch Miracle: Job Growth, Welfare Reform and Corporatism in the Netherlands* (Amsterdam: Amsterdam University Press).

Vitols, S., Casper, S., Soskice, D. and Woolcock, S. (1998) *Corporate Governance in Large British and German Companies* (London: Anglo-German Foundation for the Study of Industrial Society).

Vogel, S. (1996) *Freer Markets, More Rules: Regulatory Reform in Advanced Industrial Countries* (Ithaca: Cornell University Press).

Wade, R. (1998) 'From "Miracle" to "Cronyism": Explaining the Great Asian Slump', *Cambridge Journal of Economics*, 22(6), pp. 693–706.

Wade, R. and Veneroso, F. (1998) 'The Asian Crisis: The High-debt Model vs. the Wall Street-Treasury-IMF complex', *New Left Review* (228).

Wakita, S. (2001) 'Why has the Unemployment Rate been So Low in Japan? An Explanation by Two-Part Wage Bargaining', *Japanese Economic Review*, 52(1), pp. 116–33.

Wallerstein, M. and Golden, M. (2000) 'Postwar Wage Setting in the Nordic Countries', in T. Iversen *et al.* (eds), *Unions, Employers and Central Banks* (Cambridge: Cambridge University Press).

Walsh B. and Leddin A. (1992) *The Macroeconomy of Ireland* (Dublin: Gill and Macmillan).

Walters, A. (1986) *Britain's Economic Renaissance* (Oxford: Oxford University Press).

Webb, M. (1995) *The Political Economy of Policy Coordination: International Adjustment since 1945* (Ithaca: Cornell University Press).

Weber, S. (1997) 'The End of the Business Cycle?', *Foreign Affairs*, 76(4), pp. 65–82.

Webster, D. (2000) 'The Geographical Concentration of Labour-market Disadvantage', *Oxford Review of Economic Policy*, 16(1), pp. 114–28.

Weinstein, D. and Yafeh, Y. (1998) 'On the Costs of a Bank-centered Financial System: Evidence from the Changing Main Bank Relations in Japan', *Journal of Finance*, 53(2), pp. 635–72.

Weiss, L. (1998) *The Myth of the Powerless State: Governing the Economy in a Global Era* (Cambridge: Polity Press; Ithaca: Cornell University Press).

Weiss, L. (1999) 'State Power and the Asian Crisis', *New Political Economy*, 4(3), pp. 317–42.

Weiss, L. (2000) 'Developmental States in Transition: Adapting, Dismantling, Innovating, Not "Normalizing"', *The Pacific Review*, 13(1), pp. 21–55.

Weiss, L. (2003) 'Guiding Globalisation in East Asia: New Roles for Old Developmental States', in L. Weiss (ed.), *States in the Global Economy: Bringing Domestic Institutions Back In* (Cambridge: Cambridge University Press).

Whitley, R. (1994) 'Dominant Forms of Economic Organization in Market Economies', *Organization Studies*, 15(2), pp. 153–82.

Whitley, R. (1998) 'Internationalization and Varieties of Capitalism: The Limited Effects of Cross-National Coordination of Economic Activities on the Nature of Business Systems', *Review of International Political Economy*, 5(3), pp. 445–81.

Whitley, R. (1999) *Divergent Capitalisms: The Social Structuring and Change of Business Systems* (Oxford: Oxford University Press).

Wilkinson, B. (1996) 'Culture, Institutions and Business in East Asia', *Organization Studies*, 17(3): 421–47.

Wilks, S. (1993) 'Economic Policy', in P. Dunleavy *et al.*, *Developments in British Politics 4* (London: Macmillan).

Williams. J., Williams, K. and Haslam, C. (1999) 'The Organization of American Production', in G.F. Thompson (ed.), *America in the Twentieth Century – Markets* (London: Hodder and Stoughton).

Williams, K., Williams, J. and Thomas, D. (1983) *Why are the British Bad At Manufacturing?* (London: Routledge).

Williamson, O. (1975) *Markets and Hierarchies: Analysis and Antitrust Implications* (New York: The Free Press).

Windolf, P. (2002) *Corporate Networks in Europe and the United States* (Oxford: Oxford University Press).

Woo, J. (Meredith Woo-Cumings) (1991) *Race to the Swift* (New York: Columbia University Press).

Woo-Cumings, M. (1998) 'Industrial Policy and Corporate Governance in East Asia', Paper Presented to the Asia Development Forum, Manila, 12 March 1998.

World Bank (1993) *The East Asian Miracle: Economic Growth and Public Policy* (Oxford: Oxford University Press).

World Bank (1993) *The East Asian Miracle: Economic Growth and Public Policy* (Oxford: Oxford University Press).

Wormack, J.P., Roos, D. and Jones, D. 1990. *The Machine that Changed the World.* (Basingstoke: Macmillan).

Yafeh, Y. (2000) 'Corporate Governance in Japan: Past Performance and Future Prospects', *Oxford Review of Economic Policy*, 16(2), pp. 74–84.

Yasui, T. (2001) 'Corporate Governance in Japan', in OECD, *Corporate Governance in Asia* (Paris: Organisation for Economic Co-operation and Development).

Yoshitomi, M. (1996) 'On the Changing International Competitiveness of Japanese Manufacturing since 1985', *Oxford Review of Economic Policy*, 12(3), pp. 61–73.

Zarnowitz, V. (1999) 'Theory and History Behind Business Cycles: Are the 1990s the Onset of a Golden Age?' *Journal of Economic Perspectives*, 13(2), pp. 69–90.

Zuckerman, M. (1998) 'A Second American Century', *Foreign Affairs*, 77(3), pp. 18–31.

Zukin, S. and DiMaggio, P. (1990), 'Introduction', in S. Zukin and P. DiMaggio (eds), *Structures of Capital: The Social Organization of the Economy* (Cambridge: Cambridge University Press), pp. 1–36.

Zysman, J. (1983) *Government, Markets, Growth: Financial Systems and the Politics of Industrial Change* (Ithaca: Cornell University Press).

Index

296   *Index*